W9-CDB-270

POPULAR CULTURE IN
SEVENTEENTH-CENTURY ENGLAND

POPULAR CULTURE
In
Seventeenth-Century
England

Edited by Barry Reay

CROOM HELM
London & Sydney

Wingate College Library

© 1985 Barry Reay
Croom Helm Ltd, Provident House, Burrell Row,
Beckenham, Kent BR3 1AT

Croom Helm Australia Pty Ltd, Suite 4, 6th Floor,
64-76 Kippax Street, Surry Hills, NSW 2010, Australia

British Library Cataloguing in Publication Data

Popular culture in seventeenth- century England.
1. England – Populat culture 2. England –
Social life and customs – 17th century
I. Reay, Barry
306'.1   DA380

ISBN 0-7099-2268-X

Printed and bound in Great Britain
by Billing & Sons Limited, Worcester.

CONTENTS

To KEITH THOMAS and EDWARD THOMPSON

PREFACE

This book would not have been possible ten,
perhaps even five, years ago, for the seventeenth
century has proven particularly hidebound as far as
'history from below' is concerned - despite the
efforts and influences of Christopher Hill and Keith
Thomas. For a while it seemed that England's
'century of revolution' would remain, in terms of
social history, a poor relation to the eighteenth
and nineteenth centuries. Thankfully, things have
changed. It is dangerous to single out names, for
someone is inevitably left off the list, but in
their various ways Charles Phythian-Adams, Peter
Clark, David Cressy, Caroline Davidson, Ralph
Houlbrooke, William Hunt, Ann Kussmaul, Michael
MacDonald, Alan Macfarlane, Paul Slack, Margaret
Spufford, John Walter, Keith Wrightson, and, of
course, the contributors to this volume, are opening up new areas of enquiry in seventeenth century
English social history. Others contribute or
stimulate from different countries or centuries
of expertise: John Brewer, Bob Bushaway, Robert
Darnton, Natalie Davis, Carlo Ginzburg, J. F. C.
Harrison, Douglas Hay, Rab Houston, Peter Linebaugh,
Robert Malcolmson, James Obelkevich, John Rule,
Robert Scribner, John Styles, Edward Thompson and
David Vincent. This volume builds upon the work of
these people. It combines original research with
an up-to-date synthesis of important new work in
early modern English social history. As I say in
the Introduction, our point of departure is Peter
Burke's <u>Popular Culture in Early Modern Europe</u>
(1978); and if we can do for the history of popular culture in seventeenth-century England what
Burke has done for Europe, our book will have been
a success.

To my surprise, this volume has been a joy to

edit. It has been something of a co-operative
effort from the start. We have agreed on the joint
dedication to the great pioneers in our subject
area. Each chapter has been read and criticised by
at least two of the contributors (as well as the
editor of course), and then re-written in the light
of these comments; the introduction was seen by
everyone. Co-ordination between the U.K., the U.S.
and Australasia has not been too taxing, and while
the various contributors differ in interpretation
and approach, the end-product coheres, I think, in a
way rarely true of collections of essays.

Individual contributors record their own
acknowledgements at the start of the notes to their
respective chapters. As editor, I would particularly like to thank Freda Christie for typing (and
indeed sub-editing) the whole book with awe-
inspiring efficiency and good humour; William Hunt
for having read and commented on almost every
chapter; Paul Baker, Michael Belgrave and Keith
Thomas who have likewise encouraged and helped in a
variety of ways; and Athina Reay for her reminders
about the more important issues in life - she was
not much interested in Muggletonians and Quakers;
she is interested in popular culture.

Barry Reay
Auckland

NOTES ON CONTRIBUTORS

Jonathan Barry is completing an Oxford D.Phil.; he
is also Research Assistant at the Wellcome Unit for
the History of Medicine.

Peter Burke is Lecturer in European History at the
University of Cambridge and Fellow of Emmanuel
College.

Bernard Capp is Senior Lecturer in History at the
University of Warwick.

Martin Ingram is Lecturer in History at The Queen's
University of Belfast.

Barry Reay is Lecturer in History at the University
of Auckland.

Buchanan Sharp is Associate Professor of History at
the University of California, Santa Cruz.

James Sharpe is Lecturer in History at the
University of York.

ACKNOWLEDGEMENTS

Peter Burke's chapter, 'Popular Culture in Seventeenth-Century London', is an amended and expanded version of an article which appeared in the London Journal, iii (1977); we are grateful for permission to use this material.

ABBREVIATIONS

The place of publication in all footnotes is London unless otherwise stated.

APC	Acts of the Privy Council
BAO	Bristol Archives Office
BCL	Bristol Central Library
BIHR	Bulletin of the Institute of Historical Research
BL	British Library
Burke, Popular Culture	P. Burke, Popular Culture in Early Modern Europe (1978)
Child	F. J. Child (ed.), The English and Scottish Popular Ballads (NY, 1965)
Cressy	D. Cressy, Literacy and the social order. Reading and writing in Tudor and Stuart England (Cambridge, 1980)
CSP	Calendar of State Papers, Domestic Series
DNB	Dictionary of National Biography
DR	Diocesan Records
ERO	Essex Record Office
Hill, World Turned Upside Down	C. Hill, The World Turned Upside Down (1972, and 1975 Penguin edn.)
HJ	Historical Journal
HMC	Historical Manuscripts Commission
Index	H. E. Rollins, An Analytical Index to the Ballad Entries (1557-1709) in the Register of the Company of Stationers in London (Hatboro, Penn., 1967 edn.)
JFHS	Journal of the Friends' Historical Society
JSH	Journal of Social History
Latimer, Annals	J. Latimer, Annals of Bristol in the Seventeenth Century (Bristol, 1902)
NY	New York
P. and P.	Past and Present
PRO	Public Record Office

Abbreviations

QS	Quarter Sessions
RB	The Roxburghe Ballads, ed. W. Chappell and J. W. Ebsworth (1871-99)
RO	Record Office
Rollins, Garland	H. E. Rollins, A Pepysian Garland (Cambridge, 1922)
RS	Record Society
Rump	Rump: or an Exact Collection of the Choycest Poems and Songs relating to the late Times, ed. H. B[rome] and H. M[arsh] (1662)
Sharp, In Contempt	B. Sharp, In Contempt of All Authority. Rural Artisans and Riot in the West of England, 1586-1660 (Berkeley, 1980)
Spufford, Small Books	M. Spufford, Small Books and Pleasant Histories. Popular Fiction and its Readership in Seventeenth-Century England (1981)
SRO	Somerset Record Office
TBGAS	Transactions of the Bristol and Gloucestershire Archaeological Society
Thomas, Religion and Decline	K. Thomas, Religion and the Decline of Magic (1971, and 1973 Penguin edn.)
TRHS	Transactions of the Royal Historical Society
WRO	Wiltshire Record Office

Introduction

POPULAR CULTURE IN EARLY MODERN ENGLAND

Barry Reay

I

    This book does not deal with the peerage and
gentry of the rural areas of early modern England
or the pseudo-gentry and wealthy merchants of the
towns, but rather with the other 90 to 95 per cent
of the population. They were a heterogeneous lot,
comprising what were known as the 'middling' and
'lower sort of people'. We know most about the
middling sort, the 30 per cent, or perhaps 40 per
cent of the nation's population who were relatively
comfortably off, ranging from yeomen and prosperous
tradesmen to husbandmen and craftsmen. We know
least about the culture of the bottom 50 per cent
(possibly 60 per cent) of the population, the
labourers, cottagers, paupers; those at or below
subsistence level.
    In many respects the seventeenth century is the
century of the middling sort. They took advantage
of the socially selective 'educational revolution',
and improved their literacy.(1) They made up the
expanding electorate, perhaps up to 40 per cent of
the adult male population - and those who did not
would have been included in a Leveller franchise.(2)
They joined the sects and the radical movements of
the 1640s and 1650s.(3) They petitioned, demonstrated and agitated in London in 1640-2, forcing
the pace of the English Revolution.(4) Appropriately, then, the middling sort have a high profile in
this volume: as the consumers of popular print
(chapter 6), as the organising core of charivaris
(chapter 5), as participants in the legal process
(chapter 7), as guild members (chapter 2), and as
those who committed their religious, political and
social beliefs to the historical record (*passim*).
Nonetheless, I trust that we have also penetrated

1

the world of the labourer and pauper (e.g. chapter 8), although it must remain true that, along with plebeian women, they remain the least culturally visible sections of society.(5)

Our point of departure in this volume is Peter Burke's pioneering work, <u>Popular Culture in Early Modern Europe</u> (1978). Burke ranges across three centuries (1500-1800), and over an impressive number of different countries. We concentrate on one country, England, and a limited span of time, the seventeenth century. If our scope is in some respects more limited than that of Burke, in other respects it is wider. Like Burke, we define popular culture as the culture of the non-elite, the 'little' as opposed to the 'great tradition': 'a system of shared meanings, attitudes and values, and the symbolic forms ... in which they are expressed': the 'structure of feeling' of the 'subordinate classes'.(6) But within our ambit we include topics which are covered lightly or not at all in <u>Popular Culture in Early Modern Europe</u>: sex and marriage, religion, popular protest, the law. Indeed Burke's chapter on London in our volume examines values and world views in the very widest sense. Our self-imposed limitations, then, permit a greater depth of coverage. And, of course, we have <u>Popular Culture in Early Modern Europe</u> to build upon.

II

In 1723, in a fascinating though incomplete autobiography, a Yorkshire Friend, Josiah Langdale, recounted the experiences of his pre-Quaker youth. As a child Langdale had attended school, but he was forced to return home to the family farm when his father died. By the age of ten he was keeping cows and ploughing. Husbandry had interrupted his formal education, but he tells us that he could read the Bible and had managed to learn some Latin (which he 'soon forgot'). At the age of thirteen he was an expert at the plough and could 'go with Four horses, & plow alone.... I very much delighted in holding the Plow, It being an Employment Sutable to my Mind, & no Company to disturb my Contemplation'. We catch glimpses of life in Josiah's parish, Nafferton, in the 1670s and 1680s. He looked back with disapproval on a youth which had been spent in 'Wrestling, Lea[ping], Football playing and going to Horse Races'. He recounted an obsession with dancing ('Dancing took much with the young People of our Town'), taught locally by a dancing-master who

tripled as a fiddler and juggler. He also remembered the time that the local bishop came to confirm
the area's eligible children. It was harvest time,
but 'Abundance of all Sorts of People ... flock'd to
our Town to see the Bishop, and those qualified to
be confirmed'. Langdale recalled a folk belief that
it was better to get under the bishop's right hand
than his left during the ritual of the confirmation
ceremony.

Josiah did not become a Quaker until he was
twenty, though as a youth he was, as he puts it,
'religiously inclined'. He took his first communion
at the age of fifteen, and 'diligently kept to
Church, both on Sundays & Holidays' - which he
implies was unusual for boys of his age. When
Langdale was sixteen his mother remarried so he
hired himself out by the year as a servant in husbandry. His second employer was a Quaker. Among
his workmates was a blind thresher called Thomas
Hewson:

> a young strong Man ... but he was blind,
> and had been so for about Twenty Years,
> who had lost his Sight when about Ten Years
> of Age; He was never taught further than
> the Psalter ... yet this Man taught our
> Master's Children, and afterwards became a
> famous Schoolmaster ... he was a Man of
> great Memory, and of good Understanding,
> a faithful Servant, and religious.

The two men became close friends: 'indeed we loved
entirely'; 'being Bedfellows sweet Communion &
Fellow Ship we had, yea more than ever'. Sometimes
they would sit in a field with a Bible and Josiah
would read for a while. Sometimes they would debate
the relative merits of the religious alternatives of
the time - the Church of England, the Presbyterians,
the Baptists and Quakers. Or they would discuss the
proficiency of various preachers:

> One time as we were coming home from
> hearing one of the most famous and learned
> of those Priests in our Country, Well said
> he Josiah I am weary with hearing these
> Priests, they are an idle Generation, they
> cannot be Ministers of Jesus Christ; This
> Sermon that we heard to Day I heard this
> Man preach some Years ago; as soon as he
> took his Text I thought how he would manage
> it, and accordingly as I thought he would

go on so he did.(7)

I have used Langdale elsewhere as an entry into a discussion of later-seventeenth-century Quakerism, but I think that he provides us with an equally vivid glimpse into the world of early modern English popular culture, the 'little tradition'. Many of the components are present: recreations, education (formal and informal), folk belief, religion.

The other important aspect of Langdale's autobiography is that it tells us about communication in the early modern period. Langdale was well aware of the world of books: he read the Bible; he was careful, he tells us in another passage, not to read books owned by his Quaker employer lest he should be 'drawn to the Belief of the Quakers'. And yet the autobiography - a scriptive cultural product - reveals the importance of orality and non-literate modes of communication: listening to and memorising passages of Scripture, listening to preachers (indeed remembering the structure of sermons over a number of years), debating, discussing, contemplating at the plough. Langdale's autobiography reminds us that the seventeenth century was a time of transition from oral to print culture; indeed the work itself is in manuscript - it was never printed. We should think (as many of the contributors to this volume will stress) in terms of interaction between the old and the new forms, an interaction encapsulated perfectly in the image of Langdale reading aloud from the <u>printed</u> Bible.

At the time of the Civil Wars about 30 per cent of English men and 10 per cent of English women were able to sign their names: the functional definition of literacy. Greater percentages would have been able to read (a skill taught before writing); and the literacy rates were higher for particular social groups (yeomen, tradesmen and craftsmen) and for certain areas of England (Bristol and London, for example).(8) Throughout our period of interest there was a developing literate culture; ideas and values were being transmitted through books and print instead of verbally. The printing presses, as Bernard Capp demonstrates in chapter 6, were able to turn out cheap pamphlets at an impressive rate; and this cheap literature was distributed reasonably efficiently throughout the country by networks of petty chapmen. It is indeed possible to follow Margaret Spufford in thinking in terms of a 'literate world of yeomen, tradesmen and craftsmen'.(9) Book ownership in towns, reflected in wills and inventories, was on the increase. People with small libraries - often the local minister or landlord - would lend books to their friends and tenants; the Muggletonian Thomas Tomkinson borrowed Henry Hammond's <u>Works</u> and St Augustine's <u>City of God</u> from the neighbouring lord of the manor.(10)

Yet this literate culture was faced everywhere with a resilient, and predominant, oral culture (see chs. 2, 5 and 6 below). What Robert Malcolmson has said of the eighteenth century is equally applicable to the seventeenth:

> Communications were overwhelmingly by word of mouth, through face-to-face contacts; and since the culture of the written and printed word was weakly developed, especially in rural areas, literature was of negligible importance in most people's lives. The popular 'literature' that did exist was still, for the most part, unrecorded: it was transmitted orally from generation to generation, in the form of folk stories, proverbs and legends, and much of the poetry of the people was expressed musically through the lyrics of ballads and songs.(11)

There was a richness and variety in this oral culture which is difficult to recapture. Keith Thomas has shown in his latest book <u>Man and the Natural World</u> (1983) that the agricultural workers of our period had a large vocabulary which enabled them to draw subtle distinctions between various kinds of flora and fauna. They had a detailed knowledge of the natural world - often highly localised - which could be handed on from generation to generation. There were, for example, some fifty different names for the marsh marigold. Eighteenth- and nineteenth-century guardians of morality were to use print to sanitise and standardise the often graphic popular terminology for plants, insects and places.(12)

As in any oral culture, proverbs were important. They provided rough guidelines to popular ethics and morality: 'Who Bulls the Cow, must keep the Calf', 'Love thy neighbour, yet pull not down thy hedge', 'There must be more than four leggs a bedd to keep a houshold'. They could 'define the rules' and transmit collective wisdom: 'Who follows Truth too close at the heels, she may chance dash out his teeth', 'Need hath no law', 'Possession is eleven points of the Law', 'He that hath an ill

name is half hanged', 'You may lend your arse, and
shite thorough your ribbs'. Sometimes proverbs
helped a woman or man cope with life's adversity,
reinforcing and reflecting the limitations of popular aspirations: 'Of sufferance cometh ease',
'Somewhat is better than nothing', 'Of a ragg'd Colt
cometh a good Horse', 'Better half a loaf than no
bread', 'Look high and fall into a Cow-turd'. And
they could mock and deflate: 'He strutteth like a
Crow in the gutter', 'One may get a fart from a
dead horse, as soon as a farthing from him', 'Newes,
newes, the skin of your arse will make a new pair of
shooes'. Culture was transmitted by formula.(13)

In oral culture, Walter Ong has explained,
words 'have no visual presence'; 'they are
sounds'.(14) And so auditory memories seem to have
been highly developed. The father of the eighteenth-
century poet, John Clare, knew over one hundred
ballads. Robert Pasfield, a seventeenth-century
servant, was

> a man utterly unlearned, being unable to
> read a sentence or write a syllable, yet he
> was so taught of God that by his own industry
> and God's blessing upon his mind and memory
> he grew in grace as he did in years and
> became ripe in understanding and mighty in
> the Scriptures. He was so well acquainted
> with the history of the Bible, and the sum
> and substance of every book and chapter,
> that hardly could any ask him where such a
> saying or sentence were but he would with
> very little ado tell them in what book and
> chapter they might find it.(15)

As I intimated earlier, the old and the new
could not maintain separate existences. Throughout
England people were struggling to come to terms with
the new medium. Some could read but not write.
Many of the religious radicals who were presumably
at ease with oral forms of communication were push-
ing themselves both technically and intellectually
to make the most of the world of writing and printing. The sectary, Lodowick Muggleton, was aware
that some of his followers were not able to decipher
'print-hand' and would therefore have to have his
books read to them.(16) When Quaker meetings
established self-censorship they rejected a number
of would-be authors because their manuscripts were
too tedious or too muddled.(17) People did not seem
to read as much as they do today. Work on Quaker

meeting-house libraries hardly indicates a thirst
for the printed word; the avid readers borrowed
eight books in ten years, ten books in nineteen
years, and twelve in eight years.(18) Once we begin
to take into account the survival of pre-literate
frames of mind, the tone and flavour of the popular
literature of the seventeenth century makes more
sense. Its repetition, its use of epithet, its
strange rhythm and use of cliché, its lack of historical specificity, reflect oral influences;
pamphlets were often either written by people who
were used to <u>hearing</u> words rather than seeing them,
or they were designed to be read aloud.(19) Again
and again one can see the interaction of oral and
print culture in simple events during the English
Revolution. In 1652 a radical penned a declaration
against the payment of tithes, and arranged for the
town crier to read it in the market place. In 1653
a Quaker who had been distributing radical literature in a northern market town pinned one of the
pamphlets to the market cross and then read it
aloud.(20)

If popular culture in seventeenth-century
England was predominantly oral, it was also extremely visual. Obviously the two were linked, for the
non-literate were at home with visual images.
Smaller inns and alehouses were compelled by law to
have signs. Every shop hung out its own particular
set of pictorial signs to advertise, without words,
its location to an illiterate population.(21) When
the Essex forger Thomas Whiting visited a village,
he chalked the outline of a fish (a whiting) on the
outside wall of his temporary accommodation so that
people knew he was in business.(22) Working men had
their own marks which they could use in place of
signatures; a tailor might sketch the likeness of a
pair of shears, a thatcher a rake, a brickmaker a
brick shape.(23) At hiring fairs for labourers men
lined up with ribbons in their caps to indicate
their specialities. Or they held 'something in
their hands, to intimate what labour they are
particularly qualify'd to undertake; as the carters
a whip, the labourers a shovel, the wood men a bill,
the manufacturers a wool comb, and the like'.(24)

Ritual, visual imagery, symbolism and festival
were important at all levels of society in a way not
true of England today. Knowledge, acquired wisdom
and experience were passed on from generation to
generation by what Rhys Isaac would call 'drama-
turgical forms of expression'(25) rather than by
writing and reading books. When older members of

the community wanted to provide younger members of
the community with a mental map of the parish
boundaries they imparted the message visually or
physically, escorting them around the perimeters,
striking them about the head at strategic points,
tripping them by the heels, or throwing them money.
One boy was made to sit on the village boundary
stone with 'his bare buttock' that he might 'remember the same so long as he should live'.(26)   Hence
the perambulations of the parish by minister and
parishioners during Rogation week.   As a Gloucestershire vicar recorded in his register: 'I ... went
in perambulation with some of my parishioners, on
Rogation Monday and Tuesday, 1606 ... to the utmost
confines of our parish ... not for any superstitious
sake, but to see the bounds of the parish.'(27)   But
the church was not the only source of mental mapping;
it could be carried out by the manor court or on an
individual basis from, say, grandfather to grandson.
In all cases, the theory was that drama would
imprint the memory.

What Edward Thompson has called the theatre and
counter-theatre of popular culture runs through the
seventeenth century like a brightly coloured thread:
the symbolism of charivaris with pots and pans,
effigies, dung and clamour, mock trials and mock
church ceremonies (see ch. 5);   the ritual of
popular protest (see ch. 8);   the theatre of insult
with crudely constructed pudenda and horn motifs;(28)
the orderly, graded, colourful Lord Mayor's pageants,
testimonies to hierarchy and order (see chs. 1 and
2);   the ritual of Tyburn, described so graphically
by Peter Linebaugh, with the condemned arriving at
the gallows dressed in white as if going to a
wedding.(29)   A certain poverty of imagination in the
sphere of print was more than compensated with a
richness in festivity.   For what can be best described as the carnivalesque was surprisingly strong
in early modern England.   A selective list of some
of the days of the calendar shows that England was
by no means bereft of feasts and festivals: the
Twelve Days of Christmas, New Year's Day, Plough
Sunday and Monday, Shrove Tuesday, Mid-Lent Sunday,
All Fools' Day, Easter, Hock Monday and Tuesday,
Rogationtide, May Day, Whitsuntide, Midsummer Day,
various Harvest Days, All Souls' Day, and on to
Christmas again.(30)   Particular trades had their
days of festivity: St Crispin's Day for shoemakers,
St Paul's day for tinners.   Parishes held annual
feasts - wakes or revels - which were times of
great celebration and conviviality, of eating and

drinking, bringing the parish together.(31) Shrovetide was a time of eating: pancakes, and in the
North, eggs and slices of bacon.(32) To steal a
phrase from Malcolmson, such entertainments were
petty carnivals, times for self-indulgence and
letting off steam.(33) May Day was another outlet
for merriment, and generally acknowledged to be a
period of sexual licence. 'Lords' and 'Ladies' or
'Kings' and 'Queens' from the ordinary population
would be elected for the day.(34) Celebrations at
Whitsun and Midsummer Day likewise involved the
choice of Lords of Misrule, 'Grand-captains of mis-
chief', or Lords and Ladies of the Ale; rules were
suspended temporarily, the lowly reigned, the world
was turned upside down.(35) Indeed if one considers
the evidence for the eighteenth and nineteenth
centuries, there is little support for the common
misconception that carnival was weak in England.
The Autobiography of Samuel Bamford demonstrates the
richness of popular ritual.(36) The problem lies
with demonstrating that this range existed in the
earlier period. One suspects that it did, though
the sources are not always forthcoming.
  From the Combe Martin 'hunting the Earl of Rone'
to the Abbots Bromley Horn Dance, English calendar
rituals were extremely localised in character. This
brings us to another dominant aspect of popular
culture in the early modern period, the importance
of regional variation (cf. chs. 1 and 2). Yet again
this was linked to orality, but it also reflected
the geographical horizons of the bulk of England's
inhabitants. England was a nation of high but
short-range geographical mobility. The median
distances travelled by masters and servants to hiring fairs was something like nine kilometres; while
it has been calculated that the social arena of the
villagers of Terling in Essex, was 'largely contained within a distance of ten miles' (approximate-
ly the drawing distance of a fair).(37)
  The phenomenon of localism had been interestingly demonstrated for the middle ages by the Corpus
Christi plays, with shepherds keeping their flocks
by night 'in the fields near Chester', or Cain
requesting that he 'be buried at the head of
Goodybower quarry' - just outside Wakefield.(38) In
the seventeenth century the regional markets and
fairs - Yarmouth's Michaelmas fishing-fair, the
Farnham corn-market, the Dorking poultry market and
lamb fair, the Penkridge horse fair - must have
provided a different ambience to popular culture in
various parts of the nation.(39) Hiring dates for

servants in husbandry ranged from Michaelmas in the
south and east to Martinmas in the North and May Day
in Lincolnshire and the West, so presumably the
pulse of plebeian festivities varied accordingly.(40)
English men and women spoke the same language, it is
true, but they did so in widely diverging dialects,
and contemporaries like Daniel Defoe spoke despair-
ingly of different races. Print and literacy would
bring a greater standardisation of English.(41)

Popular culture was not only regionally
nuanced, it was also layered and divided according
to occupation, social status and gender. To quote
Burke, there were 'many popular cultures or many
varieties of popular culture'.(42) One could pursue
subcultures indefinitely. Trades and occupations
had their own saints and saints' days, their own
superstitions (particularly miners and fishermen),(43) and sometimes, as it seems with the boat-
people of Oxford, their own artwork.(44) Each of the
Companies of London had a distinctive colour, arms
and banner.(45) And trades presumably had their own
vocabularies and rituals, intimately tied to the
processes of work.(46) Then there were the subcultures of youth,(47) criminality,(48) and religious
sectarianism (Muggletonians and Quakers, for
example).(49)

Gender differences must also have been important, though predictably we know least about the
role of women in popular culture. Sadly the women
in the pages which follow appear infrequently, and
then often as victims. (With this in mind, the
material which Ingram uncovers in his chapter on
libels and rough music makes for depressing reading.)
Male dominance was publicly proclaimed in a number
of popular rituals, including the 'wife-sales', a
plebeian form of divorce in which the wife was led
by a halter into the market place and sold.(50)
Insubordinate wives could be ritually humiliated in
the skimmington ride. 'Scolds' - women who disturbed and disrupted the community - could be
punished with a ducking on the cucking stool, or in
the north-east of England with a metal head-and-
mouth clamp called a brank.(51) Geoffrey Quaife's
work on Somerset provides some horrendous examples
of sexual violence - physical and verbal - towards
women, although it is difficult to know how widespread the phenomenon was.(52)

Women were excluded from many of the points of
contact for popular culture. Few gained apprenticeships, and those who joined guilds usually did so
through marriage.(53) Probably few unaccompanied

women would have felt at ease in the environments of
the alehouse and tavern except during the occasion
of a wake or an ale; they were, as now, male-
dominated milieus.(54) Many of the leisure activities of the period were male-oriented. The largest
role that women could hope for in sports and
recreations was that of spectator. Morris dancing,
bell-ringing, cock-fighting, pugilism and wrestling
were male affairs, as, presumably, was the 'manly
sport of football'. Women watched bull-baits, but
it was the men who handled the dogs and officiated
over the proceedings.(55) At horse races women were
also peripheral: 'You see no ladies at New-Market',
wrote Defoe (though Newmarket was in any case a
<u>gentry</u> affair).(56) Women did take part in many of
the popular festivities - in May Day and harvest
celebrations, for example, and in the various wakes
and ales. They even had their own day, at Hocktide,
when they blocked the streets and bound male
passers-by who were released on payment of a
dole.(57) In Kent they also had their own fair, the
Charlton Horn-Fair, when (Defoe noted with disapproval) 'the women are especially impudent for that
day; as if it was a day that justify'd the giving
themselves a loose to all manner of indecency and
immodesty, without any reproach, or without suffering the censure which such behaviour would deserve
at another time'.(58) However the theme of such
affairs, as with carnival, was one of temporary
madness. The world was topsy turvy, but it was for
a mere moment, a temporary inversion which threw
'normality' into sharp relief.

Women were less literate than men. The coming
of writing, as Burke has put it, merely 'added to
the list of cultural items which women did not share'
with men.(59) Although it is likely that the literacy figures hide a large number of women who were
able to read but not write, and who were therefore
not excluded entirely from the printing revolution,
it still remains true that the role of women in
popular culture was stronger in the oral realm. The
poet Clare recalled that when he worked in the
fields as a boy, the women who were helping him with
the weeding told tales of giants, hobgoblins and
fairies - 'old women's memories ... to smoothen our
labour'. In Bedford during the English Revolution,
John Bunyan came across 'three or four poor women
sitting at a door in the sun, and talking about the
things of God.'(60) We need to know more about the
contact points for female popular culture. Much of
women's labour was domestic, and collective, so

presumably the entry points for this almost invisible
cultural world are the places where, or the times
when, women gathered: the parish pump, well or
stream where they washed clothes and collected
water, at the bakery or mill; during harvesting,
spinning, or when dung and wood was collected for
fuel, or on their frequent trips to fairs and
markets. All provided opportunities for female
interaction and exchange of views.(61)

We should be wary of painting too bleak a
picture of the plight of women in Tudor-Stuart
England. Keith Wrightson has provided plenty of
evidence of caring and companionate marriages.(62)
Nor should we be trapped into thinking of female
cultural acquiescence. Indeed Martin Ingram's work
(chapter 5 below) detects an element of insecurity
in charivaris, a recognition of the gap between the
ideals and realities of a patriarchal system;
Bernard Capp (chapter 6) makes a similar comment
about popular literature. Women took part in, often
dominated, and sometimes led food riots, and were
active in the 1640s in the protests in London at the
outbreak of civil war. They found self-expression
and a measure of equality in some of the radical
sectarian movements of the English Revolution.(63)
Quaife has discovered some examples of seventeenth-
century Somerset women who revelled in their sexuality, who in outrageous ways overturned customary
expectations about the public behaviour of
women(64) - though we can assume that such characters
were rare, and that their mere existence, their
recognised oddity, served to reinforce the
traditional model of acceptable female behaviour.

The great cultural divide within the 'little
tradition' of the seventeenth century, as we shall
see in this volume, was the division between 'rough'
and 'respectable'. It reflected (though not rigidly)
socio-economic division. William Hunt and Keith
Wrightson have argued that population growth and
inflation in early modern England produced a polarisation of society between a fraction of the
'middling sort' (prosperous yeomen, substantial
tradesmen and artisans) and the poor. These parish
elites below the level of the gentry were drawing
apart from the traditional world of popular culture.
Sometimes, though not necessarily (see chapter 4),
this socio-cultural fission was sharpened by the
ideology of Puritanism, an ideology of discipline
with an emphasis on order and godly reformation,
hostile to the old popular culture, and with a
simple division of humankind into the elect few and

the reprobate many.(65)   The godly minority felt
alienated from the 'prophane, ungodly, presumptuous
multitude' who, as Richard Baxter wrote, would
travel miles to go to a market yet refused to go to
hear a minister, and who had been heard to say 'That
if the Puritans were in Heaven, and the good fellows
in Hell, they had rather go to Hell, than to
Heaven.'(66) The existence of this self-conscious
culture of a section of the middling sort suggests
that Edward Thompson's simple division between
patrician and plebeian cultures is not totally
applicable to the seventeenth century.(67)   It is a
reminder too of the importance of religion in
popular culture.

III

Burke's <u>Popular Culture</u> begins with a discussion of the concept of two cultural traditions,
first advanced by the anthropologist Robert
Redfield.   With some modifications, Burke suggests,
this concept is a useful starting point for understanding the dichotomy between elite and popular
culture in the early modern period.

> Applying this model to early modern
> Europe, we can identify the great tradition
> easily enough.   It includes the classical
> tradition, as it was handed down in schools
> and universities;   the tradition of medieval
> scholastic philosophy and theology, far from
> dead in the sixteenth and seventeenth cen-
> turies;   and some intellectual movements
> which are likely to have affected only the
> educated minority - the Renaissance, the
> Scientific Revolution of the seventeenth
> century, the Enlightenment.   Subtract all
> this from the culture of early modern
> Europe, and what residue is left?   There
> are folksongs and folktales;   devotional
> images and decorated marriage-chests;
> mystery plays and farces;   broadsides and
> chap-books;   and, above all, festivals,
> like the feasts of the saints and the great
> seasonal festivals such as Christmas, New
> Year, Carnival, May, and Midsummer.   This
> is the material with which this book will
> be primarily concerned;   with craftsmen as
> well as peasants, with printed books as
> well as oral traditions.

But, continues Burke, this is only a starting point.
Redfield's model needs to be revised; we need to
take into account cultural flow and overlap. Burke
writes in one place of a 'two-way traffic' between
the two traditions, yet the emphasis is on the
unequalness of the overlap. The elite participated
in popular culture ('popular culture was everybody's
culture'), they were 'bi-cultural', culturally
'amphibious': the people did not participate in the
great tradition. 'Thus the crucial difference in
early modern Europe ... was that between the majority, for whom popular culture was the only culture,
and the minority, who had access to the great
tradition but participated in the little tradition
as a second culture.' However things did not remain
the same throughout the period - and here Burke
introduces a further theme of social change - for
the elite gradually withdrew from the second culture
during the course of the seventeenth and eighteenth
centuries until, by the end of that period, the two
were 'now separated, as never before'.(68)
    Several of the chapters of this volume provide
examples of overlap and interaction between the two
traditions in seventeenth-century England, in some
cases to the point of questioning the viability of
a division between elite and popular culture. In
London (Peter Burke's chapter) patrician rubbed
shoulders with pleb at Bartholomew Fair and in May
Day celebrations, and both participated in the Lord
Mayor's shows. In Bristol, Jonathan Barry argues,
hierarchical civic culture was 'widely shared and
valued'; while patterns of leisure and social
zoning did not (until about 1700) imply rigid class
divisions. His chapter emphasises the weakness of
the cultural divide between the Bristol elite and
the mass of the population. When we turn to the
various spheres of popular culture, there is further
evidence of overlap. My chapter on religion refers
to popular attachment to the rituals of the Church
of England, the established church, and beliefs in
astrology, witchcraft and fairies which were by no
means limited to the lower level. Similarly Martin
Ingram's chapters on sex and marriage, and rough
music, ridings and libels provide examples of
shared values - the need for marriage in church,
belief in the immorality of adultery and bastard-
bearing, attachment to patriarchalism. Sections of
the people took part in the regulation of sexuality
and marriage; control was not (pace Robert
Muchembled)(69) simply imposed from above. The elite
tolerated and participated in charivaris; ridings,

Ingram claims, 'bore witness to a measure of consensus between rich and poor, rulers and ruled'.
Elsewhere, he has argued, like Barry, against
'insisting on too pronounced a split between "popular" and "elite" culture'.(70) In the area of
popular literature it seems that many of the cheap
pamphlets dealt with by Capp formed the childhood
reading of the elite or became entertainment for
patrician adults - it is worth recalling that one of
the best English collections of chapbooks and
printed ballads is the collection of one Samuel
Pepys. Even the content of much of this literature,
the ever-popular chivalric tales, had been discarded
by an earlier aristocratic audience. Almanacs were
often written by members of the gentry and pseudo-
gentry and have indeed been described as a kind of
bridge between high and popular culture.(71) The law
was centrally important in seventeenth-century
England, at all levels of society. James Sharpe
establishes the ubiquity of the law, and uses it to
question yet again the alleged dichotomy between the
two cultures. When we turn to food riots (Buchanan
Sharp's chapter) we find that they were usually
attempts to <u>enforce</u> officially sanctioned market
regulations: they were not attacks on the established order, but rather attempts to reinforce it.

The world of popular leisure, not specifically
covered in this book, provides one last example of
overlap. The great centres of plebeian recreation
in the seventeenth century were the alehouses, about
50,000 in all in mid-century or one for every one
hundred inhabitants. They provided the venues for
so many of the activities and games of the people,
from dancing and the performance of plays, to bowls,
marbles, dice, backgammon, cards, shove-penny and
ten-bones. The upper classes generally kept away
from this milieu, preferring the atmosphere of the
inn.(72) But the gentry were by no means excluded
from the recreational life of their inferiors.
Indeed they took part in a whole range of popular
activities: cock-fighting, bull-baiting, pugilism,
horse-racing, cudgelling, harvest festivities,
hunting. They hired morris dancers, players and
mummers.(73)

Does all this threaten the usefulness or
integrity of the term popular culture? Not, I
think, if one begins to ask questions about social
space. It is not enough (<u>pace</u> R. M. Isherwood)(74)
simply to locate patrician and plebeian in the same
place; one has to determine what they were doing
in that place, what their respective roles were,

whether they participated on equal terms. As Isaac
has put it, 'shared pastimes cut across but did not
level social distinctions', and given the right conditions shared pastimes could actually reinforce
hierarchy.(75) The gentry were the patrons of sport.
They, or the mayor or aldermen in the towns, would
donate the bull for the bull-bait or bull-running
(in some places the baiting would take place outside
the door of the donor). They owned the horses at
the horse races, the cocks at the cock fights, and
they provided the purses and the bulk of the
betting.(76) They organised the football matches
which would usually range across vast tracts of
land, with the houses of the gentry organisers sometimes forming the goals.(77) They rode in the hunt
and shot the game. The plebs, for their part,
watched. They cheered. They followed the hunt and
beat the game. In the words of George Gascoigne,
hunting was 'a sport for gentle bloods':

> The paine I leave for servants such,
> as beate the bushie woods
> To make their masters sport.(78)

Robert Malcolmson uses cock-fighting as an example
of a sport which cut across class lines; and yet
the very passage he cites to support this claim (an
extract from the diary of Oliver Heywood, 1680) dis-
tinguishes between 'gentlemens cocks' and the cocks
of the poorer sort, refers to separate days being
set aside for the respective cocking, and tensions
when 'beggars' presumed to fight 'their cocks
among gentlemen'. It may well be true that in
some cockpits, as a foreign observer noted, 'the
people, gentle and simple ... [sat] with no distinction of place' and mingled when they placed
their wagers, but the relationship was not without
its strains. And we know that in Elizabethan and
Stuart London the fashionable sat close to the ring,
the plebs sat towards the back of the pit.(79)
    At the harvest or shearing suppers the patrons,
the masters or dames, provided food and entertainment for their willing workers, sitting at the head
of the table or even, perhaps, like Bathsheba
Everdene in Thomas Hardy's Far From the Madding
Crowd, maintaining their social position by spatial
separation from the labourers. Even if there was a
brief spell of knockabout humour between patron and
worker, it was always clear that it was a temporary
matter. The social framework was always plain:
people were aware of the source of the largesse and

the provider of the venue.

> Our Master joyful at the welcome sight,
> Invites us all to feast with him at Night,
> A Table plentifully spread we find,
> And Jugs of humming Beer to cheer the Mind;
> Which he, too generous, pushes on so fast,
> We think no Toils to come, nor mind the past.
> But the next Morning soon reveals the Cheat,
> When the same Toils we must again repeat:
> To the same Barns again must back return,
> To labour there for room for next Year's Corn.(80)

One only needs to look at the morris dancers in the painting, The Thames at Richmond, to appreciate the politics of space. Gentry look on while the common people perform; largesse is dispensed but hands do not touch.(81)

If we return to some of the examples of overlap mentioned earlier and look at them in more detail the distinction between popular and elite culture seems to have more integrity. All classes participated in the Lord Mayor's shows, but the upper classes watched from the balconies and the 'blue apron' audience from the streets.(82) In the realm of ideas it is once again not enough merely to locate spheres; one has to ask what beliefs were held by whom within these broad categories? The iconography of the pageantry in London appealed at different levels - classical imagery for the 'great tradition', more simple forms for the 'little tradition'.(83) As I stress in chapter 3, values at the popular level were not necessarily at one with those proclaimed by the religious establishment, even though plebeian and patrician were nominally of the Church of England. Whether we turn to the law or politics we find that popular attitudes, opinions, expectations, were often sharply at variance with those of social superiors. What were perquisites, tolerated minor infractions, customary practices or perfectly legitimate activities for one group (trade perks, smuggling, wrecking, poaching, gleaning, coining, wood gathering) were theft, embezzlement or crime for another.(84) Protection of traditional rights (anti-improvement protest and food riots) could be seen as rebellion.

Possibly the most fruitful approach when dealing with culture and ideology in the early modern period is to think in terms of hegemony. A dominant social group or class can maintain its supremacy through force, coercion or bare-faced suppression, or it can control through what Marx and Engels called the means of intellectual production - in other words, through ideology and culture. This latter way is usually known as hegemony. The concept of hegemony, then, normally associated with the Italian Marxist theorist Antonio Gramsci, 'refers to an order in which a common social-moral language is spoken, in which one concept of reality is dominant, informing with its spirit all modes of thought and behaviour ... hegemony is the predominance obtained by <u>consent</u> rather than force of one class or group over other classes'.(85) The hegemonic group maintains its position by dominating the organisations which shape ideas: the institutions of religion, the law, education, politics and communication. So, as E. P. Thompson argues in his discussion of eighteenth-century English society, hegemony determines the parameters of the possible, it inhibits the development of social, political or cultural alternatives to the status quo and the prevailing ideology. Yet it is also an on-going process, a struggle, a striving for control which can never be all-encompassing. In other words, hegemony allows for class rule, the impulse towards domination; it helps to explain compliance and the limitations of popular thought and activity; but it also allows for, and explains, popular resistance.(86)

Seventeenth century England was a hierarchical society. It was a society in which the values of the elite, the gentlemen, were dominant. This is not to say that such values were unchallenged - they were not - and that they were universally accepted; it is merely to say that the dominant ideology was one of paternalism and deference. The stress was on order and privilege. Ideology justified, supported, legitimated social inequality, for the doctrine of 'the Great Chain of Being' bound people in superior-inferior relationships. Order was said to be divinely ordained. People were told to accept their lot on earth and they would then be rewarded in Heaven. They were informed that when the Fifth Commandment told them to honour thy father and mother it had in mind <u>all</u> superiors. The Anglican Prayer Book Catechism b̄ĭd the catechumen 'to submit myself to all my governors, teachers, spiritual pastors and masters: to order myself lowly and reverently to all my betters ... to learn and labour truly to get mine own living, and to do my duty in that state of life unto which it shall please God to call me'.(87)

The idea of order and hierarchy permeated the

structure of early Stuart law and government. In the absence of a standing army, a professional police force and an organised bureaucracy of any substance, government depended on the role of unpaid, amateur officials. These part-time officers formed a hierarchy of government which corresponded more or less to the social hierarchy in country and town, stretching from the noble Lord and Deputy Lieutenant and the gentleman Justice of the Peace, down to the more humble yeoman, tradesman, artisan or husbandman as churchwarden or petty constable. (The labouring poor and women were mostly excluded.)(88)

Hierarchy was reinforced in a multitude of ways. Status and rank were reflected in manners, speech and dress. There were correct ways to approach a social superior, appropriate forms of address which were different to those employed to a social equal or to an inferior. One of the reasons that the Quakers caused so much consternation was because they refused to acknowledge the cultural accoutrements of paternalism. The Quaker spirit within, explained the young John Locke in 1660, 'leads men from the sense of curtesy and gratitude'.(89)

As Wrightson points out, paternalism implied reciprocity: protection of inferiors by superiors, respect and support for superiors by inferiors. It was a reciprocity based on unequal power. The superior would buy a drink for the inferior - not vice versa. The landlord could look out for his tenants in times of stress, perhaps intercede for them if they got into trouble, possibly hold Christmas dinner for them. Such actions proclaimed the social order.

> Such beneficence cost little, and in return a price was tacitly demanded - in terms of deference, obedience and implicit recognition of the legitimacy of the prevailing social order. The assistance rendered might vary in its content and its regularity, and so no doubt did the degree of genuine deference elicited in return. It was, nonetheless, an exchange of essentially unequal obligations: crumbs from the table, relatively speaking, in return for at least an outward subscription to a world-view and a tacit rejection of alternative definitions of the situation.(90)

Of course, force, or the threat of force, was the ultimate legitimiser. It 'is not Devines, preaching Hell, & Damnation, or Excommunication, that can keepe a company of Rude people, From throwing him out of ye Pulpitt', the Earl of Newcastle advised Charles II, 'for without ye power of Armes, ye prentices of a Shrove tusday, would teare ye Bishopps Moste Reverent Lawne sleeves, from his Armes, & cutt his throte To Boote'.(91) But we should not forget the importance of ideology and culture as class weapons.

With some modifications, then, Thompson's gentry-plebs model for the eighteenth century can be applied to the seventeenth. This is the metaphor of 'fields of force', with the gentlemen at one pole, the plebs at the other, the middling sort oscillating between the two, and with the gentry's hegemony defining the limits of the field. The problem with the seventeenth century, I intimated earlier, is that the middling sort were emerging as a force in their own right, and the split of the ruling classes in mid-century (the 1640s and 1650s) allowed the emergence of ideological alternatives to the dominant culture.(92) The 'larger outlines of power, station in life, political authority' <u>no longer</u> seemed quite so 'inevitable and irreversible'.(93) Even so, much of the debate of the 1640s and 1650s was conducted within a conservative framework, and what break there was with paternalism merely served to reinforce it in the long run. Order was restored in 1660. For much of the Stuart century, then, Thompson's model seems applicable.

The notion of hegemony also reconciles evidence of the overlap between elite and popular cultures with evidence of popular resistance and rebellion. Apart from the ideological divisions within the ruling group, there were two main structural weaknesses in gentry hegemony during the seventeenth century. The first relates to the way in which the operation of the law permeated all or most sections of society. In theory, incorporation of most groups into the institutional processes of law and government - as jurors, constables, churchwardens - is an effective means of gentry control. But in practice the essential point about the amateur officers was their discretionary power, the fact that they could act as a buffer between the statute book or central policy and the needs of the local community and could modify or shape the law to meet their concepts of justice. The very flexibility of the law could thus operate against the desires of the ruling class.(94) The other weakness (or ambiguity) is an ideological one. Hegemony, we saw earlier, relies on consent, not just on ideological control. It is not enough to blinker the ruled, they have to be convinced. Whether they relate to salvation of souls or equality before the law, doctrines have to appeal, have actually to correspond to the needs of those who are governed. The danger for the rulers, as Thompson and others have pointed out, is that they will be trapped by the logic of their own rhetoric; 'they played the games of power according to rules which suited them, but they could not break those rules or the whole game would be thrown away ... so far from the ruled shrugging off this rhetoric as a hypocrisy, some part of it at least was taken over as part of the rhetoric of the plebeian crowd'.(95) The 'just price', the 'rule of law', 'the equality of man', were terms which could return to haunt the rulers.

We shall see in this volume that ridings and rough music could be used against unjust magistrates and enclosers (those who threatened the economic well-being of the community), and in political demonstrations.(96) Riots frequently occurred on holidays, the traditional time for ritual and festivities. As Paul Slack has pointed out recently, movements of protest were linked 'with the everyday world of popular culture'.(97) The Earl of Newcastle thought that recreations would 'amuse ye peoples thoughts and keepe them in harmless actions'. Yet an anti-improvement riot in the Lincolnshire fens in 1641 began with a game of football; the ball was kicked against a house which had recently been erected on drained land and the mob then proceeded to demolish the building ('so they have pulled down many'). The same happened several times in the fenland areas during the seventeenth and eighteenth centuries, an almost theatrical reminder that access to common land involved more than issues of bread-and-butter, and that protection of communal recreation space was at one with defence of customary rights.(98) The theatre of popular culture could also borrow from the repertoire of the elite, infusing forms with new emphases in mock trials, mock baptisms and mock burials. Early modern rebels and rioters often assembled, like the militia, to the beat of a drum, elected their own 'captain' or 'mayor' - Captain Cobbler, Captain Pouch, Captain, Lord, and Master Poverty, Captains Charity, Faith and Piety, Lady Skimmington - and some even issued 'quasi-royal proclamations'.(99)

Food or anti-improvement riots operated within the given framework. Paul Slack and Peter Clark have written of the 'conservatism of popular

aspirations'; 'rioters' objectives were usually
conservative, limited and deferential'.(100) Rioters
acted in defence of custom and traditional rights
such as those of subsistence and of access to the
common land; like the Clubmen of the Civil Wars,
they could move to protect their communities against
outsiders and disruptive and unwelcome innovation.
They acted in defence of the status quo, persuading
magistrates to intervene against grain hoarders and
speculators, fen drainers and enclosers. There is
nothing blind or unthinking about this kind of
activity, defensive and reactive though it was.
Barrett Beer is well wide of the mark with his
claims for the credulity of the commons, for their
'imperfect understanding of the past and ... limited
comprehension of the present'.(101) The point surely
is, that like today's British miners, the commons
understood the past and the present all too well.
Defence of tradition was defence of tried ways of
doing things, of accumulated wisdom. Resistance was
resistance to the market forces which threatened the
old way of life. Perhaps such women and men were
credulous in so far as they were unaware that they
were doomed by the 'onward march of history' or by
the inexorability of economic rationalisation. But
we can hardly be surprised that they resisted. Such
intransigence is not usefully described as conservative: traditionalist is a far better term.
Frequently riots were attempts to enforce the law;
to paraphrase Sharp (chapter 8), much of this
activity reflected the official point of view. Yet
it was at the same time 'a more radical restatement
of it'. The magistrate did not always find it convenient to be reminded of his duty. In the words
of Francis Bacon, 'a froward retention of custom is
as turbulent a thing as an innovation'.(102)

The popular literary forms examined by Capp in
chapter 6 show similar constraints. In this literature there was little or no direct challenge to
the political or social order. Sandra Clark's
recent study of Elizabethan pamphlets has referred
also to 'the innate conservatism of popular thought'
as it is reflected in its literature, its 'reaction-
ary tone'.(103) Even the Elizabethan and Jacobean
'bourgeois hero tale', a new type, subscribed to
the dominant ideology of the landed elite: the
heroes were merchants but they acted like knights
and were still enmeshed in the language of chivalry.(104) And yet, as Capp demonstrates, there could
be a subversive edge to popular literature, a
momentary overturning of the hierarchical order, a

carnival-like mockery of social superiors.

Finally, Sharp has reminded us that 'animosity
... could easily lurk behind the facade of deference'.(105) We catch sight of it only rarely: with
the sailor who when told that a Lord had been killed
in battle 'said in his rough country fashion that
the King could make ten lords in a single day but
that it would take more than five years to make a
good sailor';(106) with those among the lower orders
who believed that the King <u>caused</u> the disease the
King's Evil (rather than curing it);(107) or with
the doggerel overheard from a seventeenth-century
servant

> I can sowe
> I can mowe
> And I can stacke
> And I can doe
> My master too
> When my master turnes his back.(108)

IV

In 1700 many changes lay in the future. Precocious London pointed the way ahead. There would
be a greater commercialisation of popular culture,(109) although as Burke shows in this book, the
seeds were sown in the seventeenth century. Literacy rates would improve. Popular culture would
become more 'politicised' - in the sense of mass-
based parties, organisation and co-ordination, for
there was nothing non-political about defence of
custom and the 'moral economy' during the early
modern period.(110) The magical world would vanish,
though it is becoming clear that 'the disenchant-
ment of the world' was a long, drawn-out affair.
Nor can we talk, without qualification, of a
nineteenth-century decline in the influence of the
established church, for it can in fact be argued
that the bulk of the English population had never
really been <u>fully</u> integrated into the Church of
England. Leisure would be transformed, but in a
more subtle and varied way than the proponents of
modernisation theory have been prepared to
recognise.(111)

The seventeenth century was a period of transition. Yet the final message of this volume is
that we should not exaggerate the century as a great
turning point for popular culture. In several of
the cultural areas which we will examine there was
no <u>sharp</u> break with the medieval period.(112) His-

torians of early modern popular culture are aware
that they must look ahead to the modern era if they
want to explain social change. They should now be
equally concerned with things medieval, for it seems
that many of these changes had an earlier starting
point which we are only just beginning to explore.
Perhaps when one approaches the subject of popular
culture in the early modern period one should think
in terms of the *longue durée*.

Notes

1. For good summaries of this whole issue, see D. Cressy,
   'Educational Opportunity in Tudor and Stuart England',
   History of Education Quarterly, xvi (1976); K. Wrightson,
   English Society 1580-1680 (1982), pp. 183-98.
2. D. Hirst, The Representative of the People? (Cambridge,
   1975).
3. B. Reay, 'Radicalism and Religion in the English
   Revolution : an Introduction', in J. F. McGregor and B.
   Reay (eds.), Radical Religion in the English Revolution
   (Oxford, 1984), pp. 18-19.
4. B. Manning, The English People and the English Revolution
   1640-1649 (1976), chs. 1-5.
5. See, however, the suggestive studies by A. Everitt, 'Farm
   Labourers', in J. Thirsk (ed.), The Agrarian History of
   England and Wales ... 1500-1640 (Cambridge, 1967), ch. 7;
   A. Kussmaul, Servants in husbandry in early modern
   England (Cambridge, 1981); M. Prior, Fisher Row.
   Fishermen, Bargemen, and Canal Boatmen in Oxford, 1500-
   1900 (Oxford, 1982).
6. Burke, Popular Culture, Prologue.
7. Friends House Library, London, 'Some Account of the Birth
   Education ... of Josiah Langdale' (1723).
8. Cressy, Literacy; Spufford, Small Books, ch. 2; and pp.
   49, 62-3 below.
9. Spufford, Small Books, chs. 1-5; *idem*, 'First steps in
   literacy', Social History, iv (1979), p. 430.
10. P. Clark, 'The Ownership of Books in England, 1560-1640:
    The Example of Some Kentish Townsfolk', in L. Stone (ed.),
    Schooling and Society (Baltimore, 1976), ch. 4; T.
    Laqueur, 'The Cultural Origins of Popular Literacy in
    England 1500-1850', Oxford Review of Education, ii
    (1976); B. Reay, 'The Muggletonians', in C. Hill, B.
    Reay and W. Lamont, The World of the Muggletonians
    (1983), pp. 48-9.
11. R. W. Malcolmson, Life and Labour in England 1700-1780
    (1981), p. 99.
12. K. Thomas, Man and the Natural World (1983), pp. 70-87.
13. These English proverbs come from J. Howell, Proverbs

(1659). For discussions of the role of proverbs, see N. Z. Davis, <u>Society and Culture in Early Modern France</u> (Stanford, 1975), ch. 8: 'Proverbial Wisdom and Popular Errors'; E. Weber, <u>Peasants into Frenchmen</u> (1979), ch. 25: 'The Oral Wisdom'.

14. W. J. Ong, <u>Orality and Literacy</u> (1982), p. 30.

15. Malcolmson, <u>Life and Labour</u>, pp. 96, 99; R. C. Richardson, <u>Puritanism in north-west England</u> (Manchester, 1972), p. 102.

16. Reay, 'Muggletonians', p. 48.

17. Friends House Library, London, MS. Morning Meeting Minutes 1673-1692, pp. 22, 24, 61, 73.

18. H. Forde, 'Derbyshire Quakers 1650-1761' (Univ. of Leicester Ph.D. thesis, 1977), ch. 7, p. 217.

19. Ong, <u>Orality</u>, pp. 23, 26, 34, 38, 45, 70.

20. PRO, ASSI 44/5, Yorks 1652; ASSI 45/4/3/103, 108.

21. P. Clark, <u>The English Alehouse</u> (1983), pp. 67-8; R. F. Bretherton, 'Country Inns and Alehouses', in L. Reginald (ed.), <u>Englishmen at Rest and Play. Some Phases of English Leisure 1558-1714</u> (Oxford, 1931), pp. 196-7; C. Phythian-Adams, 'Milk and Soot. The Changing Vocabulary of a Popular Ritual in Stuart and Hanoverian London', in D. Fraser and A. Sutcliffe (eds.), <u>The Pursuit of Urban History</u> (1983), p. 84.

22. W. Hunt, <u>The Puritan Moment</u> (Cambridge, Mass., 1983), p. 51.

23. Cressy, <u>Literacy</u>, pp. 59-60 (for some examples).

24. Everitt, 'Farm Labourers', p. 435; D. Defoe, <u>A Tour through the Whole Island of Great Britain</u> (1974 edn.), ii, p. 31.

25. R. Isaac, <u>The Transformation of Virginia 1740-1790</u> (Chapel Hill, 1982), p. 122.

26. B. Bushaway, <u>By Rite. Custom, Ceremony and Community in England 1700-1880</u> (1982), pp. 81ff.; Everitt, 'Farm Labourers', p. 405.

27. T. F. Thiselton-Dyer, <u>Old English Social Life</u> (1898), p. 196.

28. G. R. Quaife, <u>Wanton Wenches and Wayward Wives. Peasants and Illicit Sex in Early Seventeenth Century England</u> (1979), pp. 168-9, 199; and p. 170 below.

29. P. Linebaugh, 'The Tyburn Riot Against the Surgeons', in D. Hay and others, <u>Albion's Fatal Tree. Crime and Society in Eighteenth-Century England</u> (1977), pp. 111-15.

30. Bushaway, <u>By Rite</u>; C. Phythian-Adams, <u>Local History and Folklore</u> (1975); A. R. Wright, <u>British Calendar Customs</u> (3 vols., 1936-40).

31. R. W. Malcolmson, <u>Popular Recreations in English Society 1700-1850</u> (Cambridge, 1973), pp. 16-19, 52-6.

32. Wright, <u>British Calendar Customs</u>, i, pp. 2-3, 8-10.

33. Malcolmson, <u>Popular Recreations</u>, p. 19. For the carnivalesque generally, see Burke, <u>Popular Culture</u>, ch. 7. For

a later period, see J. K. Walton and R. Poole, 'The
Lancashire Wakes in the Nineteenth Century' and D. A.
Reid, 'Interpreting the Festival Calendar : Wakes and
Fairs as Carnivals', in R. D. Storch (ed.), <u>Popular
Culture and Custom in Nineteenth-Century England</u> (1982),
chs. 5-6.

34. Phythian-Adams, 'Milk and Soot', pp. 85-92; P. Stubbes,
<u>The Anatomie of Abuses</u> (1583), no pagination: 'May-
games'.

35. Stubbes, <u>Anatomie of Abuses</u>.

36. <u>The Autobiography of Samuel Bamford</u>, ed. W. H. Chaloner
(1967), i, pp. 131-58.

37. Kussmaul, <u>Servants in husbandry</u>, p. 60; K. Wrightson and
D. Levine, <u>Poverty and Piety in an English Village</u> (NY,
1979), p. 76; E. W. Moore, 'Medieval English Fairs', in
J. A. Raftis (ed.), <u>Pathways to Medieval Peasants</u>
(Toronto, 1981), p. 285.

38. V. A. Kolve, <u>The Play Called Corpus Christi</u> (Stanford,
1966), pp. 111, 112, 114.

39. Defoe, <u>Tour</u>, i, pp. 66, 129, 142, 153, ii, p. 78.

40. Kussmaul, <u>Servants in husbandry</u>, p. 50.

41. Defoe, <u>Tour</u>, i, pp. 218-19; Malcolmson, <u>Life and Labour</u>,
p. 94; D. Leith, <u>A Social History of English</u> (1983),
p. 34. I have also benefited from hearing Keith Thomas's
talk 'Speech and its social implications in early modern
England'.

42. Burke, <u>Popular Culture</u>, p. 29 (and ch. 2).

43. P. Thompson, T. Wailey and T. Lummis, <u>Living the Fishing</u>
(1983), ch. 11; J. Rule, 'Methodism, Popular Beliefs and
Village Culture in Cornwall, 1800-50', in Storch (ed.),
<u>Popular Culture</u>, p. 62. These are, of course, more
recent examples.

44. Prior, <u>Fisher Row</u>, p. 5.

45. A. Plummer, <u>The London Weavers' Company 1600-1970</u> (1972),
pp. 225-6.

46. For some recent examples, see the glossaries in Thompson,
Wailey and Lummis, <u>Living the Fishing</u>; D. Douglass and
J. Krieger, <u>A Miner's Life</u> (1983). See also B. Gilding,
<u>The Journeymen Coopers of East London</u> (Oxford, 1971).

47. B. Capp, 'English Youth Groups and <u>The Pinder of Wake-
field</u>', and S. R. Smith, 'The London Apprentices as
Seventeenth-Century Adolescents', in P. Slack (ed.),
<u>Rebellion, Popular Protest and the Social Order in
Early Modern England</u> (Cambridge, 1984), chs. 10-11 (both
first appeared in <u>P. and P.</u>)

48. J. L. McMullan, 'Criminal Organization in Sixteenth and
Seventeenth Century London', <u>Social Problems</u>, xxix (1982);
M. Rediker, '"Under the Banner of King Death": the Social
World of Anglo-American Pirates, 1716-1726', <u>William and
Mary Quarterly</u>, xxxviii (1981); J. A. Sharpe, <u>Crime in
Early Modern England 1550-1750</u> (1984), ch. 5.

49. Reay, 'Muggletonians'; *idem*, The Quakers and the English Revolution (1985), ch. 6.
50. Work on the eighteenth century suggests that sales probably took place with the wife's consent in many cases, and were to her lover: Malcolmson, Life and Labour, pp. 103-4; see also S. P. Menefee, Wives for Sale (Oxford, 1981). However, Martin Ingram has informed me that there is very little reliable evidence of wife-sales (in the sense of the transfer of a wife after a marriage had actually been solemnised) before the end of the seventeenth century, and that he knows of no evidence for that century to support the claim that women consented and were sold to their lovers.
51. J. W. Spargo, Juridical Folklore in England Illustrated by the Cucking-Stool (Durham, Nth Carolina, 1944), pp. 27-8, 121-2; C. Davidson, A Woman's Work is Never Done (1982), p. 194. For the skimmington, see ch. 5 below.
52. Quaife, Wanton Wenches, pp. 168-70, 173-4, and index: 'violence'.
53. V. Brodsky Elliott, 'Single Women in the London Marriage Market', in R. B. Outhwaite (ed.), Marriage and Society (1981), p. 91.
54. Clark, English Alehouse, pp. 131-2; K. Wrightson, 'Alehouses, Order and Reformation in Rural England, 1590-1660', in E. and S. Yeo (eds.), Popular Culture and Class Conflict 1590-1914 (Brighton, 1981), pp. 5-10.
55. Malcolmson, Popular Recreations, pp. 56 and illustration of a bull-bait (facing p. 117).
56. Defoe, Tour, i, p. 76.
57. Wright, British Calendar Customs, i, pp. 124ff.
58. Defoe, Tour, i, p. 97.
59. R. O'Day, Education and Society 1500-1800 (1982), ch. 10; Burke, Popular Culture, p. 50.
60. Malcolmson, Life and Labour, p. 98; J. Bunyan, Grace Abounding to the Chief of Sinners, ed. R. Sharrock (Oxford, 1962), p. 14.
61. A. Clark, Working Life of Women in the Seventeenth Century (1982 edn.), pp. xxxiv (introduction by M. Chaytor and J. Lewis), 51; Davidson, A Woman's Work, pp. 8-9, 76, 77, 138-9.
62. Wrightson, English Society, chs. 3-4.
63. For food riots, see ch. 8 below, and J. Walter, 'Grain riots and popular attitudes to the law', in J. Brewer and J. Styles (eds.), An Ungovernable People. The English and their law in the seventeenth and eighteenth centuries (1983), pp. 62-3. For the 1640s and the sects, see P. Higgins, 'The Reactions of Women', in B. Manning (ed.), Politics, Religion, and the English Civil War (1973); K. Thomas, 'Women and the Civil War Sects', P. and P., 13 (1958).
64. Quaife, Wanton Wenches, pp. 156-8. Cf. J. Nestle, 'My

Mother liked to Fuck', in A. Snitow, C. Stansell and S. Thompson (eds.), Powers of Desire (NY, 1983).

65. Wrightson and Levine, Poverty and Piety; Hunt, Puritan Moment; Wrightson, English Society; D. Underdown, 'What was the English Revolution?', History Today, xxxiv (March 1984).

66. R. Baxter, The Saints Everlasting Rest (1677) (original edn. 1649/50), pp. 294, 354.

67. E. P. Thompson, 'Eighteenth-century English society: class struggle without class?', Social History, iii (1978), p. 151; idem, 'Patrician Society, Plebeian Culture', JSH, vii (1974), p. 395.

68. Burke, Popular Culture, pp. 24, 28-9, 58, 270.

69. R. Muchembled, Culture populaire et culture des élites dans la France moderne (XVe-XVIIIe siècles: essai (Paris, 1978).

70. M. Ingram, 'Ridings, Rough Music and the "Reform of Popular Culture" in Early Modern England', P. and P., 105 (1984).

71. B. Reay, 'Popular Literature in Seventeenth-Century England', Journal of Peasant Studies, x (1983); Wrightson, English Society, p. 197.

72. See Clark, English Alehouse, pp. 44, 123-5, 152-5.

73. Malcolmson, Popular Recreations, pp. 67-8.

74. R. M. Isherwood, 'Entertainment in the Parisian Fairs in the Eighteenth Century', Journal of Modern History, liii (1981), pp. 27-30.

75. Isaac, Transformation of Virginia, p. 104.

76. Malcolmson, Popular Recreations, pp. 56-7, 66-7.

77. N. Elias and E. Dunning, 'Folk Football in Medieval and Early Modern Britain', in E. Dunning (ed.), The Sociology of Sport (1971), ch. 7.

78. M. Vale, The Gentleman's Recreations (Cambridge, 1977), p. 28.

79. Malcolmson, Popular Recreations, pp. 49-50; R. Ashton, 'Popular Entertainment and Social Control in Later Elizabethan and Early Stuart London', London Journal, ix (1983), p. 9.

80. Malcolmson, Popular Recreations, pp. 59-64 (p. 61 for the quotation from Stephen Duck); Phythian-Adams, Local History, p. 26. And see Bushaway, By Rite, ch. 4.

81. See cover of this volume.

82. See p. 44 below.

83. P. 45 below.

84. Brewer and Styles (eds.), An Ungovernable People, Introduction, and chapters by Malcolmson and Styles; Hay and others, Albion's Fatal Tree, chapters by C. Winslow, J. G. Rule, and Hay (on poaching); J. Styles, 'Embezzlement, industry and the law in England, 1500-1800', in M. Berg, P. Hudson and M. Sonenscher (eds.), Manufacture in town and country before the factory (Cambridge, 1983), ch. 7;

J. G. Rule, 'Social Crime in the Rural South in the Eighteenth and Early Nineteenth Centuries', Southern History, i (1979); P. Munsche, Gentlemen and Poachers. The English Game Laws 1671-1831 (Cambridge, 1982); J. A. Sharpe, Crime in Seventeenth-century England: A county study (Cambridge, 1983), pp. 98, 100, 168-70, 176; idem, Crime in Early Modern England, ch. 6.

85. J. V. Femia, Gramsci's Political Thought (Oxford, 1981), ch. 2 (p. 24 for the quotation): an excellent account of the concept of hegemony.

86. Thompson, 'Eighteenth-century English society'; idem, 'Patrician Society, Plebeian Culture': two extremely important articles.

87. J. Schochet, 'Patriarchalism, Politics and Mass Attitudes in Stuart England', HJ, xii (1969), p. 429.

88. Wrightson, English Society, ch. 6.

89. The Correspondence of John Locke, ed. E. S. De Beer (Oxford, 1976), i, p. 145.

90. Wrightson, English Society, pp. 57-65 (p. 58 for the quotation).

91. Bodleian Lib., Oxford, MS. Clarendon 109, p. 39.

92. Hill, World Turned Upside Down; idem, The Experience of Defeat (1984); Manning, English People and the English Revolution, chs. 9-10; McGregor and Reay (eds.), Radical Religion.

93. Thompson, 'Patrician Society, Plebeian Culture', p. 388.

94. For the way in which the 'legal fabric ... was shot through with discretion' (Brewer and Styles), see K. Wrightson, 'Two concepts of order: justices, constables and jurymen in seventeenth-century England', in Brewer and Styles (eds.), An Ungovernable People, ch. 1; J. A. Sharpe, 'Enforcing the Law in the Seventeenth-Century English Village', in V. A. C. Gatrell, B. Lenman and G. Parker (eds.), Crime and the Law. The Social History of Crime in Western Europe since 1500 (1980), ch. 4. See, too, an important article for the eighteenth century: P. King, 'Decision-Makers and Decision-Making in the English Criminal Law, 1750-1800', HJ, xxvii (1984). The (now classic) best account of law as a weapon of the ruling class is D. Hay's 'Property, authority and the criminal law', in Albion's Fatal Tree, ch. 1.

95. E. P. Thompson, Whigs and Hunters (1977), p. 263.

96. N. Rogers, 'Popular Protest in Early Hanoverian London', in Slack (ed.), Rebellion, Popular Protest, ch. 13 (first published in P. and P.)

97. Slack (ed.), Rebellion, Popular Protest, Introduction, p. 11.

98. Bodleian Lib., MS. Clarendon 109, pp. 74-5; C. Holmes, Seventeenth-Century Lincolnshire (Lincoln, 1980), p. 155; Malcolmson, Popular Recreations, pp. 39-40.

99. P. Zagorin, Rebels and rulers, 1500-1660 (Cambridge, 1982), ii, p. 25; and see pp. 171, 281, 286, 294 below.

100. Slack (ed.), Rebellion, Popular Protest, p. 6; P. Clark, 'Popular Protest and Disturbance in Kent, 1558-1640', Economic History Review, xxix (1976), p. 378.
101. B. L. Beer, Rebellion and Riot. Popular Disorder in England during the Reign of Edward VI (Kent, Ohio, 1982), p. 6.
102. F. Bacon, Essays (1962 edn.), p. 74.
103. S. Clark, The Elizabethan Pamphleteers (1983), pp. 36, 215.
104. L. S. O'Connell, 'The Elizabethan Bourgeois Hero-Tale', in B. C. Malament (ed.), After the Reformation (Manchester, 1980).
105. P. 287 below.
106. The Diary of Thomas Isham of Lamport (1658-81) (Farnborough, 1971), p. 127.
107. B. Capp, Astrology and the Popular Press. English Almanacs 1500-1800 (1979), p. 212.
108. Kussmaul, Servants in husbandry, p. 45.
109. N. McKendrick, J. Brewer and J. H. Plumb, The Birth of a Consumer Society (1982).
110. For a useful survey of change over several centuries, see J. Stevenson, Popular Disturbances in England 1700-1870 (1979).
111. H. Cunningham, Leisure in the Industrial Revolution (1980).
112. See chs. 4, 7, 8 below; and J. A. Sharpe, 'The History of crime in late medieval and early modern England: a review of the field', Social History, vii (1982). This is the theme too of Ralph Houlbrooke's new book on the family: The English Family 1450-1700 (1984).

Chapter One

POPULAR CULTURE IN SEVENTEENTH-CENTURY LONDON*

Peter Burke

I

The aim of this essay is to describe the
culture of the ordinary Londoner in the seventeenth
century, and to discuss the changes which this
culture underwent between 1600 (or a little before)
and 1700 (or a few years later).   It is intended at
once to fill a gap between, and in certain respects
to take issue with, two well-known studies of London
culture by Professors L. B. Wright and J. H.
Plumb.(1)   It overlaps rather than coincides with
Wright's book not only for reasons of chronology
(his chosen period being from 1558 to 1640), but for
reasons of sociology as well. Wright chose to confine himself to 'the literate common people' while
this study is also concerned with the illiterate.
It makes use of the concept of 'the commercialisation
of leisure' which Plumb applied to the eighteenth
century, while remaining somewhat sceptical of his
view of the 'cultural poverty' of the decades before
1700.
       It is at once necessary and impossible to
define the term 'culture' before proceeding to employ
it.   I shall use the term to refer to attitudes and
values, or world-views. These attitudes and values
may be embodied in artifacts, such as images and
texts (including broadsides, chapbooks, and, where
they have been recorded, even graffiti).   They may
also be expressed in performances, whether formal
(plays or pageants); or informal (the semi-
ritualised attacks on brothels, for example). Any
institution and any form of behaviour has a place at
the edge of the definition, for they can all be
regarded as cultural artifacts, but images, texts
and performances will occupy the centre.
       As for the 'ordinary Londoner', he or she is

31

perhaps best defined in negative terms. Ordinary Londoners were the unlearned, the non-elite, the people who had not been to grammar school or university, who did not know Latin, who were not members of the king's court or the Inns of Court, and who could not afford to visit a private theatre or buy many books. The upper classes called these people 'the vulgar', 'the multitude', or 'the mob'. Their culture might be described as 'blue-apron culture', for in the seventeenth century 'blue-apron' carried associations similar to the more recent coinage, 'blue-collar'.(2)

I shall be equally concerned with culture which came _from_ the people and with culture which was intended _for_ the people. Literary critics and sociologists have tended to operate with two opposed models of popular culture, 'Folk' and 'Mass'. As Dwight Macdonald puts it, 'Folk Art grew from below. It was a spontaneous, autochthonous expression of the people, shaped by themselves ... to suit their own needs. Mass culture is imposed from above. It is fabricated by technicians hired by businessmen; its audiences are passive consumers.'(3) This typology has its uses, but it is important not to mistake it for reality. In seventeenth-century London, as indeed in Western Europe more generally, what one would have found would have been something in between, or more exactly, a whole spectrum of arti-facts and performances with a greater or less degree of participation from below or imposition from above. So much so that it might be useful to build this tendency into the model, and to think, as historians and sociologists are increasingly coming to do, in terms of interaction between the two cultures, learned and popular, dominant and dominated. Whether one is considering songs or stories, images or rituals, it may be useful to ask: 'who is saying what, to whom, for what purpose and with what effect?'(4) However, in asking this question we must not let ourselves assume that the message trans-mitted was necessarily the message received. Recent research on popular culture has underlined the fact that receivers are not passive but active, that they consciously or unconsciously reinterpret the messages sent to them, seeing or hearing what they want to see and hear.

It cannot, of course, be assumed that ordinary Londoners were either socially or culturally homo-geneous. London was by seventeenth-century standards an unusual environment. At a time when only a dozen or so European cities had populations of 100,000 or more, London stood out. The population of the urban agglomeration, both inside and outside the limits of 'the City', was about 200,000 at the beginning of the century and nearly 600,000 at its end. The eastern suburbs - to some extent still villages - grew still faster, from about 20,000 to about 90,000 in the course of the century.

Parts of this agglomeration had distinct characters of their own. Joseph Addison wrote in 1712 that London was like 'an Aggregate of various Nations distinguished from each other by their respective customs, Manners & Interests'. (5) The centre, both literally and metaphorically, was the City, with its privileges and traditions, its lord mayor, aldermen, livery companies, wards and precincts. However, something like half greater London was outside the City. To the west there was Westminster, in the shadow of the court and the Houses of Parliament. To the east there was a relatively poor area - Whitechapel, Spitalfields, Stepney - with a high proportion of unskilled workers and immigrants and also of centres of entertainment - theatres, brothels, etc. - which were there to escape central control. (6)

The diversity of London was not simply topographical. As a port it contained a fair number of sailors; as a centre of fashion and conspicuous consumption it was full of servants and of craftsmen working in the luxury trades, from goldsmiths to peruke (or periwig)-makers. From the cultural point of view it is particularly relevant to note that most English printers and booksellers were established in London; those producing for the cheap end of the market were generally to be found, in the late seventeenth century, either in West Smithfield or on London Bridge. (7) There were, of course, the usual divisions, cultural as well as social, between men and women, skilled and unskilled, old and young, natives and immigrants; London had more than its fair share of the young, come to better themselves or simply to find work. Modern estimates of the seventeenth-century apprentice population vary between 10,000 and 20,000.

To what extent true subcultures existed in this period is a question which the fragmentary evidence does not allow us to answer with confidence. Sailors and thieves each had their own jargon, unintelligible to outsiders. So did homosexuals, who also employed hand signals to identify each other in public. (8) The Huguenot silk weavers of Spitalfields differed from their neighbours in trade, language and religion. A particularly strong case can be made, and indeed has been made, for describing London apprentices as a subculture, with a strong sense of fraternity, a tradition of collective action (usually violent), and a literature specially designed to appeal to them, whether its form was escapist, like The Valiant London Prentice, or godly, like The Apprentice's Faithful Monitor (c.1700). (9) One might even talk of a 'subculture of heresy', noting, for example, that the area around Coleman Street, not far from the Guildhall, where Independents and Fifth Monarchists flourished in the middle of the century, had been associated with Lollards around 1520.(10) All the same, I have the impression that subcultures were less clear-cut in the seventeenth century than they have since become, and that the cultures of different subordinate groups overlapped to a large extent. Even learned and popular cultures were not hermetically sealed off from one another, as we shall see. Hence there is a case for drawing on the researches of specialists in bibliography, drama, nonconformity and political history in order to present blue-apron culture as it was experienced, as a whole. In doing this it may be useful to begin with traditional popular culture, and then to examine what was new.

II

Any picture of the traditional popular culture of seventeenth-century Londoners is bound to be as fragmentary as the surviving evidence, most of which takes the form of tantalisingly brief allusions to what was so well-known at the time that there was no need to describe it. At least the fragments are more numerous for the seventeenth century than for the years before 1600. For example, there are a fair number of references to witchcraft and magic. Cunning men practised their trade in the heart of London. In 1614 John Wheeler of Grub Street, apothecary, was accused of 'seducing the king's subjects by making them believe that by erecting a figure he can help them to (find) stolen goods'.(11) Accusations of witchcraft not infrequently came before the Middlesex justices. In the reign of James I, for example, Alice Bradley, a widow of Hampstead, was accused of bewitching hogs, heifers, a man and a woman; Agnes Godfrey, a yeoman's wife of Enfield, of bewitching a steer, a pig, a mare and a person. While accusations of witchcraft against people were made against Anne Beaver, widow, of

Edmonton; Dorothy Magicke - was this an occupational
nickname? - of Holborn; William Hunt, a yeoman of
Finchley, and his wife Joan; Elizabeth Rutter, widow,
of Finchley; Anne Branche, a yeoman's wife of
Tottenham; Agnes Berry, a widow of Enfield; and
Agnes Miller, another yeoman's wife of Finchley.(12)
In 1621, there was the *cause célèbre* of Elizabeth
Sawyer, commemorated in a pamphlet and also in
Thomas Dekker's play The Witch of Edmonton. Between
1652 and 1657 seven accusations of witchcraft came
before the Middlesex justices, including those
against Temperance Fossett, a yeoman's wife of
Whitechapel; Grace Boxe, widow, of Whitechapel; and
Elizabeth Kennit, spinster, of Stepney.(13) As late
as the year 1700, a blacksmith's apprentice of
Southwark claimed to have been bewitched by the wife
of a waterman.(14) To the evidence from judicial
records may be added that of material culture, like
the bottle found in the Thames, and dating from the
second half of the century, which contained a piece
of felt in the shape of a heart, pierced by five
pins.   It is said to be a piece of protective
rather than destructive magic.(15)

Wives who beat their husbands were still paraded
through the streets to the raucous music of a
charivari. John Stow describes an occasion, one
Shrove Monday at Charing Cross, when he saw 'A man
carried of four men. And before him a bagpipe
playing, a shawm, and a drum beating. The cause was
his next neighbour's wife beat her husband.'(16) At
the end of the century a French visitor to London
recorded having seen this several times.(17) The
initiation of journeymen still involved elaborate
rituals. That of the printer, Thomas Gent, about
1713, at an inn in Blackfriars, took the form,
according to his own account, of a kind of dubbing,
'striking me kneeling with a broadsword', and a kind
of christening, in which ale was poured on his head
and he was given the name 'earl of Fingall'.(18)
There is also some indication that prisoners condemned to be hanged at Tyburn dressed as if they
were going to a wedding, as their successors were to
do in the better-documented eighteenth century.   A
group who were executed in 1690 called for sack and
drank the health of the king - King James.(19)

The evidence is richest, or rather, least poor,
for traditional calendar festivals, five of them in
particular.(20)

First, Shrove Tuesday. It may well be the case
that Carnival was taken less seriously in England
than in most parts of the Continent, but it was, all

the same, a major festive event of the London year.
In his <u>Jack a Lent</u> (1620), the London waterman-poet
and comic writer, John Taylor (1580-1653), gives a
vivid description of Shrove Tuesday as a time of
'boiling and broiling ... roasting and toasting ...
stewing and brewing'. London apprentices had their
pancakes subsidised by the Eyre bequest. Shrovetide
was also the time for whipping cocks and for ritualised but nonetheless violent attacks on brothels and
other places of entertainment. As Taylor puts it,
'Youths arm'd with cudgels, stones, hammers, rules,
trowels and hand-saws, put playhouses to the sack
and bawdy-houses to the spoil'. If readers are
inclined to suspect the testimony of literary
sources, and wonder whether John Taylor had made
these incidents up, some details from the Middlesex
sessions records may serve to allay their doubts.
In 1614, for example, the apprentices rioted and a
number of silk-throwsters and other craftsmen were
accused of 'assisting the apprentices in pulling
down Joan Leake's house in Shoreditch on Shrove
Tuesday, being in their riotous company.' The
modern editor of this document comments coyly that
'the significance of Mrs Leake's house is quite
unknown to me', but Dekker knew better and refers to
Shrove Tuesday as the day when apprentices 'did
always use to rifle Madam Leake's house at the upper
end of Shoreditch'.(21) Shrove Tuesday riots can be
documented for at least twenty-four of the thirty-
nine years from 1603 to 1642.(22)

In the second place, there was Ascension Day, a
parish festival which involved beating the bounds, a
procession and a feast. The churchwardens' accounts
record payments for wands, laces, ribbons, nosegays,
bread, cheese and beer. On the basis of this
evidence it has been suggested that 'In the
seventeenth century in many parishes it became the
most considerable procession of the year'.(23) On
the other hand, it does not bulk large in literary
sources.

May Day was celebrated in London, as elsewhere,
with maypoles (the one in the Strand was traditionally important), and with dancing. On his way to
Westminster on 1 May 1667, Samuel Pepys recorded
'meeting many milkmaids with their garlands upon
their pails dancing with a fiddler before them', and
this seems to have been an annual custom. By the
end of the century the milkmaids were wearing or
carrying silver for the occasion. It was in the
eighteenth century that they would be joined by the
chimney sweeps to produce the ritualised contrast

between 'milk and soot' which impressed visitors to London.(24)   There was also a May Fair, held where Curzon Street now runs, with rope-dancing and puppet-shows.   On occasion, in the reigns of Charles I and Charles II, there were May Day riots, reminiscent of the notorious 'evil May Day' of 1517, but they were less frequent by far than Shrove Tuesday disturbances.(25)

Then there was Midsummer, the eve of St John the Baptist.   Following a tradition of 'Midsummer Shows' which went back to early Tudor times, if not further, the mayor and the watch went in procession through the City, and there were pageants with 'great and ugly giants marching as if they were alive and armed at all points'.   Londoners decorated their houses with 'green birch, long fennel, St John's wort'; and in 1694, John Aubrey saw some twenty young women 'in the pasture behind Montague House ... looking for a coal under the root of a plantain, to put under their heads that night, and they should dream who would be their husbands'.(26)

Finally, St Bartholomew's Day (25 August) was the occasion of the great Bartholomew Fair at Smithfield, with all the attractions so vividly evoked by Ben Jonson's play on the subject: plays, puppets, waxworks, rope-dancers, and - appropriately enough in London's meat market - the consumption of roast pork on a gargantuan scale.   In this case the commercialisation of the festival is already apparent; the shift from wrestling and archery, in which all able-bodied men could participate, to displays by professionals.(27)   There were other festivals in the Londoner's year; Christmas, St George's Day, Pentecost, and St Luke's Day (18 October, marked by a Horn Fair outside the village of Charlton, near Greenwich), but the five which we have discussed seem to have been particularly important and distinctive.

Who was saying what to whom in these festivals? What did they mean? Ascension Day was surely an affirmation of community solidarity at the parish level, and suggests that this solidarity could survive the pressures of the big city, as does the continued existence of the wardmotes, assemblies of all householders of the ward.(28) Milkmaids and green birch suggest that Londoners were not yet cut off from their rural roots.   Many of them were first-generation townspeople, and in any case the villages of Islington, Kensington, Stoke Newington and so on were near at hand.   The Midsummer pageants, on the other hand, were an affirmation of civic

pride; the giants were probably Gog and Magog.
Whether everyone felt this pride, or only the
members of the City companies, it is impossible to
say. Not everyone was equally active on these
festive occasions. The apprentices seem to have
been more active than most, as one might have
expected, for in many parts of traditional Europe it
was the young adult males, often organised into
clubs like the 'Abbeys of Misrule', who took the
initiative in organising festivals. But for whom?
It is impossible to give a precise answer to that
question because popular culture (unlike learned
culture) was open to all, as open as the streets in
which so much of it took place. Members of the
upper classes still participated in this popular
culture. Pepys, for example, was no 'ordinary'
Londoner in the sense of this essay, but a member of
the upper classes; yet his Diary makes his enjoyment
of May Day and Bartholomew Fair clear enough. 'All
the nobility in town' attended May Fair in 1701,
according to a contemporary report.(29)
    These traditional festivals seem to have been
less important in London than in the great cities of
Catholic Europe like Paris, Madrid, Rome, or Naples,
where feast-days were marked by great processions of
fraternities behind crucifixes, images of saints,
holy relics, or the blessed sacrament. Italian
cities in particular offer much richer evidence than
London does of a popular culture based on local
communities within the city, communities such as
parishes, wards or quarters. Thus it was the
quartieri who organised the highly spectacular
celebrations of St John the Baptist's Day in
Florence; the *rioni* played a prominent part in the
Roman Carnival; while the *contrade* arranged the Palio
of Siena (they still do). In Protestant London,
things were different. The traditional Corpus
Christi processions and plays had ceased after the
Reformation, and so had the parish Dedication Day
festivals.(30) Shops remained open during all
festivals except Christmas and Easter, which must
have reduced participation. If parishes and wards
had relatively little cultural importance, this may
be because seventeenth-century London, unlike Venice
or Florence, Siena, or Rome, was growing fast by
immigration, and so contained a substantial number
of people who had been uprooted from their home
community but were not yet accustomed to London
traditions. One is left with the impression - the
evidence is too fragmentary to permit firmer
conclusions - that, despite the milkmaids and the

green birch, traditional festivals were in decline, allowing opportunities for the rapid penetration of newer forms of popular culture.

III

It is probably accurate to imagine the inhabitants of English villages and small towns in the seventeenth century as living out their year in remembrance of festivals past and in anticipation of festivals to come.(31) In London, on the other hand, there was no lack of shows to fill up the spaces between festivals. In a town which trebled in the seventeenth century from about 200,000 to very nearly 600,000 people, it was worth the while of a variety of professional entertainers - acrobats, actors, ballad-singers, bear-wards, clowns, fencers, puppet-showmen - to put on a virtually continuous performance. Villagers might see this kind of show a few times a year, but Londoners could see them all the time. If they wanted to hear the latest ballad, they would go to London Bridge; if they wanted to watch a bull-baiting, they would go to Southwark. The existence of professional entertainers was no new phenomenon; medieval minstrels had been professionals. What was new was that popular entertainers were no longer forced to take to the road. They could now make a living by staying in the same place.

The change was most obvious - not to say 'dramatic' - in the case of the theatre. In 1576 the first permanent theatre in London was opened (outside the City, in Shoreditch), and it was quickly followed by several more. These public theatres were open to anyone who could afford the entrance fee of one penny. It has been calculated that by 1600, from 18,000 to 24,000 Londoners were going to the theatre every week, including 'Tailers, Tinkers, Cordwayners, Saylers' according to an informed (if prejudiced) contemporary, Stephen Gosson. It is difficult to tell whether or not he was right. Apprentices are often mentioned in contemporary descriptions of audiences, but it is unlikely that their masters would have let them go (since performances took place in working hours), and equally unlikely that they could have very often afforded the entrance fee, unless they were gentlemen-apprentices, for a penny would have been real money to them. Sailors ashore, on the other hand, probably did have the time and the money.(32)

In the early seventeenth century the so-called

'private' theatres began to be built, nearer the
centre than the public theatres, in Drury Lane,
Fleet Street and elsewhere. They were in fact open
to the public, but the cheapest seats cost sixpence.
Despite Ben Jonson's reference to '6d mechanics', it
is unlikely that very many ordinary people
frequented them.(33) However, some public theatres
remained open until the middle of the seventeenth
century, when they were shut down by decree. They
included the Red Bull, in Clerkenwell, and the
Fortune, these two theatres being 'mostly frequented
by citizens and the meaner sort of people', although
gentlemen could also be seen there. Their
repertoire included plays which 'dramatized the
criticisms and grievances of Londoners against the
prerogative government'.(34)

After the Restoration, when the theatres tended
to serve a limited public of courtiers, aristocrats
and officials, the audience might widen at Christmas
to include, as Pepys more than once complained,
'ordinary prentices and mean people'. (35) In this
period, however, ordinary people generally saw their
plays in the street or in taverns, which reverted in
this respect to their Elizabethan function, or at
fairs. 'Drolls' (in other words short dramatic
pieces, usually but not always comic), could be seen
in Lincoln's Inn Fields in the 1650s and in the
Queen's Arms at Southwark in the 1690s. At least
seventeen plays are known to have been performed at
Bartholomew Fair between 1661 and 1699. There were
puppet-plays at Charing Cross in the 1660s and
1670s, and at the Duke of Marlborough's Head in
Fleet Street early in the eighteenth century.(36)

Who was speaking to these audiences? Among
others, Shakespeare. A list of the plays known to
have been performed at the Red Bull and the Fortune
in the years 1600-41 includes pieces by such
talented authors as Thomas Dekker, John Webster, and
Philip Massinger, although the staple fare was
provided by lesser men like Henry Chettle, Richard
Hathway, and Samuel Rowley. (37) Better-known by the
public were the performers, some of whom achieved a
kind of stardom, like William Kemp, who flourished
about 1600, and was particularly famous for his jigs,
satirical song-and-dance acts at the end of plays
which sometimes, according to the JPs who ordered
their suppression in James I's reign, led to breaches
of the peace. (38)

As for the repertoire, so many of the pieces
performed at the Red Bull and the Fortune have been
lost that it is necessary to rely on the slippery

evidence of titles. These suggest what one might have expected, that plays with a London topic appealed to the audience; Dekker's <u>Match Me in London</u> (1611), for example, or his <u>The Late Murder at Whitechapel</u> (1624), or Chettle and John Day's <u>Blind Beggar of Bethnal Green</u> (1600), Thomas Heywood's <u>Four Prentices of London</u> (1600), Day and Hathway's <u>The Boss of Billingsgate</u> (1603), the anonymous <u>Whittington</u> (1605), or Thomas Jordan's <u>The Walks of Islington</u> (1641). More surprising, perhaps, is the substantial number of plays with subjects taken from ancient history and classical mythology, suggesting that the hegemonic culture exercised a fascination over people who had never been to grammar school, let alone university. Thus the Red Bull staged Heywood's <u>Rape of Lucrece</u> (1607), while the patrons of the Fortune could have seen William Boyle's <u>Jugurth</u> (1600), or Chettle, Day and Dekker's <u>Cupid and Psyche</u> (1600), Hathway and William Rankins's <u>Hannibal and Scipio</u> (1601), and <u>Caesar's Fall</u> (1602), by five authors, including Dekker. (39)

In the late seventeenth century, the repertoire of drolls included a number of traditional popular subjects, dealing with the adventures of such well-known heroes and heroines as St George, Guy of Warwick, King Solomon, Friar Bacon, Dick Whittington, Robin Hood, Judith, and Griselda. There were also comic scenes taken from early seventeenth-century plays, notably from Beaumont and Fletcher and from Shakespeare - Falstaff disguised as a robber, for example, or the gravedigger's scene from <u>Hamlet</u>. Themes from the old public theatre had clearly passed into popular tradition. The tastes and prejudices of an urban audience are indicated by the regular appearance of a stage peasant, who may be called 'Bumpkin' or 'Simpleton' or provided with a thick West Country accent. There are also references to drolls concerned with the more sensational current affairs, such as the massacre of Amboina and the siege of Vienna. (40)

The rise of the theatres illustrates the professionalisation of entertainment. The role of the audience was becoming more passive. In the case of popular religion, however, the trend was the other way. It was becoming de-professionalised, taken away from the clergy, and the opportunities for active popular participation increased to a peak in the middle of the century.

The most obvious examples to take are those of the separatist congregations. A few existed before

41

1641. In 1616, a secret congregation was founded by
Henry Jacob. Discovered in 1632, its members were
imprisoned. They included the Southwark cobbler,
Samuel How, who became notorious for a sermon he
preached at the Nag's Head Tavern in the
traditionally heretical parish of St Stephen's,
Coleman Street, defending the right of laymen to
preach. After 1641, separatist congregations came
out into the open and multiplied; six separate
churches split off from Jacob's original foundation.
These 'gathered' or 'private' churches, or
'conventicles' as they were called, which met in
shops or private houses, were generally led by
craftsmen or shopkeepers, such as How and John
Spilsbury, who were both cobblers; Praise-God
Barbon, a Baptist leather-seller of Fleet Street;
Samuel Eaton, button-maker; John Green, hat-maker;
Thomas Lambe, a soap-boiler whose Baptist congregation was in Bell Alley, off Coleman Street; and
Lodowick Muggleton, a tailor who founded his own
sect, the Muggletonians.(41) In London houses in the
1630s and 1640s it was possible to hear men asserting 'that perfection is and may be attained in this
life', that there was no Hell except in this life,
or that Christ was not God.(42) Women were
prominent among the separatists; the visionary Anna
Trapnel, the lacewoman, Mrs Attaway, who preached in
Lambe's church, and others.(43) Recent research on
the Quakers, the Ranters, and the Fifth Monarchy Men
suggests that all three sects derived a good deal of
their support from ordinary people in London. The
Quakers recruited their members mainly from tailors,
shoemakers, weavers, sailors and carpenters - but
not, apparently, from unskilled labourers. The
Ranters, we are told, addressed themselves to 'the
slum dwellers of London and other cities'. The
leaders of the Fifth Monarchists included a master
cooper (Thomas Venner), a ribbon weaver (John
James), and a bricklayer (John Belcher), while their
followers were drawn from shoemakers, tailors, silk
throwsters, shipwrights and labourers.(44)

Opportunities for religious self-expression were
at their greatest in the 1640s and 1650s, but they
did not disappear thereafter, despite persecution of
dissent. The religious census of 1676 revealed that
7 per cent of the population of London were
nonconformists, but this figure may well be too
small. There were probably from 8,000 to 10,000
Quakers alone in London at this time. In 1711,
there were 26 Presbyterian meeting houses in London
and its suburbs, 23 for the Baptists, 14 for the

Quakers and 12 for the Independents, and a
population of about 100,000 dissenters altogether,
about one Londoner in six.(45)
It is worth reflecting for a moment on the
significance of these statistics and trends for the
history of popular culture. They suggest that after
1640 it was possible for ordinary Londoners to
choose their religious community in a way which
would have been unthinkable in 1600. In a European
perspective, London stands out in this respect. The
only great city on the Continent in which a similar
choice was possible would have been Amsterdam. It
is true that in London the less respectable forms of
dissent faded into obscurity in the later seventeenth
century - the Fifth Monarchists, for example, are
last heard of in 1682, meeting in a cellar on London
Bridge. However, we do not know whether ordinary
people abandoned the more radical doctrines or
simply kept quiet about their adherence, while the
doctrines remained an underground part of popular
culture. Whichever it was, popular attitudes to
orthodox Christianity could never be quite the same
again. Even popular Anglicanism (about which we
know less than about dissent, though it was probably
more important in numerical terms), changed its
significance when adherence became a matter of
individual choice, rather than something which was
automatic and taken for granted.
As striking a new development as the emergence
of alternative forms of Christianity was the rise of
political consciousness, of popular participation in
politics, of a popular 'political culture'.
It was of course nothing new for Londoners to be
on the receiving end of official political messages.
They were exposed to them in a way in which other
ordinary Englishmen and women were not. They had
front seats at traditional political performances
like royal entries and coronation processions.
James I entered London in state in 1604, Christian
IV of Denmark in 1606, and so on. Charles II's
progress through the City for his coronation was an
elaborate happening in which the Great Conduit at
the entrance to Cheapside ran with wine, and there
was a pageant devised by John Ogilby (1600-76), with
music by Matthew Locke (c.1630-77), all at a cost -
to the livery companies - of some £11,000. There
were bonfires and other celebrations on 17 November,
the anniversary of the accession of Queen
Elizabeth.(46) All these performances were obviously
designed to show the monarchy in a favourable light.
Political messages in support of the

establishment were also part of the Lord Mayor's
Show on 29 October, a festival which was at its
height in the seventeenth century, or, more exactly,
between 1585 and 1708. It was customary to lay on
four pageants in St Paul's Churchyard, Cheapside and
elsewhere, through which the new mayor and his
procession moved in triumph, as in a royal entry.
The scenery would normally include arches, chariots
and temples furnished with saints, goddesses, and
virtues. A recurrent scene represented a forest or
wilderness with singing and dancing shepherds,
nymphs, blacks, and wild men of the woods.(47)
    These shows were devised by pageant poets, with
the help of a team of painters and other artificers.
The poets included Thomas Middleton (1580-1627),
Anthony Munday (1553-1633), John Tatham (fl.1632-
64), Thomas Jordan (1612?-85), Matthew Taubman (died
c.1690), and Elkanah Settle (1648-1724). They were
men on the margin between learned and popular
culture. Munday, for example, was an actor, a
translator, and a draper; Middleton was the son of
a London bricklayer but went to Queen's College,
Oxford; Jordan was an actor at the Red Bull before
becoming poet to the corporation; while Settle who
went to Oxford but left without taking a degree, was
once considered a rival to Dryden, but ended writing
drolls for performance at fairs and even (so it was
said) playing the part of the dragon. Behind these
poets stood the twelve great livery companies, one
of which would provide the mayor and pay for that
year's pageants.
    The pageants were open to all, rich and poor,
learned and unlearned; the upper class watching from
balconies, and the 'blue apron auditory' in the
streets. To appeal to both audiences at once posed
serious problems. Which of the groundlings would
have recognised Mercury, let alone understood that
he symbolised trade? In a similar context, that of
providing street entertainments in honour of James
I, Dekker and Jonson have left us their reactions to
this problem. Dekker reluctantly admitted that 'The
multitude is now to be our audience, whose heads
would miserably run a wool-gathering if we do but
offer to break them with hard words.' Jonson
admitted that the multitude would be there, but
refused to write for them. His declared aim was to
present shows which 'might, without cloud or
obscurity, declare themselves to the sharp and
learned: and for the multitude, no doubt but their
grounded judgments did gaze, said it was fine, and
were satisfied'. He refused to introduce an

interpreter, as Munday was to make St George interpret the Lord Mayor's Show of 1609, or to hang notices on the different figures, a practice mocked by Jonson with his 'This is a dog; or, This is a hare'.(48)

In practice, the shows tended to draw on two different iconographical and mythological traditions, learned and popular respectively; the classical tradition, and the 'trades' tradition of craftsmen in general and the City companies in particular. One might see Astraea but also Jack Straw, Janus but also the City giants, who appeared in 1672 sitting in chariots 'moving, talking and taking tobacco as they ride along, to the great admiration and delight of all the spectators'.(49) The two traditions were mobilised for the same purpose - panegyric. The actors quite literally sang the praises of the new mayor, of his company, of trade, of London, and of the king. Their function was legitimation. Sir William Walworth the fourteenth-century Mayor was more than once represented in the shows. This was partly to compliment his company, the Fishmongers, but also to symbolise the victory of order over sedition - for it was Walworth who killed the rebel Jack Straw.(50) Thomas Jordan's show for 1678 revealed an Indian plantation in which the workers sang a song including the improbable couplet:

> With mattock, spade, pruning-hook, shovel
> and sieve,
> What a life of delight do we labourers live!

This was at once an exotic variation on the pastoral, a compliment to the Grocers (who had provided the mayor that year), and an attempt to persuade ordinary Londoners of the delights of hard work.(51) Legitimation was never more necessary than in 1689, when the City poet, Matthew Taubman (who had mocked the Whigs in his Lord Mayor's Show of 1686), produced <u>London's Great Jubilee</u>, which presented William III as a hero

> Sent by Indulgent Heaven to set us free
> From Arbitrary Force and Slavery.(52)

So much for political messages from the authorities to the people. Perhaps the most important comment to make about them is that they were contradictory, because the ruling class was divided. This meant that opportunities for active popular participation in politics as in religion were increasing in the seventeenth century. The best evidence for this participation comes from happenings which, if not entirely unplanned, were rather more spontaneous and rather less carefully scripted than the Lord Mayor's Shows: from riots and from organised non-violent happenings which it is convenient, if technically anachronistic, to call 'demonstrations'.(53)

Urban riots were nothing new and they were not a particularly English phenomenon, but on several occasions they reached important dimensions; at Fleet Street in 1629, at Charing Cross in 1638, and over much of London in the case of the London weavers' riot of 1675 and, above all, in the Sacheverell riots of 1710. In the first two incidents, apprentices, soldiers and sailors were involved; in the third, weavers; in the last, apprentices and servants, amounting to some five thousand people altogether.(54)

From the point of view of this essay, it is important to decide whether or not these disturbances reveal political consciousness on the part of the participants, as opposed to blind fury, manipulation from above, or 'pre-political' reactions to hard times. In the first two cases, where documentation is thinner, the attitudes of the crowd can only be characterised in negative terms; they were against foreigners and against Catholics.(55) In the last two cases, the most obvious comment to make is again negative. The weavers were against engine looms, which they smashed, and the Sacheverell rioters were against dissenters, whose meeting-houses they attacked. In these two cases, however, it is possible to go just a little further.

The weavers' riot was described by a contemporary diarist as a 'Rebellion begot in the Belly not the Braine', a 'gut reaction' one might say in modern terms, rather than a rational one. The comment neatly illustrates the upper-class view of crowd action as 'spasmodic', which has been pilloried by Edward Thompson. If we follow him in attributing political consciousness to the Luddites, then we shall have to attribute it to the seventeenth-century weavers as well. Wearing green aprons which 'symbolised their allegiance', a recent account informs us, groups of weavers smashed the engine looms which were robbing them of work and then took the fragments outside to burn them 'in an atmosphere of celebration'.(56) If this smashing and burning was not 'political' in the narrow sense of the term, it was at least an example of direct action in the service of collective bargaining. The Sacheverell riots might be dismissed as an example of manipulation, since some gentlemen have been identified among the crowd and the riots were a response to Sacheverell's fiery sermon on the subject of 'The Church in danger'. All the same, if it was so easy to persuade some five thousand people to attack dissenters, that argues considerable popular identification with the Church of England. The study of late seventeenth-century demonstrations points to the same conclusion.

Demonstrations were, if not uniquely English, at least something of a London speciality in the period 1640-80. In the early 1640s, for example, one thinks of the crowd which escorted Burton, Bastwick and Prynne into London in triumph, in a kind of unofficial pageant modelled on royal entries or the Lord Mayor's Show. Again, there was the crowd which brought the Root and Branch Petition, with its more than 15,000 signatures, into Parliament. During the 'December Days' of 1641, crowds demonstrated against bishops and there was, according to one contemporary, 'a kind of discipline in disorder, tumults being ready at command, upon a watchword given'.(57) In 1647, the apprentices organised both petitions to Parliament and demonstrations outside Parliament, in support of the Presbyterians and to claim a holiday to replace the traditional religious holidays they had lost.(58)

During the Exclusion Crisis, demonstrations were organised again, and some took the form of pageants, notably the pope-burnings of 1679 to 1681. The pope had been burned in effigy in Cheapside in 1673, but what happened in 1679, 1680 and 1681 was something much more elaborate. The demonstrations were organised and paid for by the Whig Green Ribbon Club. Their leader, Shaftesbury, hired the playwright Elkanah Settle to design the pageants, of which there were nine in 1680. They featured the pope, cardinals, bishops, friars, inquisitors, nuns, and a bellman crying out, 'remember Justice Godfrey'. There were allusions to the Pope's presumed responsibility for the Great Fire of London as well as to the Popish Plot. The figures were labelled so that the spectators would be in no doubt about the message - Settle does not seem to have shared the objections voiced by Ben Jonson. The pageants were a kind of inverse Lord Mayor's Show, designed to criticise rather than to justify the authorities, and after the regime changed in 1688, Settle was in

fact asked to design Lord Mayor's Shows. The day
chosen for the Whig demonstrations was 17 November,
the accession day of Queen Elizabeth, so that an
official festival was appropriated by the opposition.
The printed version of the 1680 procession presented
it as a spontaneous affair in which 'the multitude'
cried out 'no popery' and other slogans 'of their
own accord', but it does admit that wine was
distributed to the crowd. In any case it is clear
that however much ordinary people may have enjoyed
or participated in the proceedings, they did not
originate them.(59) The same might be said of the
pope-burning processions revived by the Whigs in the
last years of Queen Anne.(60)

An important but elusive topic which has
attracted much attention from historians in recent
years is the nature and extent of popular support
for king or parliament, Presbyterians or
Independents, Whigs or Tories.(61) It seems that
both sides could appeal with success to ordinary
Londoners, but to different groups. The 'radicals',
so it has been argued, appealed to such groups as
weavers, shoemakers and printers, especially to
those who were less well off and who lived in the
City, with its tradition of independence, or in the
east of London. The 'conservatives', on the other
hand, appealed to the inhabitants of Westminster,
whose luxury trades depended on court patronage, and
to the Thames watermen, who also needed the court.
As for arguments other than self-interest, the Whigs
could appeal to popular anti-Catholicism, the Tories
to hostility to dissenters, and also to the excise.
This picture is doubtless too simple, as current
research indicates.(62) However, it does suggest two
interesting conclusions. The first is that popular
political consciousness was negative rather than
positive. Perhaps this is still true today, but it
is easier to find evidence of positive political
ideals among Londoners today than in the seventeenth
century. The second conclusion is that popular
political consciousness increased during the period,
indeed that it was raised dramatically. As a late
seventeenth-century witness remarked with some
sourness, 'Every little blue-apron boy behind the
counter undertakes as boldly as if he had served an
apprenticeship at the council board'.(63) The Civil
Wars of the 1640s and the crises of 1679-81 and 1688
made a great contribution to the political education
of the ordinary Londoner. The impact of these
events was made stronger and also more permanent by
the fact that they were recorded in print. A new

medium reinforced the new messages.

IV

Between 1600 and 1700 there was a vast increase in the amount of cheap printed literature available to the English public; broadsides, pamphlets, newspapers and chapbooks. It was intended for a wide audience, rural as well as urban, but Londoners probably saw far more of it than anyone else, since most booksellers and nearly all printers lived in the capital. Broadside ballads sold at a penny, the same price as admission to a performance at a public theatre. Almanacs cost twopence, while chapbooks varied between threepence and sixpence. As for the literacy rate, it appears to have been high and growing. In the early seventeenth century, 76 per cent of a sample of craftsmen and shopkeepers in the City could sign their names. Women's literacy rose dramatically from 10 per cent in the middle of the century to 48 per cent at the end.(64) The illiterate could of course listen to others reading aloud.

This cheap printed literature was far from homogeneous. A traditional genre was the black-letter broadside ballad, the great age of which lasted from 1550 to 1700. In this period some 3,000 ballads were licensed, but it is likely that another 9,000 were in circulation. The House of Commons forbade ballads in 1647 - which is some testimony to the power of the ballad - and none were licensed till 1656. In the later seventeenth century, the ballad trade was in the hands of a small group of booksellers, among them the Coles family, the Wright family, John Deacon, Thomas Passinger, and William Thackeray. (65) Some of these ballads were old ones, including Little Musgrave and Lady Barnard (Child 81), Barbara Allen (Child 84), Chevy Chase (Child 162), and a number of ballads from the Robin Hood cycle (Child 122-4, 126, etc.) However, traditional ballads seem to have been swamped by new ones, which often dealt with current events; battles, murders, witchcraft, monstrous births and other prodigies. Famous political ballads include A New Song of an Orange and, of course, Lilliburlero.

English chapbooks are best known in their eighteenth-century form, when they were standardised in a twenty-four page format and distributed from Bow Lane and elsewhere. They were the English equivalent of the French *Bibliothèque Bleue*, which has attracted much interest from historians in the last twenty years. However, chapbooks, in the sense of small cheap books distributed by hawkers or chapmen, already existed in the seventeenth century. They seem to have increased in numbers quite suddenly in the 1650s and 1660s, and to have been produced by the same entrepreneurs who had cornered the ballad market; Deacon, Passinger, Thackeray and the rest.(66)

Chapbooks dealt with a wide range of subjects. A recent analysis of the 114 examples in the Pepys collection at Cambridge noted that 44 were humorous, 36 practical, and 29 works of fiction, while 5 offered social comment.(67) In the 1680s, the publisher, William Thackeray, produced a catalogue of 145 chapbooks under four headings: 'small godly books', 'small merry books', 'double books' and 'histories'. However, it may be more useful to divide them into religious or secular books, fiction or non-fiction. Broadly speaking, 95 of the books were secular in content, 50 were religious; in other words, religious books were only about 35 per cent of the total. Of the 95 secular books, about 10 were practical, ranging from the care of horses to the writing of letters, and the remaining 85 were works of fiction, including the exploits of such traditional heroes as St George, King Arthur, Guy of Warwick and Robin Hood.(68)

Almanacs were more varied than the modern reader might expect. If they were fundamentally compendia of practical information about the weather, medicine, or markets and fairs, they did not limit themselves to those topics. They popularised history and the new science, and they often dealt with religion and politics. Given what has already been said about riots and demonstrations, it is interesting to note the xenophobia of the almanacs, the hostility to Scots, Dutchmen, and Frenchmen in particular.(69)

For evidence of popular political culture, however, the almanacs and ballads are less useful than the news-sheets and pamphlets which proliferated during the seventeenth century, especially in its middle years. The London book-seller George Thomason collected nearly fifteen thousand pamphlets between 1640 and 1663, together with over seven thousand news-sheets. These news-sheets were both regular and frequent, although they did not appear every day; London's first newspaper in this narrower sense, the Daily Courant, did not appear till 1702.(70) It cannot be assumed that all this literature was popular, but some of it certainly appealed to a wide audience.

As in the case of the crowds, some of which demonstrated in favour of the Whigs, while others favoured the Tories, it cannot be assumed that the values expressed in this cheap literature were homogeneous. Londoners were exposed to contradictory messages. On the traditional or conservative side there were the ballads and chapbooks presenting lord mayors such as William Walworth, Simon Eyre or Richard Whittington in a heroic light, or telling stories of valiant and honourable apprentices who took part in tournaments and carried off the prizes. In works like these, written by craftsmen for craftsmen (Richard Johnson, one of the best-known authors, had been an apprentice in London), we see, as a recent student of the subject puts it, 'bourgeois pride ... expressed in terms of the values of the elite'. (71)

For an instance of the popularisation of radical values, we may turn to the Leveller movement of the 1640s. The Levellers appealed, as a pamphlet of William Walwyn's has it, to 'all the plain people of London'. They had links with the separatist congregations, and Richard Overton had a secret press in Coleman Street. The Levellers also had links with the theatre; John Harris was a professional actor before turning Leveller and pamphleteer. It has recently been argued that Overton was also involved with the popular drama. The anti-Laudian pamphlet Canterbury his Change of Diet, which has been ascribed to Overton, reads very much like a piece of popular theatre. Among other pieces of political slapstick, it shows Archbishop Laud cutting off the ears of a doctor, a lawyer and a divine and ordering them to be dressed for his dinner, and then, his fortunes reversed, being forced into a cage and having his nose put to the grindstone. (72)

Which set of values appealed more to ordinary Londoners, we do not and cannot know for certain. However, as in the case of religion, it may be argued that the significant fact was that ordinary people had a choice of political allegiance, that the media were no one's monopoly.

The discussion so far has suggested a number of ways in which the ordinary Londoner's culture differed from popular culture elsewhere. Were these differences connected? To what extent did London culture grow out of London society? The topic needs to be treated in depth and detail, but here there is space for no more than a few suggestions. For example, the mockery of the country 'bumpkin' by the sophisticated townsman or 'cit' is what one might expect to find in urban popular culture. There are obvious sixteenth-century Italian and German parallels, notably in the Carnival plays of Hans Sachs, the Nuremberg shoemaker. (73) The importance of the professional entertainer is what might be expected in a city with several hundred thousand inhabitants; the obvious parallel here, though far from the only one, is seventeenth-century Paris. At the Pont Neuf, as on London Bridge, one could be sure to find a performance of some kind in progress. (74) Again, the lack of great religious processions through the streets is what might be expected in a Protestant city. In this case London is matched by Amsterdam. The commercialisation of festivals in seventeenth-century London is matched by Venice: the feast of the Ascension by Bartholomew Fair.

Other features of popular culture in London may be in need of a more elaborate explanation. For example, there is the relative weakness of cultural activities based on parishes or wards; the importance of cheap literature; the degree of penetration of popular culture by ideas and themes from learned culture; the emergence of the entrepreneur as popular hero, a type apparently without any contemporary European parallel, even in the Dutch Republic; and the importance of popular participation in politics, and in particular of non-violent demonstrations against the authorities.

A brief and schematic explanation of these special features of London culture might stress the following factors. London was a large Protestant city; both urbanisation and Protestantism favour literacy and Protestantism favours popular religious participation. All this was equally true of Amsterdam. However, political participation was greater in London than in Amsterdam. We might relate this to the fact that London was the political centre of England, while it was The Hague, small as it was, and not Amsterdam which was the political centre of the Dutch Republic. London was also the printing centre of England, and printers, who are craftsmen yet involved intimately with book-learning, are the most obvious intermediaries between learned and popular culture. Servants are also important intermediaries because of their opportunities for sharing in the culture of their masters by listening to their conversation or reading their books. The concentration of important people in seventeenth-century London involved an equal concentration of

servants; in 1695, servants formed 20 per cent of
the population of forty London parishes.(75) A third
kind of intermediary, unique to England, was the
gentleman apprentice. Thanks to primogeniture, the
younger sons of gentlemen often found themselves
sent to London to learn a trade. Of the 1,850
admissions to the freedom of the City of London in
1690, 179 concerned the sons of knights, esquires or
gentlemen. The existence of this social group helps
explain the appeal of stories like The Honour of the
Tailors (1687), in which an apprentice - the future
Sir John Hawkwood - makes his career by feats of
arms. This social group also provided political
leadership. Samuel Barnardiston, a London apprentice who was a younger son of a Suffolk gentleman,
led the demonstrations in the 'December Days'. The
Leveller Walwyn was the younger son of a Worcester
gentleman, and had served his time as apprentice to
a silk merchant in Paternoster Row.(76)

A last point deserving emphasis concerns the
relation between cultural and social change. As we
have seen, popular culture did change a good deal in
London in the course of the seventeenth century.
This was also a time when the City was growing
extremely fast, thanks to massive immigration. This
means that it will at any one point have contained a
substantial number of people who had been uprooted
from their traditional community but were not yet
familiar with London ways. It has been suggested
that 'When the number of migrants into a locality
increases, there must be a critical point at which
the increase will place such a strain upon the
system as to prevent its operation'. (77) There are
reasons for thinking that this critical point was
indeed reached in London in the seventeenth century,
perhaps in the 1650s, when the wardmotes went into
decline.(78) Traditional popular culture was
associated with traditional communities, and is
likely to have declined with them, producing a kind
of cultural vacuum in which it was easier than before
for new forms of popular culture to take hold - the
culture of print, for example, or politics, or that
of the separatist congregations. These congregations, and perhaps the Whig and Tory parties, with
their local infrastructure of clubs, taverns and
gangs seem to have offered some Londoners the
substitute they needed for the traditional community
they had lost. It has also been remarked that
immigrants to London in this period 'shed many of
the traditions of authority and deference into which
they had been born in their villages.... They were

open to new impressions and to radical notions ...
they felt more of a sense of solidarity with others
in their own condition and less of a sense of loyalty towards superiors, and out of this was born
class-consciousness'. (79) It is impossible to
verify these suggestions directly, but they are
hypotheses which make more intelligible the direction
which we know change to have taken in the period.

Two points might be added in support of this
general argument. The first is that some of the
popular literature of the period appealed directly
to immigrants. The ballad version of Dick
Whittington presents London as a paradise of social
mobility and ends with the moral:

> And you poor country boys
> Though born of low degree
> See by God's Providence
> What you in time may be.

The second point is a comparative one. There
was another part of the world where rags-to-riches
success stories of the Whittington type were part of
popular culture in the seventeenth century; Japan,
where Ihara Saikaku (1642-93) published his
Japanese Family Storehouse in 1688. Subtitled The
Millionaire's Gospel Modernised - a reference to an
earlier chapbook - it consists of a number of Samuel
Smiles-like stories of entrepreneurial success
thanks to diligence, thrift and native wit. Japan
too was in rapid social change in this period, and
three of its cities - Osaka, Edō (the modern Tokyo)
and Kyōtō - were growing fast as a result of
immigration. A new form of culture was developing,
which appealed not so much to the samurai or the
peasants as to the townsmen, the *chōnin*. This new
popular culture included chapbooks (*kana zōshi*),
kabuki theatre, puppet plays, and coloured woodblock
prints. (80) The parallel should not be pushed too
far, for there were important differences. For
example, there seems to have been little popular
political culture in Japan at this time. Yet there
are sufficient similarities between the popular
culture of London and that of Edō, in particular,
to high-light the connexion between changes in
culture and changes in society.

*   I should like to thank the editor, Barry Reay, and my
     Emmanuel colleague, Tim Harris, for their help in
     revising this article.

1.   L. B. Wright, <u>Middle-Class Culture in Elizabethan England</u>
     (Chapel Hill, 1935); J. H. Plumb, <u>The Commercialization
     of Leisure in Eighteenth-Century England</u> (Reading, 1973).

2.   E. Ward, <u>The London Spy</u> (1699), p. 2, refers to a ballad
     singer's 'blue-apron auditory'.

3.   D. Macdonald, <u>Against the American Grain</u> (NY, 1962),
     p. 60.

4.   The formula is that of the American political scientist,
     Harold Lasswell, as revised by Raymond Williams, in his
     <u>Television: Technology and Cultural Form</u> (1974), p. 120.

5.   <u>Spectator</u>, 403 (1712).

6.   R. Ashton, 'Popular Entertainment and Social Control in
     Later Elizabethan and Early Stuart London', <u>London
     Journal</u>, ix (1983).

7.   Spufford, <u>Small Books</u>, pp. 111, 115.

8.   On the jargon of London thieves, Thomas Dekker, <u>Lantern
     and Candlelight</u> (1608). On 'the homosexual subculture'
     of the eighteenth century, R. Trumbach, 'London's
     Sodomites', <u>JSH</u>, xi (1977).

9.   S. R. Smith, 'The London Apprentices as Seventeenth-
     Century Adolescents', <u>P. and P.</u>, 61 (1973).

10. A. G. Dickens, <u>The English Reformation</u> (1967), p. 28.

11. <u>Calendar to the Sessions Records, Middlesex 1612-14</u>, ed.
     W. Le Hardy (1935), pp. xv, xx, 199. A cunning man who
     practised not far from Cheapside is described by Richard
     Johnson, <u>The Pleasant Conceits of Old Hobson the Merry
     Londoner</u> (1607), no pagination.

12. <u>Middlesex County Records</u>, ii, ed. J. C. Jeaffreson (1888),
     pp. 8, 58, 73, 91, 96, 108, 112, 116, 143.

13. <u>Middlesex County Records</u>, iii, ed. Jeaffreson (1888),
     pp. 208, 223, 278.

14. <u>DNB</u>: Hathway, Richard.

15. R. Merrifield, 'The Use of Bellarmines as Witch-Bottles',
     <u>Guildhall Miscellany</u>, iii (1954).

16. J. Stow, <u>A Survey of London</u> (2 vols., 1908), i, p. 190.

17. F. M. Misson, <u>Memoires et Observations</u> (The Hague, 1698):
     'Cornes'.

18. T. Gent, <u>The Life of Mr T. Gent</u> (1832), p. 16.

19. G. F. Gemelli Carreri, <u>Viaggi</u> (Naples, 1701), letter xxi,
     p. 328 (he was in London in 1686). On the eighteenth
     century, see P. Linebaugh, 'The Tyburn Riot against the
     Surgeons', in D. Hay and others (eds.), <u>Albion's Fatal
     Tree</u> (1975), pp. 112-17.

20. A useful collection of Dekker's references to these
     festivals is to be found in M. T. Jones-Davies, <u>Une
     peintre de la vie londonienne</u> (Paris, 1958), pp. 307-8.

21. J. Taylor, <u>Jack a Lent</u> (1620); <u>Calendar to the Sessions
     Records</u>, pp. xv, 371; T. Dekker, <u>Owl's Almanac</u> (1618);

Middlesex County Records, iv, p. 118, 146, 341.

22. K. J. Lindley, 'Riot Prevention and Control in Early Stuart London', TRHS, xxxiii (1983).

23. C. Pendrill, Old Parish Life in London (1937), p. 44.

24. C. Phythian-Adams, 'Milk and Soot', in D. Fraser and A. Sutcliffe (eds.), The Pursuit of Urban History (1983), pp. 83-104.

25. Ward, London Spy, p. 134; S. Rosenfeld, The Theatre of of the London Fairs in the Eighteenth Century (Cambridge, 1960), ch. 6; Lindley, 'Riot Prevention', notes that there were eight May Day riots from 1603 to 1642.

26. Stow, Survey, p. 101; Aubrey is cited in P. Clark and P. Slack (eds.), English Towns in Transition (1976), p. 81.

27. Rosenfeld, Theatre, chs. 1-3; H. Morley, Memoirs of Bartholomew Fair (1859).

28. V. Pearl, 'Change and Stability in Seventeenth-Century London', London Journal, v (1979).

29. Letter of B. Fairfax, cited in W. Hone, Everyday Book (1831), p. 572.

30. Stow, Survey, p. 230 refers to Corpus Christi plays at Skinner's Well, Smithfield, in 1381 and 1409.

31. On popular festivals in rural England c.1600, see N. J. O'Conor, Godes Peace and the Queenes (1934), and C. L. Barber, Shakespeare's Festive Comedy (Princeton, 1959), ch. 3.

32. A. B. Harbage, Shakespeare's Audience (NY, 1941), argues that the audience was a wide one; the narrower view is put forward by A. J. Cook, The Privileged Playgoers of Shakespeare's London (Princeton, 1981), ch. 6.

33. W. A. Armstrong, 'The Audience of the Elizabethan Private Theatres', in G. E. Bentley (ed.), The Seventeenth-Century Stage (1968), pp. 215-34.

34. M. Heinemann, 'Popular Drama and Leveller Style', in M. Cornforth (ed.), Rebels and Their Causes (1978), pp. 69-88 (the passage quoted is on p. 70). On the audience at the Red Bull and the Fortune, J. Wright, Historia Histrionica (1699), p. 5.

35. Samuel Pepys, Diary, 27.12.1662, 1.1.1663, 1.1.1668; H. Love, 'The Myth of the Restoration Audience', Komos, i (1967).

36. A. B. Harbage, Annals of English Drama (1964), pp. 74-142; J. J. Elson (ed.), The Wits (Ithaca, 1932), introduction; Rosenfeld, Theatre, ch. 8.

37. Harbage, Annals of English Drama.

38. DNB: Kemp, William; C. R. Baskervill, The Elizabethan Jig (Chicago, 1929).

39. Harbage, Annals of English Drama.

40. Elson, Wits, and G. Speaight, The History of the English Puppet Theatre (1955), Appendix B.

41. M. Tolmie, The Triumph of the Saints (Cambridge, 1977); C. Hill, B. Reay and W. Lamont, The World of the Muggle-

tonians (1983).

42. Richard Lane, tailor, 1631, quoted by Hill, World Turned Upside Down (1975), p. 148; Marshall, a bricklayer of Hackney, quoted by T. Edwards, Gangraena (1646), i, p. 112; an anonymous man, quoted ibid., p. 113.

43. K. V. Thomas, 'Women and the Civil War Sects', in T. Aston (ed.), Crisis in Europe (1965), pp. 317-40.

44. A. Cole, 'The Social Origins of the Early Friends', JFHS, xlviii (1957); A. L. Morton, The World of the Ranters (1970), pp. 71, 101; B. S. Capp, The Fifth Monarchy Men (1972).

45. English Historical Documents, 1600-1714, ed. A. Browning (1953), pp. 413-15, 427; on the Quakers, W. Beck and T. F. Ball, The London Friends' Meetings (1869), p. 32.

46. R. Withington, English Pageantry (2 vols., Cambridge, Mass., 1918), i, ch. 5; E. Halfpenny, 'The Citie's Loyalty Display'd', Guildhall Miscellany, x (1959); J. E. Neale, 'November 17th', in his Essays in Elizabethan History (1958), pp. 9-20.

47. F. W. Fairholt, Lord Mayors' Pageants (2 vols., 1843), i; S. Williams, 'The Lord Mayor's Show: Peele to Settle', Guildhall Miscellany, x (1959); D. M. Bergeron, English Civic Pageantry 1558-1642 (1971).

48. T. Dekker, Dramatic Works, ed. F. Bowers (4 vols., Cambridge, 1953-61), ii, pp. 229f; B. Jonson, Works, ed. C. H. Herford and P. and E. Simpson (11 vols., Oxford, 1925-52), vii, pp. 67-9.

49. T. Jordan, London Triumphant (1672).

50. Examples are the 1590 Show for Mayor Allot, and the 1616 Show for Mayor Leman, both of the Fishmongers.

51. T. Jordan, The Triumphs of London (1678).

52. M. Taubman, London's Great Jubilee (1689), p. 2.

53. The Oxford English Dictionary's first instance of the term 'demonstration' in its political sense dates from 1839. The term is described as an example of Whig 'cant', so it may not be inappropriate to use it of the period when the Whig party was coming into being.

54. Lindley, 'Riot Prevention'; R. M. Dunn, 'The London Weavers' Riot of 1675', Guildhall Studies in London History, i (1973-4); G. Holmes, 'The Sacheverell Riots', P. and P., 72 (1976).

55. Lindley, 'Riot Prevention', p. 112.

56. Dunn, 'Weavers' Riot'.

57. B. Manning, The English People and the English Revolution (1976), ch. 4 (the comment from Dudley Digges is quoted on p. 91).

58. S. R. Smith, 'The Apprentices' Parliament of 1647', History Today, xxii (1972); I. Gentles, 'The Struggle for London in the Second Civil War', HJ, xxvi (1983).

59. G. Sitwell, The First Whig (Scarborough, 1894), chs. 5-7; J. R. Jones, 'The Green Ribbon Club', Durham University

Journal, xlix (1956), pp. 17-20; S. Williams, 'The Pope-Burning Processions of 1679-81', *Journal of the Warburg and Courtauld Institutes*, xxi (1958); O. W. Furley, 'The Pope-Burning Processions of the Late Seventeenth Century', *History*, xliv (1959); T. Harris deals with this subject in his Cambridge Ph.D. thesis, still (1983) in progress.

60. N. Rogers, 'Popular Protest in Early Hanoverian London', *P. and P.*, 79 (1978), pp. 77-8.

61. N. Rogers, 'Aristocratic Clientage, Trade and Independency: Popular Politics in Pre-Radical Westminster', *P. and P.*, 61 (1973); L. Colley, 'Eighteenth-Century English Radicalism before Wilkes', *TRHS*, xxxi (1981); Gentles, 'Struggle'.

62. T. Harris discusses this question in his thesis.

63. Quoted in Pearl, 'Change and Stability', p. 6.

64. Cressy, *Literacy*. His principal references to London occur on pp. 72-5, 144-9.

65. H. E. Rollins, 'The Black-Letter Broadside Ballad', *Proceedings of the Modern Language Association* (1919), pp. 258-339; C. Blagden, 'Notes on the Ballad Market', *Studies in Bibliography*, vi (1954).

66. R. Mandrou, *De la culture populaire aux xviie et xviiie siècles* (Paris, 1964); Spufford, *Small Books*, ch. 4.

67. R. Thompson, 'Popular Reading and Humour in Restoration England', *Journal of Popular Culture*, ix (1976); Spufford, *Small Books*, chs. 7-9.

68. Spufford, *Small Books*, reprints Thackeray's catalogue in an appendix.

69. B. Capp, *Astrology and the Popular Press* (1979).

70. *Catalogue of the Pamphlets ... collected by George Thomason, 1640-1661* (1908).

71. L. S. O'Connell, 'The Elizabethan Bourgeois Hero-Tale', in B. C. Malament (ed.), *After the Reformation* (Manchester, 1980), pp. 267-87.

72. W. Walwyn, *The Poor Wise Man's Admonition unto all the Plain People of London* (1647); Heinemann, 'Popular Drama'; *Canterbury his Change of Diet* is no. xv in *Occasional Facsimile Reprints*, ed. E. W. Ashbee (1868-72).

73. H. Sachs, *Der Rossdieb zu Fünsing* is one example.

74. F. Boucher, *Le Pont Neuf* (2 vols., Paris, 1925-6).

75. P. Clark (ed.), *The Early Modern Town* (1976), p. 228.

76. Manning, *English People*, pp. 93, 114; Smith, 'London Apprentices'.

77. M. Stacey, 'The Myth of Community Studies', *British Journal of Sociology*, xx (1969), proposition 3.

78. Pearl, 'Change and Stability'.

79. Manning, *English People*, p. 71.

80. I. Saikaku, *The Japanese Family Storehouse*, trans. G. W. Sargent (Cambridge, 1959).

Chapter Two

POPULAR CULTURE IN SEVENTEENTH-CENTURY BRISTOL

Jonathan Barry

I

Although Bristol was England's third largest
city, with a population rising from about 12,000 in
1600 to around 21,000 by 1700, it remained (by our
standards) a small community which was only just
starting to outgrow its medieval boundaries.
Bristol was one of a number of major ports,
industrial centres and provincial capitals which
grew, particularly after 1650, faster than other
provincial towns, but whose character remained more
akin to their smaller counterparts than to the
highly populated metropolis. Like most of the large
provincial centres, Bristol was a corporate town
with extensive powers of self-government; but
unlike many, it was not the focus of county or
regional government. Perched on the borders of
Somerset and Gloucestershire, Bristol was a regional
capital in economic terms, and strong enough to
assert its political and cultural independence from
its rural neighbours. But it was far from
dominating the countryside around - apart from the
immediate hinterland.(1)
Bristol's steady growth in the seventeenth
century depended on immigration from the neighbouring counties and the Severn valley; the city's
native population was only just able to reproduce
itself. By and large, immigrants entered the city
through apprenticeship or marriage, rather than
drifting in without a prepared niche in town life.
In the 1630s about two thousand apprentices were
active in the city, and even at the end of the
century, when the number of non-Bristolian
apprentices had fallen to just over 50 per cent, two
hundred outsiders were apprenticed each year. Both
apprenticeship and marriage into a family in Bristol

could lead to the freedom of the city, although many apprentices never took it up because they either left the city or became journeymen. In the early seventeenth century about 20 per cent of the population were freemen, including (presumably) at least half the adult males. (The elections at the end of the century (in 1696) saw about three thousand freemen voting at a time when the city contained only 4,560 households, 19 per cent of which were headed by widows.) Most household heads must have been freemen, and many of the others had shared the experience of apprenticeship.(2)

Although the late seventeenth century saw the growth of new industries such as sugar-refining, pottery- and glass-making, and metal-working, the scale of such enterprises was small; the characteristic forms of production remained those of the artisan and shopkeeper, together with mercantile and port activities. Although the gradual decline of the weaving industry in the parishes south of the river did cause social unrest and led to efforts to promote work for the poor, there is little sign of a concentration of labourers or underemployed poor - at least until the 1690s. In 1695 Bristol pioneered the development of the city-wide Corporation of the Poor, but this was probably a reaction to the short-term dislocation caused by the Nine Years' War and the problems of allocating poor relief between parishes rather than to the overwhelming burden of the permanently impoverished. The Corporation of the Poor catered mainly for the old and infirm and the young, offering the latter education and then apprenticeship.(3) Despite evident strains, Bristolians remained confident that apprenticeship and work could provide the social discipline necessary to hold the community together.

Religious and political changes in the city offered a challenge to such cohesion. The city's internal government was firmly in the hands of the rich, with a self-perpetuating common council and aldermen ruling over eighteen select vestries in the parishes. The council was increasingly controlled by the mercantile interest in the city, although leading retailers and manufacturers were also part of the governing elite. The mass of the freemen do not seem to have challenged this characteristic form of local government, but after the Restoration they were successful in broadening the parliamentary franchise to include all the freemen as well as freeholders and councillors. Late seventeenth-century Bristol saw bitter struggles between Whigs and Tories for both parliamentary and local control. Religion was the most divisive issue. Although Bristol was a cathedral city, it was in a poor diocese which yoked the Bristol area together with Dorset. Compared to the council, the church authorities had little power in the town, for the former owned many of the livings and even had its own private chapel opposite the cathedral. The council's support of lecturers and active preachers in the town before 1640 did nothing to prevent the early emergence of separatist groups and, in the upheavals of the Civil War, Independent and Baptist congregations. In the 1650s, Bristol proved a fertile field for the Quakers. After 1662 these dissenters were joined reluctantly by the Presbyterians. All in all, dissenters and sectaries formed a good quarter of the city's late seventeenth-century population.(4)

Seventeenth-century Bristol can still be characterised as a 'face-to-face' society where great premium was placed on corporate unity. Socially, the town was highly inegalitarian; with a wealthy mercantile elite at one extreme and much poverty at the other, but with a large middle ground of masters, apprentices and journeymen. In the daily business of government, and in religious and political battles, the city's rulers could not afford to alienate this middling group.

It is in this context that I shall explore the nature of 'popular culture' in Bristol and, in particular, the recent suggestion by Keith Wrightson that in the seventeenth century (in the countryside at least) cultural forces came to reinforce social divisions, creating a growing gulf between respectable and plebeian, or elite and popular cultures.(5) What effect did cultural changes have in Bristol; and what can this example tell us about the nature of popular culture in seventeenth-century provincial towns?

II

The shortage of direct evidence concerning the nature of popular culture - as marked for Bristol as anywhere - has forced historians to speculate about the implications for popular culture of other trends which we <u>can</u> recapture, if only partially. The most obvious of these are the developments in educational provisions and the growing importance of the printing press. Together, these might suggest the establishment of a cultural barrier

between the literate, who were able to participate
in a broader world of knowledge, and the illiterate,
who were trapped in a traditional world of oral culture and custom.

Seventeenth-century Bristol still contained
many illiterate people. For their benefit, the
streets were overhung with sign-boards which bore
the emblems of each man's trade; each tradesman had
his own 'mark'. But the majority of Bristol's <u>adult</u>
<u>males</u> were not illiterate. Figures are hard to
establish before 1660, but we do know that in the
1620s and 1630s 75 to 80 per cent of the witnesses
to probate inventories could sign their names. A
survey of the signatures on marriage licence bonds
of the 1660s and 1690s shows a literacy rate of over
80 per cent, still rising, though very gradually.
Neither of these sources offers a perfect cross-
section of Bristol society, for both are biased
towards the better-off. But a comparison between
marriages by licence and all marriages in the next
century suggests that when the figures are corrected
for social bias about 65 per cent of adult males
could sign their names in the 1660s, and 67 per cent
in the 1690s. Evidence from guild and vestry
records indicates steadily improving literacy over
the period, and that by 1700 illiteracy was
extremely rare among the wealthier inhabitants.(6)

Although the majority of Bristol's adult males
could sign, literacy varied greatly with occupation.
Near-complete literacy among merchants, professional
men and retailers, contrasts with an illiteracy rate
of 50 per cent or more among labourers and unskilled
men, and with below-average figures for those in
rough, outdoor crafts and agriculture. The vast
majority of those recorded in the licence bonds were
artisans and sailors whose literacy rate varied
between 70 and 90 per cent. Interestingly, the
sailors, who form the largest single occupational
group, came high in the literacy ranking: at 87 per
cent in the 1660s (although this fell to 82 per
cent in the 1690s, perhaps because the wars of that
decade brought less skilled men into service). The
traditionally contemplative shoemakers and cord-
wainers were also highly literate: 86 to 87 per
cent.

Whilst these Bristol figures for male literacy
may seem surprisingly high, they accord with
findings for other English cities and also with
rural figures from nearby counties for the same
trades.(7) Contemporaries recognised that city trades
required the skills of literacy, and apprentices

were already expected to have mastered the three Rs before they were indentured.(8) Unapprenticed labourers and unskilled men formed only a small proportion of the city workforce in comparison to the artisans and shopkeepers for whom literacy constituted a vocational advantage.

If we are looking for a large group excluded from literacy, then the women of the city seem likely candidates. Women were not often asked to sign or mark, but occasional listings suggest that only 20 to 35 per cent of women could sign. Female standards appear to have been rising faster than male, but even in the 1750s only 43 per cent of women could sign (compared to 71 per cent of men). Women may have learned to write at later ages than men; at home rather than at school. The wives of men from the literate occupations were more likely to be literate than others, although we know of merchants' and retailers' wives who were unable to write.

We should be hesitant to conclude from this that they could not read, which is, after all, what matters in cultural terms. We assume that reading and writing go together. Yet in the seventeenth century children learnt to read before they began to learn to write. Reading could be taught at home, or by dames charging as little as 2d a week, who doubled as child-minders before the child was old enough to contribute to the family economy. Writing with a quill was a complex art (comparable perhaps to typing today) taught by writing masters along with arithmetic and merchant's accounts.(9) Writing cost more to learn than reading; and writing lessons began only when children were old enough to earn money at work, which meant that schooling hit at the earning capacity of the family. The occupational stratification of the ability to sign reflects the vocational purposes for which writing was valued. We can assume that more people had a basic grasp of reading, and that the social distribution of reading ability was not necessarily the same as that for writing. This applies particularly to girls, for whom the desired vocational skills were reading, sewing and housewifery - but not writing.(10)

As education had a largely vocational aim, it is not surprising that schooling was usually the result of private demand not public provision. Bristol had many schoolteachers, few of whom depended on public funding. The council administered two schools established by charity for orphan boys and girls; while the Merchant Venturers ran another small school for the children of poor seamen. Two uncertainly financed parish schools for the poor were started in 1654 and 1670, and some of the parishes helped to educate the occasional poor child, as did some of the sects. No more than a hundred children a year were being educated in this fashion before 1700. A series of initiatives to reach the children of the poor were then started, reaching perhaps three hundred children by 1710.(11)

The primary motive for these efforts was to inculcate religious and moral discipline, although learning to read the Bible obviously offered access to other reading as well. When Bristolians discussed the role of education, they recognised its vocational usefulness; but they mainly saw it as a process of socialisation which moulded children into virtuous citizens and good Christians. Mere learning was regarded with suspicion; and schooling in itself played no greater part than apprenticeship or the example of one's peers and betters. The school curriculum reflected these aims.(12)

Schools of all sorts, like parents at home, began teaching with the hornbook, spelling-book and primer, then moving on to catechism, psalter and Bible. Since the chief motive for teaching reading was to introduce the Bible, it seemed natural to teach children to read from it. Large classes, shortages of texts, and rote methods of learning meant that reading was acquired through a process of oral recitation and memorisation of a sacred text, and experienced as part of an oral tradition in the classroom and the church. Although pious children were steeped in the Bible by the time they finished school, such education did not nourish an active, critical attitude to print. Nor did it furnish any guide to the wider world of secular literature, which children were left to discover on their own, outside school. An uneven and often brief period of schooling by such methods probably led to most children being semi-literate: able to read, but ill-equipped to digest any sophisticated, literary products.

If 'primary' education left most children semi-literate, should we view 'secondary' (that is, grammar school) education as a crucial dividing-line in cultural experience? Certainly, only a small minority received a classical education. In theory the three grammar schools were all free to the sons of freemen, although attendance obviously involved many hidden expenses apart from loss of earnings.

These three schools probably taught a hundred boys at any one time; but others could attend the schools of private masters, notably the parish clerks and clergy, and, after 1662, nonconformist ministers. (Even the Quakers sponsored masters able to teach both Latin and vocational subjects.) But most parents did not want to educate their sons in the classics at the expense of more vocational training. Although the grammar schools offered writing lessons, many parents only sent their children for a few years to gain a smattering of Latin before they moved on to vocational training and into apprenticeship. The City School had a good library, traditions of oration and versifying, and could offer children scholarships to university; yet the vast majority of its pupils left to take apprenticeships in the mercantile or retail trades. Those who went on to university nearly all became clergymen, whilst another tiny band went to the Inns of Court to study law. Medical apprentices also found a humanistic education vocationally useful. Although these groups undoubtedly imbibed a knowledge of, and an admiration for, the classical heritage, one must question the long-term effect of a few years of the classics. The council clearly valued the City School, and saw the classical tradition as the appropriate grounding for future governors of the city. But the credentials of the rulers of Bristol depended on custom and experience - and wealth - rather than learning.(13)

This brief survey of education and literacy has shown that although most Bristolians were technically able to read, their educational experience did not establish any clear pattern for future reading habits beyond exposure to the Bible. Unfortunately the material available on the nature of reading habits can do little to fill in the picture, and we are forced to draw implications from very partial evidence.

There are clear indications that the book trade was assuming a more significant role in Bristol life. The number of booksellers and others connected with the book trade increased between the 1630s and the 1670s, and then declined again before another upswing in the early eighteenth century.(14) The inhabitants of Bristol could also buy printed matter from petty chapmen and hawkers in the streets, from grocers and other shopkeepers, and from the London booksellers who had stalls at the two annual fairs. Few small towns today would support so many retail outlets for books. But we

must bear several caveats in mind. The Bristol
book traders, like the Londoners at the fairs, were
catering to a regional market, and even to export
demand. None of the booksellers depended for their
livelihood solely on sales of printed material, as
all were also stationers and bookbinders. The most
common label used for such men was 'stationer',
indicating that the most important part of their
business was the retailing of paper and paper
products, writing utensils, and account books. The
trade boom from the 1650s, and the growth in
government bureaucracy, are more likely causes of
the increase in numbers than an increased demand for
literature. The late seventeenth-century trade only
supported two major bookshops whose owners regularly
engaged in publishing ventures or subscribed to
serious works.

Until the first local printer, William Bonny,
set up business in 1695, after the lapse of the
Licensing Act, all books and other printed matter
had to be ordered from London, and were sent
unbound to save carriage costs. Books were only
bound when bought, which accounts for the close
links between the book trade and the leather and
gilding trades. Shops with small stocks of largely
unbound stock can hardly have attracted customers to
browse and discover new areas of knowledge. The
poor and ill-educated were probably too timid to
enter the bookshops which were mostly located in the
mercantile and administrative heart of the town;
perhaps they preferred the market stalls at fair-
time. And, apart from the market bargains, books
were expensive.

Unfortunately, the only quantitative evidence
of book ownership that survives, namely references
in probate inventories, is only reliable in its
coverage of the more expensive sorts of reading
matter. Probate assessors were not interested in
worthless, unbound items, and judged books more by
size and binding than content. Chapbooks and
pamphlets are rarely mentioned, and broadsheets
never. When book titles or genres are specified
they are mostly religious works, above all the
Bible, followed in popularity by works on history,
especially chronicles, or blends of religion and
history such as Foxe's <u>Book of Martyrs</u>. There are
also some navigational books, maps and charts,
medical and legal treatises, but almost no secular
literature, except for a few chivalric romances
amidst the works of piety and history owned by a
woollen-draper. It is likely that this apparent

devotion to serious works reflects the kind of material published in the large volumes which caught the appraisers' attention.(15) Only one extensive listing has survived from this period, in the printed catalogues of the books of Thomas Palmer, rector of the central parish of St Werburgh's, whose library was sold in London in 1694. Among the more than eight hundred titles are 128 'great folios', mostly of divinity, but also covering history, the classics, and both moral and natural philosophy. Among the smaller volumes, however, are many school-books, practical guides, and a range of secular literature - from Francis Quarles's <u>Argalus and Parthenia</u> (1629) to the pornographic <u>Venus in the Cloister</u> (1683) and the intriguing <u>Tryal of old Father Christmas</u> (n.d.)(16)

Selectivity in the recording of books may help to explain the overall pattern of book ownership found in the inventories. Only the professions, and above all the clergy, invested a considerable part of their wealth in books. Otherwise the likelihood of leaving books increased with wealth, although with no clear threshold to suggest a dramatic social division between a reading and a non-reading class. Even in the wealthiest class only a slender majority of Bristolians left books; and the figure for all classes was only just over 25 per cent.

More difficult to explain, given the evidence for a more extensive book trade, is the decline in the overall number of inventories which mention books: from 34.6 per cent for the period 1620-60, to 21.8 per cent for 1660-1710. The trend is exaggerated by the rising proportion of inventories for poorer people at the end of the century, but the same pattern is clear within most valuation ranges. It is tempting to suggest a shift in reading habits towards the cheaper ephemeral literature not appraised in the inventories. But if this is the explanation, then it must have occurred at all levels of wealth, implying that the rich were also reading chapbooks and pamphlets. An alternative explanation could lie in the apparent decline in ownership of religious books. Service books are rarely mentioned after 1640, and the number of Bibles which are specified falls sharply from the 1670s (although the Bible is still by far the most commonly recorded book). Civil war and religious pluralism may have lessened the number of Bibles in households which owned no other books, in which case the evangelists of the 1700s were justified in their efforts to reverse such a development. But perhaps religious literature had also become cheaper and escaped appraisal!

If print was to have any effect upon the lives of ordinary Bristolians, it would almost certainly have to be the cheaper literature of broadsheet, chapbook and pamphlet.(17) These were sold in the streets, and advertised vocally so that all knew their contents. When all but the wealthiest worked from dawn to dusk, and candlelight reading was expensive and tiring, the brief tract was much more easily digested than the bulky folio. Artisans and shopkeepers could read to themselves or to their companions at work, but they could hardly concentrate on long and complex arguments.(18) For this reason, Sunday was officially set aside for the whole household to listen to readings from religious works. Another centre where reading was possible was the alehouse; it was a place of leisure where ballads and other forms of print were often available. Almost all these settings involved experience of the printed word as part of an oral culture, read or sung aloud and shared with others – including the illiterate.

One of the most important developments of the eighteenth century was the combination, in periodicals and serial publications, of serious content with ephemeral packaging. The almanac, perhaps the single most popular printed item in seventeenth-century Bristol, probably attracted an audience of all classes in this way; and the early newspapers may have had a similar effect. From the Civil War onwards, concern was repeatedly expressed at the popularity of news among the people. The London newspapers and newsletters were too expensive for any but the richest to buy, and only after 1702, when the first local paper offered a weekly digest of national news for ½d or 1d, did buying a paper become feasible for the average inhabitant of Bristol.(19) But those of the middling-rank could afford to go to the new coffee houses, where they read and discussed the news. The first coffee house was licensed in 1666, and by the 1680s there were two or three near the Tolzey, where the merchants traded, and others south of the river and near the cathedral. In 1676 one coffee seller was put on a bond of £500 not to supply seditious news or pamphlets to his customers, and to report all seditious talk. It is clear that books in general, and pamphlets and newsletters in particular, were vital aspects of coffee house life. During the Exclusion Crisis of 1679-81 several coffee houses were raided or closed down.(20)

Here again we must set reading in its social context. Coffee house news was not absorbed privately but discussed publicly, and indeed the cryptic, often allusive character of the reporting required such public interpretation. Oral and printed culture were still closely interdependent. Printed newsletters still imitated and travelled alongside private letters, and they were discussed together as letters were opened and rumours were repeated. The reputation of the source mattered more than whether or not the news was printed.(21) Traditional means of communication in the city remained of major importance, even after 1695 when the first press was set up. The city bellman walked the streets, proclaiming local and national news, and, for a fee, making announcements for private citizens. To make a public announcement, one could stand on the High Cross at the city centre and declaim, or fix a written notice to the Cross or on the Tolzey. The council did the same on a grander scale when it proclaimed major news from the High Cross and other crosses, as well as from those other focal points of city life, the pumps and conduits. Public attention was assured by the lavish use of music, costume, and free food and drink. Church bells proclaimed major events, and parishioners used the bells and elaborate processions to proclaim their rites of passage, lavish funerals for example. During the heightened political tension of the years 1679-89, there were fierce struggles to control such oral, ritual vehicles of propaganda, for many were convinced that such forms carried more weight than the printed word.(22)

The use of publication to convey a political or religious message in Bristol during this period further illustrates this point. The use of print did certainly increase, starting with pamphlet controversies between the denominations in the 1650s, and then reviving with the reprinting of sermons and the first electioneering literature in the late 1670s and 1680s (although it is worth recalling that all such works had to be printed in London). By 1700 the local Society for the Reformation of Manners saw the distribution of broadsheets to a thousand city households as one way to reform the city, and the council were beginning to use printed notices to citizens about local regulations and standards of behaviour. But such material was still produced on a very small scale, supplementing rather than replacing other techniques.

The most commonly published items were reprints of
important sermons, showing that print was still
linked to older forms of communication.(23)

III

Two distinct but linked hypotheses have been
proposed whereby the Reformation and the subsequent
pattern of religious change affected the nature and
status of popular culture. The first stresses the
replacement of ritual and magic, through which the
Catholic church had appealed to popular beliefs and
needs, by an austere religion of the word and
personal salvation. The second argues that
Protestantism became associated with a godly lifestyle, and alienated from the sports, drinking, and
'good cheer' of popular culture, which it
endeavoured to suppress by a 'reformation of
manners'. Both hypotheses find expression in the
connotations of the term 'Puritan'. Some historians
have seen this 'Puritanism' as an expression of
urban values which were battling against a popular
culture deeply rooted in the practices and beliefs
of an agrarian society.(24) How useful are these
concepts to an analysis of urban popular culture?
The Reformation had clearly damaged the
religious ritual life of Bristol, and Protestantism
contained a legacy of distrust for the calendrical
festivals which had survived. Although scarcely
Catholic, the festivals of Shrove Tuesday and May Day
were clearly popular with the people, and were
disliked by Puritans. The sharpest attacks on
popular practices came during the 1650s. It was no
accident that the apprentice riots of 1660, which
the Bristol royalists guided towards demonstrations
for a free parliament, incorporated Shrove Tuesday
games of football and throwing stones at <u>hens</u> and
<u>bitches</u> (thence both obeying and ridiculing the
Council's proclamation against the abuse of <u>cocks</u>
and <u>dogs</u>, a traditional Shrove Tuesday pastime).(25)
The nonconformist sects distinguished themselves by
their hostility, not only to the ritual of church
services but to the whole notion of the 'holiness'
of days or places: thus they opened their shops at
Christmas. In so doing they were well aware that
they were offending the sensibilities of the mass of
citizens, and so were not surprised when they were
physically assaulted in response.(26)
This does not mean that the bulk of the Bristol
population were not committed Protestants. Rather
it seems that the sectarians were unusual in

interpreting the Protestant religion of the word as a reason to reject the use of symbols and rituals to convey religious and moral messages. Christmas, Easter and Whitsun continued to provide the backbone of both the church calendar and public leisure. Most parishes still held perambulations on Holy Thursday, led by the vestry elite of the parish. The old saints' days were still favoured as dates on which to establish gift sermons or annual doles of bread. The city guilds still had their patron saints. Although the churches were whitewashed, and images had been replaced by written texts and tables of benefactors, these and other church furnishings were lavishly gilded and well maintained.(27)

Throughout the seventeenth century the council showed great devotion to the idea of a preaching ministry, and clashed with successive bishops over cathedral services, in part because they wanted to hear sermons without enduring the full church service. But they were hardly hostile to ritual. The clashes at the cathedral were over rival claims to ritual precedence of clergy and magistracy. The corporate year involved an elaborate round of visits to the parish churches on Sundays and other church festivals, as well as perambulations of the city boundaries. There is no sign that such activities worried Puritan councillors, and the Presbyterian Council of the 1650s was as enamoured of pomp as any other. The Council was as hostile as the crowd to the sectarian rejection of public holidays. The culmination of this came in 1656 when James Nayler, surrounded by Quaker disciples, rode into Bristol on a donkey. The horrified reaction of the Bristol leaders (and Parliament) reflected belief that such an act was not merely blasphemous, but also a parody of the civic ritual of Bristol and other towns in which great visitors were met outside the gates and ushered in by a procession of notables.(28) In short, the calendar and rituals of religion were so inter-woven with the civic establishment in Bristol that rejection of all such ritual was only possible for those - a minority in the sects - willing to cut themselves off from civic life. With their appearances in sackcloth and ashes, and their ritual warnings of the fate of Bristol, the Quakers seemed to challenge the whole meaning of civic life. But the increasingly introspective leaders of the sect soon rejected such methods.(29)

Even if most of the godly elite in Bristol were still committed to the use of ritual, did this ritual also have popular appeal; or did it merely represent the self-congratulation of the city's rulers? Both city and parish government were oligarchic; and commentators on civic ritual stressed its orderly expression of social distinctions and hierarchy. A corporate gallery in the cathedral, or special pews in church, made clear who was important in the city and gave them privileged access to the word of God. Enthusiasm for civic ritual did not necessarily mean sympathy for the ceremonial outlets of ordinary people; to the city rulers Shrove Tuesday marches and games appeared as threats to public order, not affirmations of social cohesion.(30)

Although there is no simple way of proving this interpretation, there are several pieces of evidence which suggest that civic culture was quite widely shared and valued. In the first place, the council and vestries were not the only participants in city rituals. A major role was always played by the guilds, which marched before the council, merchants, clergy and others on civic holidays and on royal visits. The guilds of Bristol still seem to have been significant occupational and social groupings in the seventeenth century, maintaining their numbers and role in economic life at least until 1700. A dozen guilds had their ordinances granted or reformulated in the middle decades of the century, and new guilds in the 1670s included such humble groups as porters and hauliers. The majority of the city's middling classes were still participating in guild life, and this was intimately associated with the wider life of the community.(31) It was compulsory for the guilds to appear at civic ceremonies, with their gowns and banners indicating their guild allegiance. When the Soapboilers' Company, a guild with strong Whig connections, failed in 1684 to participate in the Fifth of November procession, their absence was immediately reported to the central government, and was taken very seriously.(32) Although this indicates the pressures on the guilds to participate, it also shows that the council needed public support to legitimate their claim to represent the whole community.

This need for popular legitimation can be seen in many aspects of civic culture. The government of the city was essentially a matter of magistracy, symbolised by the dispensing of justice; and civic ritual appealed to the citizens to acknowledge that their magistrates were living up to the high standards of justice. The council was enormously sensitive to the possibility that its public reputation might be tarnished, and such 'ceremonial' matters as precedence, wearing the correct robes, and the proper entertainment of civic guests, were very important in this respect.(33) Whilst such efforts were probably intended chiefly for the middling and elite of the community, the crowd was also an important ingredient. Its presence, and popular acclamations of joy and approval, were always noted. The crowd had to be attracted by free drink, bonfires, music, gunfire and bells, but there is no sign of popular rejection of such activities. Visitors to Bristol noted (not always with approval) the fierce civic pride of the average Bristol freeman.(34)

The civic traditions of Bristol were important for the social identity of both the elite and ordinary Bristolians. In the absence of any ties to the rural areas, Bristol people looked to their occupations, their city, and their church, for a sense of belonging. The membership and trappings of the city guilds and militia were much prized, for there were as yet few voluntary societies or clubs through which those who had recently arrived in the city could establish an identity. One such grouping did emerge in our period, with the establishment (around 1658) of four charitable societies, each with an annual feast when the natives of Bristol, Gloucestershire, Somerset and Wiltshire, respectively, could meet, hear a sermon, dine, and give money to support the apprenticeship of poor boys from their counties. Significantly, these societies, run largely by retailers and skilled craftsmen rather than the merchant elite, chose to express their solidarity in the style of civic ceremony: with processions through the city to and from sermons, followed by dinners. Equally importantly, they identified apprenticeship as the key institution for transmitting the civic values of virtue and industry.(35)

As we have seen, apprenticeship was the single experience common to most Bristol men, and it was clearly assigned a central place in socialisation. This does not mean that apprentices did not pose problems to public order and morality. As individuals they were often accused of disobedience to masters, immorality and so on; and as groups they formed a powerful force which the city's rulers could not easily control. The apprentice riots of 1660 were only quelled by the appearance of troops, and on other occasions the magistrates had to appeal the apprentices, and negotiate with them. If we an trust the propaganda of 1660, the apprentices saw themselves as representing, in some sense, the opinions of a city silenced by the lack of a parliament, particularly on such subjects as high taxation. Apprentice attacks on Quakers in the 1650s, and against brothels in 1685 and papist houses in 1688, also saw the city's youth take the law into their own hands in a way unacceptable to the city leaders.(36) Yet we should not ignore the fact that the apprentices were engaged in defence of civic values (as they saw it) and that they often had the tacit or even active support of some of their masters, as well as the knowledge that the civic authorities were themselves officially opposed to sects, prostitution, and popery. The willingness of the elite to use apprentice support in the establishment of the society of the Loyal Young Men of Bristol as junior partner to the Tory Artillery Company during the reaction to the Exclusion Crisis, indicates the ambivalence of their attitudes (although that society was carefully controlled by its elders, and probably consisted largely of apprentices from the prosperous trades).(37) Even the more boisterous marches of apprentices from the poorer guilds - coopers, carpenters, butchers - bearing their occupational emblems before them on Shrove Tuesday and clashing with rival trades, reinforced vertical loyalties to the trade rather than solidarity between workers in different occupations.

Nor can concern for the 'reformation of manners' in Bristol be explained simply as an effort of the city's elite to impose an alien lifestyle on the mass of citizens. It was, on the contrary, an attempt by the magistrates to live up to the role expected of them by the wider citizenry, who shared an image of the city's needs. In a small trading community, personal credit and reputation were vital to both trader and artisan, and public order and morality were seen chiefly in terms of individual morality and the correct relations of master to servant or apprentice. Only the 'virtue and industry' of the citizens, to quote the city's motto, caused Bristol to prosper. The primary method by which such virtues were inculcated was personal example, enhanced by the effects of work. The role of the magistrate was to control potential trouble-spots such as alehouses, whose excessive numbers or abuses might subvert the natural social ties. It was also the magistrate's task to enforce social discipline on the unemployed and poor who, as masterless men and women, had escaped the usual channels of social control. This does not seem to have been a major problem in Bristol, until the 1690s when opinion of all kinds seems to have been unanimous that new, formal mechanisms of reformation were needed. Schemes then poured forth from Quakers, Presbyterians, and Whig and Tory Anglicans to meet this need. There was no agreement on the best solution - workhouse, reform society, charity school, etc. - and there was feuding between the rival groups who realised that power would accrue to those who ran the schemes. But there is little sign of disagreement over basic aims; there was a clear sense that the party solving the problem would win esteem from the general citizenry.(38)

If the reform movement had a civic inspiration, where does this leave its supposedly 'Puritan' motivation? There is certainly evidence that the 1650s were a period when the city authorities were particularly keen to enforce moral standards, focusing especially on behaviour which threatened the sanctity of the sabbath; disorderly conduct in the streets, alehouses opening during service hours, citizens travelling into the countryside. But these concerns were by no means unique to this decade, and much of the appearance of activity may reflect the need to reimpose old disciplines after the hiatus of the Civil War, when Bristol was occupied in turn by Royalist and Parliamentary forces, and civil authority was consequently weakened.

There is little evidence that the Anglican Tories who dominated the council after 1660 repudiated the reformation of manners in favour of an alliance with popular culture. It was the ultra-Tory mayor, Sir John Knight, who issued the first printed broadsheet calling for moral reform, and similar calls are contained in the addresses of grand juries of varying political hues, and of clergymen of all persuasions. The Anglican clergy were convinced that moral laxity was the reason why God had visited England with the scourge of Whig radicalism. The only case I have discovered of a Tory promoting plebeian culture came in 1697 when the Mayor used corporate funds to support a bull-baiting in the city. This mayor was engaged in a single-handed campaign to block the opening of the Corporation of the Poor workhouse, and it seems reasonable to view the bull-baiting as a symbolic act of defiance against the moralists. But this was very much an isolated incident, and the bulk of Tories sought to claim the moral approach as their own, rather than to oppose it.(39)

This does not mean, of course, that everyone in Bristol was respectable, or even that everyone welcomed interference with their right to get drunk, break the sabbath, or engage in rough sports. Rather than seeing a simple antithesis between two outlooks, we need to view 'respectability' as one pole of communal life, with sociability as the other. The council themselves engaged in an elaborate round of feasting and recreation, including regular expeditions to hunt ducks and fish in pools near the city. The life of the guilds and other societies revolved around breakfasts, dinners and suppers, in which occupational solidarity was reinforced by common cheer. The apprentice marches performed the same function. Nevertheless, all these groups were also aware of the dangers of excessive sociability. Guild regulations laid down elaborate rules to ensure the maintenance of good fellowship, and these centred on the very problems that obsessed the reformers, namely drunkenness, slander, blasphemy, and sabbath-breaking as a form of unfair competition. Even the most zealous reformers opposed drunkenness rather than drinking, and accepted the lawfulness of moderate recreation, although they balked at such activities as gambling and dancing, which to most Bristolians were legitimate pursuits.(40)

One final point might be made about the reform of manners: it was not called for exclusively from the top downwards. Not only were the city elite constantly warned that the citizens would only respect them if they behaved respectably, but the probity of the city could itself act as a badge of honour, implicitly criticising the lifestyle of the great. Such provincial moralism is very evident in the attitudes of the so-called 'country party' of the eighteenth century, and was doubtless part of the civic self-image earlier.

IV

Much of the recent literature on provincial towns, particularly in the post-Restoration period, has been preoccupied with the role of the towns as entrepôts, for the countryside, of a metropolitan culture, a culture based on the consumption, by the well-off, of luxury goods and services. This is thought to have given the towns a renewed cultural

importance after a period of depression caused by
the Reformation's erosion of the towns' religious
and educational roles, and by the weakening of civic
strength *vis-a-vis* the countryside during the period
of agricultural and gentry prosperity from 1540 to
1640. Accounts of this 'commercialisation of
leisure' have tended to focus on the experience of
the gentry, or the pseudo-gentry, rather than on its
impact on the cultural experience of ordinary town-
dwellers, although it has generally been assumed
that these developments widened the gap between
'polite' and 'plebeian' culture. For the better-
off, it is suggested, work and leisure became
increasingly differentiated, and status was sought
through adoption of a certain lifestyle, which
could be purchased, both directly by buying certain
cultural items, and indirectly by devoting one's
time to culturally prestigious, voluntary
activities. (41)

The dominant position of London, both as a
population centre and as a focus for the activities
of the wealthy, had by 1600 led to an unprecedented
concentration of cultural production in the capital.
No other town could hope to support similar professional standards in theatre, music or the arts,
and in some cases, such as printing, they were
legally prohibited from even trying. How far were
the elite of Bristol investing in cultural goods
from London which set them aside from the 'vernacular' tastes of ordinary Bristolians?

A major change appears to have occurred in this
area during the seventeenth century. The merchant
elite of 1600 were investing heavily in rich furnishings and plate, and they were more likely than
others to possess pictures and musical instruments.
Their houses were resplendent with complex plaster-
work and elaborate carving in both wood and stone.
Carved mantelpieces offered a setting for ornaments,
such as the delftware which was produced locally
from the 1640s onwards. But, as this last example
suggests, many of these cultural items were produced by local craftsmen, and reflected local tastes
and methods. Only at the very end of the century
did the wealthy abandon the 'Tudor', vernacular
style of architecture for the neo-classical style.
The elaborate monuments in churches look similarly
old-fashioned, while the stone carving, in part
reflecting classical influences to be sure, was
still predominantly concerned with heraldic devices,
reflecting the civic and guild position of the
owner. It was not until the eighteenth century that

wealthy households began to be filled with prints
from London and Holland, or with the tea and coffee
equipment associated with a round of polite visiting.
Although the council employed London-based or itinerant artists to paint portraits of notables, local
painters were used for other commissions, as well as
to gild and paint the countless boards, crosses and
insignia, largely heraldic in inspiration, which
brightened city life. These artistic activities
were accessible to ordinary Bristolians, as guild
and church members, and for the decoration of their
sometimes elaborate funerals.(42)

A similar point can be made about the theatre
and music. There was no fashionable world of
assemblies, balls and concerts until the early
eighteenth century. Music was chiefly heard in the
churches, the alehouses and the streets. Church
organists and choristers provided the chief reser-
voir of musical talent in the town, along with the
city waits, or musicians, whom the council retained
to perform at civic functions. Music was popular in
alehouses, and was also a feature of barbers' shops.
The probate inventories indicate a fairly broad
ownership of instruments in the early seventeenth
century, and the town supported several instrument-
makers; but both seem to have lessened in later
years, suggesting perhaps a rise of the professional
musician at the expense of the amateur. Nevertheless, the great growth in music teaching, sale of
sheet music, and concerts manned by itinerant
musicians, occurred after 1700. (43)

The only plays to be seen were put on by itinerant players at the two fairs; or at least this was
so after the 1620s when the council ceased to wel-
come troupes of players, and the playhouse in Wine
Street fell into disuse. The plays at the fairs
attracted the crowds as well as the better-off, and
from the 1690s the council began a campaign to ban
plays at the fairs as well, on the grounds of morality and public order. The plays which the council
objected to were not confined to rope-dancing,
pantomime and other 'popular' performances, but
included Shakespeare and Dryden. In the eighteenth
century some commentators supported theatrical
attendance as part of polite culture, but sought to
prevent apprentices or the lower classes from
attending, on the grounds that it would encourage
absenteeism and inculcate values inimical to honesty
and sobriety. We lack the evidence to discover
whether this view existed earlier and affected
seventeenth-century attitudes; the material avail-

able for this period stresses moral objections to
the plays - these objections applied to all
ranks.(44)

The merchant elite of the town were accustomed
to considerable leisure. It enabled them to fill
posts in local government and to lead the lives of
gentlemen, engaging in such noble pursuits as
hunting and fencing.(45) For the middling and lower
classes, work was more all-encompassing, stretching
in theory from dawn to dusk, rather than according
to the clock, and punctuated only by Sundays and
public holidays. In practice, leisure was probably
available in the interstices of the working day,
since few were yet involved in capitalised industries where time literally meant money. Major
events, such as the launching of a warship, could
attract vast crowds.(46) There was a considerable
number of public holidays, and summer evenings were
rarely wholly occupied by work. The two fairs, each
of which lasted eight days, offered a rich range of
popular entertainments at the end of each January
and July, including plays, monsters, menageries,
working models, puppet-shows, and a great range of
exotic stalls.(47) Sundays, too, offered a regular
break which many used as a chance to get out into
the streets and countryside, or into the
alehouse.(48)

This pattern of leisure seems too haphazard to
encourage divisions of experience according to
class. The official Sunday and holiday pursuits of
church attendance and household worship were intended for all classes, and Bristol was noted as a city
of regular sermon-going. Complaints of non-
attendance do not suggest that the problem was confined to any one social group. There was no doubt a
whole range of social gradings between the inn or
tavern, at one end of the social scale, and the
humblest alehouse at the other; but most men must
have patronised their local alehouse. Social zoning
in the city was not yet sufficiently sharp for
neighbourhood to imply class segregation. The rich
still lived mostly in the central parishes, with the
poor in the back streets of the same areas. Public
spaces were also relatively accessible, as the city
was compact enough for all classes to be close to
the Marsh and the meadows by the rivers.(49) Fishing
and walking, if not riding, were open to all, as
were the humbler forms of shooting and hunting in
the neighbouring countryside.(50)

There are clear signs that this communal access-
ibility was becoming weaker by 1700. The rich began

to own houses on the outskirts of town as well as in the centre, or they moved to new suburban developments. One public resource, the Marsh, was reserved for the use of the wealthy, first by the establishment of a bowling-green which was used for exercises by the Tory Artillery company from 1678, and then by the building of the fashionable Queen Square from 1700. The surge of building after 1660 filled up the green areas of the city; and the wealthy were thereafter increasingly catered for by squares and other areas with gardens, whilst the poor were gradually confined to the poorer suburbs.(51)

The point has already been made that seventeenth-century Bristol lacked a rich array of voluntary associations. The city elite met socially at the council, or at the Merchant Venturers' Hall, or as officers of the city militia or Artillery Company. The most important associations for the middling groups were probably either the guild, whose activities blurred the distinctions of work and leisure, or else the 'church', where they might exercise authority as vestrymen or leading figures in a nonconformist society. Both parish and sect still sought to control many aspects of their parishioners' lives beyond the purely religious. Although the later seventeenth century did see the establishment of charitable societies, these met infrequently and cannot be compared to the plethora of clubs, freemasons' lodges, benefit societies and other groups established in the next century. This fact, together with the apparent absence of a tradition of entertaining at home, supports the image of an essentially public culture, constantly affected no doubt by social distinctions, but still played out in the public gaze.

V

Given the paucity of direct evidence for the cultural experience of the middling and lower orders of Bristol society, this chapter has concentrated on exploring the implications for popular culture of the cultural developments widely held to have intensified the gap between popular and elite culture. I have suggested that the socio-economic conditions of Bristol, together with the strong sense of communal and civic identity, militated against any clear division between popular and elite culture. Both education and the use of print developed only fitfully, adapting to traditional modes of communication and vocational needs rather than overthrowing

existing patterns. 'Godliness' was generally pursued in areas where it reinforced existing civic
norms, affecting attitudes concerning the proper
balance of respectability and sociability; it was
not, I believe, pursued along simple social lines.
Commercialisation and developments in polite culture
introduced cultural forms which were less rooted in
the local community, but this process was only just
beginning in 1700. In some ways, moreover, the
commercialisation of culture could weaken cultural
divides, for it encouraged entrepreneurs to develop
cheap versions of elite culture at prices which
ordinary consumers could afford.

There are, of course, many other elements of
popular culture of great importance which have not
been considered here. By focusing on overt forms of
cultural activity I have ignored the possibility
that ordinary Bristolians had distinctive values
regarding such private matters as family, work, and
health, which led them to see the world very
differently from their civic rulers. Yet I suspect
that the common experiences of apprenticeship and
work in the peculiar circumstances of town life made
even these differences much less marked than in the
industrial city or the large metropolis. There is
ample evidence to demonstrate that the elite felt
sufficiently close to the anxieties of ordinary life
to share popular notions regarding what E. P.
Thompson has called 'the moral economy'.(52)

The cultural developments of the period certainly affected the growth of political and religious
divisions within Bristol. A stress on reading and
above all on the Bible, provided the religious sects
with a cultural inheritance sufficiently strong for
them to be able to cast off both the religious and
the civic establishment. Literature, mostly from
London, and education became central to the preser-
vation of their way of life against the pressures of
society, even if pamphlets were of little use in
converting others. In a similar fashion the
divisions of Whig and Tory, derived largely from
religious allegiance, encouraged the exploitation of
the new means of communication, and brought new
intensity to the battles to control education and
moral discipline. Neither party, however, felt able
to repudiate publicly the civic inheritance which
offered support from the mass of freemen. In the
struggles for popularity the old methods were still
judged the most effective. It is in the aspects of
city life where divisions were greatest that we can
see most clearly the weakness of the line between

popular and elite culture.(53)

Notes

1. For Bristol's population and history in the seventeenth
   century, see: Latimer, Annals; Merchants and Merchandise
   in Seventeenth-Century Bristol, ed. P. McGrath (Bristol
   RS, xix, 1955); W. B. Stephens, 'Trade Trends at Bristol
   1600-1700', TBGAS, xliii (1974); D. H. Sacks, 'Trade,
   Society and Politics in Bristol 1500-1640' (Harvard Univ.
   Ph.D. thesis, 1977); W. Minchinton, 'Bristol metropolis
   of the West in the eighteenth century', TRHS, iv (1954).
2. Sacks, 'Trade, Society and Politics in Bristol', pp.
   205-54, 498, 752-60; J. R. Holman, 'Apprenticeship as a
   factor in migration: Bristol 1675-1726', TBGAS, xcvii
   (1979); Inhabitants of Bristol in 1696 (Bristol RS, xxv,
   1968), Introduction.
3. J. Cary, Account ... Corporation of the Poor (1700); E.
   Butcher, Bristol Corporation of the Poor (Bristol RS, iii,
   1932). For general comments on the occupational structure of early modern towns, see J. Patten: 'Urban
   occupations in the pre-industrial town', Transactions of
   Institute of British Geographers, ii (1977).
4. Apart from the sources in note 1, see B. D. Henning (ed.),
   History of Parliament: The Commons 1660-90 (1983), i,
   pp. 237-40; R. C. Latham, Bristol Charters 1509-1899
   (Bristol RS, xii, 1947). For nonconformity: Records of
   a Church of Christ in Bristol 1640-87, ed. R. Hayden
   (Bristol RS, xxvii, 1974); Minute Books of the Men's
   Meeting of the Society of Friends in Bristol ed. R. S.
   Mortimer (Bristol RS, xxvi, xxx, 1971, 1977); M. Caston,
   Independency in Bristol (1860); J. G. Fuller, Rise and
   Progress of Dissent in Bristol (1840).
5. See K. Wrightson, English Society 1580-1680 (1982), ch.
   7. The best studies of English urban culture 1500-1700
   are Units 7 and 8 of English Urban History 1500-1780,
   Open University A322, by Peter Clark, and his intro-
   duction to P. Clark (ed.), County Towns in Pre-Industrial
   England (Leicester, 1981). For four important studies of
   specific towns: C. Phythian-Adams, 'Ceremony and the
   Citizen', and P. Corfield, 'A provincial capital in the
   late seventeenth century', both in P. Clark (ed.), The
   Early Modern Town (1976); D. M. Palliser, 'Civic
   Mentality and the Environment in Tudor York', Northern
   History, xviii (1982); V. Pearl, 'Change and stability
   in seventeenth-century London', London Journal, v
   (1979).
6. The literacy material has been drawn from many sources in
   the Bristol Archives Office (BAO): Marriage Licence
   Bonds EP/J/3/1; Parish Registers 1753-60; Probate

Inventories; Churchwards' Accounts and Vestry Books;
Bristol Apprentice Books 1636-1700; Bristol Court
Recognizances O4417 (2-3), O4434 (1-3), O4435 (1-2);
Guild Records O4370 (Soapmakers), 28156 (1-2) (Felt-
makers), O8155 (Bakers), 4954(3) (Taylors). Bristol
Central Library (BCL) also has guild records: 4939
(Mercers), 4765-6, 6529 (Taylors). The British Library,
Add. MS. 28100 contains Tylers' Company records.

7. D. Cressy, 'Levels of Illiteracy in England 1530-1730',
    HJ, xx (1977); L. Stone, 'Literacy and Education in
    England 1640-1900', P. and P., 42 (1969); R. Houston,
    'Development of Literacy in Northern England 1640-1750',
    Economic History Review, xxv (1982); *idem*, 'The Literacy
    Myth', P. and P., 96 (1982). But for evidence of lower
    literacy in other towns see W. B. Stephens, 'Illiteracy
    and Schooling in the Provincial Towns', in D. Reeder
    (ed.), Urban Education in the Nineteenth Century (1977).

8. A. Yarborough, 'Bristol Apprentices in the sixteenth
    century', TBGAS, xcviii (1981), p. 122 notes that in the
    Tudor period boys' indentures included education, but
    BAO, Apprentice Books 1636-1700, provide no similar
    cases. P. McGrath, Merchant Venturers of Bristol
    (Bristol, 1975), p. 209 notes the assumption that only
    boys fluent in the three Rs could expect to be
    apprenticed.

9. For vocational schools, see McGrath, Merchant Venturers,
    pp. 84-5; and for Bristol masters and texts of this
    kind, see J. Brown, The Merchants Avizo (1607); S.
    Sturmy, Mariner's Magazine (1669); Records of a Church
    of Christ, ed. E. B. Underhill (1847), pp. 58-67.

10. See Cressy, Literacy; T. W. Laqueur, 'Cultural Origins
    of Popular Literacy in England 1500-1850', Oxford Review
    of Education, ii (1976); M. Spufford, 'First Steps in
    Literacy', Social History, iv (1979).

11. For the problem of orphans, see J. R. Holman, 'Orphans in
    pre-Industrial Towns', Local Population Studies, xv
    (1975). Accounts of efforts to educate the poor or
    orphaned, include H. Larcombe, 'Progress of Education in
    Bristol' (Univ. of Bristol M.A. thesis, 1924); D. J.
    Eames, 'Contributions made by Society of Merchant
    Venturers to the development of education in Bristol'
    (Univ. of Bristol M.A. thesis, 1966); F. R. E. Bowen,
    Queen Elizabeth's Hospital (1971); W. A. Sampson's
    histories of Red Maid's School (1908) and Queen Elizabeth
    Hospital (1910); D. G. Cooke, Story of Temple Colston
    School (Bristol 1947); Latimer, Annals, pp. 31-2, 64,
    78, 84-5, 96, 249, 394, 479, 488; Butcher, Bristol
    Corporation of the Poor; Minutes, ed. Mortimer.

12. The fullest material on the early education of ordinary
    Bristol children can be found in the Minute Book and

Register Book for Temple Colston School, in BAO, Temple
Ka 1(1) and Ka 3. Scattered references to the cost and
nature of education occur in Churchwardens' Accounts and
many other sources, e.g. the account of the schooling of
the Freind family in Bodleian Library, MS. Top. Oxon. f.
31. For the ethics of education, see Brown, <u>Merchants</u>
<u>Avizo</u>; S. Crossman, <u>Young Man's Monitor</u> (1673); T.
Hardcastle, <u>Christian Geography and Arithmetic</u> (1674);
H. Waterman, <u>Sermon ... Corporation of the Poor</u> (Bristol,
1699); J. Cary, <u>Account ... Corporation of the Poor</u>
(1700). For an example of the assumption that all
teachers would take their pupils to church on Sunday, see
BAO, O4417(3), 21.10.1667.

13. C. P. Hill, <u>History of Bristol Grammar School</u> (1951);
E. T. Morgan, <u>History of Bristol Cathedral School</u> (1913).
For the ethos of the City school in the early eighteenth
century, see W. Goldwin, <u>Poetical Description of Bristol</u>
(1712), preface; A. S. Catcott, <u>Exercises performed at</u>
<u>visitation</u> (Bristol, 1737); Bodleian Library, G.A.
Gloucs. B4a, fos. 85, 328-34, 519-26. For university
experience, see J. R. Holman, 'Some aspects of higher
education in Bristol and Gloucestershire 1650-1750',
<u>TBGAS</u>, xcv (1977).

14. It is not possible to list all the sources used for this
analysis. Further details will be found in my forthcoming <u>Directory of the Bristol Booktrade 1640-1775</u>, to
be published as a <u>Factotum Occasional Paper</u>. For comparisons with other towns, see J. Feather, 'Cross-channel
currents', <u>The Library</u>, ii (1980); D. Stoker, 'A
History of the Norwich book trades' (Library Association
thesis, 1975).

15. BAO, Probate Inventories. The only detailed study of
book ownership in inventories is P. Clark, 'Ownership of
Books in England 1560-1640', in L. Stone (ed.), <u>Schooling</u>
<u>and Society</u> (Baltimore, 1976); although J. R. Johnson,
'Worcestershire Probate Inventories 1699-1716', <u>Midland</u>
<u>History</u>, v (1978) does tabulate the books recorded in
inventories. Johnson's figures for the late seventeenth
century are lower than Clark's for the earlier years, but
different probate collections are never directly
comparable. Both Clark and Johnson record the same
social stratification and the frequent mentions of the
Bible. Clark finds a stress on service books, theological works, chronicles and legal works, and concludes that
the absence of vocational titles, stories, ballads and
almanacs probably indicates their ephemerality and
cheapness.

16. <u>Bibliotheca Palmeriana</u> (1694). The owner is wrongly
identified in R. Thompson, <u>Unfit for Modest Ears</u> (1979),
pp. 209-10.

17. For popular literature, see Spufford, <u>Small Books</u>; V.
    Neuburg, <u>Popular literature</u> (1977); B. Capp, <u>Astrology</u>
    <u>and the popular press</u> (1979); G. A. Cranfield, <u>Press and</u>
    <u>Society</u> (1978); C. Shepard, <u>History of Street Literature</u>
    (Newton Abbot, 1973).
18. Occasionally, printed works refer to the limited leisure
    and capacities of the average reader: Hardcastle,
    <u>Christian Geography and Arithmetic</u>, pp. 95-6; A.
    Bedford, <u>Serious Reflections</u> (Bristol, 1706), p. 4;
    R. Grove, <u>Every Christian's Capacity</u> (Bristol, 1711),
    preface.
19. For Bristol interest in London news, see P. Fraser,
    <u>Intelligence of the Secretaries of State</u> (Cambridge,
    1956), p. 140; J. G. Muddiman, <u>King's Journalist</u> (1923),
    pp. 284-8; <u>Williamson Letters</u> (Camden Soc., ix, 1874),
    pp. 161-4; <u>CSP, 1665-6</u>, p. 116. For the background, see
    Cranfield, <u>Press and Society</u>. The early history of
    Bristol's press is summarised in D. F. Gallup, 'Chapters
    in the history of the provincial newspaper press' (Univ.
    of Bristol M.A. thesis, 1954).
20. Some of the evidence for early Bristol coffee houses has
    been collected in BCL, 22709; other evidence comes from
    BAO, Letters, Presentments, Court Orders, and Inventories.
    For coffee house culture generally, see A. Ellis, <u>The</u>
    <u>Penny Universities</u> (1957) and P. Kaufman, 'Coffee houses
    as reading centres', in his <u>Libraries and their users</u>
    (1969).
21. Examples include HMC: <u>xxvi</u>, pp. 76-81; HMC: <u>li</u>, pp.
    142-5; <u>Massachusetts Historical Society Collections</u>,
    viii, pp. 328-36; BCL, 11154, 16.6.1690; J. Holloway,
    <u>Free and Voluntary Confession</u> (1684), pp. 11-12; <u>CSP,</u>
    <u>1680-1</u>, p. 250.
22. The Bristol bellman is illustrated in E. Ralph,
    <u>Government of Bristol</u> (Bristol, [1973]), p. 19.
    Bellmen's activities can be traced in the Mayor's Audits
    and Corporation Vouchers in BAO, Churchwardens' Accounts.
    For public announcements and ritual, see <u>Two State</u>
    <u>Martyrs</u> (Bristol, 1643), p. 8; J. Whiting, <u>Persecution</u>
    <u>Exposed</u> (1715), p. 59; <u>CSP, 1667</u>, p. 448; <u>CSP, 1681(1)</u>,
    p. 141; HMC: <u>Finch ii</u>, p. 57; M. de 1. Laudon, 'The
    Bristol Artillery Company and the Tory triumph in
    Bristol', <u>American Philosophical Society Proceedings</u>,
    cxiv (1970).
23. BAO, O4217 and the Corporation Vouchers from 1696 show
    the limited extent and nature of corporate expenditure on
    printing until the 1740s. For earlier comments on the
    use of print locally, see (for the 1650s) R. Farmer,
    <u>Great Mysteries</u> (1655), p. 31; and W. Grigge, <u>Quaker's</u>
    <u>Jesus</u> (1658), p. 62. Apart from polemical sermons,
    several grand jury addresses and at least one election

leaflet were published in the years 1679-83; whilst BAO, Quarter Sessions Orders 1682-1705, letters 30.4.1685, 27.5.1693 and 17.8.1697, refer to later distribution of political propaganda. For reform literature, see BL, 816 m 16(27), BCL, 10162, 1.10.1700, 26.8.1701, 16.8.1702, 13.10.1702.

24. See the works cited in note 5, and P. Clark, 'The Alehouse and the Alternative society' in D. Pennington and K. Thomas (eds.), Puritans and Revolutionaries (Oxford, 1978); Clark, 'Ramoth-Gilead of the Good', in *idem* and others (eds.), The English Commonwealth 1547-1640 (Leicester, 1979); the essays by I. Luxton and W. J. Shiels in F. Heal and R. O'Day (eds.), Church and Society in England (1977); R. W. Malcolmson, Popular Recreations in English Society 1700-1850 (Cambridge, 1973). The continuity of the reform tradition in the late seventeenth century has been stressed by D. W. R. Bahlman, Moral Revolution of 1688 (Yale, 1968), and T. W. Curtis and W. Speck, 'Societies for the Reformation of Manners', Literature and History, iii (1976). Much of this work has stemmed from the suggestions in Thomas, Religion and Decline.

25. For pre-Reformation ritual, see J. H. Bettey, Bristol Parish Churches during the Reformation (Bristol, 1979); J. Latimer, Annals of Bristol in the Sixteenth Century (Bristol, 1908), pp. 4-12. For the 1650s, see BAO, 04417(1), 26.2.55, 12.2.57, 6.3.60. For the 1660 riots, see A Letter of the Apprentices of the City of Bristol (1660); BCL, 10166(1) and 4502 (accounts for 1660); HMC: li, pp. 160ff; HMC: lxxi (2), pp. 57ff; Diurnal of Thomas Rugg (Camden Soc., xci, 1961), p. 42; J. Corry and J. Evans, History of Bristol (1816), i, pp. 477-9.

26. Popular and elite hostility to the separatists' attitudes to church and ritual can be traced in Records, ed. Hayden, pp. 89-96; Minutes, ed. Mortimer (1977), p. 107; J. Besse, Collection of Sufferings (1753), i, pp. 39, 63; and in court orders to close shops on holidays. See also CSP, 1665-6, p. 116.

27. This picture of church ritual and life is based on study of the Churchwardens' Accounts in BAO, together with the summaries of local charities in W. Barrett, History and Antiquities of the City of Bristol (Bristol, 1789). See also A. Harvey, 'Church Furnishings', TBGAS, xxxii (1909). For an elaborate round of holiday keeping by Bristolians abroad, see T. James, Strange and dangerous voyage (1633).

28. Latimer, Annals, describes with Victorian liberal disgust the range of civic ritual at this period, which is best reconstructed from corporate accounts. For the Nayler incident, see Grigge, Quaker's Jesus; R. Farmer, Satan Inthron'd (1657), and J. Deacon, Grand Impostor Examin'd (1656). Compare Nayler's entrance with the reception of

Richard Cromwell two years later, recorded in Corry and
Evans, History of Bristol, i, p. 472; or Latimer, Annals,
pp. 42-50 on Queen Anne's visit in 1613.

29. See the references in note 26. The 'warnings' and prophecies of George Bishop and others died out after 1665,
until the 1690s when they were revived by a radical
fringe of Quakers and French prophets. See R. Mortimer,
'Warnings and Prophecies', JFHS, xliv (1952).

30. Corry and Evans, History of Bristol, i, p. 472, or HMC:
lxxviii, p. 142, for examples of the stress on orderly
ritual. The guilds always marched in order of historical
precedence, followed usually by the clergy, merchants and
gentry, and, finally, the corporation, so that the most
important groups were placed nearest to the mayor or the
honoured visitor.

31. For the guilds, see Sacks, 'Trade, Society and Politics',
pp. 123-61; F. H. Rogers, 'Bristol Craft Guilds during
sixteenth and seventeenth centuries' (Univ. of Bristol
M.A. thesis, 1949). BAO, O4369(1) contains all the guild
ordinances.

32. For the political connotations of guild celebration, see
CSP, 1684, pp. 240-1; Bodleian Library, MS. Gough
Somerset 2, fo. 99. For a portrait of civic ritual
stressing the guild role, see Goldwin, Poetical
Description.

33. For the notion of magistracy see CSP, 1680-1, p. 681;
Barrett, History, pp. 120-1; S. Crossman, Sermon (1676),
p. 28. For council touchiness about ritual and precedence: CSP, 1663-4, p. 477; CSP, 1667-8, pp. 423-7;
CSP, 1684, pp. 240-1; CSP, 1689-90, p. 241; Latimer,
Annals, pp. 109, 277-8, 295, 312-15, 357, 461. The civic
chronicles which were still kept by many Bristolians
indicate belief that corporate justice and hospitality
brought the city privileges and hence prosperity. Latham,
Bristol Charters, p. 40, records that the charter of 1663
was given on the grounds that the King had been royally
entertained on his recent visit.

34. For two hostile comments on Bristolian pride, see R.
North, Lives of the Norths (1890), i, p. 284 and Life of
Marmaduke Rawdon, ed. R. Davies (Camden Soc., lxxxv,
1863), p. 173. For an early example of the popularity of
public events, see the account of the reception of Paul
Ferris after rowing from London to Bristol: An English
Garner (1907), pp. 110ff.

35. Bristol's charities can be studied from Barrett, History,
and T. J. Manchee, Bristol Charities (2 vols, Bristol,
1831). See W. K. Jordan, 'Forming of the charitable
institutions of the West of England', American
Philosophical Society Transactions, 1 (1960), pt. 8;
City Chamberlain's Accounts in the sixteenth and

seventeenth centuries, ed. D. M. Livock (Bristol RS, xxiv, 1966), Introduction. Many of the charity records are in BAO. The most important of the 'immigrant' societies, the Gloucestershire Society, is still in existence and has most kindly given me access to records dating back to its foundation.

36. For apprentice activity on Shrove Tuesday, see CSP, 1669-70, p. 76; CSP, 1671, p. 127; Latimer, Annals, p. 434; BCL, 10163(2), 1685; Bodleian Library, Gough MS. Somerset 2, fos. 80, 99. For Tudor comparisons, see A. Yarborough, 'Bristol Apprentices in the sixteenth century' (Catholic Univ. of America Ph.D. thesis, 1977); and *idem*, 'Apprentices as adolescents in sixteenth century Bristol', JSH, iv (1979). On apprentice culture generally, see S. R. Smith, 'London apprentices as seventeenth-century adolescents', P. and P., 61 (1973); D. V. Glass, 'Socio-economic status and occupations in the city of London at the end of the seventeenth century', in Clark (ed.) Early Modern Towns; L. S. O'Connell, 'The Elizabethan Bourgeois Hero-Tale', in B. C. Malament (ed.), After the Reformation (Manchester, 1980).

37. Richard Roberts, Sermon (1685); The Brave Boys of Bristol (n.d.)

38. The 'reformation of manners' theme can be traced in Anglican literature - e.g. T. Thompson, Diet for a Drunkard (1612), or the sermons of Crossman (note 33) or Waterman (note 12), or the broadsheet of Mayor Knight (note 27); in dissenting works - e.g. E. Hancock, Pastor's Last Legacy (1663), T. Speed, Reason against Rage (1691); in corporate records - e.g. Presentments by parishes and the Grand Jury and Court convictions - e.g. BAO, O4452(1) (mostly against blasphemy and drunkenness 1695-1728). The reform plans around 1700 are summarised in J. Latimer, Annals of Bristol in the eighteenth century (Bristol 1893), pp. 32-5, 46-8, 60, 80-1; see also notes 11 and 23.

39. Latimer, Annals, pp. 485-6, records the bull-baiting incident, which is then quoted by Malcolmson (see note 24) and others to illustrate typical corporate attitudes, thus completely misjudging the significance of the event.

40. For the dangers of gambling, see CSP, 1663-4, pp. 433-82; BAO, Quarter Sessions Orders 1653-71, Jan. 1668-9; BAO, Grand Jury Presentments, April and July 1682, April 1685, Jan. 1689-90. The grand juries were particularly concerned that 'the children and servants' of merchants and tradesmen might gamble away their parents' and masters' money. The years of youth and service were seen as dangerous for all classes, not just the poor; although one presentment did refer to 'divers artificers and labouring men' mis-spending much of their time and money in drinking and gambling. Apart from dice

and cards, the gaming seems to have consisted of
skittles, shuffleboard and, after about 1680, billiards.

41. J. H. Plumb, The Commercialization of Leisure in
     Eighteenth-Century England (Reading, 1973); P. Borsay,
     'Culture, status and English urban landscape', History,
     lxvii (1982); *idem*, 'English urban Renaissance', Social
     History, v (1977). Both see the vital change as
     occurring around 1700. See also the works cited in note
     5, and, for wider perspectives on leisure: K. Thomas,
     'Work and Leisure in pre-Industrial Society', P. and P.,
     29 (1964); F. Redlich, 'Leisure-Time activities',
     Explorations in Entrepreneurial History, iii (1965);
     M. R. Marrus (ed.), Emergence of Leisure (NY, 1974).
42. Most of the remarks on the arts are based on probate
     inventories, and the bills of painters in corporate,
     church and private accounts. For the characteristic
     artistic products of the area, see: I. M. Roper,
     Monumental Effigies of Gloucestershire and Bristol
     (Gloucester, 1931); F. Britton, English Delftware in the
     Bristol Collection (1982); A. Ray, English Delftware
     Pottery (1968), pp. 39ff; A. C. Powell, 'Glassmaking in
     Bristol', TBGAS, xlvii (1925); and for the stone
     chimneypieces, the numerous 'Archaeological notes' in
     TBGAS early this century.
43. Considerable work has been done on music in Bristol;
     e.g. J. G. Hooper, 'A survey of music in Bristol' (BCL,
     unpublished typescript, 1963); W. L. Goodman, 'Musical
     Instrument-makers in Bristol Apprentice Books 1536-1643',
     Galpin Society Journal, xxvii (1974). For the barber-
     shop connection, see E. Phileroy, Satirical Vision
     (1684), p. 11, and the inventories of medical men in BAO.
     BCL, 5030 shows that the Wiredrawers' Company hired the
     city musicians to perform at account dinners during the
     mid-seventeenth century. For complaints of the increased
     proliferation of secular musical professionals and sheet-
     music by 1700, see A. Bedford, The Great Abuse of Music
     (1711).
44. G. T. Watts, Theatrical Bristol (Bristol, 1911) summar-
     ised most of the records of early Stuart theatricals and
     the struggles over an attempt to re-establish a permanent
     theatre after 1700. For plays at the fairs see
     Massachusetts Historical Society Collections, viii, p.
     329; BCL, 10162, 6.8.1700, 23.6.1702.
45. J. Aubrey, Brief Lives (Harmondsworth, 1972), p. 367,
     describes the lifestyle of his merchant godfather, John
     Whitson, who kept hawks and was leader of the city
     militia.
46. Latimer, Annals, p. 349; T. Godwin, Phanaticall
     Tenderness (1684), p. 6.
47. Scraps of information on the fairs can be found in Temple
     and St James Churchwardens' Accounts; BAO, 14417(1),

5.8.1654; 14417(3), 10 and 13.7.1668; British Library, Add. MS. 19256f.57; Bodleian Library MS. Ashmolean 1815 f.200; Thomas, Rayling Rebuked, Epistle and p. 5; Latimer, Annals, pp. 83, 193, 351, 462, 636. Bristol Fair was still a major economic as well as cultural event, drawing merchants and traders from all over the West Country and Ireland. The fairs were so integral to Bristol's image that when Sir Ferdinando Gorges and Humphrey Hooke of Bristol planned their colony in Maine (first called Bristol) they proposed two annual fairs on exactly the same dates as their home city.

48. Sabbath profanation is discussed in Latimer, Annals, p. 58; BAO, O4417(1), 5.10.1657, 27.11.57, 12.4.59; Grand Jury Presentments, Aug. 1680, Jan. 1693, Oct. 1694; Quarter Sessions Orders, Jan. and Sept. 1655, Oct. 1657, Jan. 1658; Minutes, ed. Mortimer (1977), pp. 166, 180; Some Reasons briefly stated (1675), p. 3 (where Bristol nonconformists justify public conventicles on Sunday on the grounds that if they met privately others might use the cover of religion to idle at home, walk in the fields, work, or converse, either idly or on business).

49. Peter Clark has summarised the statistics for Bristol alehouses, as well as discussing alehouse culture generally, in his The English Alehouse (1983), pp. 51-6. BAO, O5062 contains regulations for alehouses and records of licensing, for which see also the parish presentments in BAO. For the changing topography of the city, see Sacks, 'Trade, society and politics', pp. 244ff; B. Little and others, Bristol: An Architectural History (Bristol, 1979).

50. Probate inventories reveal a number of fowling pieces and other guns owned by Bristolians of varying wealth, including many shopkeepers and craftsmen. The Latin mottoes on Millerd's 1673 Map of Bristol refer to the riverside meadows as places for walking and fishing. Riding in the Marsh was repeatedly deplored in the Grand Jury Presentments of 1678-85.

51. For bowling-greens and Marsh development, see Latimer, Annals, pp. 272, 396, 490.

52. E. P. Thompson, 'The Moral Economy of the English Crowd', P. and P., 50 (1971).

53. In a recent study of charivaris Martin Ingram has similarly questioned a rigid dichotomy between elite and popular culture: M. Ingram, 'Ridings, Rough Music, and the "Reform of Popular Culture" in Early Modern England', P. and P., 105 (1984).

Chapter Three

POPULAR RELIGION*

Barry Reay

I

The subject of this chapter is the religion of
the popular classes as opposed to official,
institutionalised, established religion and theology.
The religion of what were known as the lower and
middle sorts of people, those who, as Marc Venard
has put it, 'without being necessarily the most
deprived do not touch the levers of power, whether
economic, political or cultural'.(1) But people mean
different things when they employ the term popular
religion - just as they do when they use the
description popular culture. For some it means
religion produced by the people, usually in
resistance to the ideology of the elite: religion
'coming from and belonging to the people', 'culture
actually made by people for themselves'.(2) In this
narrower sense - religion as an 'oppositional form'
- it can also refer to religion taken up at the
popular level, having been produced, perhaps, by
what could be called 'the ideologists of the common
people', those who stood on the edges or even
outside the popular classes but who felt that they
were attuned to their needs and aspirations.
Historians who deal with sixteenth- and seventeenth-
century sectaries and heretics or the radicals of
the English Revolution of 1640-60, are usually
discussing popular religion in this narrow sense.
But for others 'popular religion' means quite
simply the religion of the vast mass of the people;
popular in the sense of 'widely favoured'.(3) In
the pages which follow I am going to explore popular
religion in its wider sense - which in any case
incorporates the narrower usage - attempting to
survey how much we really know about the religion
of the people in sixteenth- and seventeenth-century

England.

So we know what is meant by the term popular; but what is meant by <u>religion</u>? Again I use the word in its widest sense: that is beliefs and practices associated with the supernatural, 'a response to the sacred'. My definition would include beliefs in witchcraft, magic and spirits; established as well as sectarian or heretical Christianity, but also what Jean Delumeau has called folklorised Christianity (more of which later). So I do not mean religion in the sense of mainly conventional Christianity, which is the way in which it is used in Patrick Collinson's chapter on popular religion in his <u>The Religion of Protestants</u>.(4) As David Clark has demonstrated in his fascinating study of folk religion in a present-day, Yorkshire fishing village, a great deal of religious activity takes place outside the church and chapel.(5)

II

The church was centrally important in Tudor and Stuart society. Its calendar punctuated the year and it permeated conceptions of time. It supervised the rites of passage of each individual (baptism, marriage and death), and it reinforced class and village identities in church-ales, wakes, and in Rogationtide beatings of parish boundaries. Church and churchyard were intimately linked to the life of the community: from the organising of the destruction of vermin in the parish to the care of the parish bull (the 'comyn bull'). Church bells summoned people to work and mobilised them at times of danger. Elections were held in the church and debts were collected there. The church was used to store fire fighting equipment and also served as the parish armoury. During an emergency occasioned by a snowstorm, the rector of Langdon Hills in Essex actually used the church building to house his sheep. In West Ham in 1577 plays were held in the church, and people stood on the communion table to watch.(6) Indeed as Alan Macfarlane has pointed out, it is difficult when we turn to the church court records for our period to think in terms of an all-abiding reverence for the sanctity of holy space.(7) Fighting, spitting, letting off guns, vomiting, urinating, farting, knitting, sewing, trading, playing cards, singing and practical joking.(8) These were the kinds of behaviour that sometimes went on in church during divine worship. In 1628, the salt-petre projectors wanted to dig under churches because 'the women piss in their seats, which causes excellent saltpetre'. (9) A South Ockenden parishioner who had been drinking before he arrived for Easter communion, became inebriated after he quaffed a whole cup of communion wine. Another Essex man urinated in his neighbour's hat while the minister was trying to deliver a sermon. People talked ('Its sharp shiting in a frosty morning'). They slept; ministers complained that people only seemed to come to church to sleep.(10) The churchyard was also used for a variety of purposes, including community amusements - in Earls Colne for activities as diverse as playing football and grazing pigs.(11)

Each church was society writ small. In many churches the men sat on one side, women on the other. The gentry sat at the front, sometimes in upholstered and locked pews, while poorer cottagers and artisans sat at the back. In St Edmunds, Sarum, in 1629 the poor were made to sit on specially made seats which were branded in 'great Red letters': 'For the Poore'. Boys were baptised before girls. Money spoke, even in death, for it determined whether one was buried inside or outside the main body of the church and the kind of passing bell which was to be tolled. Social deviants were either buried in certain sections of the churchyard or else were excluded entirely from the community and interred at the side of the road or in wasteland. Community divisions could also be reflected in the communion wine, with claret for the poorer sort and muscatel for the gentry. Keith Thomas refers to a Kentish parson who thought that there were three heavens - one for the poor, one for the middling sort, one for the rich.(12)

Throughout our period the law compelled people to worship at their local church. Church courts, with debatable degrees of effectiveness, continued their involvement in the policing and self-policing of popular morality - adultery, gossip, swearing, working on a Sunday or holy day, drunkenness, bastardy, absence from church, nonconformity, nonpayment of tithes or church rates, defamation and slander.(13) For the elite, religion was 'the glew and soder that cements a Kingdom, or church together'. The Anglican work The Whole Duty of Man told its poorer readers to be content with their lot, for 'whatever our Estate and Condition in any respect be, it is that which is alloted us by God, and therefore is certainly the best for us, He being much better able to judge for us, than we for ourselves'. Charles I believed that people were 'governed by the pulpit more than the sword in time of peace'; James I that church and government went hand in hand - 'shake the one, and you over-throw the other'.(14)

Patrick Collinson has reminded us that we should never underestimate the strength of popular attach-ment to 'commonplace prayer-book religion'. And John Morrill has recently demonstrated that stubborn adherence to the rituals of the Church of England is an important and neglected element in the religious history of the seventeenth century. During the 1640s, he writes, the 'greatest challenge' to res-pectable Puritanism came not from the radical sects but from 'the passive strength of Anglican surviv-alism'.(15) But attachment to ritual and practice and to the celebration of Easter and Christmas is one thing; ideological conformity is quite another. If we should not be tempted to think in terms of mass disaffection, neither should we assume conformity.

III

There was tremendous potential for religious control and conformity. But the more that people work on the sixteenth and seventeenth centuries the clearer it is becoming that this was no 'Age of Faith'. If popular religion is any guide, there never was (in Marxist terms) incorporation of the subordinate classes. Although the church was socially important, it was a long way from command-ing anything approaching orthodoxy. There is plenty of evidence for this, evidence which runs the gamut from ignorance of Christian fundamentals, to indifference, to out and out hostility.

Christopher Hill and Keith Thomas have found telling evidence of 'ignorance' and indifference at the popular level in Tudor and Stuart England. Bishops and ministers bewailed the shortcomings of the laity and made comparisons with the North American Indians and Africans. Thomas Hooker wrote of the ignorance of the 'meaner or ordinary sort of people'; 'it is incredible and inconceivable, what ignorance is among them'. John Jewel said that many were so ignorant that they did not even know what the Scriptures were. At the beginning of the seventeenth century the rector of a parish in Kent found that of four hundred communicants 'scarcely 40' had any knowledge about Christ, sin, death and the afterlife. It was said of men in south Yorkshire and Northumberland that they were totally ignorant

of the Bible and did not know the Lord's Prayer.(16)
A Yorkshire boy when quizzed by a minister could not
say 'how many gods there be, nor persons in the god-
head, nor who made the world nor anything about
Jesus Christ, nor heaven or hell, or eternity after
this life, nor for what end he came into the world,
nor what condition he was born in'. Otherwise he
was 'a witty boy and could talk of any worldly
things skilfully enough'. A Lancashire woman when
asked about the Jesus Christ mentioned in the Creed,
replied 'she could not tell, but by our dear Lady it
is sure some good thing, or it should never have
been put in the Creed, but what it is I cannot tell
you'. An old man from Cartmel, also in Lancashire,
a regular church attender, did not know how many
gods there were. When Christ was mentioned by his
questioner he said: 'I think I heard of that man
you spoke of, once in a play at Kendall, called
Corpus Christi play, where there was a man on a
tree, and blood ran down.'(17) Witch-hunters, who
took a suspect's inability to repeat the Lord's
Prayer or the Creed as evidence of witchcraft guilt,
were actually more likely to be uncovering popular
religious 'ignorance'.(18)

It goes without saying that there was geographical and social variation. Labourers, servants, the
young and the very poor may rarely have attended
church.(19) In 1662 Ralph Josselin found it worth
reporting that 'divers of the ruder sort of people',
spurred on by the possibility of a one-shilling
fine, had joined the congregation of his Earls Colne
church.(20) The populations of certain areas
acquired a notoriety for their lack of religion,
particularly the inhabitants of wastes and forests.
The cottagers of Kingswood Forest, it was noted in
1667, 'generally live there without government or
conformity' and are 'not responsible to any Civil
Officer or Minister for their behaviour or
Religion'. The people of the New and Windsor
Forests, an observer said in 1617, 'go ten times to
an alehouse, before they go once to a church'. The
inhabitants of the Forest of Knaresborough were
thought to be attached more to wisemen and wizards
than to the Christian religion.(21) Historians
working on Lancashire, Cheshire, and Derbyshire
have made the point that some of the parishes were
so large that regular attendance and clerical supervision would have been improbable.(22) Richard
Clark and others have worked out that some churches
were just not large enough to accommodate all their
parishioners, so regular attendance was logistically

impossible.(23)

Peter Laslett, who tends to stress conformity,
cites parishes in seventeenth-century Kent, Notting-
hamshire and Northamptonshire where either most or
large numbers of the eligible population communicated at Easter. There are similar examples from
the diocese of Oxford.(24) Yet we also have information from other parishes - in Kent, Essex and
Oxford - where few bothered to turn up at Easter.
'Not above 20 or 40 people' were at church in Great
Bardfield (Essex) in 1599 out of a possible 200
communicants. In a visitation of the Kentish town,
Cranbrook, in 1663 it was claimed that of 3,000
potential communicants 'not above 200 usually come
in a yeare'. (The parish also contained some 500
unbaptised.)(25) In Earls Colne, with a population
of 1,000 and a theoretical congregation of 500,
attendance at church was not exactly high: 70-100
in 1662, 100 in 1663, 80-90 in 1664, 30 in 1680.
The figures for holy communion were far worse: 14
at Easter sacrament in 1668, 20 in 1669, 14 in 1670,
15 in 1671, 12 in 1674, 12 in 1678, 16 in 1679, 17
in 1680, 11 in 1681.(26) Peter Clark estimates that
a fifth of the population of later sixteenth-
century Kent were regular absentees.(27) During the
first half of the seventeenth century in the dioceses of Norwich, York and Chester up to 2,000
people were excommunicated each year; perhaps 15
per cent of the population at any given time was
out of favour with the church.(28)

It is extremely difficult to know the extent of
basic religious knowledge in Tudor and Stuart
England, how informed people were about the official
religion. The various ecclesiastical changes - in
language, liturgy, ceremony, architecture and
doctrine - imposed from above with amazing regu-
larity, particularly in the mid-sixteenth century,
must have bewildered the ordinary parishioner.
Visitations in Cambridgeshire recorded marks where
the seemingly constantly moving altar had once
stood.(29) At Norwich and Chester in the 1630s four
or five different catechisms were being taught in
churches.(30) At the very least this would have been
a time of uncertainty.

Proficiency must have been affected by the
quality of ministers, or by whether or not a parish
even had a resident incumbent, for at the beginning
of the seventeenth century at least one out of
every six parishes had no priest.(31) As Thomas has
pointed out, there were difficulties in the
transition from Latin to vernacular religion,

difficulties which affected the clergy no less than their parishioners.(32) A Protestant survey of the diocese of Gloucester (1551) found that of 311 clergy more than half were unable to repeat the Ten Commandments accurately, thirty-three could not locate them in the Bible, and nine were unable to count them. Ten could not repeat the Lord's Prayer, thirty-nine failed to find its scriptural location, thirty-four did not know its author.(33)

Under Elizabeth and the first Stuarts the standard of the clergy improved, both financially and educationally, until by 1640 they were a fully developed profession. With this change to a largely graduate ministry the problem seems to have been no longer clerical ignorance but clerical exclusivity. This caste-like group, more socially select than ever before, seemed to set itself apart from the community. Rosemary O'Day suggests that this elitism may have provoked some of the anticlericalism of the Revolution years.(34) How it affected the religious erudition of the common people is far from clear. University degrees do not guarantee efficient teachers. John Dod claimed that the majority of English ministers preached over the heads of their hearers. There were complaints about 'tortuous analogies and obscure Greek phrases', learned allusions and complicated metaphors.(35) Hostile clerical comment spoke of congregations who sat through sermons 'more like stockes than men, conceiving no more than the very stooles they sit upon'. Richard Younge wrote of 'those blocks that go to Church as dogs do, only for company'.(36) But this may have been a reflection on the preacher rather than his listeners. As an Oxfordshire minister reported to his bishop in the 1680s: 'I read, as sent by your Lordship St. Cyprian's tract, and sent word about the parish I had, such a day, something to communicate to them from their Bishop, very few came more, and of those that did, 5 or 6 went out of the church before I had read halfe of it, which used not to do so; and reported there was only a homily which they understood not.' In Suffolk a century earlier, a Yoxford man had said that he did not attend church because he could not understand the rector.(37)

According to the canons of 1604, parsons, vicars and curates were expected to instruct 'the youth and ignorant persons' of their parishes in the rudiments of Anglican practice and dogma: the Ten Commandments, Articles of Belief, Lord's Prayer, and the catechism set out in the Book of Common Prayer.

(Puritan ministers taught their own catechisms.)
How successful were the ministers? Did they manage
to impart some basic religious knowledge?
Christopher Haigh's work on Lancashire during the
sixteenth century and John Pruett's work on
Leicestershire during the late seventeenth and
early eighteenth centuries suggest that ministers
had trouble getting children to come to be catechised. But unfortunately there is nothing for the
Church of England equivalent to Gerald Strauss's
superb account of the impact of the Lutheran
catechism on sixteenth-century Germany.(38) All that
can be said at the moment is that the story does not
seem to have been one of success. Whenever her
minister took 'his greene book in hand', complained
Susan Kent in 1624, she knew that she was in for
'such a deale of bibble babble that I am weary to
heere yt & I can then sitt doune in my seat & take
a good napp'.(39)

IV

We talked earlier of 'ignorance'; yet ignorance
is not really a very helpful term. E. P. Thompson
has warned that what is sometimes taken to be
mistaken doctrine is in fact doctrine translated
into more meaningful terms, adapted to the
'life-experience of the poor'. He cites the
seventeenth-century case (taken from Thomas's
Religion and the Decline of Magic) of an old man who
visualised God as 'a good old man', Christ as 'a
towardly young youth', the soul as 'a great bone in
his body', and who thought that when he died 'if he
had done well he should be put into a pleasant green
meadow'. He also refers to an eighteenth-century
gamekeeper who upon hearing the minister talk about
a place called Paradise, observed that it 'seemed to
be a desperate pleasant place ... but if there was
but a good trout-stream running down Chicken Grove
Bottom, Fernditch Lodge would beat it out and
out'.(40) A Romford weaver who had trouble with the
doctrine of the Trinity in 1583 is probably another
example of the same type. When he said that 'the
Sonne' was 'lesse than the Father, and can do
nothinge without the Faither geve him leave', he was
probably thinking of his own upbringing rather than
the finer points of Trinitarian dogma.(41) But such
information is rare.
It is in fact extremely difficult to enter the
minds of ordinary people of the past, even with
regard to such fundamental religious concepts as

God, Christ, Heaven and Hell. In traditional
iconography God was a 'Venerable old man sitting in
a chaire, with a severe aspect, wrinkled forehead,
circumflext eie-browes, great white curled
beard'.(42) This was more or less how the future
Muggletonian Laurence Clarkson visualised him in his
Church of England days, 'a grave, ancient, holy, old
man, as I supposed sat in a Heaven in a chair of
gold'. But Clarkson was still young and his view of
Heaven reflected a child's horizons. Heaven was a
house, 'a glorious place with variety of rooms
suitable for Himself, and his Son Christ, and the
Holy Ghost'.(43) Clarkson's ideas changed during the
Revolution. When he was a Ranter he saw God as 'an
infinite all', in all things; as a Muggletonian, he
again saw him as a distinct person, this time 'five
foot high'.(44)

A seventeenth-century Welshman visualised Christ
as exactly like 'Old Rice Williams of Newport',
including the large grey beard. For a future
Quaker, a woman, he was 'a fresh lovely youth, clad
in a grey cloth, very plain and neat'.(45) Ralph
Josselin's son, Tom, had a dream in which Christ
appeared all dressed in white. As for God, the boy
seems to have conceived of him as 'a great man as
big as a house ... with a great fire on his head'
(though the entry in Josselin's diary is somewhat
ambiguous).(46) The period of the Revolution was a
time of intense speculation. An erstwhile Quaker
and Baptist, Rice Jones of Nottingham, reached a
position where he thought in terms of an internal
crucifixion and resurrection; 'there never was such
a thing' 'as a Christ that died in Jerusalem'.
Jacob Bauthumely preferred to see God as 'one
individed essence', 'in all Creatures, Man and
Beast, Fish and Fowle, and every green thing, from
the highest Cedar to the Ivey on the wall'. Some
were less certain, notably John Boggis of Great
Yarmouth: 'Where is your God, in heaven or in
earth, aloft or below, or doth he sit in the clouds,
or where doth he sit with his arse?'(47)

According to a satirical play performed in
Kendal in 1621, Hell was filled with landlords,
Puritans and bailiffs.(48) So eschatology sometimes
reflected the concerns of the here-and-now. Thomas
Webbe was supposed to have said that there was no
Heaven but women and no Hell save marriage. The
Digger Gerrard Winstanley thought that Heaven was 'a
fancy' used by priests as a form of social control.
George Foster had a vision in which a man on a white
horse was cutting down the rich while crying out

'Equality, equality, equality'. God became 'that mighty Leveller' who would symbolically 'Levell the Hills with the Valleyes, and ... lay the Mountaines low', and 'make the low and poor equal with the rich'.(49) Socially conservative preachers, on the other hand, preferred to see God as the great landlord.(50)

As a boy in the Church of England, Clarkson did not know where Hell was, 'but judged it a local place, all dark, fire and brimstone, which the devils did torment the wicked in'. The Devil was 'some deformed person out of man', a black thing which could appear at any time and in any shape. Later, influenced by the radicals, Clarkson felt that Hell, the Devil (and Heaven) were 'all in the imagination'. The Muggletonian Clarkson took Hell to be the earth after the Final Judgement; the Devil was all those predestined to damnation.(51) Medieval sermons referred to devils flying 'above in the eyer as thyke as motes in the sonne', transforming themselves into swine, dogs, apes, horses, spiders, or taking on the form of a beautiful woman or even a parish clerk. In 1584 Reginald Scot wrote of how 'in our childhood our mothers maids have so terrified us with an ouglie divell having hornes on his head, fier in his mouth, and a taile in his breech, eies like a bason, fanges like a dog, clawes like a beare, a skin like a Niger, and a voice roring like a lion, whereby we start and are afraid when we heare one crie Bough'.(52) Puritans continued the tradition, inculcating terror of death and damnation, promoting the idea of an ever active Satan.(53) The religious chapbooks which circulated widely in the seventeenth century consisted largely of 'calls to repentance, death-bed testimonies, and meditations on death and on the Last Judgement. ... Fear was often deliberately evoked.'(54) But as always it is a large step from concepts in sermons, pamphlets, and even in chapbooks, to the notions of the mass of the population. Puritan indoctrination was not without its effects. The future Quaker, John Crook, when young, was convinced that he was being followed by Satan. John Rogers, later a Fifth Monarchist, thought he saw demons in every tree and bush. Fear of the Devil, Lodowick Muggleton wrote, 'hath caused many men and women to loose their wits'.(55) However, these are the comments of literate laymen with Puritan backgrounds. We do not have as much information about the non-literate, less obviously zealous majority.

Witchcraft trial material contains descriptions
of Satan as he appeared to the accused witches: a
dunnish coloured ferret, a boy with a cloven foot, a
tall black man, a handsome young man, a man in a
long cloak (sexually like a man but cold and heavy),
a mole with a great hollow voice, a man with a
shrill voice, a hairy black boy, a handsome young
gentleman, a black dog, a gentleman in black, a
black man on a horse.(56) Yet we have no way of
knowing for certain whether such notions were those
of the accused or merely imposed during questioning.
Christina Larner has maintained that in Scotland by
the mid-seventeenth century these images of the
Devil were part of popular culture in a way that
they had not been a century earlier.(57) We do not
yet know whether this was also the case in England.
There is of course literary evidence for the early
modern period - ballads, plays, epigrams and
proverbs - of mockery and flippancy on the subject
of the Devil and Hellfire, though this humour may
merely mask more deep-seated fears.(58) By the nineteenth century, if Lincolnshire village life is a
guide, the Devil of popular culture was certainly
not the fearful figure of earlier centuries.
People called him 'Old Harry', 'Old Sam', 'Old Nick'
or 'the old 'Un' and treated him with a mixture of
'familiarity, affection, and awe'. He had the
habit of appearing dressed as a clergyman or
bishop.(59)

V

If it existed at all, atheism as we understand
it was rare in the early modern period.(60) Normally it is better to talk of anticlericalism and
scepticism, or irreligion, none of which is
quantifiable, but all of which demonstrate popular
opposition to established dogma. Some historians
have argued for a relative absence of anti-
clericalism and unorthodoxy, particularly in Tudor
England.(61) But unless one sees the ideology of
the Revolution of 1640-60 as a total aberration,
their claims make little sense. Whereas most of
the evidence for irreligion is for the Revolution
period, there was an older (and continuing)
tradition. We catch glimpses of it during the
searches for heretics in the fifteenth and sixteenth centuries, in the church court and quarter
sessions records of the sixteenth and seventeenth
centuries, and in ballads,(62) almanacs,(63) and
jestbooks.(64)

Of the great number of examples, a small selection gives some idea of the range: Mary was not a virgin and Christ was the son of Joseph; Christ was 'no more than a good prophet'; the sacrament of the altar is not the body of Christ, 'for the bread was made of corn with man's hand, and likewise the wine made of fruit'; it is as good to confess to a tree as to a priest; holy oil is 'meet [only] to grease sheep and boots'; there is no God except the sun and the moon; malt does more to justify God's ways to man than does the Bible; priests should work with their hands for their livelihood; 'baptism could be done as well in a ditch as in a font, and marriage in church could be omitted had not the avarice of priests prevented it'; Heaven could not possibly be large enough to accommodate all souls destined for salvation; all the churches should be made into 'cowhouses and shithouses'.(65) Henry Potter of West Malling denied the resurrection of the dead, 'saying that he would not believe it until he saw it'.(66) Brian Walker of Bishop Auckland questioned the existence of God; 'if anie would show him a devill he would beleive there was a God'.(67) Thomas Sands rejected Ussher's claim that creation had taken place in 4004 B.C. and plumped instead for '20,000 years ago'.(68) A Yorkshireman said he cared 'not a fart' for any minister in Wensleydale; 'I had rather hear a cuckoo sing'.(69)

It is often difficult to determine to what extent such comment is plebeian common sense, and how much of it is proto-Protestant or Puritan theorising. Considered blasphemy, self-doubt and sheer provocativeness are often difficult to disentangle. What do we attribute to indifference, what to out-and-out hostility? Whatever the original impulses, several themes emerge from the mish-mash. Ordinary people thought about the great issues of life and death; they speculated; they questioned. They did not necessarily believe everything they were told. They showed a healthy distrust of the orthodoxies of the clerical and lay elite.

Rejection of established doctrine could take more organised forms, and England had a tradition of heresy and nonconformity: the Lollards, the Family of Love, the Anabaptists, Puritan quasi-separatism. The leaders of these groups were often university men or members of the clergy. But the rank and file were mostly craftsmen and tradesmen, men (and their wives) who were sometimes, as in the case of the

Lollards, closely linked to the highly mobile cloth and wool trade.(70)

Out-and-out separation from the established church was a comparative rarity in the period before 1640. The policies of Archbishop Laud during the 1630s had the effect of alienating those who had hitherto been reconciled to working within the church, of nudging Puritans, often reluctantly, in the direction of separatism. But it was only with the Revolution that real separatism began: in the form of Seekers, Ranters, Baptists, Fifth Monarchists, Congregationalists, Quakers, Muggletonians and a whole range of prophets and pseudo-messiahs.(71) London provides an interesting case study. With only a handful of separatist churches in the 1630s and perhaps a population of 1,000 separatists in 1641, by 1646 London could boast thirty-six gathered churches, and by the 1670s London Quakers alone possibly numbered between 8,000 and 10,000.(72). Before the Revolution, quasi- or semi-separatism was the most common form of dissent. The zealous would attend church, leaving perhaps when the Prayer Book appeared, or only turning up for sermons, but would also hold their own meetings where they would discuss various issues and read from Scripture.(73)

It is extremely difficult to establish clear-cut continuity between the earlier groups I have mentioned and the radicalism of the Civil War. Hill has traced some continuities, geographical and ideological, between the heretics of the sixteenth and the radicals of the seventeenth centuries. Michael Mullett has argued that there was consistency in what he terms the 'lay religious impulse'.(74) An emphasis on the Scriptures, a rejection of the distinction between the priest and layman and of the whole concept of an established church, hostility to tithes, anti-Trinitarianism, mortalism, unorthodox ideas about Heaven and Hell, a stress on human effort as a means to salvation, and adult baptism, were some of the connecting themes. Continuity there certainly was; but it is still impossible to say to what degree the radical ideology of the Revolution was a product of the revolutionary situation, and to what degree it was a continuation of pre-existing ideas and attitudes.

VI

Historians disagree over the nature of the English Reformation. Some say that it was a case of reformation from above, 'Reformation by royal decree'. Others see the impulse as coming from below and stress the groundwork of the Lollards. Some see it as a rapid process; others claim that it was slow in coming and never totally successful.(75) Yet although they may debate its force, extent and origins, few would deny the Reformation's eventual inroads at the popular level. And that brings us to the next important feature of popular religion in early modern England, the emergence of a Protestant popular culture during the seventeenth century.

The sixteenth and seventeenth centuries witnessed great change. Catholic England became Protestant. No longer was the dominant faith 'a cult of the living in service of the dead', a direct, visual religion with 'arithmetical piety', with its masses, votive lights, prayers, vigils for departed souls, pilgrimages, relics, devotion to the saints and the Virgin, and belief in miraculous cures. By the 1580s, and sometimes earlier, the wills of those who had something to bequeath were overwhelmingly Protestant in tone. Rather than commending their souls to God, the Virgin and all the saints, testators in Kent, York, Hull and Leeds chose Protestant preambles which trusted their souls to 'Almighty God' (without intermediaries) and which stressed salvation through the merits of Jesus Christ.(76)

Reformers moved against a whole range of popular activities and customs associated with the church: religious drama and processions, the festivals of Yule and the Boy Bishop, Lords of Misrule, church-ales and wakes.(77) The English Sunday began to establish itself at the expense of the various saints' days. By the eighteenth century the church had lost much of its control over the festivities of the poor.(78)

Puritanism, a zealous form of Protestantism, was firmly entrenched by the beginning of the seventeenth century. Its precise impact upon the laity is extremely difficult to assess, however. The old stereotype about a Puritan south and east is not really all that helpful, though accurate to some extent. True, there was regional variation, but division usually cut across rather than around counties. Sussex was divided between Puritan east and non-Puritan west. Derbyshire Puritanism was strongest in the southern half of the county. Vast areas of Lancashire and Cheshire were relatively unaffected by the Reformation. Some Cambridgeshire parishioners were 'thoroughly imbued' with Puritan doctrine while others were neutral or lukewarm.(79)

Puritanism had popular roots, but it is rapidly becoming something of established orthodoxy that those roots had definite social limits. Collinson has explained that although Protestantism enjoyed popularity in the sixteenth century as a 'movement of protest', 'cocking ... a snook at the symbols of religious tradition and authority', by the seventeenth century it had lost this image of irreverence. 'Now the Bible and the psalms were no longer exciting novelties but symbols of order, discretion, age and dominance in the local community.'(80) Puritanism clearly had possibilities as an ideology of discipline, and this was a fact not lost on the gentry and richer classes. A godly ministry, Puritans reasoned, would 'contain the common people in the duties of their subjection and loyalty to the supreme power'.(81) Later organisational forms of Puritanism, the Presbyterianism and Independency of the 1640s, would appeal to members of the gentry for similar reasons; 'these systems would do better than the king and the bishops ... in containing popular demands and disciplining the people'.(82) Perhaps more important was the way in which provincial Puritanism appealed below the level of the gentry to the parochial elites drawn from the upper and middling ranks of village society: prosperous yeomen, substantial tradesmen and artisans. Keith Wrightson and others have argued that ideological transformation went hand in hand with socio-economic change. Seventeenth-century England witnessed a widening gap between the 'better sort' and the poor. The elite distanced themselves from the culture of the poor and attempted to 'impose a new form of social discipline that would reinforce their own position as masters, employers, ratepayers and pillars of the church'. Thus Puritanism, in the words of William Hunt, provided 'theological legitimation for a cultural revolution which contemporaries called the "reformation of manners"'.(83) The result was an attempted transformation of the morality and behaviour of the poor, a move against traditional popular culture in its various forms, from the Maypole to the alehouse.

The potentials of Puritan acculturation were great. Historians talk, for the period from 1550 on, of a move towards a Bible-based culture. C. J. Sommerville has calculated that there was one Bible for every fifteen members of the population.(84)

Prayers were said twice a day in the house of the
pious William Gouge (three times on Sundays); there
was Bible-reading, and children and servants were
catechised. Oliver Heywood's mother, the wife of a
fustian-weaver, was similarly concerned with her
son's spiritual upbringing: 'She was continually
putting us upon the scriptures and good bookes and
instructing us how to pray'. 'At Calk in Derbyshire,
where people came with their victuals to spend the
whole day with the preacher Julines Herring, they
went away in the evening "in companies, repeating
the Sermons, and singing <u>Psalms</u> in their return
home".' In the Cambridgeshire village of Dry
Drayton (1570-91) there was constant preaching,
sermonising, and catechising. The minister, Richard
Greenham, would even 'walk out into the fields and
... conferr with his Neighbours as they were at
[the] plow': there was no escape.(85)
    We have stories about the conversion of 'drunken
Alcester' into reformed Alcester, of precocious
children who were familiar with the Scriptures at a
ridiculously early age, or who smiled at the thought
of death.(86) We have the Puritan baptismal names
of late Elizabethan Sussex, Kent and
Northamptonshire; whole families like the Starrs of
Cranbrook: No-strength Starr, More-gift Starr, and
their brothers and sisters Mercy, Sure-trust,
Stand-well and Comfort.(87) We find an obsession
with the imagery of the books of Revelation and
Daniel, with the symbolism of the Scarlet Whore, the
Ten-horned and Seven-headed Beasts, and with the
identity of Antichrist; in short a powerful
apocalyptic tradition.(88) Nowhere - apart from in
the language and doctrine of the Revolution sects -
are the bitter fruits of Puritan enculturation more
vividly revealed than in the millenarian dreams of
five-year-old Jane Josselin (the daughter of Ralph
Josselin) and her eleven-year-old brother Tom;
these godly children were simply steeped in biblical
imagery.(89) Though they were admittedly the
children of a minister, they were surely not unique.
The occasional hysterical outbursts of children when
prayers were said or the Bible was read, interpreted
in several well-publicised cases as evidence of
demonic possession, may well have been reactions
against endless prayers and sermons.(90) With their
doubts of salvation, and terror of impending
Judgement, several of the patients of the
seventeenth-century astrologer physician, Richard
Napier, bear witness to the sometimes traumatic
side-effects of Puritan preaching. Joan Perkins

cried out 'Christ Jesus, have mercy on me', day and
night for a whole year. George Trosse 'fancied'
that every step he took was a step backwards; 'I
was making a progress into the depths of hell'.(91)

There was also an anxious, powerful, and
widespread hatred of Catholics - although it was by
no means a purely Puritan phenomenon. Anti-
Catholicism, Robin Clifton and Derek Hirst have
argued, was a major ingredient in the religio-
political ideology of ordinary people in sixteenth-
and seventeenth-century England. It was there
throughout our centuries of interest, surfacing from
time to time in verbal and physical attacks on
Catholics, in alarms and panics, in the election
squabbles of the early seventeenth century.
Sometimes anti-Catholic feeling was stimulated from
the top, whipped up by politicians and
propagandists -`the sixteenth-century Protestant
versions of the old Catholic morality plays and the
late seventeenth-century pope-burning processions
seem to be examples of this - but always the elite
had plenty of raw material to work with.(92)

And we have that great, godly catch-all, the
doctrine of Providence. God was expected to
intervene in the daily events of life, sometimes by
fire, sometimes by plague, sometimes by fits of the
stone. The hand of God was detected everywhere. 'I
was taken ill with a cold', Josselin noted in his
diary in 1644, 'but god delivered mee'; and when
the swelling subsided after he had been stung on the
nose by a bee, the minister took it as evidence that
'divine providence reaches to the lowest things'.
More dramatically, the radical republican Edmund
Ludlow, as Blair Worden has put it, brought out 'the
entire providence detection-kit' to demonstrate the
inevitability of the destruction of the regime of
Charles II; 'storms, comets, plagues, fires, ghost
armies fighting in the sky, huge whales washed up on
beaches, children born with two heads and four arms,
millions of whitings swarming on dry land'. The
sects, too, assiduously recorded judgements upon
persecutors, as proof that the Lord was on their
side.(93)

But zealous Protestantism, whether of the
non-separatist, semi-separatist or separatist
variety, was never the religion of the bulk of the
people. As Collinson has pointed out, there 'is no
reason to believe that an intellectually demanding
and morally rigorous religion transmitted by the
written and spoken word had a broad, natural
appeal'. What Bob Scribner has said of the

Reformation in Germany is equally true of England: it was a popular movement but also 'a minority phenomenon'.(94) Research is continually exposing the limitations of the Protestant and Puritan impact.(95) Despite the above-mentioned perambulations of Richard Greenham, Dry Dayton remained cold to Puritanism. The Reformation, Christopher Haigh has argued convincingly, was extremely slow in coming to Tudor Lancashire. As late as the end of the sixteenth century, even in areas destined to enjoy reputations as Lancashire Genevas, Puritan evangelists were fighting what seems to have been a losing battle against the various 'enormities of the Sabbath': 'wakes, fairs, markets, bear-baits, bull-baits, ales, may games, resorting to alehouses in time of divine service, piping and dancing, hunting, and all manner of unlawful gaming'.(96) There are similar godly complaints for London and Kent; and church-ales, feasts, and revels were 'very common' in early seventeenth-century Wiltshire.(97) The Stuarts' Books of Sports of 1618 and 1633, and the anti-Puritan policies of Archbishop Laud during the 1630s, gave official favour to such activities. Undoubtedly there was popular support for the Laudian church, for the Royalists in the Civil Wars, and for the restoration of monarchy in 1660, precisely because of their identification with a 'cakes-and-ale' policy.(98)

If we look at the period as a whole, celebration of saints' days and church-ales declined. But historians of the eighteenth and nineteenth centuries have shown that feasts, wakes, and a variety of popular sports and customs survived well into the Industrial Revolution. The autobiography of Samuel Bamford, for instance, indicates that many of the popular cultural forms anathematised by Puritans were still thriving in early nineteenth-century Lancashire: Christmas, Shrovetide, Easter, May Day and Whitsuntide festivities, wakes, charivaris and Lords of Misrule.(99) Puritan acculturation had been only partially successful.

VII

Any discussion of popular religion in early modern England has to mention Catholicism. It too had its popular roots, potently illustrated by the Pilgrimage of Grace of 1536-7 and the South-West rebellion of 1549 when the insurgent commoners marched under religious banners and took up arms

in defence of traditional beliefs.(100) Haigh and
John Bossy have shown that there is some fascinating
work to be done on the subject of popular
Catholicism. We know that most English people were
Catholic at the beginning of the period, and we
assume that they were Protestant by the end of it:
but we are still not sure either of the veracity of
that assumption or the precise nature of the change.

It would appear that by the beginning of the
seventeenth century Catholicism was disproportionately 'a nonconformism of the gentry'. The only
real areas of popular Catholicism were in the West,
Wales, and in the North, particularly the north-east
and Lancashire.(101) In Lancashire and Cheshire from
the 1560s to the 1630s there were complaints about
the continued use of holy water, observation of
abrogated saints' days, and prayers for the dead.
Rosary beads were still used and other Catholic
practices were insinuated into the worship and
ceremony of the Church of England. Catholics buried
their own dead in the secrecy of the night, and some
went around openly sporting crosses in their
hats.(102) A Bunbury ale-seller kept relics and a
huge crucifix 'which he set before such as come to
drink at his house'. Haigh cites the case of Ralph
Mercer of Walton (1588) who did not attend church or
receive communion, who was married secretly, and who
had his children baptised illicitly.(103) There were
areas of Wales where, in the mid-seventeenth
century, people still invoked the saints and visited
holy wells and chapels. There are other
seventeenth-century examples from the diocese of
Durham, the West and North Ridings, Wiltshire and
Cornwall of popular attachment to at least the
trappings of the old religion: praying at the
stumps of old standing crosses, the use of the sign
of the cross, the telling of beads, praying to
saints, the performance of the old morality
plays.(104) In such areas it was even possible to
have whole villages dominated by Catholicism.(105)
In the south and the Midlands, however, isolated
gentry families seem to have been the norm.

Richard Clark's observations concerning
seventeenth-century Derbyshire will probably prove
typical for the rest of England: <u>independent</u> lower
class Catholicism was practically non-existent;
almost always it was dependent on the proximity of a
resident recusant gentleman.(106) So to some extent
popular Catholicism was a matter of gentry-tenant
dependence: as John Earle put it in 1628, the
religion of the husbandman was 'part of his copyhold

which he takes from his landlord, and refers to it
wholly to his discretion'.(107) This is not to argue
for an undifferentiated Catholicism in post-
Reformation England. Haigh has drawn a distinction
between the 'more public culture' of peasant
Catholics (with its masses, Latin prayers,
protective magic, and pilgrimages), and the
devotional, bookish Catholicism of the gentry
household. We should perhaps think of two
Catholicisms in sixteenth- and seventeenth-century
England, that of the people and that of the
elite.(108)

In any case, paternalism is only part of the
answer. We still need to explain what it was that
attracted, and continued to attract, ordinary people
to Catholicism. Again Bossy provides some hints,
with a passage from a Jesuit's letter which tells of
a poor woman who became a Catholic after listening
to a Protestant preacher who assigned the illiterate
to a future of eternal damnation.(109) Bible-based
Protestantism was all very well for the more
literate middling sort, but it had little meaning
for illiterate labourers. To some extent, then,
popular Catholicism may have been a reaction against
the academic pretentions and sermonising patter of
Protestant preachers. Thus a York man threw
snowballs at a congregation coming from a sermon
some time in 1615, saying that 'it was never [a]
good world since ther were so many sermons'.(110)
In popular Catholicism there may have been something
of the 'no-damn-nonsense suspicion of high-flying
scholars' that Hill has found in some of the
sectaries of the Civil Wars.(111)

There is also evidence, at least for East
Anglia, that popular Catholicism combined with
social discontent. Hunt writes of the persistence,
from the 1570s to the 1590s, of the 'fantasy of a
vagrant army, under Catholic commanders, ready to
liberate the poor of England'. Essex labourers
spoke of an Irish/Spanish invasion which would be
aided by poor Englishmen 'whereof a great part are
bored through the ears' (the penalty for vagrancy);
at least Philip of Spain would give the poor 'meat,
drink and clothes'. Such men looked back to a
golden Catholic age. 'It was a merry world when the
service was used in the Latin tongue'. 'It was
never merry in England sithence the scriptures were
so commonly preached and talked upon'; 'we shall
never have a merry world while the Queen
liveth'.(112) This brand of Catholicism was a
condemnation of the new order rather than blind

attachment to the old.

VIII

Committed Protestantism never captured the nation, and even at its peak organised dissent attracted only 6 per cent of the population. A mere 1 or 2 per cent of English men, women and children were still Catholic by the 1640s. Though nominally Anglican throughout most of the period, the religion of the bulk of the people was probably closer to Delumeau's folklorised Christianity referred to early in this chapter, syncretic in form, a mixture of Christianity, magic and folklore, blurred at the edges where it intersected the world of astrology.(113)

Non-Christian and pre-Christian beliefs survived into the sixteenth and seventeenth centuries and beyond. They can be detected in various forms. The many popular cures provide a good example: the curing of rupture by passing a patient through a split in a tree, curing wens by rubbing them with a dead person's hand, curing cattle or protecting other livestock from witchcraft by the burning or mutilation of the afflicted animals or by driving the beasts through smoke, the belief that the breath of children or animals (e.g. a white duck or drake) could suck the evil spirit out of an afflicted party, the use of a miscellany of amulets for warding off a miscellany of ills.(114) Combating witchcraft by drawing the blood of the witch, usually by scratching, the belief that it was possible to injure an individual by getting hold of an object belonging to that person, the conviction that menstrual blood had magical properties, and the practice of bathing in the dew on May Day to increase sexual vigour, are also obvious examples of non-Christian ideology.(115)

Indeed, to demonstrate the vitality of non-Christian belief systems we need only to turn to the case of astrology, the belief, widespread in the sixteenth and seventeenth centuries, that the stars and planets influence behaviour and events on earth.(116) Astrologers taught that by calculating the position and movements of the planets at certain times it was possible to determine all sorts of things: a person's character and state of health, future events, the nature of the weather or harvest. In their consulting rooms, or via the printed almanac, they provided a popular service. During the 1660s astrological almanacs were selling at the rate of 400,000 copies a year, and the most popular astrologers were handling between 1,000 and 2,000 cases a year. Their importance, Thomas has intimated, must have seemed to rival that of the nation's clergy.(117) Astrologers were consulted about medical problems; they told fortunes; they catered for the needs of an agrarian society, setting out the best times to plant crops, fell timber, castrate animals - all according to the position of the moon. People went to them for advice about the best way to conceive a male child, about future marriage prospects, even about the likely winner of a horse race. During the Civil Wars astrologers, Royalist and Parliamentarian, proclaimed that the stars predicted victory for their respective sides.(118)

It would be misleading to draw too much of a distinction between Christian and non-Christian beliefs. In many cases the two were inextricably fused. Indeed some of the 'pagan' examples given at the beginning of this section were to be found in combination with the symbolism, theology and language of Christianity. When a Somerset painter had a wen cured by rubbing it with a dead woman's hand, the rubbing was accompanied by the recital of the Lord's Prayer and the begging of a blessing.(119) Astrology was perfectly compatible with the dogmas of orthodox Christianity: God was ultimately behind the workings of the planets and thus the final arbiter; and he could use the stars to indicate his plans for humankind. More than a few ministers are known to have practised the art.(120) Sometimes the mergers between Christianity and its rivals were conscious acts of church polity, sometimes the results of unavoidable 'corruption' from below. It is well known that the cult of saints simply replaced pagan gods in some areas of Europe, and that pre-Christian curative springs became Catholic holy wells.(121) It is also generally accepted that the early church transposed the Christian calendar on to the pagan calendar - both were in any case closely linked to the agricultural year.(122) Syncretism is detectable in the Yule-logs, holly and mistletoe in Christian Christmas celebratory ritual, and in the purificatory or fertility fires which were lit on the eve of the feast of the Nativity of St John (Midsummer Day).(123) It is better, then, to use the term folklorised Christianity, for it allows for the type of fusion we have been discussing: pagan and Christian, magic and religion; the world of popular healing and belief in witches and spirits.

The popular healers of Tudor and Stuart England, the cunning folk (or white witches or wise men and women as they were also known) enjoyed a tremendous amount of popularity. Thomas has quoted contemporaries who were convinced that there were cunning folk in every village, and that they had 'as many followers as the greatest divines'. According to the calculations of Macfarlane, no one in Elizabethan Essex lived more than ten miles from a known wise man or wise woman. It is therefore no exaggeration to describe them as a kind of 'shadow clergy'.(124)

Apart from healing, they fulfilled a host of functions which included combating black witchcraft (*maleficium*), finding lost and stolen goods and treasure, casting horoscopes, prescribing charms for all kinds of things, fortune telling and advising on a range of subjects. One enterprising Newcastle cunning man 'lett leases to people for tearme of yeares and life'; 'he could take away a man's life a yeare before his appointed time, or make him live a yeare longer'.(125) People differed in their interpretations of the source of the white witches' powers. Many villagers must have merely accepted that the cunning folk had secret powers, and left it at that, but others certainly attributed their power to divine assistance. The white witches in Edward Poeton's 'The Winnowing of White Witchcraft' said that their power was God-given, and that they received help from angels who were invoked by a secret formula or by the use of prayers; in other words, they were 'illumined from above'. Richard Napier likewise turned to the Archangel Raphael when he needed help with patients.(126) The white witch was almost certainly pre-Christian in origin;(127) but by the sixteenth and seventeenth centuries Christianity was equally certainly an essential ingredient in cunning-folk lore.

The various charms and rituals of the popular healers were firmly rooted in the ceremony and prayers of pre-Reformation Catholicism, though often in combination with non-Christian techniques - sympathetic magic, for example. One healing technique from sixteenth-century Somerset was to take the girdle of the sick person, cut it into five pieces, say five Paternosters and five Aves, and then bury the pieces of the girdle in separate places. Another sixteenth-century healer, this time from London, employed a mixture of herbs and prayers. For those affected with sores, she recommended that

they 'gather herbe-grace, dyll verveye, marygoldes,
put a lyttill holy water to them, & sey sume
prayers; & when she stampethe to sey iii pater
nosters, iii aves, and a crede, in the worshyp of
our Lady, yf it be a woman that stampeth; & if it
be a man he must se [say] iii pater nosters, iii
aves, & a crede, in the worshypp of Jesus'.(128)
Divination by the use of the sieve and shears was
accompanied by the invocation of the names of the
Father, Son and Holy Ghost, or of St Peter and St
Paul. Creeds, Paternosters and Ave Marias were
repeated; the sign of the cross and the name of
Jesus were employed.(129) Christianity continued to
play a role in popular healing. Until this century,
church-window lead, rainwater from the church roof,
moss from church bells, money from the church
offertory, and stone ground from church statues were
all thought to have curative properties. The Bible
was also used to heal and to ward off evil
spirits.(130)

Apart from belief in white witches, there was
widespread belief in another kind of witch, the
black witch, one who was able to do harm by
supernatural means. 'The fables of Witchcraft have
taken so fast hold and deepe root in the heart of
man', wrote Reginald Scot at the end of the
sixteenth century, 'that fewe or none can
(nowadaies) with patience indure the hand and
correction of God. For if any adversitie, greefe,
sicknesse, losse of children, corne, cattell, or
libertie happen unto them; by & by they exclaime
uppon witches.'(131) As Scot observed, the damage
that they were thought to do varied; but most could
come under the heading of death or injury. Witches
were blamed for the death of people or livestock,
the sickness of a person or his or her cows, horses,
pigs, sheep, chickens. They were thought responsible for the burning down of a barn or house, for
beer going bad, butter or cheese spoiling, cows not
milking, a wood pile falling down, or a cart getting
stuck in the mud. The bulk of English witchcraft
accusations were far more mundane than their
counterparts on the Continent. English witches did
not start plagues; and they were seldom accused of
interfering with the weather. English witchcraft
was less sexual and demonic than the Continental
variety.

There were two conceptions of witchcraft in
early modern Europe: the view of the elite and the
view of the majority of the population. The learned
stressed the role of Satan: witches made a pact

with the Devil and agreed to serve him through the promotion of evil. The ordinary villager thought merely in terms of *maleficium*; to him or her the witch was simply someone with the supernatural ability to do harm to others: there was no idea of Devil worship or of adherence to Satan. Elite ideas were either imposed on popular conceptions in the court room or they were gradually taken up at the popular level through the influence of the pulpit or the impact of well-publicised cases. The extent to which this occurred varied, however. The evidence for popular belief in pacts with the Devil seems strong for Scotland, weak for England, and practically non-existent for Essex except for a brief period in the 1640s when a team of professional witch-hunters was at work.(132)

Then there was what has been called the 'enchanted world', the world of spirits. This belief was not confined to the popular level. Arthur Dent warned his many readers that they had 'all the divels in hell' against them, 'a very legion of divels, lying in ambush against our soules'. An English bishop said that there were evil spirits all around: 'I am not able to tell how many thousand be here amongst us.'(133) Scot wrote in 1584 of a fear of spirits, elves, fairies, dwarfs, imps, and a mass of 'other bugs'; it was widely believed, he said, that 'everie churchyard swarmed with soules and spirits'. A century later, the godly Richard Baxter was to talk in terms of the souls of wicked men lurking around graves and the like, 'near us, in the Air, Earth and sea, and not in the higher glorious Regions'.(134) Scot had felt that Protestantism was driving out such superstition, but he was over-optimistic. James Obelkevich has shown that these beliefs continued into the nineteenth century. There are both seventeenth- and nineteenth-century references to the popular notion that if one stood on a porch on the eve of the feast of the Nativity of St John or on St Mark's Eve one would see the apparitions of all who were to die during the following year. In Yorkshire in the seventeenth century it was believed that after death departed souls lingered over the moors.(135)

Witchcraft depositions and confessions, and the case-books of the physician Napier point to a popular belief in imps and spirits, usually described, like the Devil, in very physical terms as moles, spiders, bees, mice, cats, flies, dogs,

birds, rats and so on.(136) According to the elite
interpretation of witchcraft these imps or spirits
were demons or agents of the Devil. An American
historian, Richard Horsley, has suggested that
ordinary villagers may have seen them differently,
perhaps as part of pre-Christian lore, as spirits of
the weather, forest gods or the like.(137) We simply
do not know. The work of another American
historian, Michael MacDonald, seems more plausible,
for his analysis of the Napier case-books enables a
unique entry into the mental world of the
seventeenth-century villager. The picture is almost
Manichean: 'Napier's patients appear often to have
believed that they embodied both a good spirit,
associated with happiness, normality, and piety, and
an evil spirit, associated with unhappiness,
suicidal despair, and apostasy.' God and the angels
were lined up against Satan and the demons, and the
battle was within as well as without.(138)

Finally there were the fairies, ethereal beings,
sometimes small, sometimes much the same size as
ordinary men and women, 'of a stature, generally,
near the smaller size of Men' as Richard Bovet put
it in 1684.(139) But they were wicked or mischievous
spirits, a far cry from the current image in
children's fairy stories. Learned opinion differed
concerning the nature of the fairies. Some saw them
as departed souls, destined presumably for Heaven or
Hell. Another interpretation was that they were
fallen angels doomed to Hell. Yet another talked in
terms of 'a Third Kingdom', a kingdom of spirits
which was a kind of middle strata between Heaven and
Hell and, as such, unaffected by the conventions of
Christian eschatology. There is a suggestion too
that as with its interpretation of witchcraft, a
substantial body of elite opinion perceived the
fairies as agents of the Devil.(140) As far as we
can gather, this demonic element was absent at the
popular level. Fairies were merely evil spirits who
had to be placated if they were not going to inflict
harm. They were thought to have a penchant for
seizing the infants of neglectful parents and
substituting children of their own. The 'common
people, if they chance to have any sort of the
Epilepsie, Palsie, Convulsions or the like, do
presently persuade themselves that they are
bewitched, forespoken, blasted, fairy-taken, or
haunted with some evil spirit, and the like', an
observer noted of the north of England during the
seventeenth century. Edward Fairfax wrote in 1621

of 'the strange follies, rooted in the opinion of
the vulgar, concerning the walking of souls in this
or that house, the dancing of Fairies on this rock
or that mountain, the changing of infants in their
cradles'.(141) And fairies were beings who often had
a clear social function, punishing untidiness,
dirtiness and lechery.(142) In an account written at
the end of the seventeenth century by a Scottish
minister, the fairy kingdom was described as a kind
of mirror image of the terrestrial world, with fairy
doubles of living people. Fairies lived in tribes,
had their own aristocracy, married, and had
children. They fought among themselves. Other
accounts claimed that the fairies had houses and
halls, kept cattle, held fairs and markets, and
(according to James I) 'eate and dranke, and did all
other actions like naturall men and women'.(143)
Yet, as is so often the case, these may merely have
been the fantasies of king and priest; we have no
way of knowing if such day dreams were part of
village culture. We must also allow for variety
and flexibility. There is no reason to assume a
clear-cut and well-developed fairy lore. As an
authority on Irish folklore has put it, 'the word
"fairy" must communicate something, but fairy
beliefs allow for a vast range of elaboration and
interpretation ... precisely what the word means to
any one individual, and whether its meaning is
constant, even for that individual, are matters of
conjecture'.(144)

IX

What can we conclude about popular religion in
early modern England? A coherent popular
Catholicism, popular Puritanism, religious apathy,
radical sectarianism, a vast amorphous world of
syncretic or folklorised Christianity, a corpus of
magical beliefs which helped ordinary people to
cope with the vagaries of a harsh and uncertain
environment: these are the categories which would
have to be mentioned in any discussion of popular
religion during the period. Ironically we know
least about the popular conformists, those who kept
out of trouble, those who did not record their
beliefs and who were not considered worthy of
comment by their more educated contemporaries, those
who possibly (and we can be no more positive)
adhered to and internalised 'official' religion.
We still have a lot of work to do before we can talk
with any confidence about the religious beliefs of

ordinary people in the sixteenth and seventeenth
centuries.

Is it possible, then, to describe the thoughts,
activities and loyalties of the average woman or man
in early modern England? Can we come up with what
sociologists would call an 'ideal type'? If the
cheap godly literature is any guide, thoughts of
death and Judgement were never far from people's
minds. Yet such obsessions may quite feasibly
reflect the interests and intentions of the authors
of chapbooks rather than the spiritual state of a
prospective audience. Presumably our average person
believed in a God (however perceived); and almost
certainly in the existence of good and evil spirits.
Probably, like his nineteenth-century, working-class
descendants, the early modern 'everyman' lived
according to the ethical code of 'practical
Christianity'- that is 'decent behaviour', 'decent
living'(145)- believing like Keith Thomas's old man,
quoted earlier, that 'if he had done well' he would
attain salvation when he died. There must have been
many in early modern England like the character in
Arthur Dent's <u>Plaine Mans Path-way</u>:

> Tush, tush: what needs all this adoo? If a
> man say his Lords prayer, his tenne
> Commaundements, and his beleefe, and keepe
> them, and say no body no harme, nor doo no
> bodie no harme, and doo as hee would bee done
> too, have a good faith to Godword, and be a
> man of Gods beliefe, no doubt he shall be
> saved, without all this running to sermons,
> and pratling of the scriptures.(146)

A minister complained in 1602 of a parish in Kent
where nearly all were of the opinion that if a man
lived 'uprightlie' he could 'by well doeing ...
winne heaven'.(147)

Certainly our 'ideal type' would not be a
'literal Christian believer' ('all of the time') in
the way that Peter Laslett has claimed for the
inhabitants of the 'World we have lost'.(148)
Indeed we have seen that non-Christian influences,
both magical and astrological, were crucial in the
belief systems of the majority of the men and women
of the seventeenth century - not that they would
have drawn any rigid distinction between the
Christian and the non-Christian. Many, as Wrightson
has put it, would have been 'concerned less with the
path to salvation in the next world' than with
coping with the dangers and misfortunes of this

world.(149)   Magic, and what we would call 'superstitions', helped to ease the uncertainties.
    Nor should our hypothetical believer's
'Christianity' be measured in terms of familiarity
with the catechism. One should think instead of the
social importance of the church, since there is
convincing evidence for popular attachment to the
rituals of traditional Anglicanism and to the
church-supervised rites of passage. When the
reformers of the 1640s assaulted the government and
liturgy of the Church of England, Anglicanism
survived, stubbornly. Morrill has shown that the
banned festivals of Easter and Christmas were still
celebrated by communion. Although officially
replaced by the Presbyterian <u>Directory for Public
Worship</u>, the <u>Book of Common Prayer</u> continued to be
used in the majority of parishes examined by
Morrill.(150) The Marriage Act of 1653 permitted
civil marriage, but at least one vicar claimed that
'Many would not be so marryed, and such for the most
part as were so marryed, were also marryed in their
own Parish Churches by their ministers'. And we
know that church marriages persisted in Interregnum
Sussex.(151) After 1660 the nonfonformist sects were
persistently troubled by adherents who returned to
the restored Church of England when it came to
marriage or the baptism of their children: the
church was etched deep in the social fabric of the
nation.
    Yet the theme of this chapter is that when we
think of popular religion in the early modern period
we need to think in terms of a range of possibilities; of permutations rather than 'ideal types'.
Patrick Collinson and John Morrill are eager that
popular Anglicanism should not be neglected.
However, I hope that the other message of this
chapter is that we need to be sensitive to tensions,
negotiation and contestation, innovation and
resistance; sensitive to the ways in which
official ideology can be manipulated and moulded at
the popular level.(152) For we must never assume
that people conformed. In the words of Natalie
Davis, we need to be aware that people were not, and
are not, passive receptacles for the values of their
social betters.(153)

*   This chapter has benefited greatly from the comments of
      Bernard Capp, Christopher Hill, Liam Hunt and Frank
      McGregor.

1.   M. Venard, 'Popular religion in the eighteenth century',
      in W. J. Callahan and D. Higgs (eds.), Church and Society
      in Catholic Europe of the eighteenth century (Cambridge,
      1979), p. 139.

2.   P. W. Williams, Popular Religion in America (Englewood
      Cliffs, 1980), p. 5; R. Williams, Keywords (1976), p. 199.

3.   Williams, Keywords, p. 199.

4.   P. Collinson, The Religion of Protestants (Oxford, 1982),
      ch. 5.

5.   D. Clark, Between pulpit and pew (Cambridge, 1982)

6.   C. Phythian-Adams, Local History and Folklore (1975),
      pp. 21-5; P. Clark, 'The Cultural Function of the
      Traditional Town', in C. Phythian-Adams and others, The
      Fabric of the Traditional Community (Milton Keynes,
      1977); Thomas, Religion and Decline (1973), pp. 179-82;
      C. Hill, Society and Puritanism (1966), ch. 12; J. C.
      Cox, Churchwardens' Accounts (1913), pp. 295, 299, 319,
      329-31; W. H. Hale, A Series of Precedents and
      Proceedings (1847), pp. 114, 156, 158-9, 172-3.

7.   A. Macfarlane, Reconstructing Historical Communities
      (Cambridge, 1977), p. 197.

8.   Thomas, Religion and Decline, p. 191; A. Fletcher, A
      County Community in Peace and War (1975), p. 88; C.
      Haigh, Reformation and Resistance in Tudor Lancashire
      (Cambridge, 1975), pp. 54-5; The Churchwardens'
      Presentments in the Oxfordshire Peculiars of Dorchester,
      Thame and Banbury, ed. S. A. Peyton (Oxfordshire RS, x,
      1928), pp. 205, 246; Hale, Series of Precedents, pp. 241,
      260.

9.   C. Russell, 'Monarchies, Wars, and Estates', Legislative
      Studies Quarterly, vii (1982), p. 210.

10.   Hale, Series of Precedents, pp. 246, 252, 253-4; J. T.
      Evans, Seventeenth-Century Norwich (Oxford, 1979), p.
      113; P. Tyler, 'The Church Courts at York and Witchcraft
      Prosecutions 1567-1640', Northern History, iv (1969),
      p. 103; K. Wrightson and D. Levine, Poverty and Piety in
      an English Village (NY, 1979), p. 14; C. Haigh, 'Puritan
      evangelism in the reign of Elizabeth I', English
      Historical Review, xcii (1977), pp. 47-8.

11.   Macfarlane, Reconstructing Historical Communities, pp.
      197-8.

12.   Cox, Churchwardens' Accounts, pp. 57, 68, 96, 186ff.,
      191, 212; Hill, Society and Puritanism, p. 427; Thomas,
      Religion and Decline, p. 180.

13.   Hill, Society and Puritanism, ch. 8; J. A. Sharpe,
      Defamation and Sexual Slander in Early Modern England
      (York, 1980).

14.   S. Clarke, Golden Apples (1659), p. 38; [R. Allestree],

The Whole Duty of Man (1719), p. 166, C. Hill, The Century of Revolution (1972), p. 74; C. Bridenbaugh, Vexed and Troubled Englishmen 1590-1642 (NY, 1976), p. 275.

15. Collinson, Religion of Protestants, pp. 191-2; J. Morrill, 'The Church in England, 1642-9', in Morrill (ed.), Reactions to the English Civil War 1642-1649 (1982), p. 90.

16. Hill, Society and Puritanism, pp. 50, 56, 57; Thomas, Religion and Decline, pp. 195-6; C. Hill, Change and Continuity in Seventeenth-Century England (1974), p. 7. See also Collinson, Religion of Protestants, pp. 200ff.

17. Thomas, Religion and Decline, p. 179; C. Haigh, 'Some Aspects of the Recent Historiography of the English Reformation', in W. J. Mommsen and others (eds.), Stadtbürgertum und Adel in der Reformation (Stuttgart, 1979), p. 96; Yorkshire Diaries and Autobiographies (Surtees Soc., lxv, 1875), pp. 138-9.

18. See for example, C. L. Ewen, Witchcraft and Demonianism (1933), pp. 172, 177, 186, 197, 212.

19. Hill, Society and Puritanism, pp. 472-5; D. M. Palliser, Tudor York (Oxford, 1979), p. 259; M. J. Ingram, 'Ecclesiastical Justice in Wiltshire 1600-1640' (Univ. of Oxford D.Phil. thesis, 1976), pp. 90, 108; Collinson, Religion of Protestants, pp. 228-30.

20. The Diary of Ralph Josselin 1616-1683, ed. A. Macfarlane (1976), p. 500.

21. R. Malcolmson, '"A set of ungovernable people": the Kingswood colliers in the eighteenth century', in J. Brewer and J. Styles (eds.), An Ungovernable People (1980), p. 91; P. Clark, 'The Alehouse and the Alternative Society', in D. Pennington and K. Thomas (eds.), Puritans and Revolutionaries (Oxford, 1978), p. 65; [E. Fairfax], Daemonologia, ed. W. Grainge (1971), p. 35.

22. R. C. Richardson, Puritanism in north-west England (Manchester, 1972), p. 15; R. Clark, 'Anglicanism, Recusancy and Dissent in Derbyshire 1603-1730' (Univ. of Oxford D. Phil. thesis, 1979), p. 7; K. Wrightson, English Society 1580-1680 (1982), p. 208.

23. Clark, 'Anglicanism, Recusancy and Dissent', pp. 8ff.; Collinson, Religion of Protestants, pp. 209-10.

24. P. Laslett, The World we have lost (1971), pp. 74-6; Bishop Fell and Nonconformity, ed. M. Clapinson (Oxfordshire RS, lii, 1980).

25. F. G. Emmison, Elizabethan Life: Morals and the Church Courts (Chelmsford, 1973), p. 77: Lambeth Palace Library, MS 1126, p. 37r. See also C. W. Chalkin, Seventeenth-Century Kent (1965), p. 224; Bishop Fell and Nonconformity.

26. Macfarlane, Reconstructing Historical Communities, pp. 193-4; Diary of Ralph Josselin, pp. 486, 541, 546, 553,

559, 574, 608, 621, 627, 628, 631.

27. P. Clark, English Provincial Society ... Kent, 1500-1640 (Hassocks, 1977), p. 156.

28. R. A. Marchant, The Church under the Law (Cambridge, 1969), p. 227.

29. M. Spufford, Contrasting Communities (Cambridge, 1974), pp. 242-3.

30. Richardson, Puritanism, p. 39.

31. C. Hill, Economic Problems of the Church (Oxford, 1968), p. 226.

32. Thomas, Religion and Decline, p. 194.

33. P. Heath, The English Parish Clergy on the Eve of the Reformation (1969), pp. 74-5.

34. I. Green, 'Career Prospects and Clerical Conformity in the Early Stuart Church', P. and P., 90 (1981); R. O'Day, The English Clergy (Leicester, 1979), pp. 210, 211, 230, 236.

35. Thomas, Religion and Decline, p. 193; J. H. Pruett, The Parish Clergy under the Later Stuarts (Urbana, 1978), pp. 122-3.

36. Wrightson and Levine, Poverty and Piety, p. 13; Wrightson, English Society, p. 215.

37. Bishop Fell and Nonconformity, p. 23-4; A. T. Hart, The Man in the Pew 1558-1660 (1966), p. 127.

38. Haigh, 'Some Aspects', pp. 94-5; Pruett, Parish Clergy, p. 116. For Strauss, see his 'Success and Failure in the German Reformation', P. and P., 67 (1975).

39. Ingram, 'Ecclesiastical Justice', p. 106.

40. E. P. Thompson, 'Anthropology and the Discipline of Historical Context', Midland History, i (1972), p. 52.

41. Hale, Series of Precedents, p. 176.

42. J. Aubrey, Three Prose Works, ed. J. Buchanan-Brown (Fontwell, 1972), p. 161.

43. L. Clarkson, The Lost Sheep Found (1660), pp. 6-7.

44. B. Reay, 'Laurence Clarkson: An Artisan and the English Revolution', in C. Hill, B. Reay and W. Lamont, The World of the Muggletonians (1983), ch. 6.

45. Thomas, Religion and Decline, p. 566.

46. Diary of Ralph Josselin, pp. 335, 339.

47. Narrative Papers of George Fox, ed. H. J. Cadbury (Richmond, 1972), p. 51; N. Cohn, The Pursuit of the Millennium (1970), p. 304; Hill, World Turned Upside Down (1972), p. 141

48. M. Campbell, The English Yeoman (New Haven, 1942), p. 152.

49. Hill, World Turned Upside Down, pp. 179, 182; C. Hill (ed.), Winstanley: The Law of Freedom and Other Writings (Harmondsworth, 1973), p. 44; A. Coppe, A Fiery Flying Roll (1649), p. 2.

50. Thomas, Religion and Decline, p. 180.

51. Reay, 'Laurence Clarkson'.

52. G. R. Owst, Literature and Pulpit in Medieval England

(Oxford, 1961), p. 112; R. Scot, The Discoverie of Witchcraft (Arundel, 1964 reprint), p. 139.

53. Thomas, Religion and Decline, pp. 559-69; D. E. Stannard, The Puritan Way of Death (NY, 1979), ch. 3.

54. Spufford, Small Books, p. 200.

55. A Short History of the Life of John Crook (1700), p. 9; Thomas, Religion and Decline, p. 562; L. Muggleton, A True Interpretation of ... the Revelation of St. John (1808), p. vi.

56. Ewen, Witchcraft and Demonianism, *passim*.

57. C. Larner, Enemies of God (1981), pp. 144, 147.

58. See B. Capp's chapter in this volume.

59. J. Obelkevich, Religion and Rural Society (Oxford, 1976), pp. 276-8.

60. G. E. Aylmer, 'Unbelief in Seventeenth-Century England', in Pennington and Thomas (eds.), Puritans and Revolutionaries, pp. 22-46.

61. H. J. Cohn, 'Reformatorische Bewegung und Antiklerikalismus in Deutschland und England', in Mommsen and others, Stadtbürgertum und Adel, pp. 328-9; Haigh, Reformation and Resistance, pp. 62, 76-7, 85, 117.

62. J. C. Holt, 'The origins and audience of the Ballads of Robin Hood', P. and P., 18 (1960), p. 95.

63. B. Capp, Astrology and the Popular Press (1979), pp. 150ff.

64. K. Thomas, 'The place of laughter in Tudor and Stuart England', Times Literary Supplement, 21 January 1977, p. 78.

65. J. A. F. Thomson, The Later Lollards 1414-1520 (Oxford, 1967), pp. 36, 41, 62, 67, 78, 80, 106, 161; I. Luxton, 'The Reformation and Popular Culture', in F. Heal and R. O'Day (eds.), Church and Society in England (1977), pp. 66, 70; Kent Archives Office, U47/47 O1, p. 71.

66. Thomson, Later Lollards, p. 186.

67. Acts of the High Commission Court within the Diocese of Durham, ed. W. H. D. Longstaffe (Surtees Soc., xxxiv, 1858), p. 116.

68. Thomson, Later Lollards, p. 80.

69. Tyler, 'Church Courts at York', p. 102, n. 72.

70. C. Cross, Church and People 1450-1660 (Glasgow, 1976); M. R. Watts, The Dissenters (Oxford, 1978); M. Tolmie, The Triumph of the Saints (Cambridge, 1977).

71. See J. F. McGregor and B. Reay (eds.), Radical Religion in the English Revolution (Oxford, 1984); Hill, World Turned Upside Down.

72. Tolmie, Triumph of the Saints, pp. 4, 37; W. Beck and T. F. Ball, The London Friends' Meetings (1869), p. 32.

73. Tolmie, Triumph of the Saints, pp. 28ff.

74. C. Hill, 'From Lollards to Levellers', in M. Cornforth (ed.), Rebels and their Causes (1978), p. 51; M. Mullett, Radical Religious Movements in Early Modern Europe

(1980), p. 65.

75. For two good surveys, see D. M. Palliser, 'Popular Reactions to the Reformation during the Years of Uncertainty 1530-70', in Heal and O'Day (eds.), Church and Society, ch. 2; Haigh, 'Some Aspects'.

76. This is where the work has been done. See Palliser, Tudor York, pp. 249-54; Clark, English Provincial Society, pp. 58-9, 76-7; C. Cross, 'The Development of Protestantism in Leeds and Hull, 1520-1640: The Evidence from Wills', Northern History, xviii (1982); idem, 'The State and Development of Protestantism in English Towns, 1520-1603', in A. C. Duke and C. A. Tamse (eds.), Britain and the Netherlands (The Hague, 1981), ch. 1.

77. Luxton, 'Reformation and Popular Culture'; Burke, Popular Culture, ch. 8; W. A. Hunt, The Puritan Moment (Cambridge, Mass., 1982), pp. 130-6; Wrightson, English Society, pp. 211-12.

78. Hill, Society and Puritanism, ch. 5; E. P. Thompson, 'Patrician Society, Plebeian Culture', JSH, vii (1974), pp. 391-3.

79. Fletcher, County Community, p. 62; Clark, 'Anglicanism', p. 114; Richardson, Puritanism, 162ff.; Haigh, 'Puritan evangelism'; Spufford, Contrasting Communities, pp. 237, 328.

80. Collinson, Religion of Protestants, p. 238.

81. Richardson, Puritanism, p. 146.

82. B. Manning, 'Puritanism and Democracy, 1640-1642', in Pennington and Thomas (eds.), Puritans and Revolutionaries, p. 155.

83. Wrightson and Levine, Poverty and Piety, esp. pp. 171, 174, 180, 181; Hunt, Puritan Moment, pp. 124-44 (the quotation comes from p. 140).

84. C. J. Sommerville, 'On the Distribution of Religious and Occult Literature in Seventeenth-Century England', The Library, xxix (1974), p. 223.

85. Hill, Society and Puritanism. p. 455; M. Spufford, 'First steps in literacy', Social History, iv (1979), p. 435; Collinson, Religion of Protestants, p. 260; Spufford, Contrasting Communities, p. 327.

86. Richardson, Puritanism. pp. 48-9; C. J. Sommerville, 'Breaking the Icon: The First Real Children in English Books', History of Education Quarterly, xxi (1981), pp. 56, 58, 61.

87. N. Tyacke, 'Popular Puritan Mentality in Late Elizabethan England', in P. Clark and others (eds), The English Commonwealth 1547-1604 (Leicester, 1979), ch. 4.

88. B. W. Ball, A Great Expectation (Leiden, 1975); C. Hill, Antichrist in Seventeenth-Century England (1971); P. Christianson, Reformers and Babylon (Toronto, 1978); R. Bauckham, Tudor Apocalypse (Appleford, 1978).

89. Diary of Ralph Josselin, pp. 237, 335, 339.

90. D. P. Walker, Unclean Spirits (1981), pp. 50, 58; Ewen, Witchcraft and Demonianism, pp. 190-2; P. Boyer and S. Nissenbaum, Salem Possessed (Cambridge, Mass., 1976), p. 4.
91. M. MacDonald, Mystical Bedlam. Madness, Anxiety, and Healing in Seventeenth-Century England (Cambridge, 1981), pp. 139-40, 144-5.
92. C. Z. Wiener, 'The Beleaguered Isle: A Study of Elizabethan and Early Jacobean Anti-Catholicism', P. and P., 51 (1971); R. Clifton, 'The Popular Fear of Catholics during the English Revolution', P. and P., 52 (1971); D. Hirst, The Representative of the People? (Cambridge, 1975), pp. 145-6; P. Rainer, Tudor and Early Stuart Anti-Catholic Drama (The Hague, 1972); S. Williams, 'The Pope-Burning Processions of 1679, 1680 and 1681', Journal of the Warburg and Courtauld Institutes, xxi (1958); O. W. Furley, 'The Pope-Burning Processions of the Late Seventeenth Century', History, xliv (1959).
93. Diary of Ralph Josselin, pp. 15, 19; E. Ludlow, A Voyce from the Watch Tower, ed. A. B. Worden (Camden Fourth Series, xxi, 1978), p. 10; Thomas, Religion and Decline, ch. 4.
94. Collinson, Religion of Protestants, p. 201; B. Scribner, 'Religion, Society and Culture: Reorientating the Reformation', History Workshop, 14 (1982), pp. 4, 6.
95. Haigh, Reformation and Resistance, ch. 14; R. Houlbrooke, Church Courts and the People during the English Reformation 1520-1570 (Oxford, 1979), pp. 248-9, 256-7.
96. Haigh, Puritan Evangelism', pp. 51-2.
97. Collinson, Religion of Protestants, pp. 204-7; Ingram, 'Ecclesiastical Justice', p. 87.
98. Cf. D. Underdown, 'Clubmen in the Civil War', P. and P., 85 (1979), p. 35.
99. H. Cunningham, Leisure in the Industrial Revolution (1980), p. 22, and ch. 2; R. Malcolmson, Popular Recreations in English Society 1700-1850 (Cambridge, 1973), p. 13; J. K. Walton and R. Poole, 'The Lancashire Wakes in the Nineteenth Century', in R. Storch (ed.), Popular Culture and Custom in Nineteenth-Century England (1982), ch. 5; The Autobiography of Samuel Bamford, ed. W. H. Chaloner (1967), i, pp. 134-56.
100. C. S. L. Davies, 'The Pilgrimage of Grace Reconsidered', P. and P., 41 (1968); P. Williams, The Tudor Regime (Oxford, 1979), pp. 318, 321, 324, 346.
101. J. Bossy, The English Catholic Community, 1570-1850 (1976), p. 100 and ch. 5.
102. Haigh, Reformation and Resistance, pp. 218-20, 222; Richardson, Puritanism, pp. 162ff.
103. Richardson, Puritanism, p. 170; Haigh, Reformation and Resistance, p. 291.
104. C. H. Jenkins, 'Welsh Books and Religion 1660-1730'

(Univ. of Wales Ph.D. thesis, 1974), pp. 492-4; Acts of the High Commission, pp. 50, 52; Hill, Change and Continuity, p. 9; H. Aveling, Northern Catholics (1966), pp. 23-4, 289-90; Aubrey, Three Prose Works, pp. 162-3; Cornwall RO, DD SF 285/68-9.

105. Bossy, English Catholic Community, p. 176.
106. Clark, 'Anglicanism', pp. 57-8, 62ff.
107. Campbell, English Yeoman, p. 291.
108. C. Haigh, 'The Continuity of Catholicism in the English Reformation', P. and P., 93 (1981), pp. 67-9.
109. J. Bossy, 'The English Catholic Community 1603-1625', in A. G. R. Smith (ed.), The Reign of James VI and I (1973), p. 104.
110. Palliser, Tudor York, p. 259.
111. Hill and others, World of the Muggletonians, p. 102.
112. Hunt, Puritan Moment, pp. 60-1; F. G. Emmison, Elizabethan Life: Disorder (Chelmsford, 1970), pp. 47-8, 55, 57.
113. J. Delumeau, Catholicism between Luther and Voltaire (1977), pp. 166ff.; see also R. W. Scribner, 'Ritual and Popular Religion in Catholic Germany at the Time of the Reformation', JEH, xxxv (1984).
114. J. Brand, Observations on the Popular Antiquities of Great Britain (1849), ii, pp. 277-90; R. Malcolmson, Life and Labour in England 1700-1780 (1981), pp. 87-8; Aubrey, Three Prose Works, pp. 79, 321; Fairfax, Daemonologia, p. 35; Depositions from the Castle of York (Surtees Soc., xl, 1861), p. 127; E. Porter, Cambridgeshire Customs and Folklore (1969), p. 92.
115. Thomas, Religion and Decline, pp. 648-59; P. Crawford, 'Attitudes to Menstruation in Seventeenth-Century England', P. and P., 91 (1981), pp. 59-60; G. R. Quaife, 'The Consenting Spinster in a Peasant Society', JSH, xi (1977), p. 231.
116. For this subject, see Thomas, Religion and Decline, chs. 10-12; Capp, Astrology; A. Chapman, 'Astrological medicine', in C. Webster (ed.), Health, medicine and mortality in the sixteenth century (Cambridge, 1979), ch. 8.
117. Capp, Astrology, 23; Thomas, Religion and Decline, pp. 364, 434, 762.
118. H. Rusche, 'Merlini Anglici: Astrology and Propaganda from 1644 to 1651', English Historical Review, lxxx (1965).
119. Aubrey, Three Prose Works, p. 79.
120. Acts of the High Commission, pp. 34-42: the clerk of St Helen Auckland (1633) cast figures, found lost goods, and sold almanacs which he kept on the communion table.
121. Thomas, Religion and Decline, pp. 54-5; Delumeau, Catholicism, p. 165.

122. Phythian-Adams, <u>Local History</u>, p. 13; Thomas, <u>Religion and Decline</u>, p. 54.
123. Brand, <u>Popular Antiquities</u>, i, pp. 298, 303, 311, 318; Phythian-Adams, <u>Local History</u>, p. 29; Delumeau, <u>Catholicism</u>, pp. 177-9; J. Simpson, 'Rural Folklore', in J. Blum (ed.), <u>Our Forgotten Past</u> (1982), p. 168.
124. Thomas, <u>Religion and Decline</u>, p. 314; A. Macfarlane, <u>Witchcraft in Tudor and Stuart England</u> (1970), p. 120; Obelkevich, <u>Religion and Rural Society</u>, p. 291. The best account of white witches is in Thomas, <u>Religion and Decline</u>, chs. 7-8.
125. <u>Depositions from the Castle of York</u>, pp. 204-5.
126. BL, MS Sloane 1954, fos. 166, 180-80v, 182-83v; MacDonald, <u>Mystical Bedlam</u>, p. 210.
127. R. A. Horsley, 'Further Reflections on Witchcraft and European Folk Religion', <u>History of Religions</u>, xix (1979), p. 79.
128. Thomas, <u>Religion and Decline</u>, p. 218; Hale, <u>Series of Precedents</u>, pp. 107-8.
129. R. F. B. Hodgkinson, 'Extracts from the Act Book of the Archdeacon of Nottingham', <u>Transactions of the Thoroton Society</u>, xxx (1926), p. 51; Aubrey, <u>Three Prose Works</u>, p. 213; Ewen, <u>Witchcraft and Demonianism</u>, pp. 146, 158, 178; Thomas, <u>Religion and Decline</u>, pp. 210, 211, 212, 213, 215, 217, 220-1.
130. T. Brown, 'Some Examples of Post-Reformation Folklore in Devon', <u>Folklore</u>, lxxii (1961), pp. 389-90; A. W. Smith, 'Popular Religion', <u>P. and P.</u>, 40 (1968), p. 184; J. E. Vaux, <u>Church Folklore</u> (1894), pp. 300-3, 308; P. Rushton, 'A Note on the Survival of Popular Christian Magic', <u>Folklore</u>, xci (1980); Cressy, <u>Literacy</u>, 51.
131. Scot, <u>Discoverie of Witchcraft</u>, p. 25.
132. For the above, see Thomas, <u>Religion and Decline</u>, chs. 14-18; Macfarlane, <u>Witchcraft</u>; Larner, <u>Enemies of God</u>.
133. A. Dent, <u>The Plaine Mans Path-way to Heaven</u> (1601), p. 285; Thomas, <u>Religion and Decline</u>, p. 561. A French pamphlet of the sixteenth century was more specific, giving a figure of 7,405,920 (Delumeau, <u>Catholicism</u>, p. 253, n. 82).
134. Scot, <u>Discoverie of Witchcraft</u>, pp. 139, 382; R. Baxter, <u>The Certainty of the Worlds of Spirits</u> (1691), pp. 5-6.
135. Brand, <u>Popular Antiquities</u>, i, pp. 192-3, 331; Aubrey, <u>Three Prose Works</u>, pp. 143, 207; Hodgkinson, 'Extracts from Act Books', p. 52; Thomas, <u>Religion and Decline</u>, p. 286.
136. See Ewen, <u>Witchcraft and Demonianism</u>; MacDonald, <u>Mystical Bedlam</u>, p. 203.
137. Horsley, 'Further Reflections', pp. 85-6.
138. MacDonald, <u>Mystical Bedlam</u>, p. 134.
139. R. Bovet, <u>Pandaemonium</u> (1684) (Aldington, 1951 reprint), p. 124.

140. M. W. Latham, The Elizabethan Fairies (NY, 1930), pp.
     44ff., 57; [R. Kirk], The Secret Common-Wealth, ed. S.
     Sanderson (Cambridge, 1976), p. 37.
141. Aubrey, Three Prose Works, p. 203; Latham, Elizabethan
     Fairies, pp. 31-3.
142. Thomas, Religion and Decline, pp. 730ff.
143. Kirk, Secret Common-Wealth, *passim*; Latham, Elizabethan
     Fairies, pp. 104-16; Bovet, Pandaemonium, p. 124.
144. L. M. Smith, 'Aspects of Contemporary Ulster Fairy
     Traditions', in V. J. Newall (ed.), Folklore Studies in
     the Twentieth Century (Woodbridge, 1980), p. 402.
145. See H. McLeod, Religion and the People of Western Europe
     1789-1970 (Oxford, 1981), p. 125.
146. Dent, Plaine Mans Path-way, p. 27.
147. Collinson, Religion of Protestants, p. 202.
148. Laslett, World we have lost, p. 74.
149. Wrightson, English Society, p. 201.
150. Morrill, 'Church in England', pp. 104-7.
151. T. F. Thiselton-Dyer, Old English Social Life (1898),
     p. 134; Fletcher, County Community, p. 116.
152. See also the discussions in C. Ginzburg, The Cheese and
     the Worms (Baltimore, 1980), prefaces; T. Bennett,
     'Popular Culture: Theoretical and Pedagogic Strategies',
     Anglistica, xxiii, 2-3 (1980), pp. 48-50; A. J.
     Ainsworth, 'Religion in the Working Class Community, and
     the Evolution of Socialism in Late Nineteenth Century
     Lancashire', Histoire Sociale, x (1977), pp. 374-5;
     M. Aston, 'Popular religious movements in the Middle
     Ages', in G. Barraclough (ed.), The Christian World
     (1981), pp. 157-8; P. Burke, 'A Question of
     Acculturation?', in L. S. Olschki (ed.), Scienze,
     Credenze, Occulte, Livelli di Cultura (Florence, 1982).
153. N. Z. Davis, 'Some tasks and themes in the study of
     Popular Religion', in C. Trinkaus & H. A. Oberman (eds.),
     The Pursuit of Holiness in Late Medieval and Renaissance
     Religion (Leiden, 1974), p. 309.

Chapter Four

THE REFORM OF POPULAR CULTURE?   SEX AND MARRIAGE IN
EARLY MODERN ENGLAND

Martin Ingram

I

Peter Burke's seminal study, Popular Culture in
Early Modern Europe, begins by defining 'culture' as
'a system of shared meanings, attitudes and values,
and the symbolic forms ... in which they are
expressed and embodied'.(1) This notion of shared
meanings is valuable precisely because of its
inclusiveness, reminding us that culture should not
be narrowly conceived in terms of arts, crafts,
music, literature and dramatic performances, but of
the whole range of systems of ideas and patterned
behaviour which give meaning to the social life of
any human group. It should certainly include the
social organisation of human sexuality and repro-
duction, which have traditionally bulked large in
anthropological studies of 'other cultures'.
     Yet Burke himself ignores sex, marriage and
family life, save for glancing references when these
matters impinge on the festivities, songs and
stories which form the main focus of his study.
Robert Muchembled's Culture populaire et culture des
élites, by contrast, devotes considerable attention
to popular sexuality and marriage patterns,
integrating these topics into an analysis of
cultural shifts in early modern France which in
other respects has much in common with Burke's
thesis. (2) Central to both works is the contention
that from about 1500 to 1800 the world of popular
culture came under attack from elite groups (clergy,
nobility and some middle-class groups in town and
country) who gradually attenuated and transformed
many aspects of social life among the mass of the
people. This 'reform of popular culture' combined
attempts to suppress many popular activities and to
modify the behaviour of the common people,

withdrawal from and deprecation of popular
festivities, and the sponsoring of a new 'popular'
or 'mass' culture which embodied the ideologies of
the ruling elites.

Muchembled's analysis - much influenced by Jean
Delumeau and Michel Foucault(3) - portrays the movement as a process of 'acculturation' which involved
three elements. The first was the construction of
new mechanisms of power centreing on the image of the
absolutist king. The second was the 'submission of
souls', including closer ecclesiastical supervision
of social life, attempts to suppress what the
Counter-Reformation church regarded as
'superstitious' elements in popular culture, and
positive efforts to instil 'true' Christianity. The
third was a movement to establish firmer social and
personal control over the body of the individual.
All these elements, but especially the last, had
implications for popular attitudes to sexuality and
marriage practices. The new forms of power entailed
a reinforcement of paternal authority within the
family. The Counter-Reformation sought to weaken
kinship solidarities (to emphasise individual
responsibility for salvation) and to suppress
popular marriage rituals or *fiançailles*; while the
'constraint of the body' involved truly massive
changes in attitudes to sexuality.

Among the upper classes, Muchembled argues, the
two centuries after 1500 witnessed a major cultural
shift which produced a new code of civility in
sexual behaviour and family life. Privacy became
more highly valued, while modesty and even prudish-
ness replaced the Rabelaisian frankness of earlier
times. These changes in upper class circles
accentuated the cultural split between rich and
poor. The lower orders themselves experienced the
sexual revolution in negative terms. In the late
middle ages, according to Muchembled, asceticism had
been notably absent from the world of popular
culture, and attitudes to sexuality were only feebly
affected by Christian notions of sin. The
peasantry, both men and women alike, 'experienced no
shame in doing the work of the flesh' and were
'relatively free to use their bodies as they wished
and did not need constantly to restrain their sexual
and emotional impulses'. These attitudes were a
prime target for the reformers of popular culture,
and the ecclesiastical authorities working in
alliance with the secular government made determined
efforts to impose stricter standards of sexual
morality. The movement began earlier in the towns,

but in France as a whole the peak period of sexual
repression was from about 1600 to the early 1700s
when 'all the courts [both spiritual and secular]
became keen defenders of Christian morality', and
'each individual learnt that his body did not belong
entirely to himself.... He was persuaded that
sexuality was a social, rather than an individual
or erotic function.'(4)
    While Muchembled's study focuses explicitly on
France (especially the Artois region), the case it
argues plainly has wider European relevance and may
be fruitfully treated as an interpretative model to
be tested both by further exploration of the French
evidence and (with due allowance for peculiarities
of the situation in France) by studies of other
regions of western Europe. It is true that the
evidential basis for Muchembled's thesis, and in
particular those parts concerned with marriage and
morality, is in itself relatively weak. His
portrayal of late medieval attitudes to sexuality
rests largely on dubious literary materials, while
his case for a moral reform campaign in the
seventeenth century is supported only by a brief
survey of a very limited range of judicial
archives.(5) More basically, Muchembled's idea that
the campaign of moral discipline after about 1550
represented a fundamentally new departure - rather
than simply an intensification or even merely a
continuation of a process which had been going on
for centuries - is open to serious objection. So
also is the related assumption (shared by Delumeau
and others) that the pre-Reformation population of
Europe was Christianised in only the most super-
ficial sense.(6) Both questions raise even more
fundamental doubts about the applicability of the
idea of a 'reform of popular culture' to popular
marriage patterns and attitudes to extramarital
sexuality. Arguably, a more fruitful approach would
be to see changes in this area as part of an ongoing
dialogue, extending over centuries if not millennia,
between varieties of official and popular culture.
    Irrespective of such doubts, Muchembled's ideas
on changes in marriage and sexual attitudes in early
modern Europe are to some extent supported by John
Bossy's study of the impact of the Tridentine
reform movement; by the findings of some historians
working on patterns of criminal prosecutions in
various parts of Europe in this period; and by some
recent studies of family life and of the Reformation
in Germany and Switzerland.(7) It is therefore
worth asking how far the kinds of shifts in sexual

attitudes outlined by Muchembled were discernible in
early modern England; if they did occur, whether
their timing corresponded with the pattern postu-
lated for France; and how far they can be related
to a wider movement for the reform of popular
culture. Numerous recent studies bear on these
questions, and in the following pages some of their
findings will be reviewed alongside fresh evidence
from hitherto unpublished material. Of course, one
brief essay cannot deal adequately with all aspects
of popular attitudes to and official regulation of
sex, marriage and family life. This paper gives
some attention to husband/wife relationships and
related issues but concentrates mainly on attitudes
to some forms of illicit sexuality and on public
control of entry into marriage.

II

Lawrence Stone's The Family, Sex and Marriage
in England, 1500-1800 offers a valuable starting
point. Stone's major argument is that the three
centuries after 1500 witnessed a change from a
family type characterised by extensive kinship ties
and a low level of affection and individual autonomy
among its members to a more recognisably 'modern'
pattern in which love and self-determination were at
a premium. Associated with this evolution were
developments in civility, privacy and domesticity
similar to those which Muchembled (following
Philippe Ariès and Jean-Louis Flandrin)(8) postulates
for France. Even more closely linked with
Muchembled's thesis is Stone's subsidiary argument
that the period from the late sixteenth to the late
seventeenth century was dominated by a transitional
form, the 'restricted patriarchal nuclear family'.
Domestic relationships became somewhat warmer than
earlier as a result of the influence of Puritan
notions of conjugal love. But a far more striking
feature was the reinforcement of patriarchal
authority within the nuclear family paralleled by a
decline in wider kin influence. Both state and
church encouraged these developments. The Tudors
sought the erosion of kin and clientage networks
and of other 'corporate bodies' which might
challenge state power, and the 'little commonwealth'
of the family was fostered as the nursery of
obedience to the crown. The church (especially
Puritan elements within it) emphasised household
piety and the duty of the head of the family to
oversee the religious and moral lives of his

dependants. (9)

Stone probably exaggerates the strength of late medieval kinship structures even for the aristocracy and gentry - he admits that wider kin ties were of limited importance among the masses - and in that respect his analysis is misleading.(10) As regards the 'reinforcement of patriarchy' he tends to confuse ideals and reality. It is certainly true that Tudor and early Stuart official philosophies re-emphasised (though they did not originate) the ideal of a hierarchical structure of obedience within the family household. The authority of husbands over wives, parents over children, and householders over their living-in servants was seen as analogous to that of the prince over his subjects; both royal and patriarchal authority were conceived as mutually validating reflections of a divinely ordered hierarchy which stretched in a 'Great Chain of Being' from God to the lowest orders of creation.(11) There were in addition some legislative attempts to strengthen in practice the sinews of patriarchal authority - as will be seen, such ideas underlay efforts to change the law to enhance parental control over marriage. But it is highly doubtful whether such ideals and prescriptions were a true reflection of the nature of family life on a day-to-day basis, especially in the ranks below the gentry to which Stone devotes little attention. Keith Wrightson, one of the most influential of the critics of Stone's view of the family in the period 1580-1680, has suggested that, within the framework of a general acceptance of the patriarchal ideal, there was in practice great variety in the nature of affective and power relationships between husbands and wives, parents and children, with a bias towards companionate and caring relations.(12)

A variety of studies based on different kinds of evidence support this conclusion. The issue of relations between husbands and wives is approached tangentially in chapter 5: the popular ritual of 'riding skimmington' undoubtedly reflects the strength of the patriarchal ideal throughout the society, yet at the same time bears witness to the flexibility of husband/wife relationships in day-to-day living and to a recognition at some level of social psychology that women could never be dominated to the degree implied in the patriarchal schema. Direct evidence from diaries, letters and wills written by people of middling rank likewise suggests that Stone underestimates conjugal

affection and co-operation and exaggerates the
subjection of wives. Michael MacDonald's study of
the case histories of the mentally disturbed
patients of Richard Napier, an astrological
physician practising at Great Linford in
Buckinghamshire from 1598 to 1634, points in the
same direction. The general framework of the
marital relationships of the lower-class women who
consulted Napier can in some sense be described as
'patriarchal', and certainly some of them had been
ill-treated by their spouses; but MacDonald
emphasises that 'many women expected the tie between
their husbands and them to be a bond of love and not
merely of obligation', and that 'wives expected to
be treated fairly and affectionately'. (13)
      Relations between parents and children may be
approached via the question of matchmaking and the
factors which conditioned mate selection. By common
consent these issues are regarded as an important
index of the nature of family relationships.
According to Stone, before 1550 marriages were
normally arranged - at least at upper social levels
- 'by parents, kin and "friends", rather than the
bride and groom', and dynastic, financial and other
practical considerations largely dictated the
choice. In the era of the 'restricted patriarchal
nuclear family' parental influence still dominated
matchmaking and romantic love was regarded with
disapproval. But, under the influence of Puritan
ideas which stressed the importance of love within
marriage, children were gradually allowed a limited
right of veto in cases where the proposed partner
was utterly repugnant. It was not until the late
seventeenth and the eighteenth centuries that unions
based on personal selection rather than parental
dictation became at all common among the upper
classes. Stone admits that at lower social levels
(especially among the propertyless) there had always
been greater freedom of choice, for the essentially
negative reason that parents could not hope to
derive benefit from their children's marriages. But
even at this level, love and personal attraction
played little part in matrimonial calculations - it
was far more important to find a wife or husband who
could work. (14)
      Except perhaps with regard to the very highest
levels of society, Stone exaggerates the importance
of parental influence in marriage formation in
sixteenth- and seventeenth-century England. It was
evidently common at all social levels from the
lesser gentry downwards for men to take the

initiative in finding a wife. For women the
situation was more variable. Females (especially
younger ones) of more substantial families were
often very dependent on parental guidance and
suggestion - though even so their preferences were
usually consulted and they were rarely subjected to
blatantly 'arranged' marriages. But some women of
middling rank, and the majority of females of the
poorer classes, evidently enjoyed a good deal of
freedom to seek out a potential mate. Apart from
anything else, certain demographic features of the
society encouraged young people to take an active
role. By the time children arrived at the normal
age for marriage - on average the mid to late
twenties - one or both parents might well be dead,
while the practice at most social levels of sending
adolescent children out into service or apprenticeship meant that young people who had not been
orphaned were often living remote from direct
parental or other family influence when they began
to think of marriage.(15)

Admittedly it was conventional wisdom at all
social levels that children should seek the consent
or 'goodwill' of their parents (if they were alive)
before committing themselves to marriage; in other
words, that parents should at least be given the
opportunity of vetoing or persuading children out of
unions which they regarded as unsuitable. Among the
propertyless this was little more than a formality.
It mattered more in families of reasonable substance
- including such middling groups as yeomen and some
husbandmen and craftsmen - especially if the young
couple were expecting to inherit or receive at
marriage a significant amount of property. Records
of matrimonial suits in the church courts show that
some parents did veto marriages proposed by their
children, backing up their prohibitions with moral,
economic and even physical sanctions. Such records
also reveal that children of all social ranks were
sometimes prepared to defy their families, braving
the consequences or hoping that parents would change
their minds. However, both court records and other
sources suggest that in cases of conflict parents
usually won: Napier's case books, according to
MacDonald, indicate that 'habits of deference were
so strong that anguished children seldom challenged
their parents directly' when they were forbidden to
marry as they wished. (16) To this extent the
strength of parental authority and influence should
not be minimised. But the vital point to emphasise
is that conflict was abnormal and most marriages

were agreed to the reasonable satisfaction of all concerned. The dominant social ideal was not parental dictation, as Stone implies, but the multilateral consent of all the interests involved; and the comment of a seventeenth-century observer, Matthew Griffith, that this flexible system worked well is probably correct: 'on all parts there is commonly a willing consent and promise of marriage; and that most an end [i.e. for the most part] with consent of parents, and parties, some few *Individium Vagum's* only excepted'.(17)

Stone is also mistaken in supposing that love and personal attraction played little or no part in matrimonial calculations. It is certainly true that at all social levels practical considerations - money and land in the middling to upper ranks, the ability to provide somewhere to live and some kind of income among the poorer echelons - were extremely important in choosing a marriage partner. But this did not rule out love. The ideal was a union which combined both practical viability and strong affection. Even when parents played a large part in bringing a couple together they commonly took care to make sure, before the match was finally clinched, that the young people could 'find in their heart to love' each other. The sort of replies they received indicate that the measure of feeling involved in such cases was by no means minimal: in a Wiltshire case in 1588, involving families of middle rank, the couple were able to assure their parents that 'they did well fancy one the other'. But love was often an even more powerful force than this. Records of matrimonial causes reveal suitors 'inflamed with love'; some, when their feelings were not recipro- cated, were said to have sickened and nearly died of love.(18) Napier's case books again provide supporting evidence. In 1615 the physician recorded that a certain Jane Travell 'sayeth that nobody can tell the sorrow that she endureth.... Sometimes will sigh three hours until as sad as can [be].... Should have married one, and they were at words as if she would not have him. And then bidding him to marry elsewhere she fell into this passion.' As MacDonald comments, such evidence makes 'nonsense of historians' confident assertions that romantic love was rare in seventeenth-century England or that it was unimportant in choosing marital partners'. Then, as now, love could be seen as a destructive force if it totally overrode prudential considerations. But all other things being equal, it was regarded as a positive sentiment which

parents and other relatives at most social levels
were perfectly happy to accommodate.(19)
     The picture which emerges is more complex than
Stone allows. While the patriarchal ideal certainly
influenced the nature of marriage in this period, it
was much modified in practice by the strength of
personal choice in marriage formation and by
flexibility and reciprocity in husband/wife
relationships within marriage. Among the mass of
the population this flexible pattern appears to have
persisted unchanged at least through the later
sixteenth and the seventeenth centuries and had
probably existed since the late middle ages. Alan
Macfarlane argues that literary evidence, such as
the Paston letters, reveals features of family life
in the fifteenth century very similar to the pattern
found under Elizabeth and the Stuart kings.
Similarly, Kathleen Davies' study of advice on
marriage found in sermons and conduct books from the
late fourteenth to the seventeenth centuries firmly
stresses continuity, at least in the bourgeois
circles to which these works were largely addressed.
She concludes that 'the godly Puritan and the pious
pre-Reformation bourgeois may well have lived very
similar lives, at least if they practised what
their clergy preached'. At present little is known
of marriage among the poorer classes in the late
middle ages; but there is no positive evidence of
any substantial shift over the period 1400-1700.(20)

III

     Another element in Stone's thesis has strong
affinities with Muchembled's arguments. Stone
suggests that in the late sixteenth and early
seventeenth centuries there was a marked increase in
public control over sexual morality and family life.
The church successfully inculcated an increased
awareness of Christian principles and a consciousness of sin, and with the active assistance of
parish officials waged a vigorous campaign to
enforce tighter standards of Christian morality.
The chief agents of discipline were the
archidiaconal and episcopal courts, whose officials
regularly conducted visitations - usually every six
months but sometimes oftener - during which the
churchwardens and sidesmen of each parish were
required on oath to 'detect' or 'present' the
delinquencies of their neighbours. Offenders
convicted of serious sins were characteristically
ordered to perform public penance: dressed in a

white sheet and carrying a white rod, they were
required humbly to confess their sin before the
whole congregation assembled in church. By these
means the ecclesiastical authorities sought to
eliminate consensual unions unblessed by a church
wedding ceremony and to punish fornication and other
forms of sexual immorality. In the later sixteenth
and seventeenth centuries, the secular courts also
increasingly involved themselves in matters of
morality, the justices of the peace playing a
particularly important role in the investigation and
punishment of bastard-bearing.(21)

As will be seen, there is undoubtedly strong
evidence for a repressive trend in the late
sixteenth and seventeenth centuries. Much more
questionable is Stone's assumption that such
repression constituted a major new departure, a
transformation of sexual mores occurring in parallel
with the supposed changes in family life. Much like
Muchembled, Stone suggests that before the sixteenth
century the church's views on marriage and chastity
had little impact on the mass of the population.
Hence 'the lower classes were allowed a wide degree
of freedom in their sexual arrangements'. Little
evidence is cited in support of this contention, and
what there is relates mainly to the continent.(22)
But Stone's picture of medieval amoralism is
implicitly accepted by G. R. Quaife, with the twist
that the latter argues strongly that this situation
persisted largely unchanged well beyond the
Reformation. In early seventeenth-century Somerset,
according to Quaife, only the wives and daughters of
yeomen and gentry - a small minority of the
population - adhered at all strictly to Christian
sexual morality. Their menfolk actively helped to
enforce this conformity among their own family
members, but themselves felt free to depart from the
Christian moral code. No such double standard
prevailed among the mass of the population for the
simple reason that for them, men and women alike,
'sex was not a moral issue'. Fornication and
adultery aroused disapproval only when they
disrupted the peace of the community or had serious
economic implications, most notably in the case of
bastards born of poor parents.(23)

Quaife's view of the seventeenth century will
be criticised later. The point to emphasise here is
that the idea of an amoral middle ages is grossly
exaggerated. Recent work on the forms and substance
of religion in late medieval England suggests that
recognisably Christian beliefs and values had

penetrated much more deeply than some early
modernists have supposed. Charles Phythian-Adams's
studies of fifteenth-century Coventry, for example,
indicate that religion was deeply embedded in the
whole life of the community. It was the same in
country areas: Dorothy Owen's study of Lincolnshire
leaves no doubt of the importance of the *rites de
passage*, the mass, religious processions, and
devotional guilds and fraternities in the lives of
fourteenth- and fifteenth-century lay people.(24)

It is equally plain that the exercise of
discipline over the morals of the population, by
both ecclesiastical and secular authorities and by
the community at large, was by no means an
innovation of the sixteenth century. In most areas
of England in the late middle ages an elaborate
system of church courts was already in operation,
and it would seem that it was precisely their
efficiency and ability to penetrate even remote
parishes which impressed contemporaries.(25) Among
their most important functions was the supervision
of sexual morality. In the 1340s the court of the
bishop of Rochester was regularly citing couples who
were living on consensual unions, ordering them not
only to solemnise their marriage but also to undergo
a whipping. In the diocese of Canterbury, in the
fifteenth century, a 'great weight of cases of
immorality' regularly occupied the courts. Thus in
1474 the archbishop's consistory court alone (there
was also a concurrent archidiaconal court in
operation) brought over one hundred charges of
illicit sexuality.(26) Activity on this scale must
have depended on a large measure of popular support
in the detection of offenders; and this in turn
implies *prima facie* a considerable degree of
acceptance, at least at the level of ideals, of
Christian morality. Secular courts, especially in
the towns, also played a role in moral discipline in
the late middle ages. Urban authorities regularly
took action against notorious cases of prostitution,
bawdry (pimping), and - to some extent - other
sexual offences. Culprits could be punished with
banishment, whipping, branding, or shame penalties
whose efficacy must have depended on popular
approval.(27) Commenting on the ethical context of
such activities in Coventry, Phythian-Adams has
remarked: 'If the tradition of Puritan respectability had a long pre-history, it was because the
medieval urban elite jealously guarded the dignity
or "worship" of the group ... by identifying itself
with the contemporary religious order'. An ordinance

of 1492 laid down that citizens who persisted in the sins of adultery or fornication were 'never to proceed nor to be called to further worship, nor to be advanced but utterly to be estranged from all good company'. (28)

IV

Public discipline over sexual morality within a Christian frame of reference was thus well established by the fifteenth century. However, some breakdown of moral discipline may have occurred in the mid-Tudor years. Certainly the church courts were badly shaken by the religious and juridical changes of the period 1530-60 and their effectiveness temporarily declined; and Peter Clark has argued, without actually proving, that marriage as an institution was under severe threat in mid-sixteenth-century Kent. (29) Efforts to strengthen the public control of morals in the later part of Elizabeth's reign may thus have represented, in the first instance, an attempt to make up lost ground. But the movement gathered momentum in the century after about 1580, consolidating earlier developments and in some respects intensifying and extending public moral discipline. The overall result was to alter significantly (though not dramatically) popular marriage practices and attitudes towards extra-marital sexual activity. The context of these changes was a combination of demographic and economic shifts, especially the rapid increase in population in the period from about 1570 to 1640 and an associated growth in the numbers of the poor; religious developments, particularly the spread of committed Protestant ideas among the middling and upper classes; cultural changes, especially socially differential shifts in literacy levels; and some increase in the regulatory activities of the central government and of the church. (30) As will be seen, however, the relative importance of these factors remains in doubt, and in any case probably varied in different regions and even between individual parishes within particular localities.

One change was tighter public control over entry into marriage. From the twelfth century, in England as in Europe, the law of the church prescribed that a couple could contract a binding union by means of a simple pledge in words of the present tense. The marriage did not depend on the consent of parents or other interests, on the presence of witnesses, or on a church ceremony. To be sure, an unsolemnised or unwitnessed marriage was regarded as irregular and the couple were liable to punishment, especially if they cohabited; while the church regarded the consent of parents as desirable so long as parental influence did not amount to the coercion of the couple. Nevertheless, a simple, unpublicised contract could make a marriage.(31)

Extra-ecclesiastical marriage contracts, called 'spousals' or 'handfastings', have for long attracted the attention of folklorists and historians, and provide one of the most colourful veins of information on popular marriage practices in early modern England. The following example (which further illustrates the importance of love and self-determination in mate selection in this period) is fairly typical. One holiday afternoon around 1 July 1576, Andrew Meten of Rampton (Cambridgeshire) and Agnes Cropwell of Cottenham discussed marriage. 'Can you find in your heart to love me and to have ... me to your husband?' Andrew asked Agnes. 'Andrew', she replied, 'You know I love you well and I can find in my heart to take you to my husband, if my mother's good will can ... be gotten'. But, according to Andrew's story, they did not wait to get this parental consent, and before they parted that evening Agnes committed herself:

> 'Andrew, before these folks here, I give you
> my faith and my troth.' And then the said
> Andrew taking her again by the hand said
> thus, viz. 'I Andrew Meten take thee Agnes
> Cropwell to my wedded wife till death us
> depart, and thereto I give thee my faith
> and my troth.' And they holding hands
> still together, the said Agnes Cropwell
> said to him thus, viz. 'And I Agnes
> Cropwell take thee Andrew Meten to my
> wedded husband, and thereto I give thee
> my faith and my troth till death us
> depart, and I promise thee I will never
> have other husband till death depart us.'

In 'sign and token' of the contract they kissed, and Andrew gave her four silver sixpences - which she promptly put in her purse.(32)

But how common were such contracts and how were they regarded? Were they seen as a preliminary to marriage in church or as a substitute for it? Was the church's view that an unsolemnised contract was binding and irrevocable fully accepted? How easy

was it to get an unsolemnised contract recognised in
the eyes either of the ecclesiastical authorities or
of relatives, neighbours and the community at large?
The case of Agnes Cropwell illustrates some of the
difficulties. She denied the contract with Andrew
Meten, claimed a prior contract with another man,
and by the time Andrew's case came to court had
secured a church wedding with his rival and had
started living with him.(33)

Mindful of the possibilities of confusion and
deceit, the church had campaigned for centuries to
ensure that matrimonial intentions were properly
publicised, preferably by the calling of banns;
that contracts should be witnessed; and, above all,
that marriages should be solemnised in church. The
church's task was aided by the common lawyers who,
faced with problems which depended on the existence
or otherwise of a marriage but themselves unable to
determine the validity of unions, used the church
ceremony as a touchstone for presuming whether or
not a marriage had taken place. In particular, it
was established that no woman could claim dower
unless she had been endowed at the church door.
For the property-owning classes - including some
middling groups - this was a powerful incentive in
favour of church marriage. In any case, the
certainty of a church wedding was of potential
benefit to everyone, whether rich or poor.(34)
Ralph Houlbrooke believes that already by the early
sixteenth century the vast majority of couples
(whether or not they contracted 'spousals') thought
it necessary to solemnise their union.(35) The same
is unquestionably true for the late sixteenth and
early seventeenth centuries. By that time, when
people talked of 'marriage' they normally meant
marriage in church; and a church wedding was
generally regarded as the only satisfactory
guarantee of a socially and legally acceptable union.

In Catholic Europe the law was rationalised by
a decree of the Council of Trent (1563) which
declared that marriages not performed in public
before a parish priest were henceforth invalid. In
England, despite attempts at reform around the mid
sixteenth century, the old law continued to apply
till 1753.(36) But judicial practice in the church
courts tended increasingly to strengthen the
principle that solemnisation was what mattered.
Even in the sixteenth century, judges were unwilling
to pronounce in favour of disputed contracts except
when both parties confessed the existence of the
union or, in cases where one party denied the

marriage, on the basis of extremely strong evidence. Most plaintiffs claiming marriage contracts were unsuccessful in securing a confirmatory sentence. In the seventeenth century, sentences in favour of disputed contracts became even harder to obtain, in some areas virtually impossible.

Given these social and legal circumstances, extra-ecclesiastical marriage contracts inevitably declined. Some indication of the diminishing importance of spousals in social life is provided by trends in the numbers of contract suits which came before the church courts. Such cases appear to have been fairly common in the fourteenth century but their numbers had fallen considerably by the early sixteenth. Evidence from a number of different dioceses reveals a further decline in the period 1560-1640, with only a trickle of cases occurring in the early seventeenth century and even fewer after the Restoration. Moreover, close examination of evidence other than contract suit papers in the diocese of Salisbury in the early seventeenth century reveals that references to 'contracts' gradually gave way to references to what were presumably legally formless, non-binding <u>promises</u> of marriage. A similar change apparently took place in the diocese of York. By 1686 the writer of the preface to Henry Swinburne's sixteenth-century work on the law of spousals was constrained to admit that the custom was 'now in great measure worn out of use'.(37) It is true that there are signs of a resurgence of consensual unions among the poorer ranks towards the end of the seventeenth century.(38) But at any rate around 1640 the need for marriage in church seems to have been very widely accepted at all social levels except, perhaps, among the vagrant poor; and it may be fairly said that the wedding service of the Church of England had been absorbed as part of popular culture.

In the late sixteenth century, when the centuries-long campaign to secure popular recognition of the need for solemnisation seemed all but won, the church turned its energies to another problem: clandestine marriage ceremonies. These were marriages that were properly solemnised in the sense that they were conducted by ministers, usually in church but sometimes in private houses, but which sought to evade the safeguards of publicity. In other words they were marriages performed without banns or licence, at irregular hours or in some parish remote from the couple's place of residence. Ecclesiastical law had for

centuries proscribed clandestine ceremonies - though
such marriages were regarded as valid - but in
Elizabeth's reign the church was prodded into
measures to make the regulations more effective.
Part of the pressure came from lay interests in
parliament, reflecting concern among the propertied
classes that the ease of clandestine marriage
undermined parental influence and encouraged
fraudulent elopement. More generally there were
fears that irregular marriages facilitated bigamy
and other forms of immorality; and, as will be
seen, there was probably also concern about the
marriages of very poor people.

The power of this movement for reform was
reduced by disagreements among the elites: the
church hierarchy proved unwilling to countenance any
change which unduly restricted freedom to marry. It
was, however, ready to tighten up the safeguards
against clandestine ceremonies in the interests of
good order and public morality. Stricter regulations were embodied in the canons of 1604, while
the Bigamy Act passed in Parliament in the same year
was probably related to the same issue. In
particular, the regulations governing the issue of
marriage liences were strengthened, with safeguards
to ensure that couples had parental consent and that
no impediments (such as consanguinity, precontract,
or a former spouse still living) existed to bar the
marriage. Clandestine marriages continued to
occur, and there was no change in the law which
regarded such unions (as long as they were not
actually incestuous or bigamous) as valid and
indissoluble. But individuals who resorted to
clandestine ceremonies, and the ministers who
conducted them, were increasingly harassed by the
courts. The information at present available
suggests that in the early seventeenth century a
reasonable balance was achieved. The problem of
clandestine marriage was contained, but the possibility of obtaining a secret ceremony provided a
useful safety valve whereby determined couples could
evade unreasonable family or other pressures. It
was only in the late seventeenth and early
eighteenth centuries, especially with the growth of
a large-scale clandestine marriage business in the
Fleet Prison and elsewhere, that a major social
problem developed.(39)

Emphasis on church marriage and tighter
regulations against clandestine ceremonies may have
done something, within the limits of parental
control outlined earlier, to bolster family

influence in marriage formation. But probably a
more important effect among the poorer ranks was an
increase in <u>parochial</u> rather than parental control.
In this period ministers and parishioners sometimes
intervened to stop couples getting married, either
by refusing publication of the banns or by
preventing a ceremony from taking place. The normal
motive was economic prudence: the more substantial
parishioners regarded the couple as too poor to
marry and feared they would burden the poor rates.
A case from North Bradley (Wiltshire) in 1618 at
first sight suggests another motive. A certain
Richard Guy claimed that the minister had refused to
read the banns because 'the parishioners were
unwilling that he ... being very old, vizt. of the
age of three score and thirteen years and upwards,
should marry with his now wife being but young'.
While it is probably true that January-and-May
marriages were generally regarded with disfavour,
another reference to this case reveals that, as
usual, economic competence was basically at issue.
Guy was not only old but also very poor, and the
parishioners naturally feared that he would soon die
and leave his widow on the parish.(40)
　　Concern over poor marriages was no new thing,
and was one of the reasons why contemporaries at all
social levels were suspicious of the marriages of
very young people before they had had time to
establish themselves economically. Apprenticeship
regulations clearly functioned to limit (amongst
other things) premature marriage: ordinances concerning the Wiltshire clothing industry in 1603
explicitly stated that 'no apprentice shall come
forth of his apprenticeship before he be four and
twenty years of age, to avoid young marriages and
the increase of poor people'.(41) But direct intervention to bar the union of people who, whatever
their age, simply happened to be poor seems to have
been an innovation associated with the growing
problem of poverty. The cases which have so far
come to light date from the late sixteenth and more
especially the seventeenth centuries. After about
1650 they were sufficiently common to excite
literary comment. Actively discouraging the poor
from marriage may eventually have become an
important mechanism whereby the more tightly controlled parishes of seventeenth-century England
imposed a check on population growth and kept their
poor relief accounts in balance.(42)
　　Preventing the poor from marrying was
undoubtedly against the law of the church, directly

contravening the principle that matrimony should be available to all who lacked the gift of continence. But the authorities apparently did little to stop it. Their complaisance and the heartless attitude of wealthier parishioners may be condemned, but they are readily understandable since without parochial support the marriages of the very poor were often extremely vulnerable. A considerable proportion of cases of unlawful separation reported to the church courts concerned couples who had been driven apart by sheer economic necessity. Censuses of the poor indicate further that in some towns abandoned wives formed a major social problem, and the phenomenon was not unknown even in small villages. Contem-. poraries of the 'better sort' took the hard-nosed view that prevention was better than cure. (43)

In these various ways public control over entry into marriage was strengthened in the sixteenth and seventeenth centuries, paving the way for Lord Hardwicke's Marriage Act of 1753 which finally did away with the old law of spousals and invalidated marriages not performed in church according to a strict set of regulations. But the degree of innovation involved should not be exaggerated. Apart from the unofficial (and technically illegal) practice of restricting the very poor from marriage, these developments represented not a dramatic new departure but the culmination of a process which had been in train for centuries. Moreover, it would be misleading to see these changes simply in terms of the imposition of elite ideas on the masses. The decline of spousals, for example, was to a large extent a spontaneous development based on a recognition at all levels of society that the certainty of marriage in church had obvious bene- fits. Only in a very qualified sense do these changes in marriage practices accord with Muchembled's model of social change.

V

Changes in the regulation of marriage entry were complemented by a somewhat more rigorous church policy towards prenuptial fornication and bridal pregnancy and by associated adjustments in popular attitudes. The pioneer researches of P. E. H. Hair demonstrated that in late sixteenth- and seventeenth-century England roughly a fifth of all brides were pregnant when they got married in church. (44) Peter Laslett related this to the custom of spousals, but it is plain that by no means

all prenuptial fornicators could appeal to the
existence of a binding contract. Many couples
proceeded to have sex after merely promising each
other marriage, while in some cases the decision to
marry was precipitated by the fact of pregnancy.
The most important factor leading to bridal pregnancy was simply that young people in the middling
to lower ranks of society were customarily allowed
a good deal of freedom in their courtship behaviour.
Couples were often described as being 'familiar
together and loving one towards the other', kissing
and cuddling, often in private, and sometimes
spending whole nights in one another's company with
little or no supervision.

This did not necessarily mean, however, that
prenuptial sex was regarded as wholly licit.
Laslett cites an interesting case from
Leicestershire which suggests that popular custom in
that area did explicitly sanction intercourse after
a formal contract. But the allegation of established custom in this case is unusual and, since it
occurred in the plaintiff's statement, must be
viewed with caution: prosecution documents in
lawsuits of all kinds often claimed the existence of
'customs' which were vehemently denied by the
defence. Study of the background of a large number
of marriage contract suits and of church court
prosecutions for prenuptial fornication suggests
that attitudes to sex before marriage were
ambivalent. Everyone knew that not only formally
espoused people but also courting couples often had
sexual relations before marriage in church, but few
were prepared to say unequivocally that this was the
right and proper thing to do. If things went wrong,
and the marriage either did not take place or was
postponed till the bride had a 'great belly', the
couple were liable to be upbraided or mocked by
their neighbours. But otherwise little shame seems
to have attached to bridal pregnancy or prenuptial
incontinence. Through the sixteenth and seventeenth
centuries the issue was rarely the subject of
defamation suits. (45)

The strict view of the church had long been that
a properly solemnised marriage ceremony alone made
sexual intercourse fully licit. Medieval moralists
and legal commentators forbade, or at least strongly
discouraged, sexual relations between contract and
solemnisation; sixteenth- and seventeenth-century
moralists firmly reproved couples who took 'liberty
after a contract to know their spouse'. 'An
unwarrantable and dishonest practice', thought

William Gouge.(46) Yet up to the mid sixteenth
century, the prosecution of antenuptial fornication
in the church courts seems to have been fitful.
Houlbrooke found that in Winchester diocese in the
1520s the courts took a rigorous view and often
punished prenuptial fornication; yet in the diocese
of Norwich in the 1560s couples detected of
incontinence were often dismissed without punishment
if they got married. Such differences, it would
seem, depended on arbitrary factors like the
attitudes of individual judges and the heaviness of
a court's workload at a given time.(47) A development from the late sixteenth century onwards was a
more consistent concern with bridal pregnancy,
though the exact timing and intensity of this
movement did vary somewhat in different areas.   In
the diocese of Ely, antenuptial fornication was
already a staple of court business in the 1580s.   In
the archdeaconry of Chichester, in contrast, such
cases never became very numerous: there were only
seven presentments for this offence in 1622, the
same number as in 1587.(48) But by far the most
common pattern, found in the diocese of York and in
many areas of southern England, was a gradual
build-up of cases in the closing years of the
sixteenth century, accelerating in the early seventeenth till quite substantial totals were reached.
Thus in the archdeaconry of Salisbury about fifty
cases came before the courts in 1627, compared with
only two in 1573. (49)

Admittedly there remained limits to the church
courts' rigour. Although churchmen proscribed
bridal pregnancy, they could recognise a difference
between this offence, the understandable if
regrettable result of strong passions between loving
couples, and bare-faced fornication or adultery.
Hence the informal comments of clergy and church
court officials sometimes reflect a certain degree
of tolerance. William Gager, official of the
consistory court of Ely, was willing in 1614 to show
favour to a man who had been 'over-bold with his
wife ... a little before marriage'; while in 1633
the minister of Chardstock (Dorset) wrote to the
court of the dean of Salisbury on behalf of a man
who fully intended marriage but had, as this cleric
humorously put it, 'begun at the wrong end, and ...
acted the last part of the scene first'.(50) Even in
official court proceedings allowances were made to
the extent that culprits were normally treated more
leniently than bastard-bearers or adulterers. In
Salisbury diocese, for example, offenders were

usually let off with a mild form of penance, either
a simple confession before the minister and churchwardens or, at most, confession before the
congregation without the ignominy of wearing a white
sheet. (51) But within these limits the increase in
prosecutions for prenuptial fornication can be seen
as a repressive development whereby the church tried
to impose more rigorous standards of personal
conduct on the mass of the population.

On the whole the authorities' success was
limited. Detailed analysis reveals that, even in
dioceses where prosecutions had become relatively
numerous by the early seventeenth century, many
parishes still only reported a minority of offenders
to the church courts. A culprit before the archdeacon of Salisbury's court in 1637 who remarked
that the offence 'was but a small matter to be
called up to the court for' was expressing an
opinion which undoubtedly was and remained
widespread in many parts of England.(52) But in some
localities churchwardens were much more co-operative
in detecting culprits; and this suggests that,
within the broad framework of tolerance outlined
earlier, there was among at least some social groups
in certain areas a perceptible hardening of
attitudes towards prenuptial incontinence. Demographic studies also indicate some shift in
attitudes and behaviour. Whereas Hair found no real
change in the incidence of bridal pregnancy in
England as a whole before 1700, more detailed
studies do show significant falls in some parishes
in the seventeenth century. (53) What areas and what
social groups were affected? More research is
needed on this issue, but some of the available
findings are suggestive. In Wiltshire in the early
seventeenth century, prosecutions for prenuptial
fornication were most intense in the clothmaking
areas. These parishes were particularly affected by
worsening economic conditions and the problem of
poverty, and it seems likely that a stricter view of
bridal pregnancy was bound up with harsher attitudes
to bastardy (an obvious threat to the poor rates)
and with tighter control over the marriages of the
poor. Detailed parish studies in Wiltshire and
elsewhere suggest that falling rates of bridal
pregnancy to a large extent reflected changes in the
behaviour of the middling to wealthier sections of
parish society, who inevitably bore the main burden
of administering and funding poor relief. In the
parish of Terling (Essex), for example, Wrightson
and David Levine have found that in the course of

the early seventeenth century bridal pregnancy
became increasingly confined to poorer couples.
There was a similar change in the parish of Keevil
in Wiltshire. By the 1620s bridal pregnancy had
declined to the unusually low figure of 10 per cent,
and the culprits were mainly poor cottagers and
undertenants. In villages like this the church's
increasing rigour towards antenuptial fornication
clearly struck a responsive chord.(54)

VI

How strict were official and popular attitudes
to other forms of illicit sexuality, and how far did
they change in the course of the sixteenth and
seventeenth centuries? It is impossible in this
short space to discuss the whole range of sexual
offences. The main target of prosecutions in both
the ecclesiastical and secular courts were cases of
sex with unmarried women, especially when they led to
the birth of bastard children; and it is to such
cases that the discussion here is mostly confined.
It is worth stressing at the outset, however, that
the general context was one in which sexual probity
(apart from bridal pregnancy) was a major touchstone
of respectability, and that it would be quite wrong
to imagine that adultery, fornication and other
forms of sexual immorality were rife or generally
condoned. One indication of this, the existence of
popular customs to deride blatant immorality, is
discussed in chapter 5. Another is the popularity
of lawsuits for redress against slanders of a
sexual nature. Such suits appear to have become
increasingly numerous in the sixteenth century and
to have remained popular until well after 1700.
They were resorted to by both men and women, but
especially the latter; and involved a range of
slanders from such generalities as 'whore',
'whoremaster' and 'cuckold' (the commonest forms of
sexual defamation) to highly circumstantial
accusations of sexual misconduct. The specific
background to such suits often turns out to be
complex and they cannot be taken simply as an index
of sexual attitudes. But it is plain that the
general background was one in which sexual 'credit'
or 'honesty' - the lower class equivalents of gentry
notions of honour - really mattered, especially to
married people of middling rank who formed the
majority of litigants. As one Yorkshire woman
commented in 1696 when she heard another woman
defamed: 'they might as well take her life as her

good name from her'.(55)

Specific accusations of bearing a bastard were relatively rare in these defamation suits. One reason for this was simply that the offence was so clear-cut: a fact so obvious that it could rarely be denied. The visibility of bastardy means that it has left abundant traces in the records and has been much studied by historians. It is therefore possible to speak of the circumstances surrounding bastardy with more confidence than in the case of most sexual offences.

In terms of the behaviour of the women concerned, there was no clear-cut dividing line between bridal pregnancy and illegitimacy. Some women who gave birth to bastards had clearly intended marriage, only to be frustrated by circumstance or betrayed by the man. Denise Hewitt of Chichester, for example, plausibly claimed in 1604 that 'William Wood of Westminster did beget her with child upon promise to her first made that he would marry with her, and that they did intend to have been married ere this time had not the sickness [plague] in the city hindered them.'(56) More generally, it is striking that the mothers of bastards were of much the same age as the bulk of women when the latter bore their first child in wedlock; while a high proportion of women brought in question for bastard-bearing claimed that the men had promised them marriage. Although some of these claims were no doubt disingenuous or irresponsibly naive - like that of a Wiltshire labourer's daughter in 1629 who contended that the holiday attentions of one of the most substantial bachelors in the parish were equivalent to an offer of marriage - it does seem likely that many bastard-bearers differed from pregnant brides only in that they had enjoyed worse luck.(57)

This was not true of all, however. A sizeable proportion of bastard-bearers - up to 30 per cent in some samples - could not reasonably have hoped for marriage for the simple reason that their sexual partner already had a wife. Some of these were tragic cases where defenceless servant girls had been ruthlessly seduced by their masters, sometimes after considerable harassment or even the use of force. But there were some, too, who apparently played a willing role. Catherine Jones of Keevil, for example, a servant who accused a married man of fathering her child in 1620, was said to have drunk to 'all the merry conceits' which had passed between

them. (58) A small minority of unmarried mothers
were 'repeaters', often closely related to other
bastard-bearers, fathers of illegitimates or actual
bastards, who produced more than one illegitimate
child. Some of them clearly served as village
whores. Elizabeth Long or Longynough, the daughter
of a poor tiler of Wylye (Wiltshire) who was himself
in trouble for sexual immorality, bore three
illegitimate children between 1611 and 1620 (with
fathers unknown in two cases); though she did claim
to have married the father of her fourth child when
she became pregnant again in 1626. (59) Whether they
were 'innocent maidens' cruelly seduced, or 'loose
women' of wide experience, the mothers of bastards
tended on the whole to be poor; and the phenomenon
may well reflect the difficulties which indigent
spinsters found in securing a marriage partner. The
males involved were drawn from a wider social
spectrum; although, as will be seen, this pattern
changed somewhat over the late sixteenth and early
seventeenth centuries. (60)
     Popular attitudes to bastardy and to forni-
cation unrepaired by speedy marriage were complex.
Views differed to some extent at different social
levels, but also between people of the same rank;
and individual attitudes were sometimes downright
ambivalent. To a degree a double standard operated,
among the masses as among the upper ranks of lay
society, and women were more likely to be censured
than men. (61) A further complication was that
private, informal attitudes (to bastardy in one's
own family, for example) undoubtedly differed to
some extent from 'public' attitudes - to other
people's bastards and the 'bastardy problem' in
general. Private attitudes were on the whole more
tolerant, or at least more humane, than public
attitudes; and they probably changed less over the
period.
     Private attitudes may be illustrated by family
reactions to bastardy. In some cases parents or
other relatives were sufficiently scandalised to
turn the woman out; but it is clear that many,
probably the majority, did not take so harsh a line.
It is not certain that there was any great
difference in this respect at different social
levels; though wealthier families were more likely
to take steps to conceal the pregnancy from their
neighbours. The degree of humiliation experienced
by the woman herself in giving birth to a bastard
doubtless varied from individual to individual, but
it does seem to have been quite powerfully

influenced by social status and also by the circumstances of the case. It would appear that hitherto
respectable widows, women made pregnant by married
men, and women from substantial and well-respected
families tended to feel shame most acutely. Elinor
Bugden, for example, a widow of some means, told in
1617 how 'finding herself ... to be with child,
intending to hide her folly and shame, she withdrew
herself from her dwelling house'. Lower down the
social scale such matters could be passed off a
little more lightly, and some women could see a
bastard child as a mere 'mishap' - especially if they
had had reasonable hopes of marrying the father. (62)
Producing an illegitimate child did not, in any
case, necessarily blight a woman's marriage chances
for life. Detailed parish studies reveal cases
where unmarried mothers, including some from
reasonably substantial families, were subsequently
able to get married to other men. There are
indications, however, that in some of these
instances they had to wait unusually long for
marriage or to make do with less satisfactory
partners than they might otherwise have expected. (63)
Mutatis mutandis, many of the foregoing remarks are
also applicable to men, with the proviso that the
double standard generally meant that males were more
sympathetically treated, while in any case men were
often given the benefit of the doubt simply because
paternity was difficult to prove conclusively.

Public attitudes to bastardy were stricter and
more straightforward. The church had, of course,
always condemned fornication and bastard-bearing,
and sixteenth- and seventeenth-century moralists
were really only continuing a long tradition in
their shrill denunciation of these sins. Such
'whoredom' was condemned not only as an offence in
the sight of God but also, more prosaically, as a
means of troubling the commonwealth through the
generation of poor bastard children. (64) The
practical effects of bastardy were the main impetus
behind a series of bills in parliament in the late
sixteenth and early seventeenth centuries to enact
harsher measures to curb the problem. Reservations
among the mass of members, especially the fear that
men of quality might be subjected to base punishments for their own sexual transgressions, led to
the failure or watering down of some of these
attempts - another example of the way in which
splits of opinion among the elites blunted the edge
of moral reform. However, measures to ensure the
maintenance of poor bastard children and the

punishment of the guilty parents were enacted in the context of poor relief and vagrancy legislation in 1576 and 1610; while for ten years after 1650, in the aftermath of the Puritan revolution which gave the zealots their chance, fornication and adultery became offences punishable respectively by three months' imprisonment and by death.(65)

Public attitudes to bastardy at the popular level do not seem to have differed much from the more moderate elite views either in nature or severity - though it is fair to say that most of the unequivocal evidence relates to the middling ranks of society and that the attitudes of the very poor remain for the most part obscure. Quaife's idea that sex was not a moral issue, and that hostility to bastardy and other forms of immorality was based purely on financial considerations, is patently mistaken.(66) To be sure, financial motives could and did act as a powerful reinforcer of moral feelings. But the vocabulary used by churchwardens, witnesses and even some offenders to describe sexual misbehaviour - 'lewd', 'filthy', 'abominable' - is strongly redolent of ethical concerns, and often very similar to that employed by clerics and moralists. Moreover, references to God, sinfulness, Judgement, and the fear of Hell are not uncommon. In 1584, for example, Francis Coggens of Hanney (Berkshire) angrily rejected a suggestion that his pregnant sister should name a false father: 'My sister ... hath committed an abominable fact already and if she should father it to another man the plague of God would fall upon her and upon us all for giving her such counsel.' The case of William Yoonges, a servant of Downton in Wiltshire, illustrates how even individuals who were apparently insouciant when they committed sexual offences were not necessarily free from subsequent pangs of conscience. In 1581 it was reported that he had boasted 'that he had gartered Joan Wootton's hose above her knee that it should stick by her forty weeks after', but when he later fell ill he changed his tune. Asked by a friend how he was, he replied 'I do burn and shall burn in hell for my wicked dealing with that wicked woman'. (67)

Traditional attitudes to bastardy can thus hardly be described as tolerant. But hostility intensified in the late sixteenth and early seventeenth centuries as economic conditions worsened in many areas and the problem of poverty became more acute. To judge from figures based on parish register analysis, illegitimacy was on the increase

towards the end of Elizabeth's reign. This
phenomenon has not yet been satisfactorily explained
and the causes were no doubt complex: but one
important factor, as Wrightson has suggested, may
have been an unusual degree of insecurity and
instability in the courtship patterns of the poor in
the harsh economic circumstances around 1600. In
any event, Laslett and Karla Oosterveen's 98 parish
sample indicates that the illegitimacy ratio reached
a peak of over 3 per cent in the quinquennium
1600-4. Although this is a low figure in comparison
with nineteenth-century rates it was by no means
negligible; and it is easy to understand why
contemporaries thought themselves confronted by a
rising tide of bastardy.(68)

How could this tide be stemmed? Legal action
was stepped up, the courts apparently working in
alliance with local interests, and especially with
the middling groups who dominated office holding in
the parishes. Already parochial officials had
little hesitation about reporting cases of bastardy
to the ecclesiastical authorities; but growing
concern is indicated in some areas by greater
diligence in detecting the fathers as well as the
mothers of bastard children. In the archdeaconry of
Wiltshire in the 1590s, only about 60 per cent of
presentments named the male partner; the rest
passed over the question of paternity in silence or
stated that 'the father we know not'. By the 1620s
the father was named in over 80 per cent of
cases. (69)

At the same time, parish officials made
increasing use of the powers of the justices of the
peace. To cite yet again the example of Wiltshire -
though there were similar developments in other
counties - the numbers of bastardy orders made by
justices increased relative to the numbers of
illegitimacy cases occurring in the shire, and the
culprits were more harshly punished. Whereas in the
early years of the seventeenth century the mothers
of bastards were sometimes but certainly not always
whipped or stocked, by the 1620s they were almost
invariably sent to the house of correction for a
year. The effects of these developments can be
observed in individual parishes. In the villages
of Wylye and Keevil, no bastardy orders are known to
have been made against offenders between 1600 and
1617. Thereafter there were several cases in each
parish, and some of the offenders were treated with
extreme rigour. James Crachley of Keevil, for
example, who denied a paternity charge in 1620

and refused to pay maintenance, was at the
instigation of the inhabitants kept in prison for
several years.(70)

Such increasing rigour and associated adjustments of attitude probably contributed to a decline
in bastardy rates in the seventeenth century.
Laslett and Oosterveen's figures indicate a
substantial drop to about 2 per cent in the 1630s
and about 1.5 per cent in the later seventeenth
century. Wrightson and Levine's detailed analysis
of the village of Terling (Essex) suggests that in
part this fall represented a spontaneous adjustment,
one aspect of a broader pattern of increased
restraint on fertility in response to economic
conditions after 1600. But partly, too, it reflected a more rigorous pursuit of bastard-bearers,
itself contingent on a conscious shift in attitudes
especially among the wealthier sectors of village
society. In Terling the more substantial householders not only harried the sins of the poor but
also practised what they preached: in the course of
the seventeenth century wealthier men became less
likely to father bastard children.(71) A similar
change occurred in the parish of Keevil in Wiltshire.
In Elizabeth's reign, men from the middling to upper
strata of village society were not uncommonly
implicated in bastardy cases and other forms of
sexual immorality. Robert Jones, for example, a
member of one of the wealthiest and most powerful
families in Keevil, was convicted of fathering a
bastard in 1595. Robert Blagden, scion of another
wealthy family and eventually to become one of the
most dominant men in the parish, was likewise
convicted of immorality in 1592: allegedly, he
successfully enticed a poor woman to adultery by
reporting that her absent husband was dead and
promising to marry her himself. The behaviour of
William Prior, a yeoman, was even more extreme. In
the 1590s he fathered a succession of bastards on
his maidservant Welthian Vaughan: he was evidently
keeping her as his concubine, in defiance of his
neighbours who repeatedly detected the matter to the
church courts and eventually forced the couple to
marry. The marriage of Prior may almost be seen as
a watershed. Over the next quarter century the
moral tone of the upper echelons of Keevil society
altered perceptibly, and bastardy became increasingly the preserve of the poor.(72)

VII

A hardening attitude to bastardy; some decline
in tolerance towards bridal pregnancy in certain
areas; tighter public control over marriage entry:
these changes add up to a significant adjustment in
popular marriage practices and attitudes to extra-
marital sexuality, especially among the middling
groups in society - yeomen and the more substantial
husbandmen and craftsmen. It remains to investigate
more fully the nature of the factors which produced
these shifts and how far they were related to the
social processes which Burke has characterised as
the 'reform of popular culture'. From the foregoing
discussion it is plain that economic pressures were
a major stimulant to change. It is less clear how
decisive a part was played by changing cultural
horizons and new religious ideas - especially
Puritanism. William Hunt has argued that in the
county of Essex economics and Puritanism were
intimately connected, the two fusing to create an
ethos which he labels 'social puritanism'. The
'godly' tended to perceive poverty as a result of
sin. Hence 'the way to reduce poverty, or ... to
check its growth, was to reform the outlook and
behaviour of the poor'. Thus Puritan preachers
provided a theological legitimation for what
amounted to a 'cultural revolution': an assault not
only on behaviour that had traditionally been stig-
matised, such as fornication, but also the whole
structure of popular sociability and festivities.
Hunt thus firmly locates the tighter regulation of
sexuality in the context of a wider programme of the
reform of popular culture whose ideological basis was
Puritanism. Puritanism likewise figures prominently
in Wrightson and Levine's study of Terling. They
stress that the intensification of sexual discipline
depended on a reorientation of values among the more
substantial inhabitants. This change was made
possible by an increase in literacy among these
groups, which made them receptive to the ideas of
the Puritan clerics who were urging moral reform.
In the early seventeenth century the 'better sort'
of Terling villagers became dominated by a coherent
group of 'godly' laymen; and the programme of moral
discipline in the village embraced not only sexual
immorality but also lax religious observance,
drunkenness, the playing of games and dancing - all
the characteristic *bêtes noires* of Puritan preachers.
Terling thus emerges as a rural counterpart of those
urban communities like Bury St Edmunds (Suffolk) and

Rye (Sussex) where determined efforts were made in
the late sixteenth and early seventeenth centuries
to convert the towns into 'godly commonwealths'. (73)
      The Wiltshire village of Keevil provides an
interesting comparison with Terling which puts the
changes in sexual morality into a rather different
perspective. As will be plain from the previous
discussion, Keevil offers an excellent illustration
of hardening attitudes to bridal pregnancy and
bastardy in the early seventeenth century. But
these changes were not contingent on the inculcation
of distinctively 'Puritan' religious and moral
attitudes: other elements of what are generally
regarded as the distinguishing characteristics of a
Puritan reformation of manners were only fleetingly
in evidence and do not seem to have attracted much
support even in the upper ranks of village society.
The ministers who served Keevil in the period
1588-1640 were Francis Greatrakes and his son
Stephen. Both were constantly resident, diligent,
preaching ministers (though apparently only Stephen
Greatrakes was a graduate); but there are few
grounds for describing either as a Puritan. During
their incumbency there was a slow increase in
prosecutions for lax religious observance, but in
absolute terms the numbers of cases remained small
and it is hard to see them as a major campaign to
raise religious standards. Indeed there is no
compelling evidence that the religious complexion of
the village altered very markedly once the shift
from Catholicism to Protestantism had been achieved
in the course of the sixteenth century. The
evidence of wills indicates the existence within the
village of a number of particularly pious
individuals. But they were widely scattered over
time and in the social spectrum. There was no distinctively Puritan movement, and no godly group
emerged to dominate the village either through
office holding or in any other way.
      Equally there was no sustained drive to reform
personal conduct other than sexual behaviour.
Dancing and summer festivities were subjected to two
isolated attacks in 1611 and 1624. The first was
probably instigated by Frances Greatrakes; the
second may have been merely a spin off from a long-
standing feud, of a personal rather than ideological
nature, between certain of the parish notables. In
any event, both attacks proved ineffectual and
festivities continued to flourish, apparently with
the support of some of the more substantial inhabitants. These summer sports were, of course, mainly

the resort of the young. The adult leaders of the
village were addicted, despite statutory
prohibitions, to bowling. There were frequent
presentments for this offence in the manor court
(even Stephen Greatrakes was prosecuted on one
occasion); but these routine presentments should be
seen as a minor source of revenue for the lord of
the manor, of no deterrent value whatsoever, rather
than as any serious attempt to reform behaviour.
There were occasional prosecutions for drunkenness
and unlicensed ale-selling but such action was very
sporadic and largely ineffectual - there was, as far
as can be seen, no committed Puritan campaign
against the demon drink.(74)

While it is plain that doctrinal Puritanism
could (as in Terling) reinforce harsher attitudes to
illicit sexuality, the case of Keevil indicates that
the latter could occur in the absence of any strong
Puritan drive. The fact is that the tightening up
of sexual morality did not demand the blinding light
of a new ideology. A major contention of this paper
has been that the public and communal control of
sexuality within a Christian context was by no means
an innovation of the period after 1500. In the
middle reign of Elizabeth, and probably for long
before, sexual morality was already reasonably
strict, heavily influenced by Christian principles
if not wholly in accord with the stern prescriptions
of professional moralists. Only quite small changes
in attitudes and behaviour were necessary to effect
the shifts of the late sixteenth and early seventeenth centuries. When such changes occurred, as in
Terling, in association with other significant
religious and cultural movements, they are apt to
appear more dramatic than they really were. In
villages like Keevil they look more like an
unexciting process of adaptation to economic conditions and to modifications in the social structure.

VIII

Muchembled postulates, for early modern France,
a movement of sexual repression which amounted to a
major cultural revolution. For the first time the
Christian church, working in alliance with the
state, confronted and triumphed over popular
attitudes to sexuality which were largely amoral and
fundamentally non-Christian. This picture will not
do for England. There is certainly evidence of
tighter public control over marriage and greater
rigour towards extramarital sexuality in the late

sixteenth and seventeenth centuries. But these developments should be seen in long-term perspective. The pre-Reformation population of England was neither amoral nor impervious to Christian values; nor was it free from ecclesiastical, secular and communal discipline over sexual behaviour. Hence the changes of the period after 1550 should be seen simply as an intensification, perhaps merely a continuation, of processes which had been at work for centuries, and it is doubtful whether any major shift in cultural outlook was required to effect them. If changes in the public control of sex and marriage are indeed to be seen in terms of a 'reform of popular culture', it was a process which began much earlier than the sixteenth century.

Notes

1. Burke, Popular Culture, p. xi.
2. R. Muchembled, Culture populaire at culture des élites dans la France moderne (XVe-XVIIIe siècles): essai (Paris, 1978).
3. J. Delumeau, Catholicism between Luther and Voltaire (1977); M. Foucault, Surveiller et punir: naissance de la prison (Paris, 1975).
4. Muchembled, Culture populaire, chs. 2 and 4, esp. pp. 95-6, 229, 238, 240.
5. Ibid., pp. 233-40.
6. Delumeau, Catholicism, p. 161, and pt. 2, chs. 3-4. For a brief discussion of this issue, see B. Scribner, 'Religion, Society and Culture: Reorienting the Reformation', History Workshop, 14 (1982), pp. 11-19.
7. J. Bossy, 'The Counter-Reformation and the People of Catholic Europe', P. and P., 47 (1970), pp. 56-7; B. Lenman and G. Parker, 'The State, the Community and the Criminal Law in Early Modern Europe', in V. A. C. Gatrell, B. Lenman and G. Parker (eds.), Crime and the Law: The Social History of Crime in Western Europe since 1500 (1980), pp. 37-8; Scribner, 'Religion, Society and Culture', p. 14; T. Robisheaux, 'Peasants and Pastors: Rural Youth Control and the Reformation in Hohenlohe, 1540-1680', Social History, vi (1981); S. Ozment, When Fathers Ruled: Family Life in Reformation Europe (Cambridge, Mass., 1983).
8. P. Ariès, Centuries of Childhood (Harmondsworth, 1979 edn), pt. 3; J.-L. Flandrin, Families in Former Times: Kinship, Household and Sexuality (Cambridge, 1979).
9. L. Stone, The Family, Sex and Marriage in England, 1500-1800 (1977), esp. pp. 4-9 and chs. 4-5.

10. A. Macfarlane, 'Review of Stone, Family, Sex and Marriage in England', in History and Theory, xviii (1979), pp. 110-11, 125.
11. E. M. W. Tillyard, The Elizabethan World Picture (Harmondsworth, 1972); W. H. Greenleaf, Order, Empiricism and Politics: Two Traditions of English Political Thought, 1500-1700 (1964), ch. 2.
12. K. Wrightson, English Society 1580-1680 (1982), chs. 3-4. See also Macfarlane, 'Review of Stone', pp. 103-26.
13. Wrightson, English Society, pp. 89-104; M. MacDonald, Mystical Bedlam: Madness, Anxiety and Healing in Seventeenth-Century England (Cambridge, 1981), pp. 98-105.
14. Stone, Family, Sex and Marriage, pp. 5, 180-94.
15. Wrightson, English Society, ch. 3; V. Brodsky Elliott, 'Single Women in the London Marriage Market', in R. B. Outhwaite (ed.), Marriage and Society: Studies in the Social History of Marriage (1981), pp. 81-100. See also Spufford, Small Books, pp. 156-66.
16. M. Ingram, 'Spousals Litigation in the English Ecclesiastical Courts', in Outhwaite (ed.), Marriage and Society, pp. 50-1; MacDonald, Mystical Bedlam, pp. 94-6.
17. M. Griffith, Bethel: Or, a Forme for Families (1633), p. 272.
18. WRO, Salisbury DR, Bishop of Salisbury: Deposition Book 10, fo. 15v; Miscellaneous Court Papers 29/47, 14 Feb. 1586/7; Deposition Book 5, fo. 23v.
19. MacDonald, Mystical Bedlam, pp. 88-98. See also Wrightson, English Society, pp. 82-4; Spufford, Small Books, pp. 157-8; A. Macfarlane, The Family Life of Ralph Josselin (Cambridge, 1970), pp. 95-6.
20. Macfarlane, 'Review of Stone', pp. 117, 124-6; K. Davies, 'Continuity and Change in Literary Advice on Marriage', in Outhwaite (ed.), Marriage and Society, pp. 58-80.
21. Stone, Family, Sex and Marriage, pp. 143-6.
22. Ibid., pp. 603-5.
23. G. R. Quaife, Wanton Wenches and Wayward Wives: Peasants and Illicit Sex in Early Seventeenth-Century England (1979), pp. 178-82.
24. C. Phythian-Adams, 'Ceremony and the Citizen: The Communal Year at Coventry, 1450-1550', in P. Clark and P. Slack (eds.), Crisis and Order in English Towns, 1500-1700 (1972), pp. 57-85; C. Phythian-Adams, Desolation of a City: Coventry and the Urban Crisis of the Late Middle Ages (Cambridge, 1979), pp. 167-9 and passim; D. M. Owen, Church and Society in Medieval Lincolnshire (Lincoln, 1971), ch. 8. See also M. James, 'Ritual, Drama and Social Body in the Late Medieval English Town', P. and P., 98 (1983); J. Bossy, 'The Mass as a Social Institution, 1200-1700', P. and P., 100 (1983).

25. M. Bowker, 'The Commons' Supplication against the Ordinaries in the Light of some Archidiaconal Acta', TRHS, xxi (1971), pp. 75-6.

26. Registrum Hamonis Hethe Diocesis Roffensis, A.D. 1319-1352, ed. C. Johnson (Canterbury and York Society, xlviii-xlix, 1915-48),pp. 911-1043; B. L. Woodcock, Medieval Ecclesiastical Courts in the Diocese of Canterbury (1952), pp. 79, 82. See also D. J. Guth, 'Enforcing Late Medieval Law: Patterns in Litigation during Henry VII's Reign', in J. H. Baker (ed.), Legal Records and the Historian (1978), pp. 90-1.

27. For some illustrations, see English Historical Documents, 1485-1558, ed. C. H. Williams (1967), pp. 967-8, 986. See also K. Thomas, 'The Puritans and Adultery: The Act of 1650 Reconsidered', in D. Pennington and K. Thomas (eds.), Puritans and Revolutionaries (Oxford, 1978), pp. 265-6; Guth, 'Enforcing Late Medieval Law', pp. 92-3.

28. Phythian-Adams, Desolation of a City, pp. 138-9. See also E. Searle, Lordship and Community: Battle Abbey and its Banlieu, 1066-1538 (Toronto, 1974), p. 415. For further discussion of continuities in law enforcement between the medieval and early modern periods, see J. A. Sharpe, 'The History of Crime in Late Medieval and Early Modern England: A Review of the Field', Social History, vii (1982), pp. 191, 201-3.

29. R. Houlbrooke, Church Courts and the People During the English Reformation 1520-1570 (Oxford, 1979), pp. 262-3 and passim; P. Clark, English Provincial Society from the Reformation to the Revolution: Religion, Politics and Society in Kent, 1500-1640 (Hassocks, 1977), p. 156.

30. Wrightson, English Society, chs. 5-7. See also W. Hunt, The Puritan Moment (Cambridge, Mass., 1983), chs. 2-3, 6.

31. Ingram, 'Spousals Litigation', pp. 37-40.

32. Cambridge Univ. Lib., Ely DR, D/2/11, fos. 181v-82.

33. Ibid., fo. 181.

34. Sir F. Pollock and F. W. Maitland, The History of English Law Before the Time of Edward I (Cambridge, 1968), ii, pp. 380-4.

35. Houlbrooke, Church Courts and the People, pp. 56-7.

36. Canons and Decrees of the Council of Trent, ed. H. J. Schroeder (St Louis, 1960), pp. 183-4; 26 George II c. 33 (Lord Hardwicke's Marriage Act). See also Ingram, 'Spousals Litigation', p. 40.

37. Ingram, 'Spousals Litigation', pp. 42-4, 52-3, 55; R. A. Marchant, The Church Under the Law (Cambridge, 1969), p. 137; H. Swinburne, A Treatise of Spousals or Matrimonial Contracts (1686), Sig. A2v.

38. Outhwaite, Marriage and Society, pp. 12-13.

39. Ingram, 'Spousals Litigation', pp. 55-7.
40. WRO, Salisbury DR, Archdeacon of Salisbury: Act Book (Office) 12, 22 Aug. 1618, <u>Office v Guy</u>; Bishop of Salisbury: Act Book (Office) 8, 2 Dec. 1617, <u>Office v Hitch</u>. On January-and-May marriages, see K. Thomas, 'Age and Authority in Early Modern England', <u>Proceedings of the British Academy</u>, lxii (1976), pp. 41-2.
41. <u>HMC: Various Collections</u>, i, p. 75. See also <u>Tudor Economic Documents</u>, ed. R. H. Tawney and E. Power (1924), i, pp. 356, 363; Thomas, 'Age and Authority', pp. 14-15.
42. M. J. Ingram, 'Ecclesiastical Justice in Wiltshire, 1600-1640' (Univ. of Oxford D.Phil. thesis, 1976), p. 121; Wrightson, <u>English Society</u>, p. 78; Hunt, <u>Puritan Moment</u>, p. 74. For a late sixteenth-century example, see WRO, Salisbury DR, Bishop of Salisbury: Deposition Book 11, fos. 2v-3.
43. Ingram, 'Ecclesiastical Justice', pp. 150-3; Stone, <u>Family, Sex and Marriage</u>, pp. 38-40; J. A. Sharpe, 'Crime and Delinquency in an Essex Parish, 1600-1640', in J. S. Cockburn (ed.), <u>Crime in England, 1500-1800</u> (1977), pp. 99-100.
44. P. E. H. Hair, 'Bridal Pregnancy in Rural England in Earlier Centuries', <u>Population Studies</u>, xx (1966); *idem,* 'Bridal Pregnancy in Earlier Rural England Further Examined', <u>Population Studies</u>, xxiv (1970).
45. Peter Laslett, <u>The World We have Lost</u> (London, 1971), pp. 150-1; *idem,* <u>Family Life and Illicit Love in Earlier Generations</u> (Cambridge, 1977), pp. 128-30; Ingram, 'Ecclesiastical Justice', pp. 188-95, 201.
46. H. A. Kelly, 'Clandestine Marriage and Chaucer's "Troilus"', <u>Viator</u>, iv (1973), pp. 440-1; W. Gouge, <u>Of Domesticall Duties</u> (1622), p. 202.
47. Houlbrooke, <u>Church Courts and the People</u>, p. 78.
48. Based on analysis of Cambridge Univ. Lib., Ely DR, D/2/18; West Sussex RO, Chichester DR, Ep. I/17/6 and <u>Churchwardens' Presentments (17th Century). Part 1: Archdeaconry of Chichester</u>, ed. H. Johnstone (Sussex RS, xlix, 1949), pp. 27-59.
49. Marchant, <u>Church Under the Law</u>, p. 137; P. Collinson, 'Cranbrook and the Fletchers: Popular and Unpopular Religion in the Kentish Weald', in P. N. Brooks (ed.), <u>Reformation Principle and Practice</u> (1980), pp. 184-6; Ingram, 'Ecclesiastical Justice', p. 182; WRO, Salisbury DR, Archdeacon of Salisbury: Act Book (Office) 1a, fos. 2v-15v.
50. Cambridge Univ. Lib., Ely DR, B/2/34, fo. 26; WRO, Dean of Salisbury: Churchwardens' Presentments, 1633 (unnumbered), letter from John Pytt to John Johnson, 17 Sept. 1633.
51. Ingram, 'Ecclesiastical Justice', pp. 200-1. See also Marchant, <u>Church Under the Law</u>, p. 137.

52. WRO, Salisbury DR, Archdeacon of Salisbury: Act Book (Office) 15, 11 Feb. 1636/7, Office v Munday.

53. P. Laslett, 'Introduction: Comparing Illegitimacy Over Time and Between Cultures', in P. Laslett, K. Oosterveen and R. M. Smith (eds.), Bastardy and Its Comparative History (1980), p. 23.

54. Ingram, 'Ecclesiastical Justice', pp. 196-201; K. Wrightson and D. Levine, Poverty and Piety in an English Village (NY, 1979), pp. 132-3; M. Ingram, 'Religion, Communities and Moral Discipline in Late Sixteenth- and Early Seventeenth-Century England: Case Studies', in K. von Greyerz (ed.), Religion and Society in Early Modern Europe, 1500-1800 (forthcoming).

55. J. A. Sharpe, Defamation and Sexual Slander in Early Modern England (York, 1980), p. 3 and *passim*. See also Ingram, 'Ecclesiastical Justice', ch. 9; C. A. Haigh, 'Slander and the Church Courts in the Sixteenth Century', Trans. Lancashire and Cheshire Antiquarian Soc., lxxviii (1975).

56. West Sussex RO, Chichester DR, Ep. I/17/11, fo. 43.

57. Wrightson, English Society, pp. 84-5; Ingram, 'Ecclesiastical Justice', pp. 229-30, 235; Quaife, Wanton Wenches, pp. 59-63.

58. Ingram, 'Ecclesiastical Justice', pp. 226, 231, 234-5; Wrightson and Levine, Poverty and Piety, p. 128.

59. Laslett, Family Life and Illicit Love, pp. 147-51; Ingram, 'Ecclesiastical Justice', p. 233.

60. Ingram, 'Ecclesiastical Justice', pp. 226-7, 231-4; Wrightson and Levine, Poverty and Piety, pp. 127-8; Wrightson, English Society, p. 86.

61. K. Thomas, 'The Double Standard', Journal of the History of Ideas, xx (1959).

62. Ingram, 'Ecclesiastical Justice', pp. 257-8; WRO, Salisbury DR, Bishop of Salisbury: Act Book (Office) 8, 20 Mar. 1616/7, Office v Bugden; Deposition Book 9, fo. 52.

63. Ingram, 'Ecclesiastical Justice', pp. 285-7; A. Macfarlane, 'Illegitimacy and Illegitimates in English History', in Laslett and others (eds.), Bastardy, p. 75.

64. R. L. Greaves, Society and Religion in Elizabethan England (Minneapolis, 1981), pp. 203-18; Ingram, 'Ecclesiastical Justice', pp. 161-5.

65. J. Kent, 'Attitudes of Members of the House of Commons to the Regulation of "Personal Conduct" in Late Elizabethan and Early Stuart England', BIHR, xlvi (1973); Thomas, 'Puritans and Adultery', pp. 257-8.

66. Quaife, Wanton Wenches, p. 179.

67. WRO, Salisbury DR, Bishop of Salisbury: Deposition Book 9, fo. 87v; Deposition Book 8, fos. 102v, 103v-4v.

68. Wrightson, English Society, pp. 145-6; Laslett, 'Introduction', in Laslett and others (eds.), Bastardy,

p. 18.

69. Ingram, 'Ecclesiastical Justice', pp. 239-40.
70. Ibid., pp. 376-8; Hunt, <u>Puritan Moment</u>, pp. 75-6; Quaife, <u>Wanton Wenches</u>, pp. 216-20.
71. Wrightson and Levine, <u>Poverty and Piety</u>, pp. 126-32.
72. Based on collation of all readily available records relating to this parish in the period 1560-1640; I intend to publish full details of this study on another occasion. For some preliminary findings, see Ingram, 'Religion, Communities and Moral Discipline'; and Ingram, 'Ecclesiastical Justice'.
73. Hunt, <u>Puritan Moment</u>, pp. 139-40, 252 and *passim*; Wrightson and Levine, <u>Poverty and Piety</u>, chs. 5-7; P. Collinson, <u>The Religion of Protestants</u> (Oxford, 1982), pp. 158-60.
74. The comparison between Keevil and Terling is elaborated in Ingram, 'Religion, Communities and Moral Discipline'.

Chapter Five

RIDINGS, ROUGH MUSIC AND MOCKING RHYMES IN EARLY
MODERN ENGLAND*

Martin Ingram

I

    One Sunday in 1614, at All Cannings in Wiltshire,
a certain Richard Hutchins climbed into the
minister's seat in the church and pronounced: 'the
one and twentieth chapter of Maud Butcher and the
seventh verse: man, love thy wife and thy wife will
love thee; and if she will not do as thou wilt,
have her take a staff and break her arms and her
legs and she will forgive thee.' Another jape,
again involving a parody of an ecclesiastical
ritual, occurred at Calne in 1633: Francis
Wastfield 'caused the sexton to toll the bell for
Henry Vayzey his wife because she did not speak to
her husband who was at the same time in the field
milking her kine'. There was another disturbance at
Stetchworth in Cambridgeshire in 1637. Robert
Bridge innocently suggested to Francis Bradford that
he might go out of the south door of the church
where there was not such a crowd, whereupon Bradford
rudely told him to go out there himself 'if his
horns were not too big'. Stories were circulating
about Bridge: gossip said that his wife had beaten
him. In the churchyard one knowing neighbour asked
another 'if he came thither to buy chaff, looking at
Bridge and jeering at him'. More impressively, at
Salisbury in 1614, Alice Mustian erected a stage on
two hogsheads in her backyard and invited people in
to watch the play on payment of small trifles like
'pins and points'. The subject of the drama? The
adulterous liaison of her own neighbours.(1)
    These stories illustrate some of the means used
by townspeople and villagers in sixteenth- and
seventeenth-century England to mock the sins and
follies of their neighbours and, on occasion, of
their social superiors. The repertoire was wide

166

and flexible. Richard Hutchins's means of deriding
an unsatisfactory marital relationship was probably
an *ad hoc* device. On the other hand, tolling the
passing bell in mockery was a well-established
practice, used in various parts of England to deride
not only crotchety spouses but also, for example,
weavers who failed to complete a cloth in due
time.(2) Derisive playlets could be used to satirise
just about anything - they were much in vogue as a
vehicle for religious controversy during the
Reformation years - but a juicy sexual scandal provided especially good copy. Their appeal and
fabrication was not, of course, confined to the
lower end of the social scale, nor were they just a
matter for amateurs. Alice Mustian's humble provincial performance had obvious affinities with the
bawdy, satirical jigs found on the London stage, or
even with a play like George Chapman's Old Joiner of
Aldgate whose matrimonial theme was firmly based in
real life events which occurred not a hundred miles
from the theatre.(3)

There is a tendency for historians to lump these
manifestations together as 'charivari' or 'rough
music'; but ideally a more discriminating approach
is required to establish the full range and explore
similarities and differences between what was evidently a variety of customs of mockery and disapprobation. This paper focuses on two of the major
forms. One, the 'riding' and the 'rough music' and
other forms of concrete symbolism which were often
associated with it, has already been intensively
investigated, so it is possible to discuss the
phenomenom with some confidence.(4) The other, the
use of mocking rhymes, songs and other verbal
lampoons, has been less fully researched, and any
comment must be tentative. Despite this disparity,
the two forms may be fruitfully compared. The
juxtaposition illustrates the variety of popular
culture, raises interesting questions about the
relationship between oral and print culture, and
reveals how different elements of popular practices
could evoke varied responses among the ruling elites.

II

Robert Moxam, a husbandman of Marden in
Wiltshire, deposed in 1626 that

> on Saturday was sevennight last past, William
> Merrydeth, servant unto one William Hollowaie
> of Marden, and John Broadbanke, servant unto

> one William Lavington ... with many others
> in a disorderly manner came through the
> town of Marden with guns, drums, coalrakes,
> ovenlugs and staves, setting upon a horse-
> back two young fellows, one of them arrayed
> and clothed in woman's apparel; and ...
> when they came over against this informer's
> door they there made a stand, saying that
> there was skimmington, beating up the drums
> and shooting off their guns there in a
> scoffing and disorderly manner .... (5)

The event which Moxam described was known as
'riding skimmington' or a 'riding'. David Underdown has suggested that the custom was peculiarly
characteristic of the western counties and, within
that region, of forest-pastoral communities.(6) The
tradition may indeed have flourished there with
unusual vigour and elaboration, but the point should
not be pressed too far. With some variations, the
custom seems to have been well known and widely
distributed in sixteenth- and seventeenth-century
England, not only in rural areas but also in the
metropolis and other towns and cities. Wherever
they might occur, ridings could vary considerably in
scale, from minor incidents organised by a handful
of individuals, to major spectacles involving
hundreds of people. But basic to all of them was
mocking laughter, sometimes light-hearted but often
taking the form of hostile derision which could, on
occasion, escalate into physical violence.

The centrepiece of these ridings was a horse and
rider. In more elaborate versions a real horse was
used, but in many parts of England the mount was
more usually represented by a 'cowlstaff' or 'stang'
carried on men's shoulders (in the North and in
Scotland the custom was commonly known as 'riding
the stang'). Sometimes the victims themselves were
forced to ride; during the ordeal they might be
pelted with mud and filth and could end up by being
ducked in a pond or river. But often the 'next
neighbour nearest the church' or some other substitute was made to ride instead, or the riders were
represented by effigies. As in the case at Marden,
male participants sometimes dressed in female
clothes, or the rider was made to face backwards on
the horse. In addition, the horse-and-rider motif
was often supplemented by other symbols. Parades of
armed men sometimes accompanied the riders, while
'rough music' was produced by shrill cries, the
raucous playing of musical instruments, the beating

of pots and pans, and gunfire. One of the riders
sometimes carried pots of grain (or a mixture of
grain and filth according to some accounts) and
scattered the contents among the crowd. Last but
not least, the proceedings often featured the display of animals' horns, antlers, or horned heads.
In a case at Aveton Gifford (Devon) in 1738, for
example, the demonstrators carried 'a large pair of
ram's horns tipped like gold and adorned with
ribbons and flowers'. (7)

The occasions for such ridings were relatively
restricted. Both literary references to the custom
and accounts of real life incidents show conclusively that the characteristic pretext was when a
wife beat her husband or in some other noteworthy
way proved that she wore the breeches. Ralpho's
explanation in <u>Hudibras</u>, that what his master had
seen was

> ... but a riding used of course
> When the grey mare's the better horse;
> When o'er the breeches greedy women
> Fight to extend their vast dominion,
> And in the cause impatient Grizel
> Has drubbed her husband with bull's pizzle,

is supported by the comments of people who were
actually involved in ridings. In 1602, for example,
some of the inhabitants of Waterbeach (Cambridgeshire) affirmed that 'there is a custom in their
town that if a woman beat her husband, the next
neighbour towards the church must ride upon a cowlstaff'. It was the same in London in 1563: 'The
twenty-second day of February, was Shrove Monday, at
Charing Cross there was a man carried of four men,
and afore him a bagpipe playing, a shawm and a drum
playing, and a twenty links burning about him,
because his next neighbour's wife did beat her husband; therefore it is ordered that his next
neighbour shall ride about the place.' (8)

While the termagant wife and/or her abject
husband were thus pre-eminently the target of
ridings, lesser forms of female insubordination and
related offences sometimes provoked demonstrations
involving at least some of the characteristic
symbols. It was conventionally assumed - though
presumably not necessarily true in practice - that a
husband who had been beaten by his wife was inevitably also a cuckold. Hence the prominence in
ridings of horns and antlers, traditionally the
ignominious badge of the man whose wife had been

unfaithful. Cuckolds who had not suffered the additional indignity of being beaten were rarely subjected to a riding as such, but the cornute symbols alone were often used to mount some kind of hostile demonstration. Occasionally the proceedings were quite elaborate. At Beckington (Somerset) in 1611, for example, the perpetrators 'disgraced' a mare by cutting the hair from its mane, tail and ears, bound a large pair of horns to its head, and paraded it through the village with loud shouts and outcries. A particularly embarrassing form of demonstration was likely to occur if a man married a woman of doubtful morals - thus making himself, according to contemporary literary conceit, a 'cuckold incontinent ... that marries himself to a woman of light disposition, who maketh him a cuckold the very first day of his marriage'. Such unfortunates sometimes had to run the gauntlet of derision at the actual wedding. In 1616, for example, when Richard Tomes of Catcombe (Wiltshire) went 'with a great company of young fellows in his company' to fetch his bride from a neighbouring parish, a buck's horn stuck with a wisp of hay and a 'picture of a woman's privities' were set up by the roadside to greet the bridal party on the way back. Similarly, at Arlington (Sussex) in 1639, Henry Hall and his newly wedded wife were met in the churchyard by a man with 'a great pair of horns upon his head ... showing thereby that the said Hall was like to be a cuckold'. But most symbolic demonstrations against cuckolds were less spectacular. Neighbours grimaced and made horn signs with their fingers or, at most, horns were hung, often under cover of night, at the victim's gate, gable-end or windows. (9)

Blatant sexual immorality (irrespective of cuckoldry) was another form of behaviour which, while not a normal occasion for ridings as such, sometimes provoked recourse to one of the supplementary symbols - in this case the rough music of pots and pans. At Burton-on-Trent in 1618, a couple who had been posing as brother and sister aroused the suspicions of their neighbours, and were eventually discovered in bed together. Thereupon they were dragged out of their house, paraded through the streets to the sound of rough music and cries of 'A whore and a knave! A whore, a whore!', set in the stocks overnight, and then expelled from the town. Similarly, around 1615, a Wiltshire woman was said to have been 'rung out of Seend with basins', a fate which apparently befell 'none but whores'. (10)

While female domination and immorality were the

characteristic pretexts for ridings, there were
other occasions. A simple form of riding was sometimes used in a holiday context in 'trick or treat'
games, and to punish people who refused to join in
the festivities or who in other ways offended the
holiday spirit. At Chichester in 1586, a game of
'tables' on New Year's Eve was rudely interrupted
when 'William Brunne who then played the part of a
lord of misrule came in ... and said that that game
was no Christmas game and so perforce took [one of
the players] ... from thence and made him ride on a
staff to the High Cross.' The use of ridings to
punish people who would not give money to Lords of
Misrule on holidays was denounced by Philip Stubbes.
Unfortunately, when refusal to take part in festivities (or, worse still, attempts to suppress such
festivities) were based on Puritan principles, such
ridings were apt to become distinctly less light-
hearted and more elaborate. John Hole, the Puritan
constable of Wells, discovered this to his cost in
1607. Hole and his associates tried to suppress the
city's May games, which had been organised on a particularly grand scale that year in order to raise
money for the repair of St Cuthbert's church.
Hole's interference raised a storm of opposition,
and he and his friends were savagely derided in a
series of spectacular ridings performed before
thousands of people.(11)

Since Hole was a constable, the demonstrations
against him inevitably had an anti-authoritarian
flavour. On occasion, ridings and rough music were
directed specifically against magistrates or others
in a position of authority, especially when they
were perceived to be acting unjustly. One of the
most notable examples occurred during the Western
Rising of 1626-32. Some of the leaders of these
riots against disafforestation and enclosure took
the sobriquet 'Lady Skimmington'; and what appears
to have been a riding, involving a noisy parade of
armed men bearing an effigy which they ultimately
threw into a coalpit, was directed against Sir Giles
Mompesson. Through most of the sixteenth and seventeenth centuries, however, such cases seem to have
been rare. It was only in the late seventeenth
century, when Whig and Tory demonstrations during
the Exclusion Crisis and afterwards included chari-
varesque elements such as the backward facing ride
and rough music, that political applications of
these customs became at all common.(12)

III

Just what were people doing when they performed ridings? Historians have conventionally seen these customs simply as a kind of informal sanction directed against those who offended community norms. While plainly true up to a point, this approach is inadequate and begs important questions. It does not explain why these demonstrations took the form they did, involving a specific set of symbols. Nor does it account for the fact that, at least in the early modern period (the situation was to change later), the custom was used in only a narrow range of social circumstances among which the beating of a husband by his wife was clearly predominant. These features must be explored further if the nature of ridings and rough music in early modern England is to be properly understood.

Reference to other societies offers some important clues. Riding backwards, cacophony, transvestism and animal symbolism are motifs which are or have in the past been widely current in numerous societies in virtually all parts of the globe. They are found in association with a very wide range of social situations. Yet this apparent diversity conceals an underlying coherence: these symbols are characteristically expressive of <u>anomaly</u> and/or <u>transition</u> – changes of state or the crossing of behavioural, spatial, or temporal boundaries. Depending on the circumstances, the symbols may either be used to express disapprobation or hostility; or they may occur in festive situations, especially calendar rituals and celebrations of the *rites de passage* of birth, marriage and death; or the 'ignominious' and 'festive' functions may occur in combination.(13)

In early modern England, the symbolism of ridings had links with both penal and festive practices. As regards the first, there were obvious similarities with some of the shame punishments meted out officially by some contemporary tribunals, especially borough courts and the Star Chamber. In the sixteenth and seventeenth centuries many towns still punished whoredom by ordering the delinquents to be paraded through the streets with basins ringing before them. This was evidently an official form of rough music. Indeed, some of the cases of popular demonstrations featuring rough music alone should be interpreted simply as unauthorised or imperfectly authorised applications of this penalty. This was probably the case in the incident at

Burton-on-Trent cited earlier: the constable of the
town took responsibility for the demonstration,
claiming the prescription of ancient borough custom
and alleging that, in any case, the punishment had
been subsequently approved by the Justices of the
Peace. (14)

Riding backwards also had a place in the
official legal repertoire. In the sixteenth and
early seventeenth centuries it was regularly
employed by the courts of the City of London, the
Middlesex justices and the Star Chamber to punish a
variety of offences, especially corruption, perjury
and other forms of deception. In 1510, for example,
three 'ringleaders of false quests in London rode
about the city with their faces to the horses'
tails, and were set on the pillory and brought again
to Newgate; and they died all within seven days
after for shame'. Similarly, in the Star Chamber in
1605: 'there was a purveyor censured for misdemeanour in his place, to ride with his face to the horse
tail; wherein one of the judges dissented from the
rest, and would rather have it upon an ass, and that
for two reasons: first, it would be more wonderment
and gather more boys about him; and secondly, the
slow pace of the ass would prolong his punishment.'(15)

The formal parallels between such official
penalties and popular ridings are obvious. To a
limited extent, there was also an overlap between
the offences with which the backwards ride was
associated in official usage and the occasions for
popular demonstrations; and in such cases, it seems
likely that the perpetrators consciously looked to
official legal practice as a source of legitimation.
The demonstrators against Sir Giles Mompesson, for
example, may have had recent legal precedent in mind
to justify their exposure of what they regarded as
the malfeasance of this 'odious projector': in 1621
Parliament had sentenced Sir Francis Michell, one
of Mompesson's associates and an alehouse patentee,
'to ride on a lean jade backward through London'.(16)

There was, on the other hand, no direct English
legal precedent for the use of ridings against
dominant wives, since husband-beating was not specifically proscribed by law. Common scolds -
quarrelsome women who disturbed the peace - were,
however, legally liable to be ducked in the cucking
stool, and this clearly influenced the nature of
ridings. (17) In some parts of France in the late
middle ages, the law did actually prescribe that
husbands who had been beaten by their wives should

be paraded on a horse or ass, face to tail. Given
the high degree of contact with France, especially
during the Hundred Years War, knowledge of these
practices may well have filtered through to
England.(18) In any event, the participants in
ridings against dominant wives sometimes boldly
asserted a quasi-legal purpose, in effect claiming
the right to supplement the official legal system.
Thus one of the actors in a riding at Haughley and
Wetherden (Suffolk) in 1604 claimed that their
object was that 'not only the woman which had offended might be shamed for her misdemeanour towards her
husband [in beating him] but other women also by her
shame might be admonished [not] to offend in like
sort'.(19)

In this light, ridings emerge as a form of
popular punitive action which had close parallels
with some official punishments, but which concentrated on forms of behaviour - especially female
dominance - of which the law itself took insuffic-
ient cognisance. But this legal perspective is in
itself inadequate. It is important to recognise
that, both in their ebullient informality and also
in their forms, ridings also had strong festive
associations. It was not simply that ridings could,
as noted earlier, be directed against people who
offended against the holiday spirit. Some features
of ridings, such as the parades of armed men, drum-
ming, and gunfire, linked them with the 'watches' or
parades of citizens in arms which in some cases
still occurred in towns and cities on Midsummer Eve
and other festivals.(20) More generally, the forms
of ridings connected them with a variety of festive
practices associated with Maytime, the Christmas and
New Year seasons, and parish feasts and revels.
Noisy cavalcades, marches and processions with gunfire and drums, the parading of pageant figures in
live or effigy form, transvestism, and even the
rough music of pots and pans - all these formed part
of the holiday repertoire.(21) The violence and
derision of ridings also had their festive parallels. On holidays, groups of armed men sometimes
invaded a neighbouring parish and engaged in real or
mock combat with the inhabitants. An account of a
series of clashes between groups from the villages
of Burbage and Wilton in Wiltshire in 1625 provides
explicit evidence of a link between this practice
and the custom of riding skimmington. One of the
leaders of the Burbage men asserted in court that
'the men of Wilton had before that time come in the
like manner to them, with a jest to bring skimmington into the said parish of Burbage, which this

examinate and the others of Burbage ... resolved to
carry back to them of Wilton'. There is no indication in this well-documented case that a wife had
beaten her husband; and in any event, it is plain
that hostility and derision were chiefly directed,
in this holiday context, not against an individual
victim but against a group representing an entire
neighbouring village.(22) Contrariwise, ridings
which were occasioned by termagant wives sometimes
involved the invasion of one parish by another. To
this extent demonstrations occurring outside festive
contexts were complicated by themes which were
normally associated with holidays.(23)

To a large extent, ridings may be seen as a
specialised application of holiday motifs. Moreover, they were themselves a species of festivity.
People who took part in ridings, whether or not they
claimed a corrective function, commonly described
them as 'games' or 'sports', performed 'in
merriment';(24) and, although these customs could
take place at any time of the year, they not infrequently occurred on major holidays and were probably
part and parcel of the festivities.(25) These facts
do not, of course, detract from the social significance of ridings. Festivities may articulate
important social meanings; while laughter, especially in the highly ritualised form found in
ridings, is (so to speak) a serious matter for the
historian. As Keith Thomas has reminded us,
laughter often springs from a sense of paradox and
from situations which involve anomalies or conflicts
of ideas; and may thereby reflect (and in some
measure ease) the tensions arising from structural
ambiguities in the ideal or actual social system.(26)
These insights are vital to understanding the nature
of ridings in early modern England and, in particular, their distinctive association with the wife who
beat her husband.

For the 'feminine monarch' was an ambiguous figure, evoking complex reactions in which hostility
mingled with an uneasy sense of fun. The social
meaning of ridings was, of course, rooted in the
prevailing patriarchal ideal which ascribed active,
governing roles to men and assumed that the chief
duties of wives and other women - who were,
supposedly, by nature weak in reason and apt to be
disorderly - lay in the negative virtues of chastity, obedience and silence. The wife who beat her
husband represented an inversion of the natural
order, a monstrous anomaly, the world turned upside
down. At one level, ridings simply expressed

hostility towards this gross transgression of social norms; while the laughter associated with these demonstrations stemmed, in part, from a sense of paradox at the spectacle of the wife who wore the trousers.

If this is all that was involved, however, it is difficult to explain why ridings were not also directed against sons who assaulted their fathers, for they equally transgressed the patriarchal ideal. It would seem that some deeper unease was involved. A clue is provided by the fact that some contempo-rary observers and literary commentators noted that the menfolk who performed ridings were not neces-sarily secure in their own masculine role. A by-stander at a skimmington ride at Ditcheat (Somerset) in 1653 contemptuously remarked of the mob that 'not ten of that company would charge an enemy'; while Jonathan Swift observed of those who mocked a beaten husband:

> Those men who wore the breeches least
> Called him a cuckold, fool and beast. (27)

Deep in the hearts of the organisers of ridings lay the knowledge that women could never be dominated to the degree implied in the patriarchal ideal. For that ideal was only too plainly in conflict with the realities of everyday life, and indeed with alter-native ideals. It is clear that, in practice, the balance of authority between husbands and wives in marriage varied considerably, and husbands could by no means count on female submission. Moreover, it is evident that strong, active, able wives were often prized (as an economic asset, for example) – despite the fact that the behaviour of such wives was unlikely to conform exactly to the stereotype of female virtue.(28) A contemporary proverb even opined that in the last resort it was 'better to marry a shrew than a sheep'.(29) In these circum-stances, reactions to the dominant wife were bound to be ambivalent. Certainly, skimmington rides derided extreme violations of the patriarchal ideal – actual physical assault by the wife – and thus set firm boundaries on the range of permissible behaviour. But their psychology was more complex than that of simple correction. Rather, the explos-ive laughter of ridings represented a cathartic release of tensions built up by 'everyman's' experience of the day-to-day conflicts between the dictates of the patriarchal ideal and the infinite variety of husband/wife relationships. Precisely the same tensions made representations of cuckoldry, termagant wives and the like a prime source of comic entertainment - endless permutations on these themes were staple fare in the comic theatre, broadside ballads, jest and story books, and in other forms of literature. In the real-life context, people had fun at the expense of their neighbours, savagely scapegoating the beaten husband and his rampant wife to ease their own fears.

The symbolism of ridings provides further insights into the nature of these customs. On the basis of a study of ridings and rough music in the nineteenth century, Edward Thompson has vigorously argued an anti-structuralist line and asserted that form and function were not mutually dependent.(30) But this is patently not true in early modern England. The various motifs found in ridings were not random but plainly integral to the meaning of the event. Moreover, the symbolism of ridings implied a connection, based on the principle of analogy or correspondence, between a variety of different kinds of experience; and can only be fully understood as part of a wider universe of meanings. The most important linkage (well known to students from the significant place it occupied in the official philosophy of the period) was a corres- pondence between the social and political hierarchy of the body politic and the authoritarian relation- ship between husband and wife in the 'little commonwealth' of the family household. Because political and domestic authority were conceived to be mutually validating, disturbances in the hierar- chy of the family implied a threat to the whole social order; and it was precisely this which justified communal action.

The very existence of ridings, which were in effect highly stylised representations of anarchy, pointed a contrast between order and disorder, while representations of political power (parades of armed men, etc.) and the authoritarian motif of the horse and rider demonstrated that order was to be con- ceived in hierarchical terms of dominance and subjection. Cacophony - discordant music - evoked a contrast between harmony and disharmony, whether between wives and husbands in marriage or between rulers and ruled. Transvestism symbolised the dichotomy of roles between men and women and the inversions thereof perpetrated by the termagant wife and her abject 'skimmington' and (in less blatant fashion) by the cuckold and his faithless partner. Animal symbolism evoked the contrast between human

and beast to place aberrant conduct firmly beyond
the social pale; while the symbols of mud and
excrement (cleansed by ducking) played on a contrast
between purity and filth - a distinction still current as a means of categorising sexual behaviour.
Ridings also demonstrated a contrast between the
hidden and the manifest, the private and the public.
Destroyers of privacy, they asserted the validity of
a system of collective values which were stronger
than the vagaries of individuals, and asserted that
in the last resort relations between husbands and
wives were a social, not just a personal matter.
        The existence of these polar opposites implied
a multitude of boundaries; and the motif of
boundary-crossing was so prominent in ridings as
scarcely to require emphasis. In this world of
symbols and correspondences, moreover, the overlap
between the forms associated with ridings and festive practices becomes more readily intelligible.
Festivals marked important time boundaries, a notion
evoked in concrete terms in holiday celebrations by
the crossing of boundaries between neighbouring
parishes, transvestism, the assumption of animal
dress, and so on. There was a strong logical link
between these activities and ridings: just as
special times justified licence and inversion, so
aberrant behaviour in everyday life justified practices more usually associated with holidays and a
festive release of energy.

IV

        Further information on the sociology of ridings
will be offered later, when popular and elite reactions to these customs are discussed. Meanwhile,
let us consider another widespread species of
popular disapprobation, the use of mocking rhymes
and lampoons. Sometimes such skits occurred in
association with ridings or with the exhibition of
cuckold's horns. The riding at Aveton Gifford,
cited earlier, included the reading of 'a scandalous
libellous paper'; and libels also supplemented the
demonstrations against John Hole and his colleagues
at Wells. But such lampoons could, and indeed
usually did, exist independently of concrete symbolism; they are best considered a separate genre of
mockery. These verbal productions took various
forms. One popular device was to satirise the
victim or victims in a mock litany, or in a derisive
proclamation supposedly issued by a mock court.
Even more common were elaborate rhymes, usually

designed to be sung. Characteristically scurrilous, the following example from Ogbourne Saint Andrew (Wiltshire) in 1626 will convey the flavour of these pieces:

> O hark a while and you shall know
> Of a filthy beast did her breech show,
> And of her doing and how indeed
> In this her filthiness she did proceed.
>
> She went and laid upon the ground
> And tucked her coats about her round,
> And because she is so brave and fine,
> She tucked up her heels and said she would
>   show the moonshine.
>
> My thought the same did me very much urge,
> It is a pity but she should be whipped with
>   the scourge;
> Although she be never so fine,
> I say her breech is not the moonshine.
>
> And all the rest I would beware
> And keep their coats upon their bare [sic];
> And although she be never so brave and fine,
> I say her breech is not the moonshine.
>
> And so I make an end and rest,
> And for to leave I think it best;
> Although she be never so brave and fine,
> I say her breech is not the moonshine. (31)

Like ridings, these rhymes and lampoons had festive associations. At South Kyme (Lincolnshire) in 1604, a rhyme directed against the Earl of Lincoln occurred in the context of an elaborate May game involving an armed parade, a derisive play, and a mock sermon on a text 'out of the book of Mab'. The Earl himself was not the only victim of satire; there was also a litany of the whores of the village, with *ora pro nobis* (pray for us) pronounced after each name.(32) More generally, the making or singing of ballads on strange, obscene or amusing subjects – 'Maid, carry thy cunt before thee' is one of the titles which have come down to us – was a traditional holiday occupation; and it was only a step from this to the framing of libels against specific individuals. (33)

Whether or not they occurred in the context of calendar festivities, mocking rhymes were often modelled closely on contemporary printed broadside

ballads and other products of professional entertainers. Sometimes they followed the conventional
division of ballads into 'the first' and 'the second
part'. Occasionally, they specified current tunes:
a rhyme from Compton Bassett (Wiltshire) in 1620 was
headed 'A New Song to the Tune of Roaring Tom'.(34)
There was probably also a certain amount of wholesale borrowing from professionals. <u>Tarlton's Jests</u>,
a collection of material attributed to the actor-
clown Richard Tarlton (d. 1588), included the rhyme:

> Woe worth thee, Tarlton,
> That ever thou wast born;
> Thy wife hath made thee cuckold,
> And thou must wear the horn.
>
> What and if I be, boy,
> I'm ne'er the worse;
> She keeps me like a gentleman
> With money in my purse.

This cropped up in the village of Earls Colne
(Essex) in 1588, allegedly the work of a tailor
called John Brande, in the form:

> Woe be unto Kendall that ever he was born,
> He keeps his wife so lustily she makes him
>   wear the horn.
> But what is he the better, or what is he
>   the worse?
> She keeps him like a cuckold, with money in
>   his purse.

Yet another elaborated version was to appear in the
Wiltshire village of Bremhill in 1618; and there
were no doubt others.(35) Detailed comparison
between these popular rhymes and surviving broadside ballads could well shed interesting light on
the impact of print culture at the lower levels of
society, and on borrowings - perhaps mutual -
between amateur and professional performers.
     Whether plagiarised or not, many of these popu-
lar rhymes were, artistically speaking, of poor
quality; and sometimes rhyme, metre and invention
broke down in ludicrous fashion. But some had real
force, and a wealth of imagery and allusion (homely
or classical depending on the author's background
and education) reflected painstaking composition.
A few were of real literary quality. This was true,
for example, of a rhyme composed in Nottingham in
1617 (and quoted below). Hudibrastic in content

and metre (and sung, incidentally, to the accompaniment of rough music made by candlesticks, tongs and basins) it bears comparison with Samuel Butler's subsequent efforts. Even more strikingly, the demonstrations against John Hole at Wells in 1607 generated a literary gem in the form of a satirical epigram, penned by a certain William Williams *alias* Morgan, 'gentleman', entitled <u>The Quintessence of Wit</u>. In C. J. Sisson's opinion, 'it might well ... stand up to comparison with the work of any Elizabethan or Jacobean satirist except perhaps Donne or Ben Jonson'. Not surprisingly, the authors of this and of another satirical piece produced in Wells at the same time were keen to get their products sent up to London to be printed and published.(36)

But the authors of mocking rhymes were primarily interested not in literary fame but in lambasting their victims; and were chiefly concerned to publicise their satires locally. This was achieved in a variety of ways. Sometimes the lampoons existed only in oral form, and were passed on by word of mouth in alehouses or wherever neighbours met. Written libels were sometimes merely cast abroad to be picked up by chance: 'Unfold me' was written enticingly on the outside of one surviving specimen. Often, however, libels were deliberately displayed in some prominent place - the victim's gable end, the maypole, the whipping post and the church door were favourite spots. The choice of the last three was evidently intended to suggest that the accusations contained in the libel were not merely malicious but had the force of community feeling behind them. As will be seen, this stance was sometimes disingenuous. But some cases do suggest a long build up of communal outrage which eventually exploded in the form of a libel. The neighbours of John Coren, vicar of Box in 1606, had apparently compiled a 'register' of his movements, reminded him that within living memory another offender had been lampooned in a rhyme fixed to the church door, and objected to his alleged mistress washing her linen in the town well in case she had the *morbus gallicus* (French pox). Eventually, a letter of 'friendly admonition' (signed by 'the country') was sent to Mrs Coren to warn her of her husband's misbehaviour, and the mistress was treated to a verse libel:

> Mistress Turd,
> At one bare word,
> Your best part stinketh.
> If stink be the best,
> Then what doth the rest?
> As each man thinketh.
> A pox on your arse
> You have burned a good tarse.
> A very filthy lot
> And that was all got
> With a *finis*.[sic](37)

In some cases, libels actually appealed to established authorities to take legal action. In 1604, a paper affixed to the chancel door of the church of Warminster (Wiltshire) began with the heading 'A true bederoll of the whores known in Warminster', went on to list their names, and concluded: 'We would entreat you that be officers to look to it, for you shall answer for not doing your offices before God. We wish you well'. In another Wiltshire case, at Aldbourne in 1629, it can be shown that the publication of a mocking rhyme in April of that year did indeed lead to the prosecution of the alleged offenders, hitherto unmolested, at the archdeacon's Michaelmas visitation.(38)

The sheer entertainment value of mocking rhymes, combined with the appeal to communal standards, made them a powerful vehicle for hostility and derision. The intensity of persecution to which victims might be subject is vividly suggested by a case at Bremhill (Wiltshire) in 1618, which figured an elaborate rhyme of thirty-six lines. It was alleged that eleven people were directly involved in its production and publication, and many others were implicated. Multiple copies of the verses were distributed at strategic points in the parish, neighbours were invited into houses to hear them sung, and the libel was also disseminated in the local market town and in other places round about. Publication reached a peak on the sabbath. The rhymes were read on the way to church, in the churchyard, and in the belfry, while a group of parishioners met and sang part of the verses in the nave. After evening prayer, the organisers tried to persuade the preacher to read the rhymes openly in the chancel (they were angry when he refused), and also tried to get the backing of the churchwardens. The whole episode reflects a remarkable degree of boldness and organisation; the effect on the victim must have been considerable.(39) This was a society in which, if the gentry valued their honour, at least the more substantial sections of the lower orders equally valued their 'credit' or reputation. (40)   Small wonder that the victims of these lampoons complained bitterly that they had become 'odious and contemptible persons' in the eyes of their neighbours. (41)

What kinds of behaviour were castigated in such libels? Whereas the occasions for ridings were firmly circumscribed by established custom and by the logic of the concrete symbolism they employed, mocking rhymes and other lampoons were much more flexible. The writers could, and sometimes did, make reference to traditional symbols like cuckolds' horns, but essentially they were free to spin words to the limits of their own invention. They did not even have to confine themselves to sin and folly; physical deformity or other afflictions could equally be the butt of savage satire. Hence the first impression is that the range of imputations found in mocking rhymes was very wide: from theft to gout. However, some matters were clearly of more common concern than others. Sexual offences were easily the most prominent target of satire. It is often unclear from the texts whether adultery or fornication was at issue; but the former does seem to have been especially conspicuous. One reason for this was simply that sexual reputation was much more a matter of concern to married householders than to single people.(42) Incest was only occasionally mentioned, probably because it was not a common occurrence anyway. Various matters relating to sex and sexual immorality - impotence, procuring, and especially cuckoldry - were also a popular source of copy. All these imputations were often elaborated by reference to beastliness, filth, disease and degeneracy; while disgusting behaviour or loathsome forms of illness occasionally formed the main substance of libels.

In contrast to these imputations of what we would regard as personal matters, a much smaller number of libels focussed on what may be broadly termed 'political' issues. A verse thrown into the church at Caistor (Lincolnshire) in 1607, for example, complained of rack renting and enclosure. Another, dropped into the minister's porch at Wye (Kent) in 1630, protested at the high price of corn, and warned the authorities to take care of the needs of the poor.(43) Particularly interesting examples of this genre were a series of libels nailed to the door of St Michael's church in Coventry in 1495-6, protesting bitterly against the enclosure

of the city's common lands by the richer burgesses
and against the imprisonment of Laurence Saunders,
champion of the rights of the commonalty.   They
warned the magistrates of the anger of the populace,
whom one of the libels likened to bees and wasps –
small, but numerous and potentially dangerous:

> Litell small been
> That all aboute fleen,
> They waggen their whyng.
> Where as they light,
> The been will byte,
> And also styng.
> Loke that ye do right.
> Both day and nyght,
> Beware of wappys.(44)

Religious as well as economic tensions found an
outlet in derisive rhymes.   The vicissitudes of the
Reformation years generated many popular satires
directed for and against religious change, while
under Elizabeth and the early Stuarts there were
anti-Catholic and anti-Puritan libels.   In
Stratford-upon-Avon (Warwickshire) in 1619, for
example, the induction of the Puritan, Thomas Wilson,
led to riots against the new minister and his
supporters;   and the indignation of the more
religiously conservative townsmen was further vented
in a series of derisive verses and lampoons.(45)

But it would be misleading to draw too sharp a
distinction between 'personal' and 'public' imputations.   Some libels, while basically political or
religious in intention, resorted to personal abuse
to maximise the comic effect and to puncture the
pretensions of authority by probing its weakest
spots.   Of course, this kind of levelling humour,
the appeal to the great primal joke that kings no
less than clowns were in thrall to bodily functions
and prey to earthy passions, was part of a long
comic tradition.   The J.P. in the stocks, the magistrate with his breeches down, the minister up to no
good in the privy, were stock figures on the stage
and in comic literature, and also had associations
with the rituals of festive inversion.(46)   In 1615,
some of the citizens of Warwick showed a sound grasp
of how these comic principles could be put to
political effect.   In the context of a land dispute,
troubles over the franchise and other tensions, some
of the commons of the town made show of summoning a
mock court, appointed the borough magistrates to be
members of a jury of 'whoremongers', and castigated

the members of the corporation for a variety of
sins - 'a greedy cormorant', 'a bankrupt', 'an old
gouty whoremaster', and so on - whereat the by-
standers 'did very much laugh and ... rejoice'.
Such tactics were particularly apt for attacks on
Puritans, conventionally seen by their enemies as
hypocrites and dissemblers who denounced the sins of
others while indulging their own vices in secret.
Thus at Wells in 1607, the Puritan constable Hole
was derided for impotence and his associates for
adultery. At Nottingham in 1617, the Hudibrastic
rhyme referred to earlier claimed that:

> By night they catechize each other,
> The holy sister with the brother,
> And when the high priest hath well drunk,
> Each one betakes him to his punk. (47)

In some cases the 'political' intention underlying 'personal' imputations was less visible. A
rhyme composed in the Wiltshire village of Keevil in
1611 claimed that the vicar and his wife and three
female parishioners 'beshit the king's hall',
elaborating the charge with a good deal of unpleas-
ant detail. At first sight this looks like mere
scatalogical humour, but other sources reveal that
there was more at issue. The minister and some of
the more substantial inhabitants had attempted to
suppress dancing and summer sports in the village,
and through an order in the manorial court had
caused the destruction of the bower or 'king's hall'
where the festivities took place. In brief, the
events underlying this libel paralleled on a small
scale the anti-Puritan conflicts at Wells,
Nottingham, Stratford and elsewhere.(48)
This case illustrates that mocking rhymes were
not always quite what they seem. And this was often
true in a rather different sense. As we have seen,
the authors of these libels commonly tried to appeal
to communal standards and implicitly claimed that
their accusations were just. In most cases it is
now quite impossible to determine whether or not
the numerous imputations of adultery, cuckoldry,
and so on had any real substance. But, whether
true or not, it is plain that such personal animad-
versions could, and not infrequently did, express
hostilities quite unrelated to the ostensible
charges. Examination of the background indicates
that some libels were essentially incidents in long
standing gentry feuds, faction struggles among town
oligarchs, or contests for land and status among

the sub-aristocracies of yeomen and substantial husbandmen and tradesmen who dominated many rural
communities. A few lampoons evidently served no
real social function whatsoever - they were simply
designed to stir up trouble.(49)

V

This brings us to the question of reactions to
these lampoons, and also to ridings and rough music,
both among ordinary members of local communities and
from the lay and ecclesiastical authorities. The
attitudes of the latter are of particular interest
in the light of current historical concerns. Peter
Burke has argued that the three centuries after
about 1500 witnessed a repressive movement, amounting to a 'reform of popular culture', against many
festivities and other popular practices; while
Keith Thomas has drawn attention to the political
authorities' attempts in the same period to suppress
subversive humour.(50) How far did these movements
affect the phenomena which we have been considering?
There seems to have been greater hostility towards
derisive rhymes than towards ridings; so let us
first discuss reactions to the verbal forms of
mockery.
Inevitably, the actual victims of derisive lampoons squealed in outrage, and the richer and more
important they were the louder they tended to
complain. The people who found themselves libelled
(or, at least, those who resorted to legal action)
included many humble individuals, but the upper
ranks - ministers, yeomen, substantial tradesmen or
merchants, and gentry - were disproportionately
numerous. The more socially elevated victims sometimes stressed not only their own discomfiture but
also more general dangers of political and social
disorder. The leading burgesses of Warwick in 1615,
for example, claimed that the organisers of the mock
court with its derisive proclamations intended not
only to slander named people but 'as much also as in
them lay to bring the very magistracy itself into
contempt and scorn and utterly to subvert all manner
of order and government within the said town'.(51)
How far could the complaints of victims strike a
responsive chord among the rank and file of ordinary
townsmen and villagers? It would appear that the
libellist's attempts to attract communal support
were by no means invariably successful, and many
people regarded them simply as a public nuisance.
Thus at Yatton Keynell (Wiltshire) in 1600 the

churchwardens presented the wife of William Tilie as
'a maker of rhymes and lewd songs and useth taunts,
nicknames and evil speeches against her honest
neighbours to the grief and great disquietness of
some of the better sort of people within the ...
parish'.(52)   There was, after all, no obvious
justification for resorting to mocking verses and
the like to censure immorality - except, perhaps,
when local officers had been negligent in prosecuting offenders - since the church courts and other
official agencies existed to exercise such moral
discipline; and the malicious motives which underlay some cases must have been only too apparent to
disinterested observers. Moreover, the 'foul and
filthy' nature of many lampoons could be distasteful
to honest folk. Richard Morgan got a cool reception
when he tried out a mocking rhyme in a shop in
Warminster in 1589: a bystander opined that it 'was
no less offensive to the ears of others' than it
would be to the victims themselves. People could
also be afraid of the tensions which scurrilous
matter might generate in the town or village. 'Fie
upon it', cried one Wiltshire woman when she heard a
mocking rhyme, 'What a beastly thing is this, burn
it, for there will come anger of it.'(53)
     Such reactions might be strengthened if the
actual authors of these libels, who claimed the
right to censor the morals of other people, were
themselves of dubious standing. In terms of socio-
economic status, the composers of such rhymes and
lampoons (predominantly male) spanned a wide social
spectrum - from gentry down to the level of husbandman and small craftsman, plus the occasional
labourer. Towards the lower end of this range,
craftsmen and small tradesmen seem to have been disproportionately represented, probably reflecting
differentials in literacy levels between agricultural workers and artisans - though illiterates did
sometimes compose or at least decide the substance
of libels, and got a schoolboy or down-at-heel
schoolmaster to write them out or knock them into
shape.(54) Thus in a purely socio-economic sense
our rhymsters were by no means the dregs of society.
However, preliminary investigation suggests that a
significant proportion were inveterate trouble-
makers, with a record of various criminal and
unneighbourly offences, including a number of
irresponsible youths. Some versifiers may also have
had a touch of disruptive madness in them. Thomas
Searle, author of a rather feeble rhyme against 'all
the noted whores in Ickleton' (Cambridgeshire) in

1637, 'could not sleep or say his prayers for thinking of it, and it grieved him he had not a good tune
for it'.(55)

If the attitudes of ordinary people were sometimes ambivalent or hostile towards mocking rhymes
and lampoons, the authorities took a wholly con-
demnatory view. The church courts had always
regarded such productions as defamations or breaches
of Christian charity; but in the sixteenth century
the secular courts also began to take cognisance of
them as criminal libels. Tudor fears of sedition,
religious unrest and disorder in general led to a
long string of proclamations against subversive and
libellous ballads and other forms of literature.
In the late sixteenth and early seventeenth centuries, the secular law - especially via judgements in
the Star Chamber - extended the law of libel to
include any 'epigram, rhyme, or other writing ...
composed or published to the scandal or contumely
of another'. Such libelling was regarded as a
serious matter, not only because it robbed a man of
his good name but also because 'it tendeth to the
raising of quarrels and effusion of blood, and ...
to the breach of the peace' and, when directed
against persons in authority, could be seditious.
Moreover, the covert nature of libel made it particularly reprehensible. It 'is very difficult to
discover the author', stressed Sir Edward Coke; and
he hence argued for severity in proven cases - by
fine, imprisonment, or (in extreme instances) by
pillory and loss of ears.(56)

In actual practice the operation of the law was
slightly less draconian than Coke's words might seem
to imply, but a steady trickle of cases did occur in
the secular courts from the late sixteenth century
onwards. Sampling of prosecutions in local courts
suggests that the crime was rather difficult to
prove to the satisfaction of juries, but convicted
cases were handled with moderate severity. In the
Wiltshire quarter sessions in the period 1601-50
there were ten indictments for mocking rhymes and
similar libels, one of which was rejected by the
grand jury. Seven of the accused, involved in four
of the cases, were actually found guilty, and punished with spells in the stocks or pillory, open
confession, short terms of imprisonment, and fines
ranging from six shillings to over three pounds. In
the Star Chamber, however, some serious cases were
punished with exemplary severity: the libellers
against John Hole, for example, were subjected to
massive fines.(57)

The law also developed the view that libels
might take the form of pictures or signs; and on
these grounds cuckolds' horns were held to be
libellous, though actual prosecutions in the criminal courts were rare. It might be thought that, *a
fortiori*, the elaborate, derisive spectacle of
ridings would be equally subject to censure; but
the law was slow to make the connection. It is true
that the church courts sometimes prosecuted the
organisers of ridings for defamation or breach of
charity, but the number of cases was minimal. In
the secular courts, even by the early seventeenth
century, performing ridings was not clearly defined
as a serious crime: it seems to have been generally
accepted only that participants could be bound over
to keep the peace or be of good behaviour. The key
judgements came after the Restoration, when in a
series of cases between 1676 and 1693 the court of
King's Bench decided that riding skimmington constituted a riot and also that an action for libel
could be brought on these grounds. But these legal
developments hardly constituted a frontal attack on
the custom. The changes were slow, piecemeal and
hesitant, and occurred partly by means of judgements
in cases which were not, in themselves, directly
concerned with ridings. In actual practice, prosecutions remained very rare. (58)
        The fact is that throughout this period ridings
were regarded, even by the upper ranks of society
and by the authorities, with a certain tolerance.
There were, it is true, some critical voices, but
they should not be exaggerated. Some Puritan ministers, scandalised by the festive associations of
ridings and by the use of such 'abominable' motifs
as transvestism, did inveigh against this custom;
yet critics of this type seem to have been few, and
there was no wholesale denunciation of this particular popular custom in moralist literature. (59) Other
objections may be inferred from the complaints of
victims and from other accounts of these demonstrations, amounting to the charge that ridings were
a threat to public order. However it is clear that
such objections did not apply with equal force to
all ridings: these customs had built in safeguards
which helped to limit their dangerous potential and
hence to stifle criticism.
        Potentially the most serious objection to
ridings was that they could be seditious. But, as
we have seen, politically motivated demonstrations
were in fact rare. In the usual run of cases where
husband-beating was at issue, the organisers might

be accused of seditious or anti-authoritarian intentions if the victims happened to be of high social
status or to occupy some position of authority. A
riding at Waterbeach (Cambridgeshire) in 1602, for
example, where the local vicar had been beaten by
his wife, was alleged to constitute a 'defacing of
the ministry'. But in this and similar cases the
organisers confidently appealed to established custom, affirming that it was the fact of domestic
disturbance, irrespective of the standing of the
people concerned, which provoked action.(60) In any
case, most victims of ridings were quite humble
people from the middling to lower ranks of society.
Thus the distinctive association of the custom with
female dominance helped to preserve it from charges
of seditious import.

Danger to property was another ground for
objecting to ridings. A skimmington ride at
Quemerford (Wiltshire) in 1618 did result in broken
windows, but even this degree of property damage
seems to have been exceptional.(61) The victims on
this occasion also complained of cruel physical
assault, and there were certainly other instances
of violence.(62) But mostly, it would appear,
physical abuse was avoided: the practice of using
substitutes or effigies in many cases probably
served to reduce the dangers. Yet another charge
was that the shame and trauma inflicted by ridings
were out of all proportion to the victim's
'offence', and likely to generate dangerous tensions
within the community. Ridings could, undoubtedly,
lead to bitterness and counter-violence: at a
stang-riding at Leeds (Yorkshire) in 1667 the victim, taunted beyond endurance, fired a gun into the
crowd and killed two people.(63) Such an extreme
outcome was, however, utterly exceptional. It must
be remembered, too, that the infliction of official
punishments (such as stocking or whipping) for
minor offences could equally arouse bitterness within
communities. Contemporaries always had to take
this possibility into account before resorting to
either formal or informal action against delinquent
neighbours.(64)

Ridings were less open than rhymes and libels
to the charge of malicious motivation. Far from
being based on flimsy or fabricated pretexts, many
demonstrations seem to have been stimulated by circumstances which were either particularly blatant
or scandalous or involved some especially ridiculous
element. In a Suffolk case in 1604, for example,
there was a long history of brawls between a wife

and husband, the latter being an inveterate drunkard. Not only was the man eventually beaten out of
the house by his wife, but he was also foolish
enough to exhibit his scratches to his neighbours
and to spend the night in an alehouse, drowning his
sorrows and lamenting his unhappy lot. (65)

Yet another criticism was that ridings were performed by base and disorderly members of the
community. Certainly some of the organisers were of
dubious reputation. James Jurdeine, for example,
the main participant in a riding at Cambridge in
1586, had evidently done penance in a white sheet,
and was convicted for abusing the beadle of the
University court. (66) On the other hand, many participants were, as far as can be ascertained, free of
any kind of record of criminality or disorder. As
regards socio-economic status, the evidence is somewhat complex. It is clear that the organisational
core usually consisted of the middling to humble
status neighbours of the victims, with women sometimes taking active part but, more often, serving
back-up functions like providing ale or furnishing
female garments for transvestite performances. But
young people, or desperate fellows like Jurdeine,
were often selected or hired to perform the hazar-
dous role of rider; while the performances
naturally attracted individuals of even more obscure
position - 'rude boys' and the like. Sometimes the
whole event was staged by servants. In London
(though not, apparently, elsewhere) there was in
this period a secular decline in the status of
participants, so that by the early eighteenth
century metropolitan ridings were peculiarly
associated with porters and other low status
occupational groups.

Overall, participation in ridings was predominantly plebeian. On the other hand, more substantial
members of the community often encouraged the
demonstrators and sometimes took an active part, or,
at the least, were prepared to remain neutral.
Officers of the law, including tithingmen, constables, and even justices, were sometimes
complaisant; (67) while in their private capacity,
gentry or other prominent individuals could be even
less inhibited in their support for these customs.
At Marden (Wiltshire) in 1626, a number of substantial parishioners were said to have encouraged the
demonstrators; 'the farmer of their town ... told
them it was well done of them and bade them go on'.
Similarly, at Barham (Kent) in 1643, Henry Oxinden,
the local gentleman, apparently encouraged and

possibly even took part in a riding. Dismissing the objections of a Puritan cleric, he declared that it was 'a harmless pastime, which according to the opinion of honest divines is not only lawful but in some sort necessary'. (68)

In the light of recent studies, which have stressed how far popular customs came under attack in this period from lay and clerical elites, such complaisance may at first sight seem surprising. In fact, it is readily comprehensible. In the first place, ridings were probably not frequent enough to be regarded as a major problem. Despite the flexibility of marital relationships in early modern England, it does seem likely that the actual beating of a husband by his wife was relatively unusual; and, since this was the characteristic pretext, it follows that demonstrations were by no means an everyday affair in the life of any particular community. When they did occur, however, they could be perceived as a defence of the patriarchal ideal which was shared by all ranks of society. Far from threatening the structure of social values held by the upper ranks, ridings could be seen as a gratifying endorsement of them. The fact that ridings could be plausibly seen as shame sanctions, very similar to those prescribed by official agencies, was likewise reassuring. To be sure, the fact that these customs were strictly speaking extra-legal (and eventually defined as illegal), and that they involved the assumption of quasi-judicial powers by unqualified individuals, could arouse some disquiet. But given that the legal system in any case relied heavily on local co-operation and delegated considerable policing powers to non-professional parish officers, such arrogation of authority could in the circumstances be lightly regarded. In fine, though ridings might at times appear indecorous and disorderly, fundamentally they were correctly perceived as representing no great challenge to the existing political, social and moral structure. On the contrary, they bore witness to a measure of consensus between rich and poor, rulers and ruled. In these circumstances, ridings were unlikely to come under severe attack. Whatever the degree of repression suffered in this period by other popular customs, it is plain that ridings and rough music were largely unscathed by the 'reform of popular culture'.

*   Some of the material and ideas included in this chapter were tried out in papers presented at a variety of seminars, and I should like to thank the participants for their helpful comments and criticisms. I am also grateful to Dorothy Owen, John Post, James Sharpe, Keith Thomas, Timothy Wales, John Walter and Keith Wrightson for kindly and generously communicating references to ridings and other relevant material. My thanks are also due to the staffs of the various libraries and record repositories which I have had occasion to use.

1. WRO, Salisbury DR, Bishop: Act Book (Office) 7, fo. 57; Peculiar of the Treasurer: Churchwardens' Presentments, 1630-40, Calne, 14 Jan. 1632/3; Bishop: Deposition Book 29, fos. 11-12; Cambridge Univ. Lib., Ely DR, D/2/49, fo. 93.

2. For examples, see W. H. Hale, *A Series of Precedents and Proceedings in Criminal Causes* (1847), p. 252; *The Churchwardens' Presentments in the Oxfordshire Peculiars of Dorchester, Thame and Banbury*, ed. S. A. Peyton (Oxfordshire RS, x, 1928), pp. 79, 205; WRO, Salisbury DR, Bishop: Act Book (Office) 6, fo. 13v.

3. C. J. Sisson, *Lost Plays of Shakespeare's Age* (Cambridge, 1936), chs. 2-3.

4. For a wide ranging treatment, with extensive bibliographies, see J. Le Goff and J.-C. Schmitt (eds.), *Le charivari: actes de la table ronde organisée à Paris (25-27 avril 1977) par l'École des Hautes Études en Sciences Sociales et le Centre National de la Recherche Scientifique* (Paris, 1981). See also E. P. Thompson, '"Rough Music": le charivari anglais', *Annales. E.S.C.*, xxvii (1972), and M. Ingram, 'Ridings, Rough Music and the "Reform of Popular Culture" in Early Modern England', *P. and P.*, 105 (1984).

5. WRO, QS Great Roll, Michaelmas 1626, no. 149.

6. D. Underdown, 'The Problem of Popular Allegiance in the English Civil War', *TRHS*, xxxi (1981), pp. 88-90.

7. M. G. Dickinson, 'A "Skimmington Ride" at Aveton Gifford', *Devon and Cornwall Notes and Queries*, xxxiv (1981), p. 292. The other features of ridings referred to in the preceding paragraph may be verified through citations in succeeding pages.

8. S. Butler, *Hudibras*, ed. J. Wilders (Oxford, 1967), p. 146 (Part II, Canto ii, lines 697-702); Cambridge Univ. Lib., Ely DR, B/2/18, fo. 174v; *The Diary of Henry Machyn, Citizen and Merchant-Taylor of London, from A.D. 1550 to 1563*, ed. J. G. Nichols (Camden Soc., xlii, 1848), p. 301.

9. PRO, STAC 8/92/10, m. 4; *The Cobbler of Canterbury*, ed. F. Ouvry and H. N. Davies (Cambridge, 1976), p. 21; WRO, QS Great Roll, Hilary 1617, no. 92; West Sussex RO, Chichester DR, Ep.II/9/24, fo. 3v.

10. PRO, STAC 8/104/20, quoted in J. Kent, 'The English
    Village Constable, 1580-1642: The Nature and Dilemmas of
    the Office', Journal of British Studies, xx, no. 2 (1981),
    pp. 38-9; WRO, Salisbury DR, Bishop: Deposition Book
    30, fos. 10v-11.
11. West Sussex RO, Chichester DR, Ep.I/17/6, fo. 79v;
    Phillip Stubbes's Anatomy of the Abuses in England in
    Shakspere's Youth, A.D. 1583, ed. F. J. Furnivall
    (1877-82), i, p. 148, n. 14; PRO, STAC 8/161/1 (extracts
    from this document have been printed, with a commentary,
    in Sisson, Lost Plays of Shakespeare's Age, pp. 162-85).
12. HMC. ... Manuscripts of the Earl Cowper (1888-9), i,
    pp. 429-30; N. Rogers, 'Popular Protest in Early
    Hanoverian London', P. and P., 79 (1978); and Peter
    Burke's chapter in this volume.
13. The ethnographic literature is extensive. For an intro-
    duction, see B. A. Babcock (ed.), The Reversible World:
    Symbolic Inversion in Art and Society (1978); and R.
    Mellinkoff, 'Riding Backwards: Theme of Humiliation and
    Symbol of Evil', Viator, iv (1973).
14. English Historical Documents, 1485-1558, ed. C. H.
    Williams (1967), p. 986; Middlesex County Records, ed.
    J. C. Jeaffreson, (Middlesex RS, i-iv, 1886-92),
    i, pp. 234, 287, ii, pp. 139, 228; Some Annals of the
    Borough of Devizes ... 1555-1791, ed. B. H. Cunnington,
    (Devizes, 1925), i, p. 35; PRO, STAC 8/104/20.
15. Songs, Carols and Other Miscellaneous Poems, from ...
    Richard Hill's Commonplace-Book, ed. R. Dyboski (Early
    English Text Soc., ci, 1907), p. 155; The Letters of
    John Chamberlain, ed. N. E. McClure (Philadelphia, 1939),
    i, p. 211.
16. P. Whiteway, 'Notes from a Seventeenth-Century Diary',
    Antiquary, xxxix (1903), p. 69.
17. J. W. Spargo, Juridical Folklore in England Illustrated
    by the Cucking-Stool (Durham, Nth. Carolina, 1944),
    pp. 7-8 and passim.
18. J.-L. Flandrin, Familles: parenté, maison, sexualité
    dans l'ancienne société (Paris, 1976), p. 122.
19. PRO, STAC 8/249/19, m. 18.
20. A. H. Nelson, The Medieval English Stage: Corpus Christi
    Pageants and Plays (Chicago, 1974), pp. 11-14 and passim;
    C. Phythian-Adams, 'Ceremony and the Citizen: The
    Communal Year at Coventry, 1450-1550', in P. Clark and P.
    Slack (eds.), Crisis and Order in English Towns,
    1500-1700 (1972), p. 63.
21. C. L. Barber, Shakespeare's Festive Comedy (Princeton,
    1959), pp. 18-30; Sisson, Lost Plays of Shakespeare's
    Age, pp. 159-62; E. K. Chambers, The Mediaeval Stage
    (Oxford, 1903), i, pp. 89-419, passim; Sir R. C. Hoare,
    The History of Modern Wiltshire: Hundred of Mere (1882),
    p. 20; Diary of Henry Machyn, pp. 125, 137, 162, 201-3,

283; HMC ... Manuscripts of the ... Marquis of Salisbury (1883-1976), viii, pp. 191, 201-3; Tudor Parish Documents of the Diocese of York, ed. J. S. Purvis (Cambridge, 1948), pp. 168-73; R. Plot, The Natural History of Stafford-shire (Oxford, 1686), p. 434; WRO, Salisbury DR, Dean: Churchwardens' Presentments, 1635, Lyme Regis, 20 Sept.; SRO, Q/SR 86.2/17; Birmingham Reference Lib., MS. 377993, fo. 26.

22. WRO, Salisbury DR, Dean: Act Book 28 (unfoliated), 26 Jan. 1625/6, Office v. Noyce et al.

23. For a particularly clear instance at Quemerford (Wiltshire) in 1618, where the skimmington riders invaded the place from the neighbouring town of Calne, see WRO, QS Great Roll, Trinity 1618, no. 168.

24. PRO, STAC 8/249/19; SRO, Q/SR 25/23; WRO, QS Great Roll, Michaelmas 1626, nos. 149-50.

25. E.g.,SRO, Q/SR 25/23 (day of village revel); PRO, STAC 8/249/19, p. 1 (Plough Monday); Colchester Town Hall, Colchester Borough:Records Sessions Book, 1630-63 (unfoliated), 11 May 1632 (Maytime).

26. K. Thomas, 'The Place of Laughter in Tudor and Stuart England', Times Literary Supplement (21 Jan. 1977), p. 77.

27. SRO, Q/SR 86.2/55; The Poems of Jonathan Swift, ed. H. Williams (Oxford, 1937), i, p. 221.

28. For a sensitive discussion of marital relationships in this period, see K. Wrightson, English Society, 1580-1680 (1982), pp. 89-104. See also R. L. Greaves, Society and Religion in Elizabethan England (Minneapolis, 1981), pp. 251-67. But for a rather different view, see L. Stone, The Family, Sex and Marriage in England, 1500-1800 (1977), ch. 5.

29. W. G. Smith and J. E. Heseltine, The Oxford Dictionary of English Proverbs (Oxford, 1948), s.v. 'shrew'.

30. Thompson, '"Rough Music"', p. 292 and passim.

31. WRO, QS Great Roll, Michaelmas 1626, no. 104.

32. N. J. O'Conor, Godes Peace and the Queenes (1934), pp. 108-26.

33. The Archdeacon's Court: Liber Actorum, 1584, ed. E. R. Brinkworth (Oxfordshire RS, xxiii-xxiv, 1942), ii, p. xxiii; West Sussex RO, Chichester DR, Ep.I/17/12, fo. 136v.

34. WRO, QS Minute Books (unfoliated), Hilary 1621, indict-ment of Robert Maundrell et al.

35. Tarlton's Jests, and News out of Purgatory, ed. J. O. Halliwell (1844), p. 19; F. G. Emmison, Elizabethan Life: Disorder (Chelmsford, 1970), p. 68; PRO, STAC 8/164/18.

36. Sisson, Lost Plays of Shakespeare's Age, pp. 175, 183-5, 200-2.

37. PRO, STAC 8/98/20.

38. WRO, QS Great Roll, Easter 1604, no. 124; Easter 1629, no. 101; Salisbury DR, Archdeacon of Wiltshire: Act Book (Office) 6 (unfoliated), 8 Dec. 1629, Office v. Knackstone and Haies.

39. PRO, STAC 8/164/18.

40. M. Ingram, 'Ecclesiastical Justice in Wiltshire, 1600-1640' (Univ. of Oxford D. Phil. thesis, 1976), ch. 9; J. A. Sharpe, Defamation and Sexual Slander in Early Modern England (York, 1980).

41. PRO, STAC 8/164/18.

42. Ingram, 'Ecclesiastical Justice in Wiltshire', pp. 277, 294-5, 356.

43. HMC ... Manuscripts of the Duke of Rutland (1888-1905), i, p. 406; J. Thirsk (ed.), The Agrarian History of England and Wales ... 1500-1640 (Cambridge, 1967), p. 583.

44. Tudor Economic Documents, ed. R. H. Tawney and E. Power (1924), iii, pp. 12-13; M. D. Harris, 'Laurence Saunders, Citizen of Coventry', English Historical Review, ix (1894), pp. 633-51.

45. Sisson, Lost Plays of Shakespeare's Age, pp. 188-96.

46. I. Donaldson, The World Upside-Down: Comedy from Jonson to Fielding (Oxford, 1970), ch. 1.

47. PRO, STAC 8/282/30; D. Hirst, The Representative of the People? (Cambridge, 1975), pp. 210-12; Sisson, Lost Plays of Shakespeare's Age, p. 202.

48. Ingram, 'Ecclesiastical Justice in Wiltshire', pp. 102-3.

49. For examples of the complex circumstances underlying some libels, see J. A. Sharpe, Crime in Seventeenth-Century England: A County Study (Cambridge, 1983), p. 157; PRO, STAC 8/98/20; STAC 8/79/12.

50. Burke, Popular Culture, chs. 8-9; Thomas, 'Place of Laughter', *passim*.

51. PRO, STAC 8/282/30.

52. WRO, Salisbury DR, Archdeacon of Wiltshire, Detecta Book, 1586-99, fo. 172.

53. WRO, Salisbury DR, Bishop: Deposition Book 11, fos. 5v-6, 24; PRO, STAC 8/164/18. See also Emmison, Elizabethan Life: Disorder, p. 68.

54. Emmison, Elizabethan Life: Disorder, pp. 73-4.

55. Cambridge Univ. Lib., Ely DR, K/17/94.

56. The Reports of Sir Edward Coke, 13 parts (Dublin, 1793 edn.), v, fos. 125a-6a; M. Dalton, The Countrey Justice (1622 edn.), p. 173.

57. PRO, E 159/440, Pasch. 9 Jac./256.

58. J. Keble, Reports in the Court of King's Bench ... from the XII to the XXX Year of ... King Charles II (1685), iii, pp. 578-9; The Reports of Sir Bartholomew Shower ... of Cases Adjudg'd in the Court of King's Bench (1708-20), ii, pp. 313-14; W. Salkeld, Reports of Cases Adjudged in the Court of King's Bench (1795), iii, p. [226]; A View of the Penal Laws Concerning Trade and

Trafick (1697), Appendix, s.v. 'riot'. cf. Sir T.
Raymond, The Reports of Divers Special Cases (1696), p.
401; The Reports of Sir Peyton Ventris (1696), i, p. 348.

59. The Presbyterian Movement in the Reign of Queen Elizabeth
as Illustrated by the Minute Book of the Dedham Classis,
1582-1589, ed. R. G. Usher (Camden Soc., viii, 1905), p.
63; Norfolk and Norwich RO, Aylsham 1, letter from John
Bond to Sir John Palgrave, 4 March 1660/1.

60. Cambridge Univ. Lib., Ely DR, B/2/18, fo. 174v. See
also BL, Add. MS. 28000, fo. 284.

61. WRO, QS Great Roll, Trinity 1618, no. 168.

62. E.g., SRO, Q/SR 86.2/55-6; Q/SR 152/1A.

63. PRO, ASSI 45/8/2/113-15; the indictment is in ASSI 44/13
(unrepaired and unflattened indictments).

64. M. Ingram, 'Communities and Courts: Law and Disorder in
Early-Seventeenth-Century Wiltshire', in J. S. Cockburn
(ed.), Crime in England, 1550-1800 (1977), pp. 116-18.

65. PRO, STAC 8/249/19, m. 18.

66. Cambridge Univ. Lib., University Archives, Commissary
Court, I/2, fos. 93v-5v.

67. E.g., PRO, STAC 8/249/19, m. 18; STAC 8/104/20, m. 1;
SRO, Q/SR 86.2/55-6.

68. WRO, QS Great Roll, Michaelmas 1626, nos. 149-50; BL,
Add. MS. 28000, fo. 281. For other striking examples of
upper class complaisance, see The Diary of Thomas Isham
of Lamport, ed. Sir G. Isham (Farnborough, 1971), pp. 78,
155, 277; Verney Letters of the Eighteenth Century from
the MSS. at Claydon House, ed. Lady M. M. Verney (1930),
i, pp. 367-8.

Chapter Six

POPULAR LITERATURE

Bernard Capp

I

Much of the popular literature of early modern
England was simple in style, light or sensationalist
in tone, and escapist in design. In this essay I
have taken 'popular' to mean the short tracts that
seem, by style and price, to have been aimed at the
lowest levels of the literate, cheaper and simpler
than the material described in L. B. Wright's
Middle-Class Culture.(1) The most important
categories were ballads, chapbooks (short booklets
sold by a petty chapman or pedlar), jestbooks and
almanacs; often ballads cost only a penny, smaller
almanacs and chapbooks twopence, and larger items up
to sixpence.(2) The apparent simplicity of the genre
is deceptive, however, for works aimed primarily at
the poor were not confined exclusively to them. In
the sixteenth century, and to some extent later, the
upper and lower classes shared overlapping tastes in
literature and humour;(3) even in the Civil War
period the library of the Earl of Essex,
Parliament's general, contained William Lilly's
latest almanac and a cheap, popular version of a
medieval romance. On the eve of the Restoration,
General Monck and the London City Council were
entertained by singers who performed a topical
ballad, and Samuel Pepys heard Admiral Mountagu on
his flagship singing a humorous ballad about the
fall of the Rump Parliament (sung to the tune of
Greensleeves).(4) In the earlier part of the period
it is thus difficult to speak of a wholly distinct
'popular' literature. By the term 'literature' I
mean here any printed reading material; none of
the main types listed above can be categorised
rigidly - even as fiction or non-fiction - for
adventure, love, religion, social comment and news

were jumbled together; and the news was as likely to be fiction as fact.

II

Recent research has documented the dramatic growth of literacy under Elizabeth and the early Stuarts; by 1641 30 per cent of the male population could sign their names, and Margaret Spufford has demonstrated that a far larger number of people would have learned to read without being able to write. In East Anglia a substantial·minority of literate people can be found even among the husbandmen and labourers (21 per cent and 15 per cent respectively).(5) Specialist groups of London publishers were quick to tap this new market, and ballads and almanacs appeared in large numbers from the 1560s. Over three thousand ballad titles were registered by the Stationers' Company over the next century and a half, and the total actually published is probably several times higher.(6) The Civil War boosted sales of almanacs, already high; some years in the 1660s saw over 400,000 copies sold annually, equivalent to more than one for every four families in the land.(7) The chapbook market, which was on a much smaller scale till the mid century, then expanded rapidly at the expense of the ballad. The stock of Charles Tias, a publisher who died in 1664, comprised about 90,000 chapbooks, and as he was only one of a consortium it seems likely that they were already matching the sales of almanacs.(8) The profits of the trade depended on low costs as well as high sales. An early balladeer complained with feeling about the poor ink and paper the printers used. Any available scrap paper was utilised, and a ballad might be found printed on the back of part of an old almanac or even a form issued by the Excise Office.(9) Old woodcuts appeared again and again to illustrate new titles, and printing mistakes were common. If the quality was poor, the productivity rates were by contrast exemplary: the slight earthquake which occurred on 6 April 1580 prompted an account which was printed and published within two days of the event.(10)

Of the authors who supplied the market we know relatively little. Even the most famous were of modest social standing: William Elderton, the best-known Elizabethan balladeer, was the head of a company of comic actors for some time; his successor, Thomas Deloney, was a silk-weaver from Norwich; and the most famous Stuart balladeer,

Martin Parker, kept an alehouse. John Taylor, the most prolific of all with 157 items to his name, worked as a Thames waterman. (11) The more obscure 'pot-poet' lived precariously; a sour contemporary commented that 'sitting in a bawdy-house, he writes God's judgements', turning his hand to any subject that would attract a publisher. (12) There were also many provincial versifiers, some of them professional balladeers, others artisans and tradesmen. Thomas Spigurnell of Colchester, better documented than most, began as an apprentice book-binder, became a pedlar and ballad-singer, and later kept an alehouse; versatile and opportunist, he was also ordained, probably for the fees to be picked up by illegal marriages.(13) Almanac-makers came from a rather higher background. Tudor compilers were often ministers or physicians, reflecting the link between astrology and medicine, while their Stuart successors included surveyors and teachers of mathematics. Increasingly, though, men from a lower social level came to the fore, earning their living as astrological consultants; William Lilly was typical of them, forced to make his own way in life when his father, a yeoman, was carried off to a debtors' prison. Lilly at least had a grammar-school education, unlike the leading astrologer at the close of the century, John Partridge, a London cobbler who was self-taught. (14)

The street-seller was vitally important in the distribution of cheap print, even in London. The ballad-man in The London Chaunticleers, published in 1659, offers ballads, jestbooks, prodigy stories and a collection of prayers for children. In 1641 there were said to be almost three hundred ballad-sellers working in the capital, standing at street corners and on benches and barrels to attract passers-by. Almanacs were sold in a similar way. (15) The ballad-seller's official standing was low, and he was classed by an Elizabethan statute as a vagabond, liable to a whipping unless he had a licence from two Justices. One Edmund Dun, 'a singing man', was listed among the rogues tramping the highways of Kent in the 1560s. (16) Shakespeare's ballad-seller, Autolycus, was no saint, and his counterpart in Ben Jonson's Bartholomew Fair cynically collaborated with a professional thief: while the singer distracted his audience with a moralising song on the evil ways of thieves, his colleague robbed their purses! (17) Often the ballad-seller was a young man with few resources other than his quick wits. Young apprentices were sent out 'with a dozen groatsworth of ballads. In which, if they prove thrifty, [their master] makes them petty chapmen.' At the end of the seventeenth century there were an estimated ten thousand pedlars or petty chapmen working the roads. Going on foot from house to house and to markets and bear-baitings, they took a small stock of printed works among the pins, toys and ribbons which filled their packs. If a man prospered he might in time buy a horse and pack-saddle or cart, and run a more substantial stall at markets and fairs, serving a wider district.(18) Though only the larger towns would have a specialist bookshop, cheap print was thus widely available from small chapmen and from shopkeepers dealing in other wares, who often included small books among their stock.(19)

Clearly many thousands of people, swayed by a glib sales patter, catchpenny titles and pictures, were parted from their pennies, but we have very little direct evidence as to who they were. Richard Baxter as a boy and John Bunyan were certainly fond of chapbook adventures.(20) Schoolboys have indeed been identified as an important sector of the market.(21) Surviving copies usually belonged originally to collectors like Pepys or gentry and professional men, but such people were not the typical buyers. The evidence from contemporary drama points instead to men such as Bottom the weaver or Thomas Middleton's country farmer; internal evidence from the ballads and chapbooks themselves confirms this impression, for many of the heroes are artisans, husbandmen, labourers and servants, and the landlords and other wealthy folk who appear are remote figures glimpsed from below.(22) The publishers issued different versions of the same stories in a variety of sizes and prices to reach different categories of readers, and almanacs too ranged from complex works with a serious scientific or political dimension to simple handbooks such as Erra Pater, based on folklore rather than astrology. Some tracts aimed at very specific groups such as weavers or apprentices, some at urban readers in general, and others at the rural poor; by the mid-century there were almanacs designed for different political and religious groups, and for different parts of the country, such as Apollo Northamptoniensis. Though London was no doubt the major market at every level, the provincial ballad-sellers and country chapmen make it clear that cheap print circulated throughout the country, on an increasing scale. As early as 1586 a fire at Beccles, in Suffolk, prompted two ballads which were printed in London but published by a bookseller in Norwich, clearly with a local readership in mind. (23) London publishers even catered for differing personal tastes and opinions: there were rival ballads, for example, urging the wisdom and the folly of marrying an older widow in preference to a young girl, and the enterprising Martin Parker was in the habit of replying to his own publications, stating both sides of a case with equal vehemence. (24)

The transition from an oral to a written culture was a slow and gradual process. From child-hood onwards people continued to absorb a mass of folk tales, rhymes, riddles, proverbs and aphorisms. (25) Before the Civil Wars, John Aubrey recalled, 'the fashion was for old women and maids to tell fabulous stories nighttimes, of spirits, and walking of ghosts'. (26) In George Peele's play The Old Wives Tale (1595) a blacksmith's wife entertains two lost travellers with such a tale by her cottage fireside; one of them remarks, 'When I was a little one, you might have drawn me a mile after you with such a tale'; and Peele cleverly meets his audience's continuing taste for magic, giants, ghosts and distressed damsels while simultaneously poking fun at such fare. (27) Aubrey thought these tales had flourished in 'the old, ignorant times, before women were readers', and had been 'frighted away' by the spread of education. In fact women, whose central mediating role he perceived, benefited far less than men from the educational advances, and there was probably little difference between the stories he remembered and those which John Clare found being told by village mothers to their children in the early 1800s. (28) The old fables had simply moved lower down the social pyramid, to find a final refuge in the labourer's cottage as a sub-culture of women and children. Much of what the 'old wives' told is lost for ever, and few of the fairy tales now popular appeared in print until after the seventeenth century. Tom Thumb, a major exception, was published in 1621 and described then as already an old favourite. Many other tales were almost certainly well known long before they reached print; versions of Cinderella, for example, have been discovered in most European countries and even in ninth-century China. (29)

Increased literacy thus brought about a situation where a new printed culture overlay an older oral tradition without destroying it. Eventually print, with its fixed forms, did under-

mine the creative spirit of the old minstrels, but
the art of making up rhymes and songs in simple
ballad rhythms survived for a long time among
ordinary folk as well as professional balladeers.
Boys shouting rude verses were a commonplace of
street life,(30) and many adults composed mocking
rhymes and lampoons to embarrass their enemies. A
Restoration piece which found its way into print was
written by a 'drunken and broken Oxford apothecary'
to ridicule the tradesmen of the town.(31) Many of
the political ballads composed by cavaliers during
the Interregnum were intended merely to be sung
among friends, without any plan for publication.(32)
The relationship between the spoken and printed word
was complex, for cheap print could feed an oral
culture as well as undermine it. Some of the ribald
verses which circulated by word of mouth were
modelled on printed ballads.(33) A person learning
a ballad from the printed page might then transmit
it orally to friends or children, and it might of
course have been passed down orally for generations
before reaching print.(34) John Taylor took material
for his jestbooks from stories overheard in taverns,
alehouses, tobacco shops and bowling greens.
Readers doubtless passed them on to their friends:
one jestbook was indeed said to be very useful for
millers, smiths and barbers, whose customers had to
wait on the premises till their business was
done.(35) At the smithy and the mill, work and
leisure were inseparable. Reading itself was often
not the silent, solitary pursuit we now assume. An
Elizabethan writer described a typical winter's
evening in a country manor-house, with people
sitting around the fire reading aloud from Guy of
Warwick, a jestbook or a book of riddles.(36) The
alehouse too had a central role. Thomas Nashe
complained that the tall stories of the newsbooks
would end up as country alehouse talk, and two
centuries later John Clare described the country
farmer in a village alehouse, poring over the dark
prophecies of 'politics and bloody wars' in a well-
thumbed copy of Old Moore's Almanac, 'that many a
theme for talk supplies'.(37) It was usual to find
a ballad pinned to the back of a door, and Isaac
Walton describes a country inn with twenty ballads
posted around the walls for the customers to enter-
tain themselves.(38) Many of the drinking songs of
the period are set in an alehouse; some are bawdy,
others simply celebrate ale, company and good
cheer. In Good Ale for my Money a baker, smith,
tailor and their friends pass a convivial evening:

> A good coal fire is their desire,
> whereby to sit and parley,
> They'll drink their ale, and tell a tale,
> And go home in the morning early. (39)

The Pinder of Wakefield (a jestbook hero) and his
friends met weekly in a tavern to amuse themselves
singing songs, telling stories and swapping
riddles. (40)

We need to remember that in the seventeenth
century the tune of a ballad was as important as the
words. 'If thou <u>read</u> these ballads (and not <u>sing</u>
them), the poor ballads are undone', a Restoration
editor aptly observed. (41) <u>Greensleeves</u> was
immediately successful despite its mediocre lyric,
and several new sets of words were set to the melody
within a few days; later ballads about crime,
politics and religion used the same tune.(42) Song
was an important part of social and working life.
It was remarked in 1589 that ballads were often
sung 'for recreation of the common people at
Christmas dinners and brideales, and in taverns and
alehouses and such other places of base resort'. (43)
We hear of medieval women singing the deeds of
Hereward the Wake as they danced, and medieval
ploughmen singing 'a gest of Robin Hood' as they
trudged home; a Jacobean writer referred to the
'old shepherd and the young ploughboy' singing of
Tom Thumb at the end of the day's labour. (44) In
1653 Dorothy Osborne, out walking on a common,
encountered 'a great many young wenches [who] keep
sheep and cows and sit in the shade singing of
ballads'. Ballads were indeed 'sung to the wheel,
and sung into the pail' (the spinning-wheel and the
milkmaid's pail), and sung by servants, blacksmiths
and cobblers. (45)

III

Ballads, the best known of the popular forms,
were also the most varied in content. From a sample
of the titles registered by the Stationers' Company,
love and religion emerge as the two leading themes,
roughly equal in importance. (46) Drinking-songs,
also popular, helped to 'drive the cold winter
away', as they promised; (47) while tales of Robin
Hood, King Arthur and other old heroes provided
escapist fantasy. Other ballads served as proto-
newspapers, reporting fires, floods, political
events and far-fetched accounts of monsters and
prodigies. Chapbooks covered a fairly similar

range, and also offered more specialist humour, from riddles to jestbooks, and utilitarian information on such varied matters as diet, medicine, beauty-care and the occult.(48) The almanac was also utilitarian, providing a calendar, tables of sunrise, and useful tips on gardening, medical treatment and so on, but it was usually accompanied by a prognostication which was broader in scope and more sensational in style.(49)

Ben Jonson bluntly asserted that 'a poet should detest a balladmaker', and the purely literary merits of the average printed ballad are admittedly modest.(50) Though verses by Christopher Marlowe and Robert Herrick entered the popular repertoire, they had to rub shoulders with hobbling doggerel, illustrated in the tale of a serpent born to a Hampshire woman as told by a simple balladeer from Watchet:

> The serpent had ears like a pig,
> Which was considerable big,
> It had a great long tail likewise,
> With a pair of wings, and eke two eyes. (51)

Most ballads were competent, flowing verse narratives. Some conveyed with skill an atmosphere of tragedy or suspense, and a very few possessed dramatic intensity and some emotional power, notably such traditional ballads as Johnny Armstrong and Little Musgrove, which found their way into the printed canon.(52) Though Elizabethan writers felt a regrettable need to add heavy moral glosses, usually absent in the traditional ballad, the old virtues were not altogether lost, for the short compass of the ballad encouraged authors to focus on a single episode and tell it concisely. To heighten the dramatic impact, much of the story was often told in direct speech by the hero or heroine; even a town devastated by fire might be given a voice and made to tell its own story to increase the sense of immediacy.(53) Quite often the narrator set the mood by supplying an emotional introduction:

> With sobbing grief my heart will break
> Asunder in my breast,
> Before this story of great woe
> I truly have expressed,

and sometimes he had to break off his tale in mid-course, temporarily overcome by its horror.(54) The compression of the ballad form and its use of direct

speech and dialogue gave it some of the characteristics of the drama in miniature. Further evolution
led to the jig, a ballad-interlude with several
characters, acted and sung on stage at the end of a
play; quite often these short pieces were then
published separately and enjoyed an independent life
outside the theatre.(55) Some of the better chapbooks were also in dialogue form, probably taken
over from the ballads. While a few jestbooks - for
example Dobsons Drie Bobbes - have been hailed as
proto-novels, many chapbooks had no structure at
all, as is clear from such titles as A Hundred
Notable Things for a Penny.(56) The chivalric tales
were highly compressed summaries of the original
lengthy romances, and had become absurdly crowded
narratives. But popular taste was indifferent to
such strictures; the chivalric stories had a wide
and lasting appeal, and it is to these that we now
turn.

IV

'Who is it that reading Bevis of Hampton, can
forbear laughing?' sneered the Elizabethan, Thomas
Nashe. In fact the old tales of chivalry had a
strong appeal for city shopkeepers and country folk
long after their original aristocratic audiences had
come to disdain them. Chapbook versions of Bevis
and especially Guy of Warwick were popular throughout the seventeenth century and long after, and old
continental tales (such as Valentine and Orson) were
imported and adapted for the mass market.(57) The
chapbook St George provides a typical example of the
genre: son of a nobleman, George wins bloody fights
against savages, monsters and giants. The author
introduces a romantic sub-plot when George rescues
the Egyptian princess Sabrina by killing the famous
dragon, and they fall in love. The king of Egypt
refuses his consent, which allows the plot to revert
to military heroics, for George has to wage bloody
wars throughout the Muslim lands until he is able to
claim his bride and return to England.(58) The
chivalric chapbooks were breathless gallops through
incredible adventures and vast slaughter, their
heroes usually possessing no motivation or personal
traits other than a desire for glory and the lady's
hand. The author of a cheap edition of Valentine
and Orson explained that he had designed it for
those who 'desire to hear and know the truth in few
words', and the plot is so compressed that lesser
adventures are reduced to a bald statement that the

heroes 'conquered giants, subdued saracens, overcame
cities, destroyed castles....'(59) The other most
popular heroes were the outlaws of legend, such as
Robin Hood and Adam Bell. The stories stressed
their strength, boldness and skill: Robin's concern
for the poor, and his attachment to Maid Marian,
were much later developments.(60) Very occasionally
a real figure from history joined the heroes of
legend; one example was the Elizabethan adventurer
Thomas Stukely, who served the king of Spain and the
Pope and perished in 1578 on King Sebastian's
crusade against the Moors. (The compiler of the
chapbook conceded that Stukely was a traitor and a
papist, but thought his valour was worthy of eternal
fame nonetheless.)(61) Most readers however wanted
far more incredible and bloody adventures against
larger-than-life adversaries, coupled with a
romantic element; the modern success of James Bond,
despite the veneer of sophistication, is based on a
remarkably similar formula. When the supply of old
chivalric heroes was exhausted, writers simply
invented new ones in the same mould, exaggerating
the traditional features. The story of <u>Tom a
Lincoln</u>, the most successful newcomer, had reached
its 12th impression by 1682. As a youth Tom leads a
band of young outlaws; he is next employed by King
Arthur on an expedition which conquers Portugal, and
then sets out to seek fame and adventure. In Fairy
Land he encounters the queen, who falls in love and
kills herself in despair when he leaves her;
finally he reaches the land of Prester John in
Africa, where he wins a princess and returns with
her to England. Each part of the story echoes tales
which would have been already familiar to most
readers: Tom is the unrecognised son of the legen-
dary King Arthur; his outlaw band lives on
Barnsdale Heath, a haunt of Robin Hood; the
encounter with the Queen of the Fairies parallels
the popular ballad story of Dido and Aeneas; and
winning the princess and killing the dragon, follows
St George.(62) Like many folk tales, <u>Tom</u> is a story
where the compiler has assembled his structure by
arranging a number of familiar and traditional
motifs in a particular way; the lack of originality
clearly did not disturb the reading public.(63)
     The appeal of the chivalric heroes was no doubt
the male fantasies of toughness, adventure and fame;
the reader could identify with the hero's exploits,
just as pious readers of Bunyan might identify with
Pilgrim's victories over allegorical giants and
ogres. In <u>The Knight of the Burning Pestle</u> we learn

that the young apprentice has often acted out bold,
heroic roles in his garret, to the amazement of
children and neighbours; in the play he is now
inspired by an old romance to throw off his blue
apron and become a knight errant in quest of
fame.(64) Some compilers obligingly narrowed the
social gulf between the reader and hero, and so
facilitated the process of self-identification; in
one version of Guy, for example, the hero is made to
be of plebeian instead of the traditional aristocratic birth.(65) The life of the famous medieval
condottiere John Hawkwood, who according to legend
had once been a London tailor's apprentice, had an
obvious appeal as a chapbook subject. A fanciful
ballad combined elements of Hawkwood and St George,
with an apprentice hero sent to Turkey, where he
defeats twenty knights at the tilt, kills two lions
with his bare hands and naturally wins the king's
daughter in marriage.(66) Fantasy and self-
identification were also a prominent part of Robin
Hood's appeal, reflected as early as 1400 in the
proverbial saying that 'many speak of Robin Hood
that never shot his bow'.(67) As an outlaw, with
only sketchy indications given of his original
social status, Robin was ideally adaptable to the
needs of every class of reader. The tales of much
humbler heroes also provided scope for their
readers' fantasy. For some heroes fame and fortune
come by magic, through Whittington's cat or the
bottomless purse of Fortunatus: an attractive
notion for the poor reader who recognised that hard
work alone was never likely to change his lot. But
often brute strength is the transforming agent:
thus Tom Hickathrift, the son of a day-labourer in
Saxon England, becomes famous for his prodigious
strength, and by slaying a ferocious giant and
securing his treasure is able to set up as a country
gentleman with his own deer park. Tom is shown to
have been dim-witted and idle as well as poor,
emphasising the point that his salvation was by
physical strength alone, an attribute from which
even the poorest need not feel excluded by birth.(68)
The story of Long Meg - a rare heroine - has a
similar theme. A country girl, Meg comes to London
to seek work and finds renown through her readiness
to fight and beat all comers, sometimes in disguise
as a man; finally she achieves a modest fortune as
mistress of an inn at Islington.(69) For Meg, the
Pinder of Wakefield and some other poor heroes,
fame seems to have been a greater spur than wealth;
this may reflect the youth of many readers,

or alternatively a lingering sense of realism in a
society where the prospects of upward mobility were
severely curtailed. Many other ballads and stories
catered similarly for the sexual fantasies of young
male readers, describing apprentice heroes seducing
or being seduced by their mistresses.

The late Elizabethan novels of Thomas Deloney,
glorifying the life and values of the successful
tradesman, provided a different kind of hero with
whom a more self-confident and ambitious urban
reader might identify. In Jack of Newbury Deloney
told the story of a young man who by his own efforts
becomes a rich clothier employing hundreds of
workers. Proud of his new place in society, Jack
declines a knighthood and tells his employees that
wealth and fame are available to all by hard work
and honesty. This tale, and its companions, enjoyed
a long popularity in cheap, shortened versions.(70)
Similarly a number of ballads flattered artisan
readers by heaping praise on the blacksmith or some
other tradesman, stressing his importance in the
life of society and the antiquity and honour of his
craft.

To most readers the world of their political
masters was infinitely remote. Ordinary folk,
unable to imagine its nature, seem to have been
fascinated instead by the idea of direct personal
contact on a more or less equal basis between
monarchs and the poor. It is in this setting that
kings most often appear in the popular literature,
rather than as military heroes or national leaders.
One group of stories told of kings and the low-born
women they took - or tried to take - as their
mistresses; the 'fair maid of London' virtuously
resisted the blandishments of 'wanton King Edward',
while the more popular heroine Rosamond became the
mistress of Henry II until she was tragically
poisoned by the jealous queen.(71) Another, larger
group described encounters between kings and
commoners who failed to recognise them. The
commoner treats his sovereign in a blunt and often
abusive fashion until he realises his mistake and
trembles for his life; the king always proves
gracious and forgiving, rewarding his new companion
with lands, office and sometimes an invitation to
court. There are several strands in the appeal of
these tales. The reader, knowing more than the
heroes, can watch their hapless blunders with amused
horror. The rags-to-riches ending, brought about
miraculously by the mere whim of an unpredictable
king, would have an obvious appeal. A key element,

though, is surely the carnival atmosphere which provides a dramatic reversal of roles, a world turned temporarily upside down. The carnival had an important role in early modern Europe, acting as a 'safety-valve' necessary to release the tensions built up in a rigidly hierarchical society.(72) Though carnivals developed less in England than in the south, and were in any case discouraged by Protestant reformers, it may be that popular literature provided an alternative outlet for the same pressures. In many stories the commoner becomes for a moment the equal, even the superior, of his king; King Edward swaps his rich steed for the tanner's nag, symbolising the exchange of positions. The uncouth tanner farts in the king's face as he is helped into the saddle; the king merely observes, patiently, 'You are very homely'. King Alfred even becomes servant to a shepherd at a wage of ten groats a year, and has to submit to blows and abuse. When he burns the cakes, the shepherd's 'toothless dame' warns bluntly that if it happens again, 'I'll thwack thee on the snout'.(73) Eventually the knights or courtiers arrive, the carnival is over and normality returns, but there is no retribution for the insults and abuse; what happens during the carnival period is protected by its spirit of license. A number of the Robin Hood ballads feature a strikingly similar reversal of roles: Robin encounters a poor stranger, a tanner or pedlar, picks a quarrel, and - to his own as well as the reader's surprise - the invincible hero is thrashed by a nobody. The point has often been noticed, but never satisfactorily explained. By 1600, it would appear, Robin Hood had come to be seen as a figure of authority in his own right, the king of the Greenwood; once a symbol of social defiance, he had become part of the established order, and in these tales he is shown as the victim not the perpetrator of carnival overturning. The ending is always the same: Robin blows his horn to summon his men, reveals his true identity and invites the stranger - now suitably deferential - to feast with him or to join his band.(74) There is a parallel too in the story of Tom Hickathrift, the labourer's son who slew a giant. Tom, now a wealthy gentleman, picks a quarrel with a passing tinker and is soundly beaten; the episode ends typically with Tom befriending and rewarding the stranger.(75)

There is no direct challenge to the political or social order in these tales, and their message is primarily conservative. The encounters between

kings and commoners would tend to reinforce popular
belief in the king's innate goodness and to divert
blame for any injustice on to the heads of the
traditional 'evil counsellors'. Long Meg and the
equally pugnacious Pinder of Wakefield were always
devoted to the king; even Robin Hood and the other
outlaws were far from being rebels, despite their
war with local officialdom, and stressed their total
loyalty to the king, from whom they sometimes
received pardons, favours and even office.
Similarly, the tragic stories of Fair Rosamond and
Patient Griselda suggested, among other things, the
disastrous consequences of love across the social
divide. In the few cases where it succeeds there is
often a twist to preserve social conventions; thus
in The Blind Beggar's Daughter of Bednal Green,
where a poor heroine marries a knight despite
opposition from his family and friends, the beggar
is suddenly revealed at the wedding to be a man of
aristocratic lineage and considerable wealth.(76)

Nonetheless popular literature did contain
more subversive undertones, like carnival itself.
It is clear that the poor relished glimpses of low
life in high places, and liked to hear of their
superiors' feet of clay. Even King Arthur,
according to one chapbook, abandoned his bastard
infant to keep 'his own disgrace from the murmuring
report of the vulgar people'. Tom a Lincoln, in
the second part, becomes a bloody tale of aristocratic adultery, jealousy, murder and suicide.
Valentine and Orson shows the Emperor of Greece
knocking his wife to the ground, pulling her hair
and trampling on her in his rage when falsely
informed of her adultery.(77) The ballad tale of
Queen Eleanor, wife of Edward II, gave a lurid and
detailed account of her lechery, sadism and pride,
for which God eventually caused her to be swallowed
up by the ground - a fate all the more satisfying
to a late Elizabethan audience as Eleanor was of
Spanish birth and breeding, which the author
stressed.(78) Equally important, some tales lent
themselves to more than the conventional moral
supplied in the text. Patient Griselda is the
obvious example: the story tells of her fidelity
and virtue, with no comment on the torments
inflicted on her by her jealous, aristocratic
husband, but many readers must have contrasted the
virtues of the poor woman with the callous cruelty
of the rich nobleman. There is a similar ambivalence in the humorous tale of a countryman invited
to the royal court who refuses to enter the king's

presence without his dog and staff lest he be robbed
by the courtiers. The episode is presented as an
example of rustic naivety, but it also allowed a
reader to see it as a sly dig at the rapacity of
royal officials. (79) There were also many ballads
which, as we shall see, made sharp and direct
comments about the behaviour of the landed and the
rich.

V

Love and courtship were prominent themes in
popular literature throughout the period. There
were ballads to match every mood and situation, from
the mutual compliments of adoring couples to the
desperation of the deserted; at least two were set
in Bedlam, with the lover driven insane by the
torments of betrayal. (80) Usually there was a
simple story line, sometimes tragic in mood:
balladeers told, for example, of the bride who fell
sick and died on her wedding day, the forsaken lover
who killed herself in despair, and the father who
contrived to marry the girl his son had been
courting, with disastrous consequences. (81) Others
described love triumphant over all obstacles. One
of the more ambitious, The Marchants Daughter of
Bristow, combined romance with adventure and
religious zeal. The heroine's family rejects her
lover, and when he leaves for Italy in despair she
contrives to follow him disguised as a man. She
finds to her dismay that he has been sentenced to
death as a Protestant heretic, and, unable to secure
his release, she vows to be burnt by his side; the
story has a happy ending, for the judge is moved by
such devotion and spares them both, and they return
to England to marry and live happily. (82)
Most tales reflected normal life much more
closely, and Margaret Spufford has very successfully related the courtship stories in the Pepysian
chapbooks to other evidence about lower-class
mores. (83) The wooing of two servants named John
and Kate, for example, is conducted at spare
moments in an alehouse, where they plan their
future and reckon up their modest savings and
likely expenses. From their employers' good will
they hope to obtain rented accommodation and a
little capital to set up an alehouse of their own.
The dialogue brings out their hopes, petty jealous-
ies, affection and bashfulness, and is full of
sense and warm feeling. (84) The literature suggests
very strongly that young people regarded love as

the chief consideration in marriage, in contradiction to some recent theories.(85) The author of
<u>Love in a Maze</u> made the point explicit:

> If you affect a maid regard not then her
>   portion,
> Hang ten pounds, give me the lass that
>   loves me,

and he gave similar advice to female readers.(86)
One rich girl defies her family and declares to her
poor suitor:

> If friends do frown and fret
> And parents angry be,
> And brothers' grief is great
> Yet I love none but thee.(87)

At the same time most ballads and chapbooks show a
down-to-earth, practical view of love and courtship. Several heroines clearly wish their swains
had more refined manners, but are willing to settle
for the solid qualities on offer;(88) a number of
works provided tips on courtship, designed to give
clumsy and disappointed suitors the hope of greater
success in the future.(89) Authors recognised
though that a substantial difference in social rank
posed a major and often insurmountable obstacle;
many a poor young man is shown falling in love with
a richer girl only to be scornfully dismissed by
her, or her parents, as inadequate.(90) The tales
of courtship also reflect the fact that pre-marital
sex was a fairly common practice at the time, with
some 20 per cent of brides pregnant by the time
they reached the altar. The response of the
fictional heroines to the ardour of their lovers
mirrors the varying behaviour of girls in real
life; some are determined to hold on to their
virginity till their wedding, while others are
content with a mere verbal promise of marriage. It
is noticeable that the writers (unlike the church)
rarely voiced disapproval of this latter course.(91)
Verbal promises were of course easily broken or
forgotten, and betrayal was a popular theme of
ballads. <u>The Lovely Northern Lasse</u>, for example,
tells of a farmer's daughter seduced by the
'sugared words' of a shepherd's boy while she was
milking the ewes; when she proves pregnant the boy
abandons her, and her parents drive her away. In
<u>The Western Knight</u> a young city girl is deserted by
the gallant who won her by false promises.(92)

These tales, closely based on the traditional
ballads 'Child Waters' and 'The False Lover', no
doubt appealed to a largely female audience, and
often showed the heroine winning back her faithless
lover by her determination and spirit. Thus a
soldier who plans to abandon his very pregnant girl
is eventually moved to relent by her adamant resolve
to follow him across the battle-fields of Europe.(93)
   In sharp contrast with the tales of love and
courtship, are another group which vigorously
support the bachelor's life. In a period when
marriage might well be impossible for a dozen years
after the onset of sexual maturity, their message
perhaps helped young men to reconcile themselves to
a lengthy period of enforced bachelordom. Balladeers stressed the carefree joys of the single life:

> No cradle have we to rock,
> Nor children that do cry,
> No landlord's rent to pay,
> No nurses to supply....

and they mocked the fate of the married man, 'Wedded
to noise, misery and want, ... Obliged to cherish
and to hate thy wife'. A Restoration balladeer
openly damned marriage and championed the
prostitute.(94) Several authors presented sexual
relationships in flippant terms likely to appeal to
the fantasies of young men. In one a youth wagers
with three girls by a throw at dice; if one of the
girls wins, she can claim him in marriage, but if
the youth wins - as he does - he can take all three
without any strings. Another tells of a whimsical
girl who is quite ready to sell her favours,
insisting only that the price must be fourpence
three-farthings precisely.(95) Equivalent ballads
in praise of the spinster's life are conspicuous by
their absence; instead one piece consists entirely
of 'pretty comparisons' designed to show an
unmarried woman as something unnatural and absurd,
'like a jail without a jailer'.(96) Bachelors were
warned that single women were always eager to be
married with reckless haste, driven on by sexual
cravings and hopes that marriage would bring them a
higher status and better life-style - the chance to

> flaunt it up and down,
> with some of the bravest in the town.(97)

   Cynicism also colours the treatment of
marriage, usually presented in terms of disillusion

and marital brawls. Balladeers were fond of showing
how repentance soon follows a rash and hasty
marriage. One young man, delighted by a sudden
match with a beautiful young woman who even brings
him £10, given by a friend at the wedding, regrets
his haste when he finds her to be 'but a cracked
glass' - already pregnant by the generous
'friend'.(98) Young newlyweds often faced a sharp
drop in their standard of living when they left
their masters' roofs and had to cope with new
expenses and soon a growing family. Many tales show
couples chafing at the cares and ties that marriage
has brought; the wife resents being left alone
while her husband is in the alehouse with his
friends, and he in turn resents her demands for new
clothes, delicacies and treats. (99) Sometimes the
wife repents her choice of partner when she finds
that marriage has brought merely a new master
instead of the expected independence. 'I would I
had married John Goosequill', laments an Elizabethan
bride, 'Then need I not to have made this moan, For
by him I might have had all my will.' Authors were
quick to condemn discontented wives and reinforce
patriarchal values; quarrels usually end with the
humble submission of the wife, moved by the
husband's arguments or, in one case, by his threat
to abandon her and go off soldiering.(100) A more
positive Elizabethan ballad, which shows a poor
couple discussing with sense and affection how they
can survive hard times and find some simple
pleasures in life, was a rare innovation and found
few successors. (101) Quarrels and brawls did of
course show, in much exaggerated style, the problems
both sexes would encounter in marriage; and ballads
sometimes ended with sensible words of advice. More
often, alas, the problems of marriage merely
prompted the black humour of shrewish wives and
cuckolded husbands. Thus <u>Half a Dozen of good
wives, all for a penny</u>, a savagely misogynist piece,
tells of a man's six marriages, each wife proving
disastrous in a new way - one a scold, another
miserly, a third a sot who pawns her own clothes for
drink. Another tale has two countrymen walking to
market, swapping anecdotes about the behaviour of
local women, and agreeing that they all deserve to
be pilloried, lashed, carted or worse.(102) It would,
of course, be rash to take these ballads as evidence
for the real nature of marital relationships.
Shrews and cuckolds were the traditional fare of
comedy, appealing to a basic *Schadenfreude*, and
reflecting the eternal gulf between the patriarchal

ideal and the inevitable compromises of the real
world.

VI

Many of the tales and ballads already discussed
were labelled 'merry' or 'pleasant'. The drinking
songs offered further light-hearted diversion:
'Give me some more ale, Which is meat, drink and
clothing', cries a tippler, idly spending Monday
morning in an alehouse.(103) The reader in search of
humour could however also turn to the more
specialised jestbooks and burlesque almanacs.(104)
'Jest' meant 'prank', and most jestbooks consist of
a number of humorous exploits loosely grouped around
a central character. The humour depends largely on
the situation and the ingenious ways in which the
hero outwits those he encounters by his repartee,
cunning and sheer effrontery. George Peele, a
popular hero, 'gulled' friends, enemies and
strangers indiscriminately, for 'he cared not whom
he deceived, so he profited himself for the
present'. (105) Many of the heroes are indeed
unsavoury characters, and the jestbooks complement
the popular demand for books about thieves and
roguery. The close link between 'jests' and roguery
helps explain why they came to be fathered on such
unlikely figures as the highwayman, James Hind, and
Cromwell's notorious chaplain, Hugh Peter, executed
in 1660.

As we might expect, cuckoldry was one of the
central themes of the jestbooks. The cuckolded
husband was a butt because, according to the conventions of the age, he had allowed his proper
authority to be flouted and his property stolen.
Other traditional targets were foreigners
(especially the Welsh) and clergymen.(106) Religion
itself did not escape ridicule altogether, for
alongside the many stories which stirred up terror
of the devil there were a few tales depicting Satan
as a figure of fun. In one, 'old Beelzebub, merry'
visits London to win new adherents but flees back to
Hell in panic when he encounters the brawling city
fishwives. In another, Satan disguises himself as a
horse and carries off a scold to Hell; undaunted,
she kicks his flanks and curbs him so cruelly with
the bit that eventually he is only too glad to
deliver her safely back to her doorstep. In outrageous parody of the balladeers' moralising gloss,
the author urges his readers to learn from the
woman's art so that 'when the Devil comes for you,

You need not care a fart'. (107)   The comedy The
Merry Devil of Edmonton (1608) and Ben Jonson's The
Devil is an Ass suggest that the theme had a widespread appeal. Political humour, which formed a
large part of the ballad literature of the Civil War
period, was largely absent from the jestbooks. (108)
Their compilers preferred to concentrate on more
perennial targets, among whom the mentally retarded
and physically deformed were prominent. From The
Wise Men of Gotham onwards readers found complacent
merriment in the misfortunes of the feeble-minded,
and while they may have consoled the poor by showing
heroes more disastrously unsuccessful in life than
themselves, it is impossible to disguise the
cruelty, even sadism, they contain. The eponymous
hero of Unfortunate Hodg of the South is introduced
as a person of 'little wit, crump-shouldered, crook-
backed, goggle-eyed, splayfooted, crooked legs, and
so deformed, that he was hated of man, woman and
child', and the 'pleasant history' that follows
shows Hodg being abused, beaten, set on by dogs,
whipped, thrown into an open grave, put in the
stocks and smeared with excrement. (109) In this
context at least it is hard not to feel some
sympathy with the Puritan attacks on popular
culture.
        Popular humour, then, was extremely earthy,
with many tales hingeing on sex, farting and
excrement, often combined; the humour lies in the
way their basic assault on decorum and respectability 'punctures pomposity', in Keith Thomas's
phrase. (110) Bodily functions were a great leveller,
and much jestbook humour has obvious subversive
implications. Richard Tarlton turns his wit against
Queen Elizabeth to her face, and the Pinder of
Wakefield makes a rude jest at the expense of the
Recorder of London - in open court. (111) Like
Shakespeare's fools, carnival revellers and the
commoners abusing unrecognised kings, the jestbook
heroes are licensed to insult the privileged.
Among their victims are rich yeomen farmers, likely
to be the most immediate symbols of authority to
many poorer readers. In one tale the prophetess,
Mother Shipton, mocked and abused for her deformity,
takes revenge on one of her persecutors, 'a
principal yeoman, that thought himself spruce and
fine', by magically turning his splendid ruff into
a lavatory seat as he sits at dinner in company. (112)
The assault on authority would have a special appeal
to the young, and several of the jestbook heroes are
themselves young men, such as the Pinder and Black

Tom, or even mere schoolboys, such as Dobson who
leads a band against the adult world, and Tom Ladle,
who wages an unrelenting feud against his mother's
paramour. (113)

There was also a gentler kind of humour present
in the literature, for ballads or books of sheer
nonsense delighted ordinary readers, as they still
do children, and riddles and verbal conceits were
highly popular. In the jestbooks, the pranks were
sometimes interspersed with riddles and puns, and
quick repartee was often used to give a new twist to
stale jokes. (114)

VII

Religion, largely absent from the oral ballad
tradition, was a major theme of the broadside
ballads, and probably 30 per cent of the Restoration
chapbooks were religious in character. (115) Many
almanac-makers too blended religious teaching with
their predictions, and some supplied brief summaries
of Christian doctrine in verse, and rhyming versions
of the Ten Commandments; Vincent Wing's religious
and moralising almanacs led the market in the
1660s. (116) The Poor Man's Plaine Path-way to
Heaven, a chapbook based loosely on Arthur Dent's
Puritan tract of 1603, had reached a 57th edition by
the 1670s, and the chilling Doomes-day had run to
thirty editions by 1682. Clearly this cheap print,
selling at a few pennies an item, was reaching a
vast audience, far beyond the very limited numbers
of Dissenters in the population. (117)

Ballads offered a basic religious instruction,
turning Bible stories into simple verse and setting
them to popular melodies. Though Protestant opinion
came to frown on such blurring of the sacred and
profane, these ballads may well have made a significant contribution to the planting of a Scripture-
based faith among the masses. Biblical histories
from Adam and Eve to Christ and even Antichrist were
available in ballad form, and in strong demand to
judge by the large number of versions in print. (118)
An Elizabethan 'sweet nosegay' of stories from the
'Garden of heavenly Pleasure' (Scripture) sought to
combine the new biblical faith with a more
traditional oral culture, and so did the
seventeenth-century collections of Christmas carols
set to such tunes as 'Troy Town', 'Wigmore's
Galliard', and 'Bonny Sweet Robin'. (119)

Ballad religion was strongly partisan in tone.
Anne Askew, burnt as a Protestant heretic in 1546,

became a popular heroine, and several writers took
stories from Foxe's <u>Actes and Monuments</u>. <u>The
Dutchesse of Suffolke's Calamity</u>, which recounted
the sufferings of a Protestant noblewoman fleeing
the persecution of Mary Tudor, was still popular a
hundred years after the events it described.(120)
The Northern Rising of 1569 and the papal bull of
1570 prompted a crop of ballads denouncing papists
as rebels and traitors, while other authors, in pre-
Reformation vein, mocked Catholic priests as frauds
and lechers. One warned the young Queen Elizabeth
against the treachery of the entire clerical order,
which, he claimed, had subverted almost every king
since the Norman Conquest, including even her half-
brother Edward VI.(121) Though this anti-clericalism
gradually faded from the ballads, it reappeared in
almanacs in the 1640s in virulent form, denouncing
clergymen of every denomination; in the Restoration
period <u>The Protestant Almanack</u> supplied scurrilous
abuse, slander and mockery about Catholic dogma and
practice to ten thousand readers a year.(122)

The dominant theme of all forms of popular
religious literature was the call to repentance, and
the favoured method was by trying to create a terror
of death and Hellfire. The effect of this grim
message must sometimes have been to reduce the
serious-minded reader to despair.(123) <u>The doleful
Dance and Song of Death</u>, an Elizabethan ballad, has
a woodcut illustration of Death as a skeleton with
trumpet and spade, summoning the lover, lawyer,
merchant and scholar alike; in another ballad Death
cries triumphantly, 'I will kill you all.' In <u>The
Great Assize</u> - Judgement Day - a woodcut shows Satan
and the flames glimpsed through the open jaws of
Hell.(124) Dr Spufford noted that Death was
similarly the 'hero' of the religious chapbooks.(125)
Another favourite device to encourage repentance, in
ballads and chapbooks alike, was the deathbed scene,
reporting the last, heart-felt counsel of a pious
father, mother or minister.(126) Almanac-writers
made use of the ever-changing seasons to remind
readers of the mortality of all living things.
They stressed too that judgement would fall on
sinners in this life as well as the next, explaining
comets and eclipses as signs by which an angry God
threatened retribution on a sinful nation if it
failed to repent. Many compilers claimed that the
Apocalypse itself was at hand, reflecting a widespread contemporary preoccupation, and they offered
both biblical and astrological proofs: in 1583 and
again in 1652 astrological predictions that the End

was nigh produced widespread public alarm. (127)

Satan's kingdom was by no means confined to
Hell, and he appeared on earth remarkably often in
the popular literature. He carried off the profane,
enticed people to commit crimes or witchcraft which
brought about their downfall, and possessed the
innocent, sometimes driving them to suicide. Sometimes he came merely to terrify ordinary folk, such
as the Essex labourer who encountered the Devil
while collecting acorns, and the hackney-cab driver
horrified to discover that the customer he had
picked up in Fleet Street was Satan in person. (128)
In Strange and true news from Westmorland (c.1670)
an avenging angel first appeared to judge a villager
who had killed his wife in a drunken rage; at the
angel's signal the Devil entered ('like a brave
Gentleman' - a suggestive phrase) and broke the
murderer's neck. (The names of thirteen trustworthy
parishioners, from squire to husbandmen, were listed
to testify to the truth of the story.)(129)

Though the more comforting parts of the Christian message received much less emphasis, about a
fifth of Pepys's religious chapbooks stressed
Christ's mercy and love, and the lasting success of
the Plaine Path-way to Heaven underlines the demand
that existed for such works. One ballad has Christ
appealing directly to readers to turn to him for
salvation:

> O come to me! I call again,
> Let not my passion be in vain.(130)

The nature of Heaven was generally left vague, but
John Hart, the most successful of the religious
pamphleteers, was able to translate its rewards into
terms which the poor would readily understand and
appreciate: he stressed that there were 'no
cripples, no blind, nor diseased ones in Heaven;
Heaven is an healthy country, there is no sickness
nor death, no poverty nor disgrace in Heaven'. A
balladeer emphasised that in Heaven the poor were
treated as princes, and the immense popularity of
the story of Dives and Lazarus - where the poor
cripple is saved and the rich man damned - speaks
for itself. (131)

While writers made it clear that salvation was
by faith, they stressed moral as much as spiritual
regeneration and generally ignored the theological
distinction between saving grace and the good works
that would accompany it. Salvation was to be
partly by godliness of life; the avenging angel of

Westmorland, for example, informed the crowd of
wondering onlookers that the way to reach Heaven was
by loving one another. Good deeds, it was often
added, would bring rewards in this life as well as
the next, whereas hardness of heart towards the poor
would prevent prayers from being answered. (132)
Writers attempted to reinforce traditional moral
values by denouncing pride, drunkenness and other
sins. In an age of strongly patriarchal attitudes,
they were especially shocked by grown-up children
who failed to show proper respect and gratitude to
their parents. One ballad tells of a young man who
tries to secure the whole of his late father's
estate by denouncing his mother as a whore and his
sisters as illegitimate. In another a father sells
all his goods to free his profligate son from a
debtors' prison; years later, when the son has
grown rich and the father destitute, the old man
comes to ask help and is turned away with contempt.
In both these stories, and many more, God's
avenging hand brings death or disgrace to the
miscreant.(133) Social morality was an equally
prominent theme; many ballads lament the decay of
charity and warn that the covetous belong to the
kingdom of Hell. (134) One, dating from the 1640s,
tells of a rich Norfolk farmer, a Mr Inglebread of
Bowton, who met the Devil while returning from
King's Lynn market and arranged to sell his barley
crop at the inflated price of eight shillings a
bushel. On the appointed day the Devil arrived with
a horse and cart to take delivery, but then instead
suddenly stirred up a terrible storm which destroyed
the barn and all the corn it contained. The moral
was clear, and the author pointed out its application for poor readers:

> If any misers you do know
> That hoards up corn to starve ye poor,
> If that these lines you to them show
> 'Twill make them sure bring out their store

- a comforting reflection, if not well-founded. (135)
There were many ballads denouncing grasping
landlords, and making bitter comments on the nature
of society:

> Like th' Israelites in Egypt
> The poor are kept in thrall;
> The task-masters are playing kept,
> But poor men pay for all.

221

Perhaps the bleakest tale is <u>A Lanthorn for
Landlords</u>, in which a young widow is evicted by a
harsh landlord; destitute, and cursing her
oppressor, she tramps the roads in search of work,
sometimes whipped as a vagrant, and eventually loses
her two small children who wander away in the fields
one day and, unable to find their way back, die of
starvation. Later the mother, now working on a
nearby farm, stumbles upon their decayed bodies. At
this horrific point the story takes a moralising,
implausible but emotionally satisfying turn. God
has indeed heard the widow's curse; and she returns
to her first home to find that the landlord has
killed himself, ruined when fire destroyed the grain
he was hoarding. His wife has been burnt as a
witch. And their children have perished miserably
after sinking into crime and prostitution. A ballad
by Thomas Deloney, written in the near-famine
conditions of 1596, showed country folk explaining
their plight to Queen Elizabeth, who is moved to
intervene to make sure grain will be made available
to the poor at a fair price. Though the tale
preserved the fiction of the benevolent monarch, its
implied criticism of the government's handling of
the food crisis led to the gaoling of the publisher
and the issue of a warrant for Deloney's arrest. (136)
<u>Sad and Dreadful News from Horsley Down</u> (1684) gave
an equally bleak glimpse of the social problems of
the city slums. Its subject, Dorothy Winterbottom
'alias Dirty Doll', was a foul-mouthed, greedy and
drunken woman abandoned by her husband and earning
her living as a tally-woman, a kind of petty usurer.
After swearing a blasphemous vow to have a poor
debtor arrested she was mysteriously beaten up by
the Devil and two helpers in human form, and died
miserably when her injuries turned gangrenous. The
story was based on a real incident and - apart from
the other-worldly nature of the assailants - is all
too believable. The author added a no doubt popular
warning to all tally-keepers of their probable
fate. (137)

   Besides the religious and moral tracts, there
was another sizeable body of works dealing with
other aspects of the supernatural, such as
astrology, magic and the occult. Only the
astrologers made much effort to relate their subject
to Christianity, arguing that floods, plagues and
the like were caused by the stars acting as God's
instruments in the punishment of sin; but their
predictions on the weather and harvest, and their
medical and gardening tips had no obvious link with

Christian teaching.(138) Some chapbooks were
utilitarian guides setting out the rules of
astrology, palmistry, magical divination and the
interpretation of dreams;(139) others, by contrast,
were the equivalent of the modern horror story. The
chilling tale of Dr Faustus was immensely popular,
and there were splendidly-told ballads about ghosts
and spirits. (140) The occult figured in comic guise
too, in the pranks of Robin Goodfellow, the jestbook
version of Mother Shipton, or in the bawdy <u>Friar and
the Boy</u>, where a magic pipe is used to shame a
lecherous friar. (141)

VIII

A considerable portion of popular literature
was journalistic rather than literary in design.
The popular appetite for news, including political
news, was immense and indeed became a subject for
satire. (142) Much of the news which interested the
poor, however, dealt not with politics but with
tales of the extraordinary: dramatic storms,
volcanic eruptions, human and animal freaks and
sensational crimes. Writers were ready to supply
whatever the public wanted, and the 'news' was
notoriously unreliable; the news stories offered by
Shakespeare's Autolycus are wholly absurd, and Ben
Jonson's balladeer shamelessly sells an account of
'The windmill blown down by a witch's fart'. Thomas
Nashe may have been right, though, in believing that
even far-fetched stories could excite and alarm the
credulous ploughman or shepherd, who 'in his field
naps dreameth of the flying dragon' and who
'lighteth no sooner on a quagmire, but he thinks
this is the foretold earthquake, whereof his boy
hath a ballad'.(143)
There were, however, many ballads giving a
straightforward and reasonably reliable account of
recent events, such as the fire in a merchant's
house in Cornhill, in which the seven occupants
perished. Similarly, an unusually severe winter was
described in an early chapbook, <u>The Cold Year, 1614</u>.
Anthony Wood collected a number of newsbook accounts
of natural disasters, from floods in the reign of
James I to the Jamaican earthquake of 1692. (144)
Especially popular were human dramas, telling for
example of people struck by lightning, a sea-captain
picked up alive from the water forty-eight hours
after his ship had sunk, and a group of sailors
marooned in Greenland to face an Arctic winter. (145)
Human oddities had a similar appeal: among them the

adult Siamese twins who toured England in the 1630s;
the glutton who could allegedly devour a whole pig
at one sitting; and 'Old Parr', a sprightly
centenarian who - it was said - had done penance for
adultery at the age of 105 and lived to the ripe age
of 152. (146)

Notorious crime provided, as now, another major
theme; many 'hanging ballads' were ostensibly
narrated by the contrite criminal just before his
death or even, implausibly, after it, and the
stories were meant to convey a moral lesson.(147)
The crime itself, though, was the major attraction;
almost always it concerned murder, for mere theft
was probably too commonplace to arouse the reader's
interest, and a thief did not provoke the same sense
of outrage. Indeed in one of the few ballads
reporting the execution of a man for a crime against
property (receiving stolen horses), there is a blunt
assertion that he had done nothing worthy of
death.(148) In the case of highwaymen the balladeer
almost always chose to emphasise the victims they
had killed rather than the robberies themselves.
Naturally it was the most sensational murders which
caught public attention; the mundane crime of
an unmarried servant girl who smothered her new-born
baby to escape disgrace was a very untypical
subject. The much rarer cases of wives murdering
their husbands figured more prominently; such women
were burnt for petty treason, and writers usually
stressed the unnatural character of their crime
against male supremacy by depicting the husbands as
mild and unprovocative.(149) Husbands who killed
their wives were less newsworthy. There were ballads
about multiple murders, aristocratic killers, a
female highwayman and murderess, the apparently
'perfect' murder, and a horrific story of a young
man who fell sick and was buried while still alive
by a landlord greedy for his lodger's
possessions.(150) Stories of murder by witchcraft
attracted both balladeers and chapbook-writers.(151)
The narrator generally made his horror and outrage
clear throughout his tale, and there was rarely any
attempt at a dispassionate understanding. Even in
the notorious case in 1660 of the Perry family, when
three members of a family were hanged for killing
a man later found to be still alive, the balladeer
chose to believe that Mother Perry was a witch who
had spirited away the supposed victim, and concluded that her family had deserved to die even
though no murder had occurred.(152) The most famous
exception to this general pattern was a case where

the crime of murder was overshadowed by the romantic
tragedy of the story. Eulalia Glandfield had been
married off to a wealthy old man named Page -
'married ... to muck and endless strife', as she put
it - by parents who had rejected her own choice of
partner. She and her lover conspired to kill the
unwanted husband, and they were both hanged for his
murder at Barnstaple in 1591. Narrating her tale,
Eulalia repents her crime but defiantly professes
her love for her accomplice and lays the ultimate
blame on her greedy parents. The case aroused widespread interest, prompting a pamphlet, several
ballads and a play (now lost) by Thomas Dekker and
Jonson. (153)

Just as most crime stories were given a
moralising ending, the prodigy story - a major theme
in the newsbooks - was interpreted as a manifes-
tation of divine anger. Storms, thunderbolts, the
birth of quads or deformed infants, monstrous fish
and the deformed pigs which seem to have held a
particular fascination for Elizabethan readers were
all explained in these terms. (154) Some of the
prodigy stories were blatant frauds. A gallimaufry
of amazing occurrences was reported from Hereford in
October 1661, with the names of constables and
churchwardens who could vouch for their truth; but
the author had in fact lifted the whole story from a
pamphlet published in 1580, when the very same marvels were said to have taken place in Bohemia.(155)
The story of a Hampshire woman who gave birth to a
live toad, a snake and a dead child which the snake
had partly eaten seems equally implausible, despite
the many circumstantial details supplied in the
account. (156) But there were many people in the
period, and not only among the uneducated, who took
such prodigies seriously and pondered their meaning.
The baby born with folds of skin round its neck like
a ruff was clearly a warning against vanity and
pride. (157) Miraculous rainfalls of blood and armies
seen fighting in the skies denoted wars and
desolation. A battle in the air between flocks of
starlings near Cork in 1621 was followed the next
year by a fire which destroyed much of the city:
clear proof, the balladeers claimed, of their
diagnosis.(158) Some stories of the downfall of
sinners were definitely based on real incidents,
such as the sad case of Dorothy Mattley of Ashover
in Derbyshire, who uttered foul blasphemies one day
in March 1661 as she sat at work washing lead ore,
whereupon, as the parish register records, 'the
ground opened, and she sank over head' along with

her tub and sieve. The fact that she had been working on top of an unstable slag-heap makes it for once quite plausible that she was indeed swallowed up by the earth. It was a splendid story both as news and religious *exemplum*, and received widespread publicity, making a deep impression on John Bunyan among others. (159)

The categories of popular literature were often blurred in this way, and news was frequently 'improved' to broaden its appeal and bring it more into line with popular taste. Thus the 'monstrous serpent, or dragon' of Horsham (Sussex) described in a chapbook of 1614, was probably no more than a large adder, but the author rounded off a fairly realistic account by speculating that swellings on its body might be incipient wings, and his hope that it would be killed before it could turn into a fully-fledged dragon was obviously designed to stir up maximum excitement. (160) Similarly the reports of a Dutch 'Hog-Faced Gentlewoman called Mistris Tannakin Skinker' in 1639 probably had some small basis in fact which writers then decorated with such details as the genteel way in which the lady put 'her dainty snout' into a silver trough. One pamphleteer was certainly blending the news story with traditional legend when he explained that her sad plight was the consequence of a witch's spell, and that she would turn at once into a beautiful maiden if anyone would marry her - a motif familiar from Chaucer's Wife of Bath's Tale and many other sources. (161)

Dr Spufford observed that the Pepysian chapbooks depicted a wholly non-political world in which the Civil Wars might never have happened. (162) It would be wrong though to conclude that politics was absent from popular literature, for the chapbooks' silence indicates little more than the specialised nature of the trade. Before 1640 the printed ballad was the main source of political news and comment; ballad-eers had to take account both of censorship and of the ordinary reader's sheer incomprehension of the remote world of high politics and, like modern popular journalists, they avoided complex issues and focussed instead on the personal dramas of the famous. Royal progresses and ceremonies were described in detail, and readers could find numerous accounts of, for example, the coronation of James I, the premature death of his eldest son and the marriage of his daughter to the Elector Palatine. (163) A ballad on the death of the Elizabethan magnate, the Earl of Huntingdon, said

nothing about his important political career and
told its story from the limited viewpoint of the
small country farmer: the Earl was shown as a good
and generous landlord mourned by his tenants because

> Their rents were not raised, their fines
> were but small,
> And many poor tenants paid nothing at all. (164)

The large crop of ballads prompted by the Northern
Rebellion of 1569 and Guy Fawkes's conspiracy were
wholly loyal to the crown and outspoken in their
condemnation of the traitors.
        Nevertheless the authorities were often
troubled by the activities of balladeers and
regarded politics as an unsuitable subject for
plebeian gossip. (165) Two ballads on the Earl of
Essex, executed in 1601 after an abortive rising,
had an immense and lasting appeal, and both took a
sympathetic line towards the Earl. The writers
ignored the political issues involved and presented
the story as a tragic drama in which a brave,
patriotic soldier and true Protestant was brought
low by the false tongues of envious rivals. The
many ballads published on the execution of Sir
Walter Raleigh in 1618 were promptly suppressed, and
it is likely that they too were critical of the
government. (166) The ballads about the Overbury
scandal in 1613 would inevitably damage the Court's
prestige, and several writers criticised James I's
extravagant generosity towards parvenu Scottish
courtiers; at least one rejoiced openly when
Buckingham's hated *confidant*, Dr Lambe, was lynched
by the mob in 1628.(167) It seems that even rural
audiences were eager for material of this kind; it
was said that the country balladeer would have his
merry songs 'interlarded with any thing against the
state, they are main helps to him, and he will
adventure to sing them though they cost him a
whipping'.(168) The Civil War gave far greater scope
for political and polemical songs, mostly cavalier
and often mixed with bawdy, till in 1643 Parliament
attempted to suppress ballad-selling altogether.
The rule of the Rump Parliament in 1659-60 gave rich
opportunities for obscene humour which many writers
seized with glee, and in 1660 General George Monck,
author of the Restoration, became a ballad-hero in
the guise of St George rescuing the distressed
damsel (England) from the cruel republican
dragon. (169)
        The Civil War also opened the way for wider

political coverage in almanacs and cheap pamphlets.
Instead of the old bland and vague predictions,
almanac-makers now supplied partisan prophecies and
outspoken commentaries designed to boost the morale
of their cause. William Lilly, the leading
Parliamentarian astrologer, drew on the Bible and
the prophecies of Merlin as well as the stars, and
his predictions carried weight with high-ranking
army officers and politicians as well as humble
folk.(170) Though most of the pamphlets and newspapers of the Interregnum aimed at a more
sophisticated audience than the material surveyed in
this essay, some of the cavalier news-sheets were
popular in style, and former balladeers provided
many of the topical verses they contained. (171)
Despite strict censorship of the press after 1660,
political discussion could not be suppressed
altogether; a man who sang an old Parliamentary
ballad of the 1640s in a Taunton alehouse then
launched into a vindication of Oliver Cromwell. The
years of upheaval following the Popish Plot of 1678
brought a dramatic increase in cheap tracts of a
topical and polemical nature. During the Exclusion
Crisis satirical ballads about the Duke of York were
sold openly at Bridgwater Fair.(172) A new
generation of astrologers published highly partisan
prophecy and comment; the leading Whig almanac-
maker, John Partridge, had to seek refuge in Holland
when James II came to the throne, while his Tory
rival, John Gadbury, who rashly predicted that
William of Orange would be executed on Tower Hill,
was in danger of losing his own life instead. (173)
The Civil Wars had opened up political debate to a
large public, and popular literature in the second
half of the century reflects the fierce diversity of
opinion that was now an inescapable political fact.

During the Civil War period the publisher
George Horton issued a number of non-partisan newspapers aimed at an unsophisticated readership, in
which news, prophecies and prodigies were jumbled
together. There were chapbooks of a similar kind,
such as one in 1660 which described how two armies
fought a battle in the air near Newmarket and the
victors then marched on London - an omen easy to
interpret in the confused last weeks of the
Interregnum. (174) The Restoration had little effect
on popular tracts of a patriotic type. Astrologers
'proved' that the stars foretold glorious victories
against the villainous Dutch and French. In 1665 a
balladeer told of a particularly monstrous fish with
a cannon on its back and markings guaranteeing

England's victory in the Anglo-Dutch war. In 1690 a short chapbook reported a naval battle seen in the sky in which the English and Dutch (now allies) routed the French, and supplied a full and gratifying account of the ships sunk and captured.(175) In these tracts politics and prodigies were indistinguishable. It is not hard to explain the appeal of this combination in times of war and upheaval.(176) To patriots and the committed such marvels suggested that history was in some way preordained and success guaranteed by Heaven. To the less committed and the unsophisticated they undoubtedly brought excitement and perhaps a reassuring sense that current events, however bewildering, were part of God's inscrutable, providential design.

IX

One lasting impression from this survey is of the immense diversity of popular literature and of the popular culture behind it, which absorbed bawdy jestbooks and doom-laden warnings of Hellfire in equal measure. Many of the stories and heroes are timeless in character, so that it hardly mattered that one writer placed Robin Hood in the reign of Henry VIII, several centuries too late, and another had King Athelstan reigning seven centuries too early.(177) Some of the popular ballads of love were based on stories reaching back to classical antiquity, such as the tragedies of Dido and Aeneas, and Hero and Leander. The tales of chivalric adventure originated in medieval aristocratic romances, adapted for a wider audience. The heroes and heroines belong to largely fixed types, and their adventures, sufferings and loves occurred in fairly standard situations. It was the archetypal nature of the subject and story which was important, and authors rarely bothered to give individual traits to the hero or circumstantial details to the plot. There was indeed a tendency for new subjects to be assimilated into the established and traditional patterns. Thus the news story of the 'hog-faced gentlewoman' became the tale of a beautiful maiden under a witch's curse, political events assumed the characteristics of marvels and prodigies, and the ballads of the Earl of Essex and Duchess of Suffolk remained popular as tragic tales of the noble and virtuous long after the causes of their misfortunes had been forgotten.

It may be that the stereotyped nature of hero

and plot made it easier for the reader to make the
imaginative leap of self-identification. The tales
of adventure certainly encouraged heroic fantasies,
especially when the hero began as a mere prentice or
labourer. In ballads of love the self-
identification might be more conscious and realistic:
in The London Chaunticleers a lovesick tinker asks
for a 'wooing-ballad', specifying The Ballad of the
Unfortunate Lover as matching his own unhappy
plight, and adding - to make the identification
complete - 'I would have a picture on it like
me'.(178) There is a startling example of this self-
identification in the unlikely context of the
'hanging-ballad', in which criminals facing the
gallows narrate their downfall and repentance. In
1635 one Thomas Sherwood committed three murders,
for which he was tried and sentenced to death. When
he came to the gallows he was in contrite mood, and
at his request the doleful ballad Lamentation of a
sinner (or Fortune, my foe) was performed, making a
deep impression on the crowd; Sherwood would have
been gratified to learn that his own case was to
become in its turn the subject of a moralising
ballad.(179) He chose the Lamentation because it
reflected both his situation and his mood; by
contrast a defiant highwayman went to the gallows
clutching a copy of Chevy Chase (a tale of fierce,
undaunted courage) to match his own feelings and to
keep up his spirits.(180)

Escapism and fantasy were the prevailing themes
of this literature, but throughout the period there
were also many journalistic ballads reflecting
popular interest in contemporary affairs. Though
many were non-political, some writers were willing
to comment on and criticise the government's
behaviour, and from the mid-seventeenth century
almanacs took political debate much further.
Moreover, some of the ballads and tales which were
bland and conventional on the surface had an
ambivalent flavour: even the eulogy on the Earl of
Huntingdon, stressing his benevolent paternalism,
carried an ambiguous message, for the author
pointedly contrasted the Earl's behaviour with the
harshness and greed of most landlords, and other
ballads launched direct attacks on social
oppression. Readers also clearly liked to hear
scandalous tales of aristocratic immorality, and to
see the rich and proud outwitted by jestbook
pranksters. To this extent popular literature may
have undermined the values of an ordered,
hierarchical society. The attack, however, was

limited: it has been suggested here that the spirit of this literature was closer to carnival than revolution, presenting a world turned upside down only temporarily, and only in the imagination - another form of escapist release. Though ballads may have led readers to curse some of their superiors, the implied remedy is moral reformation, not a change in the social order: the rich should behave with the honesty and benevolence of an idealised past. If they fail to do so, remedies are left to an avenging God, or a Devil who will come to claim his own. The king is usually a benevolent figure, but there is little suggestion that he will bring any general relief, and his benevolence is as unpredictable and random as life itself.

At the start of the seventeenth century there was considerable overlapping of taste between the classes. Stories ranging from King Lear, Romeo and Juliet, and Titus Andronicus to The Babes in the Wood and The Pinder of Wakefield attracted dramatists and ballad-makers alike. The tale of Dr Faustus, reaching England about 1588, inspired anonymous balladeers as well as Marlow.(181) Chivalric and romantic stories, originating among the aristocracy, slowly filtered down to reach a mass market, and Guy of Warwick, King Arthur and Patient Griselda found a new audience. Similarly works such as Holinshed's Chronicles (1577), aiming at middle-class readers, contained a treasure-store of personal dramas which Deloney and others turned into popular historical ballads.(182) But upper-class taste was now turning away from the chivalric themes which were reaching the poor probably for the first time. The gentry also began to turn away from the crude humour of the jestbooks, reflected in the way their heroes decline in social standing as the century advances; for whereas George Peele, an early jester, was an Oxford graduate, his Restoration successors were such as Poor Robin, a simple provincial saddler, and Black Tom, a negro and professional thief.(183) By 1700 the polarisation of taste was well advanced.

There were finally also important changes in the form of popular literature. The broadside ballad flourished from the mid-sixteenth to the mid-seventeenth century. At its best it combined in simple form the elements of poetry, music and drama, and its woodcuts were one of the very few kinds of representational art the poor were likely to encounter. From the mid-seventeenth century the ballad declined quite rapidly as writers turned to

prose, a process greatly accelerated by the Civil
War, and the emergence of newspapers inevitably
undermined the ballad's journalistic role. The
chapbook market increased dramatically, and the
almanac too expanded enormously in scope and sales
from the 1640s. In quality, however, the literature
does not feel richer in 1700 than a century earlier
(except for the almanacs); if anything, the reverse
is true, and many of the chapbooks seem crude and
derivative compared with earlier ballads. John
Taylor's biographer thought his writings
'contemptible', and the historian of the Pepysian
chapbooks describes them as 'crude, unsubtle,
earthy, uncompassionate'.(184) The change, if this
impression is correct, probably springs from the
polarisation of taste in Stuart England, with the
middle-classes gradually adopting the new tastes of
their social superiors. By 1700 the writers
supplying the poorer end of the market perhaps felt
a measure of contempt for the culture of their
readers, and were content merely to rework stories
handed down from a previous generation. If this
literature had become more exclusively 'popular' by
the end of the period, it was also more
impoverished.

Notes

1. L. B. Wright, <u>Middle-Class Culture in Elizabethan England</u>
    (Chapel Hill, 1935).
2. The best introduction is V. E. Neuburg, <u>Popular
    Literature: A History and Guide</u> (1977); Wright, <u>Middle
    Class Culture</u>, ch. 12; Burke, <u>Popular Culture</u>, chs. 5,
    6. On ballads, see the works of H. E. Rollins, esp. 'The
    Black-letter Broadside Ballad', <u>Publications of the
    Modern Language Association</u>, xxxiv (1919); on chapbooks,
    Spufford, <u>Small Books</u>; on almanacs, Capp, <u>Astrology and
    the Popular Press</u> (1979); on jestbooks, F. P. Wilson,
    'The English Jestbooks of the Sixteenth and Seventeenth
    Centuries', <u>Huntington Library Quarterly</u>, ii (1938-9).
3. Burke, <u>Popular Culture</u>, ch. 9; K. Thomas, 'The Place of
    Laughter in Tudor and Stuart England', <u>Times Literary
    Supplement</u>, 21 Jan. 1977.
4. V. F. Snow, 'An Inventory of the Lord General's Library,
    1646', <u>The Library</u>, xxi (1966), pp. 120, 122; <u>Rump</u>, ii,
    pp. 188-92; S. Pepys, <u>Diary</u>, 23 April 1660.
5. Spufford, <u>Small Books</u>, ch. 2; Cressy, <u>Literacy</u>, p. 119.
6. <u>Index</u>.
7. C. Blagden, 'The Distribution of Almanacks in the Second
    Half of the Seventeenth Century', <u>Studies in Bibliography</u>,
    xi (1958); Capp, <u>Astrology</u>, p. 44 and ch. 2; C.

Blagden, 'Notes on the Ballad Market', Studies in Bibliography, vi (1954).

8. Spufford, Small Books, ch. 4.
9. J. Lilly (ed.), A Collection of Seventy-Nine Black-Letter Ballads and Broadsides (1867), p. 208; Bodleian Library, Wood 401, fos. 9v-10, 39-40v, 109-10v.
10. L. B. Campbell, 'Richard Tarlton and the Earthquake of 1580', Huntington Library Quarterly, iv (1940-1), pp. 293-301.
11. See DNB for each of these; and on Deloney: The Works of Thomas Deloney, ed. F. O. Mann (Oxford, 1912); Rollins, 'Black-letter Ballad', pp. 296-306.
12. J. Earle, Micro-Cosmographie (1628), quoted in Neuburg, Popular Literature, p. 76; H. E. Rollins, A Pepysian Garland (Cambridge, 1922), p. 393.
13. For Spigurnell, see W. Hunt, The Puritan Moment (1983), p. 154; for some provincial balladeers, see The Life and Times of Anthony Wood, ed. A. Clark (1891-1900), i, pp. 352, 504-6, ii, p. 148; H. E. Rollins, The Pack of Autolycus (Cambridge, Mass., 1927), pp. 126, 185-90; Rollins, Garland, pp. 420-4; Lilly (ed.), Collection, pp. xxxvi, 220.
14. Capp, Astrology, pp. 51-9 and Appendix 1.
15. The London Chaunticleers, in Dodsley's Old English Plays, ed. W. Hazlitt, xii (1875), pp. 329, 337; Rollins, 'Black-letter Ballad', pp. 306-23; G. Puttenham, The Arte of English Poesie (Cambridge, 1936), p. 83; Spufford, Small Books, p. 118; Capp, Astrology, p. 60.
16. Works of Deloney, p. x; T. Harman, A Caveat or Warning for Common Cursitors (1566), in C. Hindley (ed.), The Old Book Collector's Miscellany (1871-3), i, p. 107.
17. Bartholomew Fair, III, i.
18. Neuburg, Popular Literature, p. 64; Spufford, Small Books, ch. 5; The Winter's Tale, IV, iii.
19. Spufford, Small Books, pp. 125-6; Rollins, 'Black-letter Ballad', pp. 323-7; Capp, Astrology, pp. 59-60.
20. Spufford, Small Books, pp. 7-8, 74.
21. Ibid., pp. 72-5.
22. A Midsummer-Night's Dream, III, i; Capp, Astrology, pp. 60-6.
23. Capp, Astrology, pp. 33-4, 59; Spufford, Small Books, ch. 3; Lilly (ed.), Collection, pp. 78-84.
24. Rollins, Garland, pp. 229-38.
25. G. F. Northall, English Folk-Rhymes (1892).
26. J. Aubrey, Brief Lives, ed. O. L. Dick (1972), p. 29.
27. Reprinted in Pre-Shakespearean Comedies (Everyman Library, n.d.), quotation at p. 134.
28. Aubrey, Brief Lives, pp. 29, 36; Clare, The Shepherd's Calendar (1827); 'January - A Cottage Evening'.
29. I. and P. Opie, The Classic Fairy Tales (1974), pp. 30-2. In 1621 the tale was said to be popular with young and

old, but in a Restoration chapbook version it was described as popular only with 'our wives and children small' (Bodleian Library, Wood 259(5), Sig. B4v). For Cinderella see Opie, op. cit., pp. 117-21.

30. Such incidents occur, for example, in the jestbook stories of Tarlton, Peele, Poor Robin, Tom Tram, the Pinder and George Dobson; see also Rollins, 'Black-letter Ballad', pp. 278-80; The Journal of George Fox, ed. J. L. Nickalls (Cambridge, 1952), p. 27; and chapter 5 in this collection.

31. Rollins, Autolycus, pp. 126-31; see also P. Clark, The English Alehouse (1983), pp. 155-6; Hunt, Puritan Moment, p. 262; chapter 5 above.

32. Rump, i, 'To the Reader'.

33. Pp. 179-80 above.

34. Spufford, Small Books, pp. 9-15, 68, 227-31.

35. Wilson, 'Jestbooks', p. 127; Spufford, Small Books, pp. 67-8.

36. R. S. Crane, 'The Vogue of Guy of Warwick from the Close of the Middle Ages to the Romantic Revival', Publications of the Modern Language Association, xxx (1915), p. 131.

37. T. Nashe, Works, ed. R. B. McKerrow and F. P. Wilson (Oxford, 1958), i, p. 23; Clare, Shepherd's Calendar: 'January: A Winter's Day'.

38. Rollins, 'Black-letter Ballad', pp. 336-8; I. Walton, The Compleat Angler, ed. A. Lang [1906], p. 52; Rollins, Garland, pp. xx; Clark, Alehouse, pp. 155, 195. Although they belong to the 18th century, most of the illustrations of alehouse interiors reproduced by Clark show ballads or other written material.

39. L. Price, Good Ale [1645?], in RB, i, pp. 411-17 (p. 414 for the quotation).

40. The Pinder of Wakefield (1632), ed. E. A. Horsman (Liverpool, 1956), pp. 6, 29.

41. Rump, i, 'To the Reader'.

42. W. Chappell, Old English Popular Music (NY, 1961), pp. 239-42.

43. Puttenham, Arte of Poesie, pp. 83-4; Chappell, Popular Music; Spufford, Small Books, pp. 170-82.

44. J. C. Holt, Robin Hood (1982), pp. 141, 142; Opie, Fairy Tales, p. 31.

45. Letters from Dorothy Osborne to William Temple, ed. G. C. Moore Smith (Oxford, 1928), p. 51; Chappell, Popular Music, pp. 55-68.

46. Based on an analysis of titles beginning with the letter 'C' in Index. Many pieces now lost cannot be classified with any certainty from the short-title alone.

47. A Pleasant Countrey new Ditty, Merrily shewing how to drive the cold Winter away (n.d.), in RB, i, pp. 84-9; cf. RB, i, pp. 475-8.

48. Spufford, Small Books, ch. 6; R. Thompson (ed.), Samuel

Pepys' Penny Merriments (1976) gives a representative sample of all but the religious chapbooks. There were often ballad and pamphlet accounts of the same episode: see Rollins, Garland, nos. 3, 4, 16, 24, 26, 35, 60, 70, 77, 79; and ballads sometimes served as 'trailers' for longer accounts (Rollins, 'Black-letter Ballad', p. 295).

49. Capp, Astrology, pp. 29-31, 33, 283-6.
50. Quoted by Rollins, Garland, p. xii.
51. Marlowe's 'Come, live with me', and Herrick's 'Gather ye Rosebuds'; T. Lanfiere, The Wonder of Wonders [c.1675], in Rollins, Autolycus, pp. 185-90 (p. 189 for quotation).
52. Child, nos. 169, 81. 'Johnny Armstrong' probably dates from soon after 1530, the date of the events it describes; 'Little Musgrove' was probably printed in 1630 (Index, no. 1506), but is much older in origin. For contrasting views of the traditional ballad, see D. C. Fowler, A literary history of the popular ballad (Durham, Nth. Carolina, 1968), and G. C. Gerould, The Ballad of Tradition (NY, 1957).
53. Lilly (ed.), Collection, pp. 78-84; Rollins, Autolycus, pp. 59-61; Rollins, Garland, p. 55.
54. RB, ii, pp. 547-53; Rollins, Autolycus, p. 66.
55. C. R. Baskervill, The Elizabethan Jig (NY, 1965); Rollins, Garland, pp. xiv-xx.
56. Wilson, 'Jestbooks', pp. 133, 141-3; Dobsons Drie Bobbes, ed. E. A. Horsman (Durham, 1955); Thompson, Merriments, pp. 175-89. A few authors told their tale in the form of allegory (Thompson, Merriments, pp. 132-7; RB, ii, pp. 372-8); mock trials (Thompson, Merriments, pp. 138-40, 260-3); and dreams (Rollins, Garland, pp. 176-8).
57. Crane, 'Vogue of Guy of Warwick', p. 141.
58. The Life and Death of the Famous Champion of England, St. George [1688/9] (Bodleian Library, Wood 254(1)); Spufford, Small Books, pp. 227-31.
59. L. Price, The Famous History of Valentine and Orson (1683), title page.
60. Holt, Robin Hood; Child, nos. 117-54.
61. The Famous History of Stout Stukeley [c.1650] (Bodleian Library, Wood 254(13)); for his life and popular renown, see DNB.
62. [Richard Johnson], The most pleasant History of Tom a Lincoln.
63. See Burke, Popular Culture, ch. 5.
64. Beaumont and Fletcher, The Knight of the Burning Pestle, 'Induction' and I, iii.
65. The Famous History of Guy of Warwick (1686); Spufford, Small Books, pp. 225-7.
66. W.V., The Honourable Prentice (1616); The Honour of an Apprentice of London [1658-64] (Bodleian Library, Wood 401, fos. 63v-4). For a Restoration chapbook version by John Shirley, The Famous History of Aurelius, the Valiant

London Prentice (n.d.), see Spufford, Small Books, p. 55. For Hawkwood, see DNB.

67. Holt, Robin Hood, p. 141.

68. The Pleasant History of Thomas Hickathrift [1686-8] (Bodleian Library, Wood 259(11)); Spufford, Small Books, pp. 247-9. Fortunatus [c.1700], is reprinted in C. C. Mish (ed.), Short Fiction of the Seventeenth Century (NY , 1968).

69. The Life of Long Meg of Westminster (1620), in Mish (ed.), Short Fiction; Spufford, Small Books, pp. 245-6.

70. Works of Deloney, pp. 1-272; Spufford, Small Books, pp. 238-44.

71. The Princely wooing of the faire Maid of London [1624, entered in the Stationers' Register 1600], in RB, i, pp. 181-5; Deloney, The Life and Death of Fair Rosamond, in RB, vi, pp. 673-5 (first published in Deloney's The Garland of Good Will (1631)). Jane Shore, mistress of Edward IV, was also a popular subject. For chapbook versions, see Spufford, Small Books, pp. 74, 221.

72. For some ballads of this type, see RB, i, pp. 520-46; for chapbooks, see Spufford, Small Books, pp. 222-4, and Thompson, Merriments, pp. 24-8; see also Burke, Popular Culture, p. 152; Fowler, Literary History, pp. 84-93. On carnival see Burke, Popular Culture, ch. 7.

73. King Edward the Fourth and the Tanner of Tamworth [1675, entered in the Stationers' Register in 1633], in RB, i, p. 535; The Shepherd and the King [1670-82] (Bodleian Library, Wood 401, fos. 1-2).

74. Child, no. 124, contains a list of the relevant ballads; Holt, Robin Hood, pp. 166-70.

75. Thomas Hickathrift, pp. 16-18.

76. [1675, entered in the Stationers' Register 1624], in RB, i, pp. 37-46; Spufford, Small Books, p. 246.

77. Tom a Lincoln, Sig. A4v; Valentine and Orson (1683).

78. The lamentable fall of Queen Elnor [1675 , entered in the Stationers' Register 1656], in RB, ii, pp. 67-73.

79. Patient Griselda, medieval in origin, was available in many cheap versions; The King and the Northern-man [1675, entered 1633], in RB, i, pp. 520-9.

80. R. Climsal, Loves Lunacy [1637], in RB, ii, pp. 6-11; H. Crouch, The Mad-man's Morrice [1637], in RB, ii, pp. 153-8.

81. The Bride's Buriall [1675, entered 1603], in RB, i, pp. 185-9; The deceased Maiden-Lover [1650?], in RB, i, pp. 249-53; M. Parker, The desperate Damsell's Tragedy [1630?], in RB, i, pp. 265-70; M. Parker, The father hath beguil'd the sonne [1629], in Rollins, Garland, pp. 309-15.

82. [1675, entered 1595], in RB, ii, pp. 86-95.

83. Spufford, Small Books, ch. 7.

84. Ibid., pp. 165-6; Thompson, Merriments pp. 116-21.

85. Spufford, <u>Small Books</u>, pp. 157-8; cf. L. Stone, <u>The Family, Sex and Marriage in England 1500-1800</u> (1977), pp. 93, 98-9.

86. [1678], in <u>RB</u>, ii, pp. 41-8.

87. <u>A new Northern Jigge, called Daintie, come thou to me</u> [1683], in <u>RB</u>, i, pp. 628-31; see also the popular story of Tommy Potts, first published in 1657; Child, no. 109; Spufford, <u>Small Books</u>, pp. 246-7.

88. E.g. <u>A mad kinde of wooing</u> [1625-38], in <u>RB</u>, ii, pp. 121-6.

89. E.g. M. Parker, <u>Good Counsell for Young Wooers</u> [1633], in <u>RB</u>, i, pp. 422-7; Spufford, <u>Small Books</u>, ch. 7; Thompson, <u>Merriments</u>, section 3.

90. M. Parker, <u>A Lover's teares</u> [1634], in <u>RB</u>, i, pp. 581-6; M. Parker, <u>The Lover's Joy and Griefe</u> [1635?], in <u>RB</u>, i, pp. 598-603; <u>The Lover's Dream</u> [1633], in <u>RB</u>, i, pp. 603-9.

91. Spufford, <u>Small Books</u>, pp. 166-8; <u>The Maids Comfort</u> [1628-9], in <u>The Roxburghe Ballads</u>, ed. C. Hindley (1874), ii, pp. 424-9 (not in <u>RB</u>).

92. [1632], in <u>RB</u>, i, pp. 587-92 (derived from the traditional 'The Broom of Cowdenknows', Child, no. 217); <u>Western Knight</u> (1629), in Rollins, <u>Garland</u>, pp. 305-8.

93. <u>The Souldiers Farewel</u> [1655-60, entered 1624], Rollins, <u>Garland</u>, pp. 173-8; Child, nos. 63, 218.

94. L. Price, <u>The Batchelor's Feast</u> [1636], in <u>RB</u>, i, pp. 46-51 (p. 48 for the quotation); <u>The Lamentation of a new-married man</u> [1624], in <u>RB</u>, ii, pp. 33-41; <u>A Broadside against Marriage</u> (1675), in BL, Luttrell Collection, ii, p. 137; Spufford, <u>Small Books</u>, p. 157.

95. M. Parker, <u>A good throw for three Maiden-heads</u> [c.1631], in Rollins, <u>Garland</u>, pp. 380-5; Parker, <u>Fourepence halfepenny Farthing</u> [1629], ibid., pp. 323-7.

96. <u>[Lacks title] or, Pretty Comparisons</u> (n.d.), in <u>RB</u>, ii, pp. 11-18 (p. 12 for the quotation).

97. Spufford, <u>Small Books</u>, pp. 63-4, 158-60; L. Price, <u>The merry-conceited Lasse</u> [1640], in <u>RB</u>, ii, pp. 111-14; <u>Lamentation of a new-married man</u>; T. W. T., <u>A mery balade, how a wife entreated her husband to have her own wyll</u> [1568], in Lilly (ed.), <u>Collection</u>, pp. 129-32.

98. R. Climsal, <u>Joy and Sorrow mixt together</u> [1630], in <u>RB</u>, i, pp. 508-14; Spufford, <u>Small Books</u>, pp. 136, 182.

99. <u>Lamentation of a new-married man</u>; <u>A Merry Jest of John Tomson and Jakaman his wife</u> [1586], in <u>RB</u>, ii, pp. 136-42; <u>Clod's Carroll</u> [1620?], in <u>RB</u>, i, pp. 201-6; <u>The discontented Married Man</u> (n.d.), in <u>RB</u>, i, pp. 294-9; Parker, <u>A Penny-worth of Good Counsell</u> [1638], in <u>RB</u>, ii, pp. 294-9.

100. Lilly (ed.), <u>Collection</u>, p. 132; <u>Merry Jest of John Tomson</u>.

101. The carefull wife and the comfortable Husband [1624, entered 1579], in RB, i, pp. 122-8; for a rare ballad in praise of marriage, see Rollins, Garland, pp. 356-60.
102. Half a Dozen of good wives [1634], in RB, i, pp. 451-6; Have among you! good Women [1634], in RB, i, pp. 435-40. For similar chapbook works, see Thompson, Merriments, section 7, and his 'Popular Reading and Humour in Restoration England', Journal of Popular Culture, ix (1976).
103. Mondayes Worke [1632], in RB, ii, pp. 148-53 (p. 153 for the quotation).
104. Wilson, 'Jestbooks'; extracts from many jestbooks are to be found in J. Wardroper (ed.), Jest upon Jest (1970). On burlesque almanacs, see D. C. Allen, The Star-Crossed Renaissance (Durham, Nth. Carolina, 1941), ch. 5; F. P. Wilson, 'Some English mock-prognostications', The Library, xix (1939); Capp, Astrology, pp. 231-5.
105. Shakespeare Jest Books, ed. W. C. Hazlitt (1864), ii, p. 297.
106. Thomas, 'Place of Laughter'; Thompson, Merriments, section 8, and pp. 200-8; The Merry Cuckold [1630], in Roxburghe Ballads, ed. Hindley, ii, pp. 463-8; Wilson, 'Jestbooks', pp. 128-9; Spufford, Small Books, pp. 182-4; Wardroper, Jest, pp. 62-73; Capp, Astrology, p. 234. A ballad in praise of the Welsh (RB, ii, pp. 328-33) suggests, though, that the Welsh community in London was large enough to attract publishers.
107. An excellent new Ditty: or, Which proveth that women the best Warriors be (n.d.), in RB, i, pp. 330-6; How the Devill, though subtle, was gul'd by a scold [1630], in RB, ii, pp. 366-71 (p. 368 for the quotation).
108. There are political comments in The Birth, Life and Death of John Frank [c.1680], Sigs. B3-3v; and the jestbook heroes James Hind and Hugh Peter had both been hanged for treason.
109. H. Crouch, Hodg (1655), p. 1 and passim; Thomas, 'Place of Laughter'; [H. Crouch?], Tom Tram of the West [1670-85]; Spufford, Small Books, pp. 182-4; Thompson, Merriments, pp. 200-8, 221-46. The Wise Men is attributed to Andrew Boorde (died 1549).
110. Thomas, 'Place of Laughter'; Spufford, Small Books, pp. 184-5.
111. Hazlitt, Shakespeare Jest Books, ii, p. 191; The Pinder, p. 50.
112. Thompson, Merriments, pp. 81-2.
113. For Black Tom, see Thompson, Merriments, pp. 209-14; for Dobson, see note 56 above; The Pleasant History of Tom Ladle [1682-1706].
114. Thompson, Merriments, pp. 173-82; Spufford, Small Books, pp. 137, 144; M. Parker, An Excellent new Medley

[c.1625] and <u>A Bill of Fare</u> [1637], in <u>RB</u>, i, pp. 52-6, 70-4.

115. Spufford, <u>Small Books</u>, p. 197, and ch. 8; Gerould, <u>Ballad of Tradition</u>, pp. 136-7; <u>Index</u>.

116. Capp, <u>Astrology</u>, pp. 144-50.

117. Both by John Hart, the second under the pseudonym Andrew Jones; Spufford, <u>Small Books</u>, pp. 196-8.

118. <u>Index</u>; for examples see Lilly (ed.), <u>Collection</u>, pp. 42-5, 125-9; <u>RB</u>, i, pp. 190-6, 270-6, 388-93.

119. J. Symon, <u>A pleasant Poesie</u> (1572), in Lilly (ed.), <u>Collection</u>, pp. 5-8; <u>Good and True, Fresh and New Christmas Carols</u> (1642); <u>New Carolls</u> (1661); cf. Burke, <u>Popular Culture</u>, ch. 8.

120. T. Deloney, <u>The Dutchesse</u>, in <u>RB</u>, i, pp. 287-94 (first published in Deloney's <u>Strange Histories</u> (1602)); <u>An Askew</u> [1675, entered 1624], in <u>RB</u>, i, pp. 29-37. Foxe's <u>Actes and Monuments</u> was first published in 1563.

121. R.M., <u>A newe Ballade</u> (n.d.), in Lilly (ed.), <u>Collection</u>, pp. 30-2.

122. Capp, <u>Astrology</u>, pp. 150-9.

123. Spufford, <u>Small Books</u>, ch. 8, esp. p. 210.

124. For various versions, undated, see Lilly (ed.), <u>Collection</u>, pp. 98-100, 173-4; Bodleian Library, Wood 401, fos. 60-1; <u>RB</u>, iii, pp. 183-6; <u>The Great Assize</u> [c.1680], in <u>RB</u>, i, pp. 394-401.

125. Spufford, <u>Small Books</u>, pp. 150, 201-4.

126. Ibid., pp. 198, 201-3; <u>A Hundred Godly Lessons</u> [1675, entered 1590], in <u>RB</u>, i, pp. 427-34; <u>A Very godly song</u> [1675, entered 1624] (Bodleian Library, Wood 401, fos. 65v-6); <u>A Godly Song, entitled, a farewell to the world</u> (n.d.), in <u>RB</u>, i, pp. 406-11; [J. Hart], <u>England's Golden Watch-bell</u> [1688-9]; <u>The Mothers Blessing</u> (1685).

127. Capp, <u>Astrology</u>, pp. 79-80, 146-50, 164-79.

128. Rollins, <u>Autolycus</u>, nos. 13, 20, 24, 37-40 (the cab-driver is no. 38); <u>RB</u>, ii, pp. 222-8 (the Essex labourer); J. E. Marshburn, <u>Murder and Witchcraft in England, 1550-1640</u> (Norman, Oklahoma, 1971).

129. Rollins, <u>Autolycus</u>, pp. 162-7.

130. Spufford, <u>Small Books</u>, pp. 208-9; <u>Glad Tydings from Heaven</u> (n.d.), in <u>RB</u>, i, pp. 401-6; H. E. Rollins (ed.), <u>Old English Ballads 1553-1625</u> (Cambridge, 1920), pp. 206-8.

131. J. Hart, <u>Christ's Last Sermon</u> (n.d.), Sig. B7v; R.J., <u>Dives and Lazarus</u> (22nd edn., 1684), originally an Elizabethan sermon preached at Paul's Cross; <u>The Dead Man's Song</u> [1675, entered 1624], in <u>RB</u>, i, pp. 223-9.

132. Capp, <u>Astrology</u>, p. 150; Spufford, <u>Small Books</u>, pp. 204-5; <u>News from Westmorland</u>, in Rollins, <u>Autolycus</u>, p. 166; J. Hart, <u>The Charitable Christian</u> (1685), Sigs. A7v-8.

133. The faire Widow of Watling Street [1624, entered 1597],
     in Lilly (ed.), Collection, pp. 157-66; A most notable
     example of an ungracious Son [1624], in RB, ii, pp. 73-9;
     The Mercer's Son of Midhurst [1624], in RB, ii, pp.
     189-97; cf. K. Thomas, Age and Authority in Early Modern
     England (1976).
134. The Map of Mock-Beggar Hall [1635?], in RB, ii, pp.
     131-6; Lilly (ed.), Collection, pp. 134-8.
135. A Warning-peice for Ingroosers of Corne [c.1643], in
     Rollins, Autolycus, pp. 31-5 (p. 32 for the quotation).
136. The Poore Man Payes for All [1630], in RB, ii, pp. 334-8
     (p. 337 for the quotation); A Lanthorne for Landlords
     [c.1640], in RB, i, pp. 547-53; Works of Deloney, p. ix.
137. Rollins, Autolycus, pp. 215-18.
138. Capp, Astrology, pp. 131-44; Thomas, Religion and
     Decline, ch. 12.
139. Thompson, Merriments, section 2; Erra Pater, a perpetual
     prognostication, went through at least 17 editions before
     1700.
140. See the ballad The Judgement of God shewed upon John
     Faustus [1658-60], and the chapbook version in Thompson,
     Merriments, pp. 98-101; L. M. Goldstein, 'An Account of
     the Faustus Ballad', The Library, xvi (1961), pp. 176-89.
     For ghosts and spirits, see Rollins, Autolycus, nos. 15,
     19, 29, 30.
141. The mad merry pranks of Robbin Good-Fellow [1675], in RB,
     ii, pp. 80-5; Thompson, Merriments, pp. 78-88, 93-4.
142. M. A. Shaaber, Some Forerunners of the Newspaper in
     England (1966); The Post of Ware [c.1621], in Rollins,
     Garland, pp. 139-43; L. Price, Newes from Hollands
     Leager [1632], ibid., pp. 399-405.
143. Winter's Tale, IV, iii; Bartholomew Fair, II, i; Nashe,
     Works, i, p. 23.
144. Shaaber, Forerunners, ch. 8; A. Miles, A Sad and true
     Relation of a great fire [1663], in Rollins, Autolycus,
     pp. 101-6; The Cold Year [1615], in Hindley, Miscellany,
     ii; Wood's collection is Bodleian Library, Wood D28.
145. Lamentable Newes, shewing the wonderful deliverance of
     Maister Edmond Pet (1613); A wonder beyond mans
     expectation (1632), in Rollins, Garland, pp. 386-92.
146. M. Parker, The Two Inseparable Brothers (1637), in
     Rollins, Autolycus, pp. 7-14; J. Taylor, The Great Eater
     (1630), and The Old, Old, Very Old Man (1635), both in
     Hindley, Miscellany, iii; cf. A wonder in Kent: Of the
     admirable stomacke of one Nicholas Wood [c.1630], in
     Rollins, Garland, pp. 342-9.
147. Marshburn, Murder and Witchcraft; Shaaber, Forerunners,
     pp. 141-4, 156-9.
148. A lamentable new Ditty, made upon the death of ... George
     Stoole [1629], in RB, i, pp. 574-81. This is a ballad of
     the Borders, and reflects the spirit of the feud.

149. M. Parker, No naturall Mother, but a Monster (1634), in Rollins, Garland, pp. 425-30; Garland, nos. 14, 49, 50, 52; in at least one of these cases the woman was in fact under strong provocation (no. 14, p. 84).

150. The Cryes of the Dead [c.1625], Rollins, Garland, pp. 222-8; Murder upon Murder (1635), ibid., pp. 431-6; A true relation of one Susan Higges [1635?], in RB, ii, pp. 531-5; A Maruellous Murther [c.1638], in Rollins, Autolycus, pp. 15-20; Misery to bee Lamented (1661), ibid., pp. 68-74 (buried alive); The Life and Death of Mr George Sandys (1626), in Rollins, Garland, pp. 248-55; A noble Dewel (1660), in Rollins, Autolycus, pp. 52-7; Marshburn, Murder and Witchcraft.

151. Marshburn, Murder and Witchcraft; Shaaber, Forerunners, pp. 156-9; Rollins, Garland, pp. 96-103.

152. Truth brought to Light [1662], in Rollins, Autolycus, pp. 93-100.

153. T. Deloney, The Lamentation of Master Page's wife of Plimmouth [c.1591]; The Lamentation of George Strangwidge [c.1591], in RB, i, pp. 553-63; Marshburn, Murder and Witchcraft, pp. 72-6.

154. Shaaber, Forerunners, pp. 144-56; Rollins, Autolycus; for pigs see Lilly (ed.), Collection, pp. 45-6, 112-13, 186-90. Pigs were kept in much closer proximity to humans than other farm animals.

155. Newes from Hereford [1661], in Rollins, Autolycus, pp. 81-6.

156. T. Lanfiere, The wonder of wonders [c.1675], in Rollins, Autolycus, pp. 185-90.

157. The true Discripcion of a Childe with ruffes (1566), in Lilly, Collection, pp. 243-6.

158. A battell of Birds [1621], and The lamentable Burning of the Citty of Corke [1622], in Rollins, Garland, pp. 150-60.

159. A most wonderful and sad judgement of God [1661], in Rollins, Autolycus, pp. 62-7.

160. True and Wonderfull ... a Strange and monstrous serpent, or dragon (1614), in Hindley, Miscellany, ii.

161. L. Price, A Monstrous shape [c.1640], in Rollins, Garland, pp. 449-54.

162. Spufford, Small Books, p. 219.

163. Shaaber, Forerunners, chs. 4-6, 8; C. H. Firth, 'The Ballad History of the Reign of James I', TRHS, v (1911); see also Firth, 'The Reign of Charles I', TRHS, vi (1912).

164. The crie of the poore for the death of the ... Earle of Huntington (1596), in Lilly (ed.), Collection, pp. 228-31 (p. 229 for the quotation); cf. ibid., pp. 260-6.

165. Index, p. 122.

166. A lamentable Ditty composed upon the Death of Robert Lord Devereux [1601?: see Index, p. 122], in RB, i, pp. 563-70; A lamentable new Balad upon the Earl of Essex

his Death [1603?], in RB, i, pp. 570-4; Firth, 'Ballad History', pp. 39-41.

167. Firth, 'Ballad History', pp. 22-5, 44-5; M. Parker, The Tragedy of Dr Lambe [1628], in Rollins, Garland, pp. 276-92.

168. R.M., Micrologia (1629), Sig. C8v.

169. H. E. Rollins (ed.), Cavalier and Puritan. Ballads and Broadsides ... 1640-1660 (NY, 1923); Bum-Fodder [1660], and Arsy-Versy [1660], in Rump, ii, pp. 54-7, 47-52. On Monck as St George see ibid., p. 62.

170. Capp, Astrology, pp. 72-88, 287-8; Thomas, Religion and Decline, pp. 313-14, 373-4.

171. Rollins, Cavalier and Puritan; J. Frank, The Beginnings of the English Newspaper 1620-1660 (Cambridge, Mass., 1961).

172. R. Clifton, The Last Popular Rebellion (1984), pp. 46, 65; H. E. Rollins (ed.), The Pepys Ballads (Cambridge, Mass., 1929-32), iii, nos. 94, 107, 108, 111, 118-21, 123, 148, 151, 154, 158-63; see also Index.

173. Capp, Astrology, pp. 91-100.

174. Frank, Beginnings, esp. pp. 235, 240, 259-60; cf. the newspapers published by John Crouch; The Worlds Wonder [1660](Bodleian Library, Wood D28(13); not in Wing).

175. Capp, Astrology, pp. 90-1, 99-101, 174-8; The Worlds Wonder! Or, The Prophetical Fish [1665], in Rollins, Autolycus, pp. 151-5; Great News from Chepstow Castle (1690) (Bodleian Library, Wood D28(30); not in Wing).

176. Thomas, Religion and Decline, ch. 13.

177. Holt, Robin Hood, p. 174; The Noble Birth of Robin Hood [c.1690], Sig. A2; A pleasant song of ... Guy of Warwick [1675, entered 1592] (Bodleian Library, Wood 401, fos. 3v-4).

178. The London Chaunticleers, pp. 329-30. The tinker was probably asking for The Unfortunate Lovers [1675, entered 1631], in RB, ii, p. 498.

179. Rollins, Garland, pp. 431-6. The Lamentation dates from 1565-6 (Index, nos. 1434-7), Fortune, my foe perhaps from 1565-6 (ibid., nos. 909, 911, 1569, 2018); see also Chappell, Popular Music, pp. 76-3.

180. The Complete Newgate Calendar, ed. J. L. Rayner and G. T. Crook (1926), i, p. 181. Chevy Chase was entered in the Stationers' Register in 1624, but was already old (c.1550); its story is set in the early fifteenth century. See Child, no. 162.

181. Goldstein, 'Faustus Ballad'; for Lear, Titus and the Babes, see T. Percy, Reliques of Ancient English Poetry, ed. H. B. Wheatley (1886), i, pp. 231-7, 224-9, iii, pp. 169-76; for the Pinder see Child, no. 124 (the ballad, entered in 1558) and The Comedy of George a Greene 1599 (Malone Society, 1911); for Romeo, Index, no. 2321 (entered 1596).

182. Crane, 'Vogue', pp. 125-45; Spufford, <u>Small Books</u>, pp. 224-37; <u>Works of Deloney</u>.

183. <u>Shakespeare Jest Books</u>, ed. Hazlitt, ii, p. 297; [W. Winstanley], <u>The Delectable History of Poor Robin, the Merry Sadler of Walden</u> [1688]; for Black Tom, see Thompson, <u>Merriments</u>, pp. 209-14.

184. <u>DNB</u>: 'John Taylor'; Spufford, <u>Small Books</u>, p. 249.

Chapter Seven

THE PEOPLE AND THE LAW

James Sharpe

I

One of the outcomes of the constitutional conflicts of seventeenth-century England was that those
social strata which we sometimes describe as the
political nation were extremely fond of English law.
The common law had been captured by the opponents of
the Stuarts, and was generally regarded as one of
the subject's major bulwarks against arbitrary
government. (1) Legal rights were among the most
important benefits that the English felt that they
had derived from the Glorious Revolution, and long
before 1688 highly-placed commentators can be found
eulogising the common law. Sir Matthew Hale was
voicing conventional wisdom rather than pleading a
special case when he wrote that the common law 'is
not only a very just and excellent Law in it self,
but is singularly accommodated to the English
Government, and to the Disposition of the English
Nation, and such as by a long Experience and Use as
it were incorporated into their very Temperament,
and, in a Manner, become the Complection and
Constitution of the English Commonwealth'. (2) On
this line of argument, all those who loved the
English constitution and, indeed, the English way of
life, also loved the English common law. It was
thought of in much the same way as religion, as an
almost mystical intellectual system which was a
central part of the ideology of the political
nation. After 1688, as one historian has recently
put it, the common law was viewed as a customary
law which 'in its infinite complexity had been
tested over many centuries and contained the accumulated wisdom of many generations'. (3)
Certainly, most eighteenth-century observers
regarded the common law, and its place in the post-

1688 constitution, as good things. Above all, the
concept of the rule of law was fundamental in contemporary political and legal thinking. Offences
should be clearly defined, not indeterminate; there
should be careful observance of the rules of
evidence; the judiciary administering the law
should be honest and learned.(4) Given such pre-
conditions, the rule of law would flourish, and
confer immense benefits upon those living under it.
Sir William Blackstone, delivering the first
Vinerian lecture at Oxford in October 1758, emphasised this point. 'Let us reflect a moment', he
urged his audience, 'on the singular frame and
polity of a land, which is governed by this system
of laws. A land, perhaps the only one in the
universe, in which political or civil liberty is the
very end and scope of the constitution. This
liberty, rightly understood, consists in the power
of doing whatever the laws permit.' (5) Another,
more recent writer, and one probably less vulnerable to complacency about the eighteenth-century
constitution than Blackstone, has also agreed that
the rule of law was one of the distinguishing
features of Hanoverian England. E. P. Thompson,
while accepting that 'the law did mediate existent
class relations to the advantage of the rulers', is
insistent on the importance of the concept and
reality of the rule of law, and that in this period
'class relations were expressed, not in any way one
likes, but through the forms of law'. (6) Eighteenth-
century thinking may have been imbued with the
rhetoric of law, but it was not an empty rhetoric.
The veneration of the common law in general, and of
the rule of law in particular, was one of the most
important intellectual legacies which the seventeenth century handed down to the eighteenth.

The importance of the common law in the political struggles of the seventeenth century and the
political thinking of the eighteenth have long been
familiar to the historian. Only recently, however,
has realisation spread of the importance of the law
and legal institutions not just to elite politics
and the political nation, but also to the everyday
life of large sections of the general population.
The functions of the law in any developed society go
far beyond the courtroom and the pages of works of
political theory. On one level, the law is about
power: it represents organised society, or powerful
groups within society, using force to regulate
individual and group conduct, and to prevent,
redress or punish deviation from the social norms

of the community in question. It is also part of culture; culture being 'the integrated sum total of learned behaviour patterns which are manifested and shared by the members of a society'. (7)   It is one of a number of sets of norms, of which social morals and custom are two of the more obvious, yet differs from most of them in that infringements of the law are met by legally prescribed and imposed sanctions. But, in general, people do not keep the law simply because they fear punishment.   Even when it is known there is little possibility of detection or punishment, most people, most of the time, do not break the law.   It has been internalised: it is part of culture.

Arguably, this was nowhere more true than in early modern England.   English society in this period had inherited the intense 'law mindedness' that has been identified as one of the distinguishing features of late medieval England. (8) Legal affairs, legal rights and legal remedies were constant preoccupations, and, even for persons of moderate property, contact with the law, via bonds, deeds and contracts, could be frequent.   Similarly, the *rites de passage* might involve contact with lawyers, for example if a marriage settlement or a will had to be made.   County society was to some extent focussed upon, and in large measure organised by, the court of quarter sessions, where many decisions about local government were enforced by indictments or recognizances.   The law was also central in dispute settlement.   Disputes over land, debts, or reputation were taken to the courts, while the activities of unruly or troublesome neighbours could be curbed by presenting them before the local manorial or ecclesiastical courts, or by having them bound over to keep the peace.   Thus the law was not merely about power: it was an influence upon the way in which innumerable men and women ordered their lives.   The point was made by Serjeant Davis in the preamble to his charge to the York Assizes in 1620.   Without justice, he told his listeners:

the land would be full of theeves, the sea full of pirates, the commons would ryse agaynst the nobylytye, and the nobylytye against the Crowne, wee should not know what were our owne, what were another mans, what we should have from our auncestors, what wee should learn to our children.   In a worde, there should be nothing certayne, nothing

sure, noe contracting, noe commercing, noe
conversing among men, but all kingdomes and
estates would be brought to confucyon, and
all humane society would be dissolved. (9)

The law was, therefore, a powerful cement of society,
virtually omnipresent in human affairs. The objective of this essay is to examine this proposition in
greater depth, and to examine the role the law
played in the lives of the popular classes, that 90
per cent of the population below the ranks of the
gentry, the professionals and the merchants.

II

This permeation of the law into the wider culture was, by the seventeenth century, a long-
established characteristic feature of English
society. As such, it demands attention in any discussion of popular culture. Although it is not part
of our intention to enter into a cross-cultural
study, it is instructive to examine some of the
conclusions which historians of French popular culture have reached about the changing relationship
between the law and popular culture in the early
modern period. According to Robert Muchembled, the
French enjoyed a developed popular culture in the
late middle ages, but this was eroded (from the
sixteenth century onwards) by steady pressure from
the state and the counter-reformed church, and
eventually went into a decline. One aspect of this
decline, he argues, was the way in which the state
emerged as the provider of the only judicial
machinery conducive to social cohesion.(10) This
seems very different from England, where, unless the
medievalists are misleading us, state law was
familiar and accepted at a very early date, the
population was 'law minded', and people were frequent litigants and active participants in the
administration of the law on a local level. Studying popular attitudes to the law in late medieval
and early modern England makes it difficult to
accept any notion that popular culture experienced
some sort of previous golden age, from which it
suffered a steady decline under the pressure of the
institutions of the state. Popular culture, in the
opinion of the present writer, is not something
which ever exists in a classic, pristine form. It
is, fundamentally, something which is dynamic, which
is in a more or less continuous state of change and
adaptation.(11)

The law in seventeenth-century England was one of the most important ways, perhaps the most important way, in which the people at large, the custodians of the 'little tradition', participated in the 'great tradition' of their social superiors.(12) That they did so presents further problems about the nature of popular culture, and about the relationship of that entity with elite culture. Behind the idea of the 'great tradition' there lies the assumption that it is essentially the culture of the elite, a predominantly exclusive and closed culture in the sense that people who had not attended those educational institutions through which it was transmitted were unable to participate in it. With the law, however, we encounter considerable difficulties with this alleged dichotomy between popular and elite culture. Members of the popular classes, as we shall argue, were heavily involved with the working of the law in a number of different capacities. This involvement, again as we shall argue, meant that the popular consciousness formulated its own ideas about the law. Thus with the law at least, to argue that the majority of the population participated only in the popular culture seems far too simplistic. As any sensitive student must realise, there is a two-way traffic between the two 'traditions'. Arguably, the law was one of the main routes through which this traffic passed. Popular attitudes towards and popular use of the law (and, one suspects, other aspects of past culture and ideology) demonstrate that popular culture does not stand in isolation: it is something which digests, adapts and assimilates from outside.(13) As one of the more perceptive students of the subject has commented: 'Given the flexibility of popular culture in appropriating and adapting models which it was hoped simply to impose on it from above, we may have to abandon altogether the search for cultural forms exclusive to specific social groups and concentrate on the category of use.'(14) Nowhere is this more true than when studying popular attitudes to the law in early modern England.(15)

But there remains a further problem, involving discussion of 'specific social groups': who were the 'popular classes' whose culture permitted so many contacts with the law? Generally speaking, historians of the subject have defined them essentially as a residual category; to Burke, for example, they were 'the non-learned, the un-lettered, the non-elite'.(16) It seems unlikely, however, that this group was homogeneous in any late medieval or

early modern European society, while there is every
indication that it was becoming increasingly diverse
in seventeenth-century England. It is now becoming
accepted that the 'non-elite' in Stuart England were
experiencing a more marked social stratification,
and, as we shall argue when discussing parish constables, this stratification expressed itself in
cultural as well as purely economic terms. If the
popular classes were not homogeneous, could it be
that popular culture was not a monolithic entity,
but was rather something which could comprehend
divergent, even contradictory, strands? If different strata within the non-elite varied so much in
their participation in the law, it becomes difficult
to accept the view that there was only one popular
culture in seventeenth-century England.

Certainly, in writing this essay it has become
obvious that not all members of 'the people' were
involved equally in either litigating, or in helping
to administer the local legal system. Women were
almost entirely excluded from the latter process;
and, apart from a few peculiar matters, were unlikely to be as frequently involved in the former as
were men.(17) There is also every indication that
they were about four times less likely than men to
be accused of felony at the assizes and quarter
sessions, unless the offence in question were witchcraft or infanticide.(18) Conversely,the labouring
poor, of either sex, were most likely to enter the
judicial record when accused of committing an
offence. Their attitude to the law remains difficult to reconstruct, although occasional glimpses
come down to us. In the 1620s, for example, we find
a cordwainer from Maldon in Essex reported for
claiming that 'in former tymes' after Sunday service
'the people did usually goe out of the church to
play at foote ball & to the alehouse & there continued till they were drunk & it ware noe matter if
they ware hanged'. Two decades earlier, another
inhabitant of the county had greeted the accession
of the Stuart dynasty by declaring that 'by God I do
not care a turd nether for the kinge nor his
lawes'.(19) Such people, it seems likely, had ideas
about the law and the wider structures of authority
which lay behind it; ideas which were far removed
from those of Hale and Blackstone.

III

Despite such reservations, it remains clear that
the law was an important element in the life of the

popular classes. Perhaps the most concrete support for this assertion lies in the sheer number of courts existing in Stuart England. At Westminster there sat the most important courts in the realm, the King's Bench, Common Pleas, Exchequer, Chancery and, until the Civil Wars, Star Chamber. Twice yearly, the assize judges rode out from Westminster into the shires, which in any case possessed their own quarter sessions. As well as these secular courts, there existed a hierarchy of church courts stretching from the archiepiscopal tribunals at Canterbury and York to the local archdeaconry courts. Many villages still possessed that most local court of all, a manorial court, while most areas enjoyed a number of tribunals dealing with small causes, the sheriff's tourn, the county court, and so on. The extent of legal services available in a provincial capital could be extensive. Seventeenth-century York, to take a slightly extreme but by no means atypical example, possessed a surprising number of institutions to which those intending to use the law could turn. Ecclesiastical courts included the court of Audience or Chancery, the Consistory court, the Exchequer court, the courts of the Dean and Chapter and other peculiar jurisdictions, and the courts of the Archdeacons. The city government rested upon a sizeable collection of civic courts, roughly as numerous. The city sheriffs held three distinct courts: a biannual tourn for the Ainsty, a wapentake of the West Riding which was under the city's jurisdiction; a monthly county court held jointly with the city coroners; and a court of common pleas, held three times a week. The lord mayor presided over a weekly court of husting or common pleas, a court of mayor and aldermen, a court of orphans, a court of chamberlains, a coroner's court and an escheator's court. There was also a court of quarter sessions for the city and Ainsty. York was an assize town; and it was, of course, the location of the Council of the North, which exercised jurisdictional powers. We must agree with the recent historian of Tudor York that the city was 'equipped with a judicial and administrative system of some complexity'.(20) The same, albeit in a diluted form in some rural areas, could be said for the country as a whole.

There is every indication that this system was used with increasing frequency in the two centuries before 1650. By the end of the fifteenth century the central courts at Westminster were already handling about 3,000 new cases a year, an impressive

total at a time when England's population was
probably not much in excess of two million souls.(21)
Between 1560 and 1640 there occurred what has been
described as a 'great, and probably unprecedented,
increase' in the amount of litigation entertained by
the two main common-law courts at Westminster, the
King's Bench and the Common Pleas. In 1580 there
were 13,300 cases at an advanced stage in these two
courts, a total that had risen to 23,453 by 1606,
and 29,162 by 1640.(22) Away from the centre, it
seems that most courts in the localities were also
experiencing an upsurge in their business. There
was a massive rise in cases coming to the church
courts at York between about 1570 and 1640.(23)
Examination of the *nisi prius* business of the
Western assize circuit (comprehending six counties)
between 1611 and 1697 shows a rise from 721 cases in
1611 to a peak of 1,024 in 1656, and a marked
falling off towards the end of the century.(24)
Little work has so far been done on seventeenth-
century manorial courts, but some idea of the amount
of business that might be handled by an active court
leet comes from the manor of Prescot (Lancashire).
Here the leet adjudicated 4,758 illegal acts between
1615 and 1660, an impressive total given that the
population of the manor in the first half of the
century was probably about 500 people.(25) Arguably,
this explosion in litigation had an impact upon the
legal system which went beyond the merely statistical: T. G. Barnes, in the course of his investigation of Jacobean Star Chamber records, has
commented that 'the litigants, not the lawyers, were
the real determinants of substantive law ... what
the litigants wanted and were prepared to pay for,
the lawyers would propose and the courts would
dispose'.(26)

But who were the litigants? So far, this
question has received little attention, but every
study yet completed suggests that they were drawn
from groups far below the very rich in wealth.
Anecdotal evidence, such as that given in depositions concerning ecclesiastical slander suits in
Yorkshire, shows people near the bottom of the
social scale initiating causes.(27) More systematic
research confirms this impression. M. J. Ingram's
work on litigation in early seventeenth-century
Wiltshire shows that although 60 per cent of plaintiffs in his sample at Star Chamber were peers or
gentry, 40 per cent of those initiating suits at the
Common Pleas were yeomen, many other litigants there
being artisans or husbandmen; while the clientele

of the Wiltshire church courts, barring gentry or
clergymen initiating tithe suits, were 'drawn overwhelmingly from the middling ranks of yeomen,
husbandmen and craftsmen'.(28) Findings from other
areas support this impression of the social background of those attending the church courts. Thus a
study of deponents in the diocese of Norwich,
1630-9, shows that of 382 men (the records do not
permit analysis of the social status of female
witnesses), 140 were described as craftsmen and
tradesmen, 90 as yeomen, and 84 as husbandmen. This
is, of course, a small and geographically limited
sample; but figures drawn from the dioceses of
Norwich, Exeter, Durham and London between 1560 and
1700, giving a good geographical spread and a sample
of 18,856 deponents, demonstrate the same result:
those involved as witnesses at the church courts
were drawn overwhelmingly from the middling ranks of
society, with tradesmen and craftsmen, yeomen and
husbandmen regularly forming about 80 per cent of
male deponents.(29) Details of occupation as given
in legal records can be unreliable.(30) Yet, if we
may discount a deliberate conspiracy by the clerical
staff of courts to mislead modern historians, it
would seem that both litigants and witnesses at
courts were drawn mainly from the middling to lower
ranks of society, from men and women of moderate or
small property. As Ingram has put it, 'in fine, the
great mass of seventeenth-century litigation, far
from affecting only the gentry and nobility, penetrated deep into society as a whole'.(31)
     There is still some uncertainty about how this
litigation should be interpreted. One view would see
it as a symptom of social disharmony, of a world in
which human relations were characteristically hostile. Lawrence Stone has interpreted the upsurge of
litigation in early modern England as one aspect of
'an abrupt rise in a wide variety of indicators of
social anomy and of a breakdown in community methods
of dealing with conflict', as a consequence of which
'both ethical and economic fissures were opening up
within the village and exacerbating conflict between
neighbours'. (32) For those, like Stone, who have
pessimistic ideas about the nature of human
relations in the period, litigation seems to provide
a handy index of conflict. Even those who do not
share these ideas, and who have different notions
about the social meaning of litigation, have commented on the way that many contemporaries thought that
the operation of the law might, under certain
circumstances, constitute a form of disorder.(33)

Work on Star Chamber records supports the view that
suits might be initiated for vexatious or malicious
reasons, and that people might litigate to continue
a conflict rather than seek justice. Hence of 8,228
actions brought into Star Chamber by information or
bill between 1603 and 1625, 4,500 contain explicit
references to other suits already in existence
between the parties involved. Yet even this
'try-on' litigation in Star Chamber was a reflection
of the state of the English law and the English
legal system rather than proof of a growth of
unpleasantness amongst the English. Star Chamber
was just part of a system of litigation which seemed
almost designed to preclude a speedy decision, in
which the substantive law was in many ways inchoate,
and in which a network of overlapping and rival
courts and jurisdictions encouraged what might be
almost endless litigation.(34) If anyone wanted to
play the system, the system was certainly there to
be played: but this did not necessarily imply that
litigation can be interpreted simply as a sign of
social tension, of Stone's 'ethical and economic
fissures'.

When we probe more deeply into litigation, and
into what can be discovered about popular attitudes
to it, we find a rather more complex picture than
one of cynical or malicious use of the law. Some
people taking cases to court were, undoubtedly,
launching malicious or vexatious litigation. One
feels that the vast majority were not. Their aim
was rather to use a suit at law as a means of resol-
ving a conflict (not invariably the conflict
recorded in the court documents), a point born out
by the frequency with which legal proceedings were
ended or accompanied by attempts at arbitration or
other forms of settlement out of court.(35) The
student of the Star Chamber, to whose work we have
referred, noted 'a flavour of negotiation' about
much of the litigation of the period, and claimed
that 'the suits were vehicles to keep open business
discussions that would issue, hopefully, in a
settlement acceptable to both parties'.(36) At the
very worst, litigation was a more acceptable social
phenomenon than violence. As Ingram has remarked,
'disagreement and conflict over a variety of issues
were common, but were to an important extent contained by the rule of law ... the multiplication of
lawsuits balanced a decline in the incidence and
social acceptability of violence, and marked an
important step towards a more settled and peaceful
society.'(37) Most people, most of the time, went to

law because they felt they had a genuine dispute
that needed to be settled: that they did so more
often in the period from 1550 to 1650 is a reflection, in large measure (leaving population growth
aside), of a growing complexity in commercial life
in a period when legal rules over many matters had
not been consolidated, and when a variety of courts
offered the person contemplating going to law a
number of alternative avenues for so doing.

Yeomen, husbandmen, craftsmen and tradesmen,
people of small property, were therefore actively
involved in the litigation of the age, either as
participants or witnesses. They were also active
participants in the actual administration of the law
at a grass-roots level. Many local courts depended
on the use of juries. Some of these - the grand
juries of the assizes and quarter sessions - were
composed of gentry; (38) but others, the trial juries
at those two courts, the juries at manorial courts,
or the coroner's jury, were formed of men of small
property. Such men also served as constables and
other parish officers, and were also involved in the
legal system as sureties. It was this participation
of members of non-elite groups in local administration which gave the English law one of its major
peculiarities. The historian has long been familiar
with the activities of the justices of the peace,
and with the significance of their contribution to
local government in the early modern period; but it
is rapidly becoming apparent that the labours of the
justices would have been fruitless without the
active co-operation of inferior officers and, indeed,
of sections of the public at large. As with suits
between parties, popular participation in the criminal and administrative aspects of the law suggests
both a familiarity with the law and a desire to use
it. Perhaps the most striking demonstration of this
latter point, a willingness to use the law, comes
with the use of binding-over to keep the peace, a
handy method of controlling a potentially violent
or disruptive neighbour. Surviving quarter sessions
records for Essex show that between 1620 and 1680
bindings-over to keep the peace or to be of good
behaviour outnumbered assault indictments by about
three to one. (39) The relevant recognizances, and
the notebook of an Essex J.P. which records many
such bindings-over, (40) show that those using this
form of legal remedy were drawn mainly from the
popular classes.

Perhaps the ultimate demonstration of a widespread willingness to participate in the enforcement

of the law, and of attitudes to the criminal law,
come with the actual indictment of criminals. Most
often, certainly when dealing with felonies other
than homicide, the decision to prosecute came from
the person offended against. As might be expected,
given the time and expense which a prosecution might
involve, scraps of evidence survive which suggest
that a formal charge was brought only after a period
of mounting tensions between the accuser and the
accused: the bringing of an indictment, in such
cases, was an episode in a whole history of deteri-
orating relationships. Thus in theft cases it is
frequently possible to find explicit statements that
an indictment was brought when the stealing of an
unusually valuable item followed a period of pilfer-
ing.(41) With witchcraft accusations, too, the law
was usually invoked only after a period of mounting
tensions and suspicions, and often only after
informal counter-action had failed.(42) More
generally, criminal charges might be brought only
after the failure of admonition and negotiation,
whether between the accused and the alleged victim,
or between the accused and the parish officers. (43)
This selective use of the criminal law is demonstrated by the profile of those who did find themselves in court. A sample of 132 persons accused of
property offences at the Wiltshire quarter sessions
in the early seventeenth century, for example,
reveals that suspects resident in the parish where
the alleged offence had been committed were less
likely to be indicted than strangers, and less likely
to be convicted: servants, interestingly enough,
enjoyed an intermediary position in both
respects.(44) Once again, the law emerges essentially as something which people used, often in an
idiosyncratic way.
  But this participation of the lower orders in
the operation of the law raises an important point:
often we are dealing not, as in litigation, with
conflicts between people of roughly equal status,
but rather with attempts by the richer members of
the community to curb the activities of the poorer.
There is some evidence that this was already being
done through the manor court in the fourteenth
century, although by the seventeenth the focus of
this type of regulation had shifted to the ecclesiastical courts and the quarter sessions. (45)
Recent research, initially on Essex parishes, but
now extending into other areas, has suggested that
in the seventeenth century constables, churchwardens
and other parish officers were recruited almost

exclusively from the upper stratum of village
society. (46)   In an age of mounting population
pressure and sharpened social stratification, it has
been argued, these officers and the social stratum
from which they were drawn became aware both of a
growing cultural gap between themselves and the
poor, and of a greater need to control that latter
group. In parishes where a godly minister managed
to imbue the parish officers with a puritanical
sense of their responsibilities, the gulf between
the 'respectable' and 'rough' could widen markedly.
The implications of this process have been
delineated most clearly in work on the Essex parish
of Terling. There the records of both the ecclesiastical courts and of the assizes and quarter
sessions show that after about 1600 cases brought
from the village increasingly involved attempts by
the richer villagers, often with the encouragement
of the vicar, to regulate the conduct of the poorer
parishioners. (47) A problem, to which we will return
later, emerges from this: for, if the law was an
important part of popular culture, it was evidently
of more importance to some sections of the popular
classes than to others. (48)

IV

     The law was, therefore, a familiar phenomenon to
the populace of Stuart England. Through frequent
contacts with the legal machine, whether as litigants, local government officers, witnesses, jurors,
sureties, or, indeed, as malefactors, the everyday
culture of the English, the way in which they viewed
the organisation of social life, the way in which
they acted and expected others to act, were informed
by notions derived and at times adapted from the law.
But ideas on the law entered popular culture through
channels other than participation: namely, through
the popular literature of the day, the vast mass of
broadsides, ballads, chapbooks and pamphlets.
     Numerous broadside ballads and chapbooks were
produced in the seventeenth century, some of them in
very large numbers; there is a tradition, for example, that 20,000 copies of Lord William Russell's
speech from the gallows were printed and sold in
1683. (49) They were normally hawked around for a few
pence or less, a price well within the power of all
but the poorest, were often illustrated with crude
woodcuts, and were almost invariably headed with a
displayed title which served the same function as
the headline does in the modern tabloid newspaper.

In so far as this literature touched on the law, it did so mainly through the description of the serious, sensational crime. The very titles of some of the relevant broadside ballads demonstrate this taste for sensationalism: The notorious robber's lamentation, or, Whitney's ditty in the gaol of Newgate (1693); A sad and true relation of the apprehension, trial and confession, condemnation and execution of two murtherers who killed a worthy knight (1675); The Bloody-minded husband, or the cruelty of John Chambers of Tanworth, Warwickshire (c.1685); The bloody-minded husband, or, the unfortunate wife (1690); The Yorkshire tragedy (c.1685). The titles of the pamphlets have much the same effect: Heaven's speedie hue and cry sent after lust and murther (1635); Murther will out (1675); The cry of blood: or, the horrid sin of Murther display'd (1692); Bloody news from Covent Garden (1683). Rarely can a reading public have been given a clearer impression of the goods it was about to purchase.

But if the tone of this literature was essentially sensationalist, its intentions were overwhelmingly normative. The objective of the ballads and pamphlets was to demonstrate that crime did not pay. Their structure normally adhered to a strict formula: whatever the details of the case in question, the main emphasis of the story was almost invariably on the gallows speech of the convicted man or woman, which normally gave an account of a slow slide into degeneracy that led to the gallows, and which was intended to be a dreadful warning to others. The gallows speeches, as reported by the hack writers composing the ballads and chapbooks, contained innumerable accounts of the consequences of youthful neglect of church attendance or of adolescent dallying in the alehouse. The general theme is stated admirably in the title of one of the ballads: A warning to all lewd livers, by the example of a disobedient child, who riotously wasted and consumed his father's and mother's goods, and also his own, among strumpets and other lewd livers, and after died most miserably on a dung hill.(50) Those who faced death on the gallows rather than the dunghill were, according to the accounts of their end, normally willing to accept the consequences of their erroneous and sinful ways, and anxious that their unhappy fate might deter others from falling into the same errors. Thus the ballad describing the execution of James Selby in 1691 has him declare:

> All you that come to see my fatal end
> Unto my dying words I pray attend
> Let my misfortune now a warning be
> To ev'ry one of high and low degree. (51)

This very conventional form which the ballads and pamphlets have provides the key to their significance. Their intention was to reinforce accepted thinking about crime and its likely end. People reading the pamphlets obviously had a fairly clear idea of what crime was about, and the objective of this popular literature was evidently to clarify this idea yet further.

Additional proof of the determination of the writers of popular literature to present a hostile view of the criminal is furnished by the almost complete absence, certainly before the last decades of the seventeenth century, of any attempt to present the malefactor as a glamorous or romantic figure. Even the highwayman was represented for what he normally was, a nasty thug. Some highwaymen, the famous James Whitney for example, were portrayed as being courageous enough, but any allusions to their fearlessness were usually compensated for by expressions of disapproval at their conduct. (52) There is the odd reference to Robin-Hood-type conduct on the part of highwaymen. Thus we find a highwayman named Biss, executed at Salisbury in 1696, enlivening his trial with accounts of his exploits, and insisting that 'the poor I fed, the rich likewise I empty sent away'. The judge, unimpressed, still sentenced him to death. (53) One senses that the nineteenth-century arrival of highwaymen as romantic figures (Dick Turpin in particular) is fairly directly related to their ceasing to be much of a problem in real life. (54)

The other great theme of popular comment on the law was the constant expression of dislike against lawyers. From the middle ages onwards lawyers had been accused of various corrupt practices: the manufacture of litigation, the prolongation of suits, the extortion of excessive fees, and the abuse of justice through taking or giving bribes. Such views were doubtless overstated, yet the popular antipathy towards the profession was remarkable. The breakdown of censorship and the general atmosphere of political and social debate in the 1640s and 1650s produced a fine crop of anti-lawyer sentiment in print. (55) But sniping at the men of law was carried out throughout the seventeenth century, and is to be found in popular literature, joke-books, proverbs, and, by the end of the century, in satirical prints. Likewise, the widely-read almanacs described by Bernard Capp are replete with jibes against lawyers. As with the general run of the popular literature of the period, criticism of the law and plans for its radical reform reached its peak in the almanacs of the revolutionary decades in the middle of the century, but the familiar themes of hostile comment were constantly expressed. Lawyers sought to 'undo the poor, and cheat the rich', and squeezed poor clients with 'fraud, delay, tricks and excessive fees'. Another almanac-writer predicted in 1617 'the terrible abusion of the laws by some double-feeing attorneys', while the persistence of such attitudes is demonstrated by a late eighteenth-century description of the archetypal lawyer as a 'monster in tufted gown'.(56) The roots of this dislike are obvious enough: the lawyer (like the doctor) was felt to be essentially somebody who profited from the misfortunes of others. There may, however, have been a deeper cause for disquiet. In a society which still viewed itself essentially in hierarchical terms, the lawyer, regarded as somebody given to upward social mobility, was something of an anomalous figure. As one writer has put it, 'in societies sensitive to social gradation, men of law regularly presented problems'.(57)

There was some degree of objective reality about contemporary beliefs about the legal profession. Certainly there was a proliferation of lawyers in the late sixteenth and early seventeenth centuries, and all too many of them were not properly qualified in anything like the modern sense. Legal practitioners included not only Sir Edward Coke and Sir Matthew Hale, but also the stewards who ran the manorial court, country attorneys, and other local men. Many of these more lowly practitioners must have stood in much the same relationship to the modern idea of a lawyer as a contemporary cunning man would have done to the modern concept of a doctor. Nevertheless, the early modern period did witness both the social rise and the increased proficiency of the English provincial lawyer. The most thorough investigation of this process is provided by Peter Clark's detailed study of pre-Civil War Kent.(58) Here lawyers became both richer and more important in the politics and society of the county as the sixteenth and seventeenth centuries progressed. Many of them, of course, remained fairly insubstantial men, having gained their train-

ing as an apprentice to an attorney rather than at
an Inn of Court. The most usual way to advancement
was by gaining a local reputation, usually as a
result of becoming one of the group of attorneys
accredited to plead at one of Kent's many town
courts. In Canterbury, the county capital, there
existed something like an informal lawyers' club,
with about seven attorneys attending to the needs of
the town court at any one time, as well as six
proctors, often notaries public, at the ecclesiastical courts. For the upper ranks of Kentish
lawyers, the material rewards of their profession
could be high. One Kent lawyer died owning an
'impressive mansion at Maidstone, £60 worth of
plate, a great deal of expensive furniture, and a
very large collection of books'. (59)

Contemporaries might complain about the proliferation of lawyers, and see in this a likely cause
of the increase in litigation. Lawyers on the other
hand, and probably with greater justification, could
claim that their numbers were increasing because of
an increased demand for their services among the
population at large. More people wanted wills made,
more people wanted contracts drawn up, and, most
notorious of all, more people were litigating.
Given that the law courts operated, in some ways at
least, as commercial clearing houses, settlers of
family disputes, land registries, and the watchdogs
of public morals and behaviour, this growing popular
awareness of and knowledge of the law should not be
surprising. The legal-mindedness of such political
and religious radicals as John Lilburne, Lodowick
Muggleton, or George Fox has long been familiar, but
it now seems safe to infer that the popular classes
as a whole shared this attribute of these well-known
figures. Certainly the English, like the peasants
of the Castilian Montes, knew what litigation was
like.(60) They also had their own ideas on the law
and on the rule of law, although these ideas only
rarely surface in the documentary record. In 1603,
for example, a number of the inhabitants of Essex
were indicted at the assizes for expressing unwelcome views on the accession of James I. Among the
run-of-the-mill anti-Scotticisms, there were a group
of statements which implied that the popular mind
thought that there was a hiatus in legal authority
between the death of the late queen and the coronation of her successor. John Sileto of Earls
Colne, a butcher, was indicted for declaring 'God
save the quene she is dead, wherefore lye I heare,
this is Nick Barley's law' (Nicholas Barley being

the constable of Earls Colne at that time). Pressed
further, Sileto told that 'I said he is no Kynge;
he is no Kinge tell he be Crowned'.(61) It was probably some such thinking which led John Walden, a
Pleshey blacksmith, to claim that 'we neither had
prince nor lawes'; while another Essex tradesman
was indicted for saying that 'there was no lawe till
our king's majestie hathe enacted a parliament but
god's lawes'.(62) Obviously, the popular consciousness was capable of forming and articulating its own
opinions on the nature of the rule of law.

Such evidence is, unfortunately, very rare.
Although something about the connection between the
law and popular culture might be inferred from the
eagerness to litigate or the willingness to participate, direct information on popular attitudes to the
law, and particularly those of the inferior craftsmen or labouring poor, is only very infrequently
available. Surviving sources, for example, make it
difficult to reconstruct anything very much about
seventeenth-century attitudes to 'social crime',
crime which is 'a conscious, almost a political,
challenge to the prevailing social order and its
values'.(63) Doubtless many of those accused of
stealing wood, stealing grain while gleaning, or
poaching, would have qualified as 'social' criminals, but the views of such offenders were rarely
recorded.(64) There is rather more information that
rioters held 'legitimising notions' similar to those
which E. P. Thompson has described for Hanoverian
England.(65) Thus apprentices rioting against new
grain-marketing practices at Sheffield in 1675 could
argue that they objected to the innovation because
it was 'not according to ye law'.(66) Legalistic
ideas sometimes informed other aspects of the 'order
within disorder' which was such a feature of the
crowd behaviour of the period. John Robinson, one
of 'a greate number of idell people' gathered for a
stang-riding in Essex in 1683, claimed that he had
'an authority for doeing it under my Lord Chiefe
Justice in Eyre's hand and under seven justices' of
the peace hands'.(67)

Perhaps the most intriguing example of popular
adaptation of legal forms comes from a late-
seventeenth-century ballad, The Brickmakers'
Lamentation from Newgate. The incident it describes
may well have been apocryphal, but nevertheless it
demonstrates how the law, or at least aspects of its
outward display, had permeated the culture of the
popular classes. According to the ballad, Dick
Lambert, one of a team of brickmakers, had stolen a

workmate's bread and cheese. The brickmakers held a mock court:

> A judge, and a jury, and clark did appear,
> A sheriff, and also a hangman was there.
> The judge being set and the prisoner brought
>   forth,
> The plaintiff he there on a brickbat took oath.

The judge, a brickmaker clad 'in a red wastecoat, which serv'd for a gown', supervised the swearing in of the jury who, like the plaintiff, took oath on a brickbat. Dick was found guilty, and sentenced to suffer a parody of the branding on the hand which was the penalty for those successfully claiming benefit of clergy: he 'had sentence, by which he was forst to be burnt in the hand with an apple hot roast'. He was also 'tried' for treason, and hanged but cut down immediately. The ballad claimed that the men playing the judge and the hangman, as well as two of the mock jurymen, had been apprehended, put in Newgate, and fined £100 apiece. The law evidently entered the popular mind sufficiently to be, or at least thought to be capable of being, represented as a subject for fairly detailed parody. It would also appear, however, that the authorities found this sort of parody, this form of order in disorder, to be unacceptable.(68)

V

Early in this essay we observed that the law, attitudes to it, and its importance in everyday life, were essentially similar to those obtaining in the late middle ages. As we begin its conclusion, it may be felt proper, not least because a descriptive and analytical approach has been adopted, to turn briefly to ideas of the role of law in eighteenth-century England, and raise some problems relating to change over time. There, certainly, impressions of the functions of the law are very different from those which have been delineated on the preceding pages. We have seen how law was a part of popular culture, at least for those plebeian strata above the labouring poor, and the law (even the criminal law) was essentially something which people used and participated in. Conversely, Douglas Hay, in what is widely (and correctly) regarded as a masterly article on law and society in eighteenth-century England, offers a rather different picture. To Hay, the criminal law (which is his major pre-

occupation) was essentially something which maintained existing economic, class and political
structures: it 'was critically important in maintaining bonds of obedience and deference, in
legitimizing the status quo, in continually
recreating the structure of authority which arose
from property and in turn protected its interests'.
Hay sees little popular participation in its
workings, since those in control of eighteenth-
century society felt that 'the common Englishman
could not be trusted to share in the operation of
the law'.(69) Undoubtedly the law, and especially
the criminal law, was upholding the existing social
structure in the seventeenth century. Yet the law,
including the criminal law, also did a number of
other things in that earlier period, possessed a
wider variety of meanings, and was well integrated
into popular culture. Hay's main concern is with
that most familiar of legislative developments, the
evolution of the 'bloody code' of capital statutes
against property offenders, and with the redefini-
tion of certain traditional or customary rights into
acts of theft. His argument, which is beginning to
attract considerable criticism, therefore addresses
only a very limited section of the problems which
arise from attempting to understand the social
meaning of the law.(70) Even if one accepts the
basic validity of his viewpoint, the impression
remains that Hay, however brilliant his answers, has
asked a somewhat limited range of questions.(71)

It may well be that the students of crime and the
law in the Hanoverian period have simply addressed
different problems and consulted different sources
from those which have concerned us in writing this
essay, and that the impression of a change between
the seventeenth and eighteenth centuries is a false
one. Nevertheless, and allowing for the patent need
for more research, there remains a sense that litigation and popular involvement in the law's workings
were declining towards the end of the seventeenth
century. The great period of expansion in business
for the courts at Westminster, as we have seen, was
the century before the Civil Wars. *Nisi prius*
actions at the assizes, in so far as record survival
makes comment possible, seem to have fallen off,
sometimes dramatically, between the mid and late
seventeenth century.(72) Evidence from such geographically removed counties as Essex and Yorkshire
indicates that the ecclesiastical courts, so active
before 1642, likewise suffered a decline in business
in the second half of the century.(73) Local manor-

ial and town courts await detailed examination, but,
if the experience of Essex was typical, they too
ceased to be used as forums for dispute settlement
as the seventeenth century progressed.(74)   Even the
criminal courts were used less in the early eighteenth than in the late sixteenth and seventeenth
centuries.   The proliferation of capital statutes
against property offences is, as we have suggested,
extremely familiar to the general historian.   Only
recently, however, has it become apparent that
(outside the London area at least) massively fewer
people were actually being tried for property
offences in the first half of the eighteenth century
than in the period c.1590-1630, and that dramatically fewer were being executed in the latter
period.(75) Popular use of the courts was slackening;
the law, perhaps, was being removed from popular
culture.   Possibly the lack of clarity in the rules
governing the types of conflict which had provoked
litigation at earlier periods had been overcome, and
no longer needed testing.   Possibly the increased
professionalisation of lawyers had decreased the use
of 'try-on' litigation at local courts.(76)   Certainly the disputes and petty crimes which had
previously been dealt with in the communal manor
court, or in the semi-communal archdeacon's court,
were now the concern of the justices of the peace,
either upon summary trial or at the petty sessions.
An important milestone had been reached in that
'millennial transition' from private, or at least
community-based, dispute settlement to the triumph
of state law.(77)

     All of which, I would contend, has important
implications for the history of popular culture in
England.   The authors of Albion's Fatal Tree, in
their introduction to the book, claim that Tyburn
Tree not only stood at the heart of the ideology of
the law but was 'at the heart of the popular
culture also'.(78)   It is to be hoped that this
essay has demonstrated that this assertion could be
expanded: public execution did constitute the most
dramatic demonstration of the contact between the
law and popular culture, but, more generally, the
law as a whole represented an important means of
transmitting the wishes and aspirations of authority
into the popular consciousness.   What is obvious is
that, in the seventeenth century at least, law,
whether it was serving to socialise, to punish, to
harass, to protect private property and private
interests, or to maintain the political and economic
status quo, was of central importance in the way in

which people went about their everyday lives. As
Alan Macfarlane has recently commented, 'English
society was based on, and integrated by, two
principal mechanisms - money and the law'.(79)

Notes

1. Much of the argument, and some illustrative documents
    relevant to this point, are collected in W. J. Jones,
    Politics and the Bench: the Judges and the Origins of
    the English Civil War (1971).
2. Sir M. Hale, The History of the Common Law of England
    (Chicago, 1971), p. 30.
3. H. T. Dickinson, Liberty and Property: Political Ideology
    in Eighteenth-Century Britain (1977), p. 63.
4. For discussions of the importance of the rule of law, see
    Dickinson, Liberty and Property, pp. 89-90; D. Hay,
    'Property, Authority and the Criminal Law', in Hay and
    others, Albion's Fatal Tree. Crime and Society in
    Eighteenth-Century England (1975); E. P. Thompson,
    Whigs and Hunters (1975), pp. 258-69.
5. Sir W. Blackstone, Commentaries on the Laws of England
    (1771), i, p. 6.
6. Thompson, Whigs and Hunters, p. 262 (author's emphasis).
7. E. A. Hoebel, The Law of Primitive Man: a Study in
    Comparative Legal Dynamics (Cambridge, Mass., 1967), p. 7.
    There is, of course, an extensive literature on the
    anthropology of the law, the best introduction to which
    is probably S. Roberts, Order and Dispute: an Introduc-
    tion to Legal Anthropology (Harmondsworth, 1979).
8. E. W. Ives, The Common Lawyers in Pre-Reformation England:
    Thomas Kebell: a Case Study (Cambridge, 1983), p. 7.
    Much of this paragraph is based upon Dr Ives's comments,
    and on W. J. Bouwsma, 'Lawyers and Early Modern Culture',
    American Historical Review, lxxviii (1973). Compare the
    comments of Thompson, Whigs and Hunters, p. 261, where he
    concludes that law 'was deeply imbricated within the very
    basis of productive relations, which would have been
    inoperable without this law'.
9. Quoted in J. S. Cockburn, A History of English Assizes
    1558-1714 (Cambridge, 1972), p. 310.
10. R. Muchembled, Culture Populaire et Culture des Elites
    dans la France Moderne (XVe-XVIIIe Siècles) (Paris, 1978),
    pp. 389-90.
11. For a statement of my belief in this tenet, in a rather
    different context, see J. A. Sharpe, 'The Impact of
    Industrial Society on English Folk Song - Some
    Observations', Contact: Today's Music, xv (Winter
    1976-7).

12. This notion of the 'two traditions' originates from R. Redfield, <u>Peasant Society and Culture</u> (Chicago, 1956).

13. A point made by R. Mandrou, <u>De la Culture Populaire au XVII et XVIII siécles: la Bibliothéque Bleue de Troyes</u> (Paris, 1974), p. 12.

14. S. Clark, 'French Historians and Early Modern Popular Culture', <u>P. and P.</u>, 100 (1983), p. 63.

15. It is instructive to find in this context that one student explicitly rejects 'any analysis in terms of opposition between a Little Tradition of local custom and informal control rejecting the Great Tradition of professional lawmen and law officers ... the self policing involved in the English system had long been one of its distinguishing and crucial features': A. Macfarlane, <u>The Justice and the Mare's Ale: Law and Disorder in Seventeenth-Century England</u> (Oxford, 1981), p. 197. For a somewhat dated, but still important, discussion of this phenomenon in a period long antecedent to the seventeenth century, see A. B. White, <u>Self-Government at the King's Command: a Study in the Beginnings of English Democracy</u> (Westport, Conn., 1933, 1974).

16. Burke, <u>Popular Culture</u>, p. 24.

17. One exception was going to law in defence of sexual reputation: J. A. Sharpe, <u>Defamation and Sexual Slander in Early Modern England: the Church Courts at York</u> (York, 1980), pp. 27-8.

18. J. A. Sharpe, <u>Crime in Seventeenth-Century England: a County Study</u> (Cambridge, 1983), table 4, p. 95 (theft), table 6, p. 108 (burglary), table 12, p. 124 (homicide), table 15, p. 136 (infanticide); A. Macfarlane, <u>Witchcraft in Tudor and Stuart England</u> (1970), p. 160. For two exploratory articles on female crime in early modern England, see: C. Z. Wiener, 'Sex-roles and crime in late Elizabethan Hertfordshire', and J. M. Beattie, 'The Criminality of Women in Eighteenth-Century England', <u>JSH</u>, viii (1975).

19. ERO, D/B3/3/149; PRO, ASSI 35/45/1/54.

20. D. M. Palliser, <u>Tudor York</u> (Oxford, 1979), p. 79, a comment which comes at the end of that author's description of the secular courts in the city, upon which my own comments are based. For the structure of church courts, see R. A. Marchant, <u>The Church under the Law</u> (Cambridge, 1969), pp. 38-41.

21. Ives, <u>Common Lawyers</u>, p. 7.

22. C. W. Brooks, 'Litigants and Attorneys in the King's Bench and Common Pleas, 1560-1640', in J. H. Baker (ed.), <u>Legal Records and the Historian</u> (1978), table 1, p. 43.

23. Marchant, <u>Church under the Law</u>, table 9, p. 68.

24. Cockburn, <u>History of English Assizes</u>, table 2, p. 137.

25. W. J. King, 'Untapped Sources for Social Historians: Court Leet Records', <u>JSH</u>, xv (1982), p. 699.

26. T. G. Barnes, 'Star Chamber Litigants and their Counsel, 1596-1641', in Baker (ed.), Legal Records and the Historian, p. 8.

27. For a number of relevant cases, see Sharpe, Defamation and Sexual Slander, p. 17.

28. M. J. Ingram, 'Communities and Courts: Law and Disorder in Early-Seventeenth-Century Wiltshire', in J. S. Cockburn (ed.), Crime in England, 1550-1800 (1977), p. 116.

29. Cressy, Literacy, table 5.3, p. 113, table 5.4, p. 114.

30. For comments on this point, and for a wider critique of of one particular class of legal document, see J. S. Cockburn, 'Early Modern Assize Records as historical Evidence', The Journal of the Society of Archivists, v (1975).

31. Ingram, 'Communities and Courts', p. 116.

32. L. Stone, 'Interpersonal Violence in English Society 1300-1980', P. and P., 101 (1983), p. 32.

33. Ingram, 'Communities and Courts', p. 110.

34. Barnes, 'Star Chamber Litigants', p. 7, table 1, p. 10.

35. Ingram, 'Communities and Courts', pp. 125-7; J. A. Sharpe, '"Such Disagreement betwyx Neighbours": Litigation and Human Relations in Early Modern England', in J. Bossy (ed.), Disputes and Settlements: Law and Human Relations in the West (Cambridge, 1983). For similar evidence from an earlier period, see E. Powell, 'Arbitration and the Law in England in the Late Middle Ages', TRHS, xxxiii (1983).

36. Barnes, 'Star Chamber Litigants', p. 23.

37. Ingram, 'Communities and Courts', p. 116.

38. J. S. Morrill, The Cheshire Grand Jury 1625-1659 (Leicester, 1976).

39. Sharpe, Crime, pp. 116-17. We look forward to the completion of Dr Tim Curtis's research in progress on this important but neglected topic.

40. ERO, D/DCv 1, passim (Notebook of Sir William Holcroft).

41. J. A. Sharpe, 'Enforcing the Law in the seventeenth-century English Village', in V. A. C. Gatrell, B. Lenman and G. Parker (eds.), Crime and the Law: the Social History of Crime in Western Europe since 1500 (1980), pp. 106-7, 109-10.

42. Macfarlane, Witchcraft, pp. 103-34; Thomas, Religion and Decline, ch. 16.

43. Sharpe, 'Enforcing the Law'; T. C. Curtis, 'Quarter Sessions Appearances and their Background: a Seventeenth-Century Regional Study', in Cockburn (ed.), Crime in England.

44. Ingram, 'Communities and Courts', table 3, p. 133.

45. E.g., J. A. Raftis, 'The Concentration of Responsibility in Five Villages', Medieval Studies, xxviii (1966); A.

Dewindt, 'Peasant Power Structures in Fourteenth-Century King's Ripton', Medieval Studies, xxxviii (1976).

46. J. A. Sharpe, 'Crime and Delinquency in an Essex Parish 1600-1640', in Cockburn (ed.), Crime in England, pp. 94-5; K. Wrightson and D. Levine, Poverty and Piety in an English Village: Terling 1525-1700 (1979), ch. 5, 'Conflict and Control: the Villagers and the Courts'; K. Wrightson, 'Two Concepts of Order: Justices, Constables and Jurymen in Seventeenth-Century England', in J. Brewer and J. Styles (eds.), An Ungovernable People. The English and their law in the seventeenth and eighteenth centuries (1980), pp. 41-4; J. R. Kent, 'The English Village Constable, 1580-1642: the Nature and Dilemmas of the Office', Journal of British Studies, xx, no. 2 (1981).

47. Wrightson and Levine, Poverty and Piety, table 5.1, p. 118, table 5.2, p. 119.

48. One section of the lower orders which experienced a peculiar position vis-à-vis the law was servants. Their legal status was in many respects unique, while there were some offences, or subdivisions of offence, which were specific to them. For a summary of their legal position (written a little after our period), see Blackstone, Commentaries, i, ch. 14, 'Of Masters and Servants'.

49. R. Thompson (ed.), Samuel Pepys' Penny Merriments (1976), p. 12.

50. RB, iii, pp. 23-5.

51. H. E. Rollins (ed.), The Pepys Ballads (Cambridge, Mass., 1929-31), vi, p. 118.

52. J. W. Ebsworth (ed.), The Bagford Ballads (1876-7), i, pp. 559, 560; Pepys Ballads, vi, p. 316.

53. Pepys Ballads, vii, pp. 202-4.

54. Despite some eighteenth-century pamphlets dealing with Turpin, it seems likely that he did not acquire his status as the prototype highwayman until he was intro- duced to the popular imagination by the historical novelist W. A. Harrison in Rookwood: A Romance (1834).

55. For some relevant quotations from this material, see D. Veall, The Popular Movement for Law Reform 1640-1660 (Oxford, 1970), pp. 201-2.

56. B. Capp, Astrology and the Popular Press: English Almanacs 1500-1800 (1979), pp. 107, 256.

57. Bouwsma, 'Lawyers and Early Modern Culture', p. 304.

58. P. Clark, English Provincial Society from the Reformation to the Revolution: Religion, Politics and Society in Kent, 1500-1640 (Hassocks, 1977), ch. 9.

59. Ibid., p. 287.

60. Many parallels and comparisons with contemporary English conditions are to be found in R. L. Kagan, 'A Golden Age of Litigation: Castile 1500-1700', in Bossy (ed.),

Disputes and Settlements.
61. PRO, ASSI 35/45/1/58.
62. PRO, ASSI 35/45/1/57; 35/45/1/55, respectively.
63. E. J. Hobsbawm, 'Distinctions between Socio-Political and Other Forms of Crime', Bulletin of the Society for the Study of Labour History, xxv (1975), p. 5.
64. For some scattered examples, see Sharpe, 'Enforcing the Law', pp. 105-6.
65. E. P. Thompson, 'The Moral Economy of the English Crowd in the Eighteenth Century', P. and P., 50 (1971). For the application of Thompson's ideas to the seventeenth century, see Buchanan Sharp's contribution to this collection; see also the studies listed in his note 4.
66. Sheffield City Central Lib., CD 509/18.
67. ERO, D/DCv 1, fo. 16v.
68. RB, iii, pp. 471-4. It is interesting to note that to a student of Spanish litigation in this period 'the law court, which was centrally placed in most villages and towns, served both as a school and a theatre, helping to teach the illiterate': Kagan, 'Golden Age of Litigation', p. 159.
69. Hay, 'Property, Authority and the Criminal Law', pp. 25, 38.
70. Notably in two very different articles: J. H. Langbein, 'Albion's Fatal Flaws', P. and P., 98 (1983); P. King, 'Decision-Makers and Decision Making in the English Criminal Law, 1750-1800', HJ, xxvii (1984). King's contribution is of considerable relevance to this present essay, as it stresses the widespread nature of the recourse to legal remedies among the lower orders in the period with which it is concerned.
71. Instructively, another first-rate collection of essays claiming to study 'the English and their law in the seventeenth and eighteenth centuries' has little to say about litigation as such: Brewer and Styles (eds.), An Ungovernable People.
72. Cockburn, History of English Assizes, table 2, p. 137, table 3, p. 138, table 4, p. 139.
73. For Essex; ERO, D/ACA 54-9. For Yorkshire: Marchant, Church under the Law; B. Till, 'The Ecclesiastical Courts of York 1660-1883; A Study in Decline' (Unpublished typescript, Borthwick Institute of Historical Research).
74. Wrightson and Levine, Poverty and Piety, p. 112; M. McIntosh, 'Central Court Supervision of the Ancient Demesne Manor Court of Havering 1200-1625', in E. W. Ives and A. H. Manchester (eds.), Law, Litigants and the Legal Profession (1983), p. 92; A. Macfarlane, Reconstructing Historical Communities (Cambridge, 1977),

p. 57. The materials I consulted for my work on Kelvedon supports the impression given by these studies of Terling, Havering and Earls Colne, and are listed in 'Crime and Delinquency in an Essex Parish', p. 317, n. 11.

75. J. A. Sharpe, <u>Crime in Early Modern England 1550-1750</u> (1984), pp. 53-63.

76. If we may again draw a comparison with Castile, Kagan attributes the decline of litigation there in the later seventeenth century (in part at least) to 'the growing professionalisation of jurisprudence' which made going to law 'unsuitable as a workaday tool of conflict': 'Golden Age of Litigation', p. 217.

77. The phrase is used by A. Soman, 'Deviance and Criminal Justice in Western Europe: An Essay in Structure', <u>Criminal Justice History</u>, i (1980), p. 5. For another essay attempting a delineation of the broad change in justice and law enforcement between the medieval and the modern periods, which also concerns itself with the transition from private to state justice, see B. Lenman and G. Parker, 'The State, the Community and the Criminal Law in Early Modern Europe', in Gatrell, Lenman and Parker (eds.), <u>Crime and the Law</u>.

78. Hay and others, <u>Albion's Fatal Tree</u>, p. 13.

79. Macfarlane, <u>Justice and the Mare's Ale</u>, p. 198.

Chapter Eight

POPULAR PROTEST IN SEVENTEENTH-CENTURY ENGLAND

Buchanan Sharp

I

   At the Wiltshire Quarter Sessions, held in
Warminster during the summer of 1614, ten clothworkers of Seend and Westbury were indicted, tried
and found guilty for the riotous seizure of grain or
for assault upon grain carriers. They were sentenced to fines of twenty or forty shillings each and
to one hour in the pillory with papers on their
heads explaining the nature of their offences. It
appears that such actions took place on as many as
six separate occasions between 15 and 29 May 1614,
and involved crowds of thirty to forty weavers, and
other clothworkers, from Seend and Westbury, accompanied (according to one account) by their wives and
children. The aim of the Westbury weavers was to
prevent the shipment of grain from the nearby town
of Warminster, probably the most important regional
grain market in the West of England at the time. In
one disturbance they stopped a load of grain at
Standerwick, four miles north-west of Warminster, on
the main road to Bath and Bristol. The clothworkers
of Seend concentrated their attention on seizing
loads of grain owned by local carriers who had, no
doubt, made purchases at Warminster for sale
elsewhere.
   Although during the course of these disturbances
the grain owners appear to have been assaulted as
they attempted to defend their property, the main
purpose of the clothworkers was not the bodily harm
of the carriers but to stop grain movement. Once
they had their hands on grain, the weavers of
Westbury delivered it, on one occasion, to the Mayor
of the town and, on another, to the constable. One
weaver told the Mayor that the rioters were acting
on behalf of the King; one half of the grain was

for his majesty, the other for themselves. The
Seend rioters took the grain that they had captured
to the house of the tithingman of the village and
divided it up among themselves. On later examination before Wiltshire J.P.s, the rioters justified
their actions in terms of simple want. When stopped,
the grain carriers offered to sell their loads at
the market price, but the weavers had no money and,
as one noted, he would 'as leaffe losse his life as
see his wife and children stearve'. A month later,
in June 1614, a weaver of Christian Malford in north
Wiltshire admitted stealing a bushel of barley and a
peck of wheat from a mill in the nearby village of
Seagry because he had no corn to feed his wife and
children, and did not have the means to buy it.(1)
   Sometime in the period immediately before the
1614 riots, the weavers of Wiltshire had petitioned
the Privy Council in London, complaining of the
activities of malsters, millers, badgers and
carriers who bought large quantities of grain in the
county's markets, thereby driving the price so high
that they could not afford to purchase enough food
for themselves and their families. The weavers
asserted that, of necessity, they must fall into
some great extremity unless the market abuses were
rapidly reformed. By the time the Privy Council
responded to the complaints, the food riots had
occurred - the great extremity mentioned in the
petition. While condemning the riots as offences
that deserved severe punishment, the Privy Council's
instructions to the Wiltshire J.P.s recommended a
milder course of proceedings. This course was a
result of the King's 'princely care' and 'gracious
clemency' towards his poorer subjects. The local
magistrates were ordered to regulate the grain market either through limiting or prohibiting completely large purchases by millers and the like. At
a minimum, the justices were to arrange market hours
so that the poor and those who bought to supply only
their own households could be served first. The
weavers had also complained to the Council that
their clothier employers paid low wages; a particular complaint was that in forty years the wage rates
had not changed, while the price of food had
doubled. In response, the Privy Council instructed
the magistrates to examine the complaint against the
clothiers. If necessary, the J.P.s were to take
remedial action, such as ordering an increase in
wages.(2) Six months later, the weavers of Wiltshire again petitioned the Privy Council asserting
that some of the J.P.s had failed to act against

market abuses. In fact, the petitioners charged
that a number of magistrates, who had substantial
amounts of corn for sale, tolerated and even encouraged the abuses of middlemen. The Council, in
reply, instructed the Wiltshire bench to enforce the
previous orders and to investigate the truth of the
allegations against some of their number. The Privy
Council, while reluctant to believe the petitioners
who were regarded as turbulent and seditious spirits,
was nonetheless convinced of the need to examine the
charges against Wiltshire magistrates, for the
matter concerned the common good of the poorer
sort.(3) What, if any, actions followed upon this
last letter remain unknown.

Many themes and topics that the historian of
seventeenth-century English popular protest would
wish to explore can be found embedded within this
somewhat minor, but quite typical, episode. While
the events that took place around Warminster in 1614
comprise an example of only one type (the most
common) of the period's popular protests, the food
riot, this kind of disturbance had a great deal in
common with the other main form of popular direct
action found in the seventeenth century, the anti-
improvement riot aimed at changes in land use such
as enclosure and drainage. For convenience sake the
two types of riot will be treated here in separate
sections; but it must be emphasised that they share
a thematic unity in terms of incidence, causes, the
aims, behaviour and social and economic position of
participants, and in the complexity of the interplay
between the actions of the protestors and the responses of those in authority who were required to
maintain order.

The typical seventeenth century popular disturbance, whether food riot or anti-improvement
riot, was concerned with subsistence matters: grain
prices, wage rates, unemployment, and common rights.
From their behaviour and what can be discovered
about their attitudes, the participants in these
disorders had quite limited and definite aims;
their needs were dramatised in acts like stopping
the movement of grain and destroying enclosures. In
the course of their actions, rioters often sought
some kind of official sanction or positive response
from magistrates or government officials. Official
response was, however, generally ambivalent. On the
one hand, when faced with manifestations of distress
in times of harvest failure or depression, central
and local government brought into operation a range
of ameliorative remedies for hunger, unemployment

and poverty. On the other hand, officials regarded certain kinds of disorder - anti-improvement riots more frequently than food riots - as threats to property rights and to social stability that demanded punitive response.

Typically, disorder occurred in areas with large populations of wage earners. Such places included market towns, ports and, above all, fen lands or wood-pasture areas, some of which were the location of industries like clothmaking, mining or ironmaking. Wage earners depended on the market for their basic bread grains; they also depended, where available, on access to common in forest and fen for important income supplements. Since the economy of wage-earning cottagers was a household one in which all the physically able members contributed to the family income, it is not surprising that women often participated in riots alongside men and that they sometimes, in fact, led protests. Food and anti-improvement riots were, in sum, as typical of the preindustrial household economy as strikes were to be of the industrial factory economy.

II

Over the past twenty years the writings of a number of scholars have contributed greatly to our understanding of the significance of food riots in the period from the early sixteenth to the late eighteenth centuries.(4) Although food riots took place in England as early as 1347, no one has so far worked systematically through the records of the medieval English kingdom to illuminate their history before the sixteenth century.(5) Outbreaks of food rioting in the sixteenth and seventeenth centuries were concentrated in the years 1527, 1551, 1586-7, 1594-8, 1605, 1608, 1614, 1622-3, 1629-31, 1647-8, 1662-3, 1674, 1681 and 1693-5. Except for 1605 and 1614, these were times of poor harvest albeit with differing degrees of scarcity.(6) The periods when outbreaks of food riots were most intense and frequent were often years of depression, especially in the cloth industry. In clothmaking areas low wages and unemployment contributed at least as much as poor harvest to the distress which produced protest.

During the seventeenth century food rioting was limited to particular areas in the south of England and was not necessarily an expression of those who were faced with outright starvation. Recent work in historical demography has demonstrated conclusively that during some harvest failures the population of the North of England suffered privation far greater than that experienced in any other region of the country. Andrew Appleby, in particular, has shown that in 1597 and 1623 the counties of Cumberland and Westmorland were afflicted by high mortality rates as a result of famine conditions.(7) While the threat of famine stalked much of the country in the years 1594-8, the north-west appears to have suffered the gravest effects; in 1623 the North, including Cumberland and Westmorland, was the one region whose inhabitants faced starvation. The north-west was a largely pastoral area with a growing population of cottagers who encroached upon the abundant waste. Even in the best of times, poor internal means of communication made it difficult for the grain needs of this population to be met from the region's limited acreage of corn growing lowlands. When the harvest failed the upland population faced starvation. This difficult situation was compounded by the north-west's remoteness from sources of supply further south that could have provided the means to alleviate the worst subsistence problems.

No doubt the region was sufficiently distant from centres of power that the government in London could safely ignore its social problems, but there is no evidence that the poverty and hunger, so graphically described by Appleby, were brought to the attention of the Privy Council. Normally during times of harvest failure or depression, J.P.s sent to the Privy Council numerous reports on local conditions and pleas for aid, often accompanied by the petitions of the hungry and unemployed, but virtually no such communications were sent by the magistrates of Cumberland and Westmorland.(8) The one report that does survive gives no indication of the level of hardship that the population was experiencing. During hard times the poor in the north-west starved to death quietly, and created no problems of order for their governors, central or local. On the basis of the lassitude that afflicts the starving, this passivity is not difficult to understand. The behaviour of the northern population does, however, raise a question about the intensity of the suffering and hunger that food rioters often pointed to as justification for their actions.

It is a truism that the food riot, as well as many other kinds of popular protest in the seventeenth century, was an attempt to preserve some traditional notion of a just price or community-based standard of a moral economy. But it also must

be emphasised that this kind of disturbance took
place in areas most affected by the market and containing large concentrations of wage earners. Overall, food riots were confined to two kinds of
locations. One was clothmaking areas, especially in
a wide arc of southern counties running from
Gloucester, Somerset and Wiltshire in the West,
through Berkshire and Hampshire, to Kent, Essex,
Suffolk and Norfolk in the east. The other location
was ports or market towns through which large quantities of grain were shipped. Ports such as King's
Lynn and Yarmouth in Norfolk, Maldon in Essex, those
along the Medway in Kent, Southampton, and Wareham
and Weymouth in Dorset, were often the scene of
riots, as were important market towns like
Warminster, Reading, Hertford, Canterbury and Wye.

Food riots were protests of wage earners who
lived in an urban or rural manufacturing world of
trade fluctuations and grain markets in which grain
moved from production point to areas of high demand
and maximum gain for the middleman. The failure of
the market to provide for the subsistence needs of
the wage-earning consumer and his family provoked
the protests. For the wage earner the failure was
measured in the gap between the level of wages and
the price of the necessary bread grains. Outright
harvest failure, accompanied by absolute scarcity of
grain and famine level prices in the market place,
was only one possible cause for food riots. Others
included low wages, unemployment, and temporary
local shortages produced by middlemen making large
purchases in the market for sale in towns, in pastoral areas, or in distant regions suffering from
poor harvest. Substantial grain purchases followed
by transportation, that resulted in locally high
prices, were particularly visible and blatant examples of the market's failure to meet the subsistence
needs of the wage earner and his family. It is not
surprising, then, that most late sixteenth- and
seventeenth-century food riots consisted of attempts
to stop the movement of grain.

There were certain market towns, ports, highways
and waterways repeatedly affected by food riots;
these were located close to concentrations of wage-
earning clothworkers. The river Severn, down which
grain moved from the west Midlands through the city
of Gloucester to Bristol and to Wales, was a regular
target for food rioters. In 1586 unemployed clothworkers twice boarded barks on the Severn below
Gloucester, and unloaded their cargoes; while in
the spring of 1622 a similar action was planned.

The corn trade of Warminster was a regular focal
point for the protests of the clothworkers of eastern Somerset and western Wiltshire. On numerous
occasions during 1595, 1614, 1622, 1630 and 1647-9
clothworkers, complaining either of unemployment or
of low wages, disrupted grain shipments from
Warminster.(9)
On a number of occasions attempts to stop the
movements of foodstuffs took place in times of ostensible plenty or before the issue of the government's
dearth measures, the Book of Orders, imposed restrictions on the normally unregulated internal grain
trade. For instance, the boarding of the barks on
the Severn in 1586 occurred eight months before the
Book of Orders was published. The riots around
Warminster in the summer of 1614 took place in a
good harvest year. The riots of the spring of 1622
in Somerset and Wiltshire and similar disturbances
along the border of Essex and Suffolk happened
months before dearth set in. Finally, the Maldon
(Essex) riots of 1629, intensively researched by
John Walter, broke out in a time of unemployment -
not harvest failure.(10) In these examples, it was
unemployment or low wages that produced disorder
among clothworkers who lived in an area with an
active grain trade. Such locations may have been
particularly sensitive to purchases made in anticipation of a poor harvest, and may have acted as a
triggering mechanism to alert the central government to prepare its responses in anticipation of
dearth.
Any treatment of popular protest and attitudes
in the period must concern itself with the government's dearth measures, because they embody so many
of the assumptions of both authorities and populace
about how the market ought to operate in hard times
to supply the poor with a subsistence. The Book of
Orders was only one of the government's weapons
against distress, there was also the Poor Law and
wage regulation. Taken together, these elements of
social policy created expectations in the wage-
earning population that their petitions, complaints
and protests would receive a sympathetic response
from central government and local magistrates. So
powerful was the effect of official policy, that,
in years of poor harvest subsequent to the central
government's last reissue of the Book of Orders in
1631, local magistrates on their own authority
attempted to implement as much as possible of the
old social policy. In those years the populace also
continued to regard the values and mechanisms of the

Book of Orders as appropriate for the regulation of the market.

The Book of Orders was first issued in January 1587 and reissued with some changes in later bad harvest years, 1594, 1595, 1608, 1622 and 1630. (11) It contained a series of regulations of the market designed to help meet the subsistence needs of the poor. To this end, heavy obligations were laid on the J.P.s of each county and their subordinate officers. The Book of Orders authorised the J.P.s to summon juries composed of constables, under-constables and other 'honest and substantial inhabitants' from each hundred or other subdivision of the county in order to discover the amount of grain available, the number of grain carriers and dealers, the number of malsters, bakers and brewers, and the amount of grain they used per week. On the basis of this information the justices imposed a series of market regulations, taking recognizances for substantial sums to ensure performance. The J.P.s bound individuals, who owned grain beyond the needs of their household and the following year's seed, to sell specified amounts of their surplus openly and publicly in the market every week. At least one magistrate was to be present at every market to see that the poor were served first and to try to persuade the sellers to lower their prices for poor customers. The J.P.s also closely regulated the activities of large purchasers of grain, such as malsters, bakers and badgers. This they did through licensing and the taking of bonds in order to impose limits on the quantities of grain purchased. Such big purchasers were not permitted to deal during the first market hour, which was reserved for the poor. Above all, the Book of Orders insisted upon public dealing in grain. All private transactions were prohibited, except for sales of small quantities to poor handicraftsmen and day labourers who lived some distance from market towns and who were unable to visit the market for their food.

Government pronouncements frequently pointed to the activities of engrossers and forestallers as a prime cause of scarcity. The Book of Orders was intended to prevent such profiteering by putting an emphasis on close regulation of grain purchases which were intended for sale out of the immediate neighbourhood. One premise of the dearth regulation was that, whenever possible, grain should be consumed locally in order to provide for the relief of the hungry and unemployed. Furthermore, prohibitions on private transactions, combined with the emphasis on public and open dealing in the market place, subjected all grain transactions to the intense glare of publicity. This reflects a widespread sixteenth- and early-seventeenth-century belief that private business transactions, especially those involving grain, were designed for individual gain at the expense of the public weal.(12)

The consuming public appears to have regarded official restrictions on grain transactions as open invitations to be watchful and to participate actively in the regulation of the market. In the hard times when these regulations were operative, the consuming public was centrally concerned with its own subsistence needs and was especially active in protesting what were considered violations of the spirit and intentions of the Book of Orders. Thus the activities of middlemen, grain carriers, large scale grain producers and lax local magistrates were frequently the objects of popular ire. In fact, food riots were often attempts to enforce officially-sanctioned market regulations and can be regarded, in many instances, not as attacks upon established order but as efforts to reinforce it.

One part of the government's dearth regulations, in particular, provided official legitimisation for popular action - the prohibitions, imposed by proclamation, on the export of grain. Such proclamations, although not included in the Book of Orders, were an integral part of the government's attempts to conserve food and to provide for the hungry.(13) In times of scarcity, the government did not impose outright prohibitions on the internal transport of grain; the licensing of large purchases and movements of grain was necessary for the supply of grain-deficient areas and towns, especially London. Crown officials faced a problem in that bulk movements of grain were generally by ship, either coastwise or down rivers with outlets to the sea, and it was virtually impossible to guarantee that the grain would not be illegally transported to foreign markets where the owners might obtain a better price. Fears of fraudulent transportation of grain overseas were widespread in official circles, especially during the dearths in the reigns of Elizabeth and the first two Stuarts. These fears were communicated to local officials in proclamations and Privy Council letters which instructed them to prohibit grain exports completely and to take substantial bonds from those engaged in lawful coastwise trade in grain to prevent illegal

transportation overseas.(14)
     The response of local officials to these
directives was a general reluctance to permit any
large movements of grain. In the Privy Council
Register there are many missives sent to J.P.s to
allow the coastal or river transport of grain cargoes that they had impounded; the cargoes had often
been bought by legally licensed dealers and were
intended for the supply of cities like Bristol and,
above all, London itself.(15) The unwillingness of
magistrates to permit such movements is understandable enough. There were no ironclad guarantees
that the cargoes would reach the urban needy at
home, or that some fraud did not lie behind the
obtaining of the licence. J.P.s, charged with the
implementation of the Book of Orders in grain producing areas, were also well aware of the shortages,
high prices and disorders created in their own
markets by large scale purchases made to supply
London, and they frequently complained to the Privy
Council about the activities of London buyers.
Many of the food riots in the port and market towns
of Norfolk and Kent were attempts to stop the
planned transportation of grain to London.(16) From
the perspective of local officials, the rebuke from
the Council that followed upon the effort to stay
shipments of grain bound for London - justified by
the claim that they might be intended for overseas -
was a small price to pay for the maintenance of
social peace in their own community. From the point
of view of the central government, the social peace
of the capital had a high priority and considerable
efforts were made to ensure that its population was
supplied with grain.(17) The success of these
efforts is perhaps best measured by the infrequency
of disturbances over food prices in sixteenth- and
seventeenth-century London. The only protests so
far discovered were some mutterings about the price
of victuals reported in 1573, a riot by apprentices
in 1595 occasioned by the price of butter in
Southwark market, and a ballad produced in 1596 complaining of the scarcity.(18)
     Popular opposition to grain transportation was
at once a reflection of the official point of view
and a more radical restatement of it. Opposition to
the export of grain from England was of long
standing, and appeared whenever food shortage
threatened. The earliest food riots for which
record has been found, those in the summer of 1347
at Bristol, Boston and King's Lynn, involved crowds
boarding and unloading ships licensed by the King to

transport grain to Gascony. (19) The 1605 disturbances in the ports on the river Medway in Kent were
provoked by large purchases of grain whose ultimate
destination was probably Spain. The first of the
two riots at Maldon in Essex in 1629 was aimed at
stopping shipment of grain to the Low Countries.
Many other food riots between 1586 and 1631 were
designed to prevent actual or rumoured export of
grain overseas. Finally, in the late seventeenth
century, when the Crown had ceased to issue the Book
of Orders in poor harvest years, and when official
policy aimed to encourage rather than prohibit the
export of grain, most of the disturbances over food,
particularly in the years 1662-3 and 1692-5, were
directed at shipments intended for export. (20)
    The people who attempted to stop the export of
grain frequently acted in an official manner or
looked to sympathetic magistrates to legitimise
their actions. The Bristol food rioters of July
1347 were accused of assuming the royal power in
issuing proclamations - no doubt prohibiting export
of grain - and ordering the unloading of the ships.
The King's Lynn rioters of the same year were
similarly accused of making 'quasi-royal proclamations', unloading grain ships, and selling the cargoes ashore 'at their own price'. The Boston
rioters elected one of their number 'to be their
captain and mayor', and also issued 'quasi-royal
proclamations'.(21) In 1596 there were large shipments of grain made from Canterbury to London;
rumours that some of it was intended for export to
France sparked disorder. Before the actual disturbance took place, one of the leading participants
sought the opinion of a local attorney's clerk concerning the legality of stopping the movement of
grain. The clerk advised that it could be stopped
'soe they tooke noe weapon in hande nor did take
any of it awaye'. When examined before magistrates
the rioters repeated this advice as legitimising
their acts; they asserted that they had stopped the
grain 'in her Majesty's behalf'. (22) In the disorders around Warminster in 1614, the weavers of
Westbury declared that one half of the grain was
for them and one half for the King. Similar statements were made by food rioters in Kent in 1631.
As John Walter and Keith Wrightson have noted, the
penalty imposed upon illegal exporters of grain was
forfeiture of their cargoes with one half to the
Crown and one half to the informants. The weavers
of Westbury and Seend deposited grain shipments with
various local officials a number of times in 1614,

thereby demonstrating the lawful nature of their acts.(23) Late in May 1629, three Somerset weavers stopped a load of barley that was being transported by water from North Curry to Bridgwater; they believed that the grain was intended for unlawful transportation overseas. The weavers returned the cargo to its point of departure, Newbridge in North Curry, tied up the boat, left the grain untouched, and went in search of the nearest J.P. to get his direction on what to do next. The justice, Robert Cuffe, told them 'he had noe authoritie either to give order for the stayinge thereof or for lettinge of it goe, but did wishe [the weavers] to be quiett and suffer the same to be carried awaie'. So the weavers went home. It is notable that the weavers appear to have been better informed than the J.P., for already on 2 May the King had issued a proclama-tion prohibiting the export of grain.(24) Finally, in May 1692 the leader of a crowd of three hundred people at Shrewsbury made a proclamation in the market place 'that the carrying of grain out of the nation would breed a famine and that they ought to hinder it'. (25)

All of these examples can be considered to be attempts by the crowd to act in a 'quasi-official' manner in order to enforce export prohibitions that had some kind of government sanction or memory of government sanction behind them. Virtually all food riots were directed against the movement of grain, but only some shipments were intended for export. No doubt ordinary people, like magistrates, were suspicious of underhanded dealing; a riot like that at Yarmouth in 1631 to prevent the export of grain on the basis of fraudulently obtained licence under-lines the real basis of such suspicions.(26) But most disorders struck at lawful transportation of grain from one region of England to another. The Crown's official opposition to export could offer some cloak of legitimacy for such acts as could the recurrent rumours that, whatever the supposed domestic destination of a particular grain shipment, it was ultimately destined for a foreign market. As Walter and Wrightson conclude: 'The fact that it is not altogether clear that the grain they had stayed was intended for export underlines the crowd's ability to exploit those ambiguities which allowed an independent role for popular initiative.'(27) Ultimately the concern of consumers, whose wages were low or who were unemployed, was with the conse-quences for local markets of large scale purchases of grain and shipment out of the area. The result

was scarcity and high prices and even greater diffi-
culty in obtaining a subsistence; this was the
reality no matter if the grain was shipped to the
Low Countries or to London. In the eyes of consumers, local supplies of grain should be brought to
local markets and sold openly in small quantities at
affordable prices.

The needs of food rioters were not always met
merely by the regulation of the market as envisaged
in the Book of Orders. Low or reduced wages and
unemployment, particularly among wage earners in the
cloth industry, were often at the heart of the subsistence difficulties that provoked food riots. The
food riot was often the final attempt on the part of
the hungry and unemployed to bring the seriousness
of their plight to the attention of those in authority after more peaceful means of seeking relief had
failed. Preceding most major outbreaks of food
rioting in cloth making areas, the unemployed or
those suffering wage cuts petitioned local J.P.s and
the Privy Council for the institution of relief
measures. Such petitioning took place before the
Gloucestershire food riots of 1586, the Wiltshire
disturbances of 1614, the outbreaks in Wiltshire and
Somerset in 1622, the disorders along the Essex-
Suffolk border in 1622, and the Maldon riots of
1629. Even when the actual documents have not survived, it is clear that petitions for relief lay
behind many of the J.P.s' reports on the state of
the cloth industry sent to the Privy Council.

Just as government dearth regulations encouraged popular self help in the market place, so other
aspects of government social policy in bad times
encouraged petitioning. Whenever grain scarcity or
depression occurred, the government brought into
operation a series of measures concerned with wages,
employment and poor relief. If the bottom fell out
of foreign markets for English cloth and unemployment or low wages resulted, the Privy Council
pressured clothiers and export merchants into continuing to produce and buy cloth in order to keep
the workers in employment. In response to complaints from the clothworkers, the Privy Council
frequently authorised J.P.s or assize judges to conduct elaborate investigations into wages or
unemployment. These inquiries were then followed by
remedial measures, including orders to raise wages
under the Statute of 1604 that authorised the paying
of minimum wages to clothworkers, or the provision
of relief for the unemployed under the Poor Law.
While the Book of Orders emphasised regulation of

markets, it also contained a section that urged
setting the unemployed to work on stocks raised
through the rates. (28)
 Government officials were conscious of the
protest and disorder that might erupt in clothmaking areas if there was no positive response to
the petitions of the unemployed and hungry. At the
same time, the petitions and protests of the unemployed contained language that spelled out the
possibility of violence if remedial measures were
not forthcoming. It has been argued, quite
persuasively, that there was a theatrical quality to
the roles would-be food rioters and the Crown played
in these circumstances. (29) Those in need were aware
that if they petitioned local magistrates or the
Privy Council, outlining their distress and threatening disorder in what strikes the modern reader as
excessive rhetorical language, the authorities would
respond with positive relief measures. Since local
and central government officials knew from past
experience that riots would follow if relief was not
provided, they were usually galvanised into taking
remedial action when faced with such complaints. At
the same time, the high flown rhetoric of the
official viewpoint came into operation. The Privy
Council, in particular, insisted on the maintenance
of order and the public peace, and threatened dire
consequences if riots took place. But the reality
of official response to the majority of food riots
was more complex. Riots usually resulted in a
redoubling of efforts to provide relief; rioters
were punished, but the punishments normally meted
out - fines, whipping, or a time in the pillory -
were not as drastic as official rhetoric would lead
one to expect. (30)
 The notion that food rioting had theatrical
characteristics, with each side playing a role whose
function and limits were well known to the other,
gains further support from the other dimensions of
food riots which we have already examined. Government dearth regulations appeared to invite popular
participation in their implementation and to give
official sanction to the forceful stopping of grain
transportation. Official regulations that routinely
blamed the corrupt market practices of middlemen for
scarcity also provided legitimisation for popular
attacks upon grain carriers. Furthermore, by
attempting to enforce official policy in stopping
grain shipments and by seeking the approval of local
magistrates for their actions, some rioters appear
to have been acting to sustain, not to overturn, the

existing social order. These actions may, in fact, have been intended to compel or shame lax magistrates into action. This appears to have been the case with two anonymous libels from the 1590s, one found in London, the other in Norwich. Both attacked the apparent failure of local officials to enforce the Book of Orders.(31)

No doubt in many instances the actions and statements of rioters and officials were governed by a set of known rules which allowed both sides to play well-defined roles and informed their acts with a kind of moderation belying the extravagance of their rhetoric. There were, nonetheless, occasions when these conventions broke down. If there was a theatre of riot, there was also a theatre of rebellion where the governing rules were quite different. In such circumstances extravagant rhetoric, particularly on the government's side, was matched by deeds. Occasionally popular protests went beyond the limits of the conventional food riot; from the late sixteenth and the early seventeenth centuries there survives evidence for three such outbreaks. First, in June 1595 some apprentices, protesting the price of victuals, seized butter in Southwark market and offered it for sale at threepence the pound instead of the fivepence that the owners had asked. A few of the participants were whipped and put in the pillory for their actions. This resulted in further disorders, including the throwing of stones at the Tower Street warders, and the assembling of a crowd of three hundred apprentices who planned the riotous rescue of their pilloried compatriots. During the rescue attempt, violence was offered to the Mayor and the sheriffs of the City. For this last action five apprentices were tried and executed for treason. The second example was an insurrection planned in Oxfordshire late in 1596 by a handful of men discontented over the high price and scarcity of food. The leaders were ultimately executed for treason. Finally, there was the Maldon, Essex, food riot of 22 May 1629, when a crowd of two hundred to three hundred people boarded a grain ship, assaulted the crew, and unloaded some of the cargo. Other rioters took grain from a storehouse, and assaulted a merchant. Five of the leading rioters were tried and found guilty of felony, four men for robbery in taking fifteen quarters of grain, and a woman as an accessory in helping assemble people from neighbouring clothing townships. Four, including Anne Carter, were hung.(32)

In each of these examples the participants

behaved in ways which the government regarded as
threatening to the existing social and political
order. The London apprentices and the men of
Oxfordshire were charged with levying war against
the Queen. They had engaged, above all, in certain
acts associated since the late middle ages with the
levying of war. The London apprentices carried a
flag, and had assembled with the sounding of a trumpet. The Oxfordshire rebels appeared armed at their
rendezvous and were led by a captain. The Maldon
grain rioters, who forcibly boarded and unloaded a
grain ship, were also led by a captain. The Maldon
crowd appeared to be acting in support of a recent
royal proclamation which prohibited the export of
grain, and they also assumed the authority to administer justice. 'In a parody of the criminal law's
sanctions, the crowd assaulted the leading merchant,
a Mr Gamble, and forced him to purchase his freedom
by the payment of a twenty pound "fine".'(33) In
their behaviour the Maldon rioters remind us of the
rioters of 1347 who were charged with misprisions and
felonies in assuming royal power. One of the participants in the Boston riots was elected captain.
At Bristol, Boston and King's Lynn the rioters
issued proclamations in a royal manner. Finally,
the King's Lynn rioters, 'on their authority without
process of law adjudged some of those bringing the
corn [to the town] to the pillory and caused execution of such judgments to be made'. (34) The
participants in these protests had crossed a fine
line between the normal food riot, that sustained
the existing social and political order, and
rebellion in which institutions of law and government were parodied and the existing social order
turned upside down.
　　　The disturbances of 1595, 1596 and 1629 also
contained political threats to the capital. The
apprentices' riot of 1595 was, of course, a London
disorder, and was aimed at important institutions of
authority in the City. In its market regulations
Tudor government was especially sensitive to the
state of the capital. There was also a long
official memory of the Evil May Day riots of 1517
when the populace of London attacked foreigners. No
disorder which posed a threat to the good government
of the capital could be tolerated.(35) Punishment
had to be swift and severe. The Oxfordshire rebels
of 1596 with their declared intention of marching on
London, and the similar threat of unemployed Essex
clothworkers made before the Maldon food riot of May
1629, triggered a fear of popular revolt that helps

explain the severity of punishments meted out to the leaders of both disturbances. Marches on the capital to seek redress of grievances had been integral to earlier popular protests such as the Peasants' Revolt of 1381, Cade's Rebellion of 1450, and Wyatt's Rebellion of 1554.

Another key to understanding popular protests that went beyond the limits of normal food riots is to be found in John Walter's study of the Maldon riot. In this instance the severity of the outbreak resulted from what the participants believed to be a failure on the part of those in authority to respond to their legitimate needs in a time of cloth trade depression. We have already noted that the transportation of grain was a particular sore spot for the unemployed; the apparent failure of Essex magistrates to enforce the recent proclamation against export provided further impetus for popular action. The Oxfordshire rebels of 1596 were also responding to official failure; they believed that lack of vigorous enforcement of the laws against the enclosure lay behind the high price and scarcity of grain. The 1595 food riot by the London apprentices can be regarded as a response to the failure of the magistracy to regulate the market. Finally, the rioters of 1347 may have been attempting to shame officials into a more vigorous policy of restraining grain exports.

The men of Oxfordshire, in their expressed aims and attitudes, reveal yet another way to understand this kind of protest. In examinations conducted by local magistrates and the law officers of the Crown, the rebels repeatedly expressed hatred for the gentry who, as producers and hoarders of grain and as enclosers, were blamed for the dearth. Similar sentiments were uttered in alehouse conversations during times of depression and scarcity. The surviving record of such statements comes from indictments for seditious words, and it is easy enough to dismiss them as merely the consequence of too much drink. It is not possible to say how typical such opinions were, and they were of course rarely acted upon. But that does not deny their genuineness or the conviction with which they were held. It simply means that drink and conversation could be a substitute for action or a way of avoiding action that was difficult to organise and fraught with danger for the organisers. Animosity, nonetheless, could easily lurk behind the facade of deference.(36)

There was always a real ambivalence in the relationship between the authorities and the people.

As long as central and local government were seen to
be attempting in good faith to provide relief then
popular protests can be regarded as quasi-official,
and supportive of the existing order. But if the
remedies failed, particularly as a result of what
was perceived to be dereliction of duty on the part
of magistrates, or if the gentry were believed to be
acting uncharitably or covetously in hoarding grain
or enclosing, then the anger of the people was
turned on them. It was not the anger of modern
class hatred but rather the kind of wrath that the
medieval moralist reserved for officials and great
men who had become corrupt and did not live up to
their duties.(37) Medieval rebels directed a similar
anger at the great who failed to carry out their
obligations. Popular animosity in the Revolt of
1381 was aimed at the symbols and persons of what
was regarded as corrupt officialdom. Thus John of
Gaunt's Palace of the Savoy was destroyed, while the
Chancellor and Treasurer of the kingdom were executed. Cade's followers also struck at official
malfeasance when they took over London in 1450.
About twenty royal servants and ministers were tried
for their misdeeds, and a number were executed.(38)
    Actions that the government considered to be
rebellious clearly reflected the same kinds of popular attitudes to be found in normal food riots.
Like food riots, they were attempts at self help that
parodied official procedures, looked to government
policies for legitimisation, and aimed to shame lax
or corrupt officials into acting according to a high
conception of the duties attached to public office.
Nonetheless, acts designed to uphold impeccable standards of official probity which involved execution
of government officers, attacks upon their persons,
marches on the capital, or the taking up of arms
were regarded as rebellions. These were qualitat-
ively different from food riots, and therefore
demanded a more severe official response.
    Fear of rebellion, however, provided the energy
which impelled government to act. No doubt officials, especially local magistrates, sympathised
with the plight of their poorer neighbours in hard
times, and regarded it as their public obligation to
take relief measures for the community of which they
were the leaders. But they were also conscious of
the inadequacy of their police powers and the lack
of ready means at their disposal to deal effectively
with riotous disorder or insurrection. Overall, the
enforcement of the Book of Orders and the other
relief measures sanctioned by the Crown proved suf-

ficient to maintain order or limit disorder to the rituals of the food riot. As historians have noted, the relative infrequency of food riots in the sixteenth and seventeenth centuries provides testimony to the government's responsiveness on behalf of the hungry and unemployed.

For a number of years after the Crown ceased to issue the Book of Orders some local officials continued to apply its provisions in time of scarcity, another indication of the importance attached locally to these regulations as a means of maintaining public peace. The last publication was in 1631, but during the hard years of 1647-8 the J.P.s of Wiltshire, supported by orders from the judges of assize on the western circuit, attempted to enforce its main provisions. In 1651 and 1656 the magistrates of Bristol similarly regulated their grain market in the interests of the poor consumer.(39) No doubt further research in local records will turn up other examples. But on the whole, despite the occasional help of sympathetic magistrates, the crowd during the late seventeenth century and throughout the eighteenth was left to enforce regulation of the market alone with virtually no support from the Crown or its officers.

III

Concern for subsistence was also central to the other major form of popular protest during the seventeenth century - the anti-improvement riot. This term is used here to include the destruction of enclosure, opposition to drainage in fens, and riotous responses to the erection of deer parks and to the rigorous enforcement of previously moribund forest laws. These protests involved resistance on the part of inhabitants in particular communities to changes in land use that adversely affected either their livelihoods or their control over the disposition of resources. Such changes were usually imposed by powerful landlords or by patentees acting on behalf of the Crown.

While the incidence of food riots was determined by the state of the harvest and the conditions of trade, that of enclosure riots 'related more to the local timing of agrarian reorganization, though on occasion riot actually occurred when a crisis such as a bad harvest year exacerbated long-standing resentment of earlier changes'.(40) The Midland Revolt of 1607 is one striking example of a disturbance caused by the conjuncture of long term agrarian change with short term crisis. This was a

series of enclosure riots that began in Northamptonshire and spread to the neighbouring counties of
Leicestershire and Warwickshire. The disturbances
lasted from the end of April until early June 1607,
and were on a large scale, involving (by contemporary estimates) crowds as large as five thousand 'of
men, women and children'. Behind the revolt lay
long-term pressure from landlords and substantial
freeholders to convert open field tillage to permanent pasture or to an improved husbandry that
involved the introduction of convertible leys - the
putting of arable down to temporary pasture for up
to ten years in order to restore fertility.
Opposition to these improvements appears to have
come from the area's growing population of marginal
small holders, labourers, and other wage earners who
were dependent on the market for most of their food.
One surviving list of 143 rebels from Northamptonshire, who submitted to the King's mercy and
received pardons, includes 62 labourers, 52 artisans
and tradesmen, 21 husbandmen and 5 shepherds. Grain
was relatively scarce in the area of the revolt in
the spring of 1607; while not at famine prices, it
was probably expensive enough to spark disorder,
especially in a situation where there was continual
pressure for enclosures that would even further
reduce local supplies. No doubt, too, the memory of
the dearth and famine prices of the 1590s was still
fresh in the popular memory. As the rebels claimed,
the aim of the revolt was 'for reformation of thos
late inclosures which made them of the porest sorte
reddy to pyne for want'.(41)
     The Midland rebels directed their ire at
enclosure of arable open fields and its permanent or
temporary conversion to pasture, but many seventeenth-century rioters against agricultural improvement aimed to destroy the enclosure of waste and
woodland or the drainage of marsh and fen which were
designed to extend improved arable and ley farming.
There are numerous examples of riots by tenants in
opposition to the efforts of private landlords to
enclose the common pastures, wastes or woodlands of
their manorial holdings.(42) But the Crown itself
was the sponsor of the largest improvement projects,
involving enclosure of waste and the drainage of
fens, and thereby encountered sustained popular
resistance.
     The government's fiscal needs provide the key
to understanding the incidence of both the improvement projects for forest and fen and the riotous
responses to projects which threatened subsistence

rights. Beginning around 1610 with a series of surveys of forests and woodlands and continuing inter-
mittently until 1659 - the end of the Protectorate -
successive English governments turned to the exploi-
tation or sale of the Crown's rights in forests and
fens in order to raise money. These rights were of
various kinds but potentially of great value. Considerable areas of England were still under the
jurisdiction of the forest law. Private landlords
and their tenants could be expected to pay for the
lifting of this law from their lands; it imposed
irksome restrictions upon agricultural activities in
the interest of preserving deer and the natural
cover in which they hid and on which they browsed.
Moreover, the Crown claimed large, but usually
poorly surveyed and vaguely specified, demesne waste
lands of its own within the bounds of virtually all
forests. Once surveyed, disafforested and enclosed
these demesne wastes could be sold or leased for
improved agriculture. A forest like Dean in
Gloucestershire was too valuable to be sold; instead,
royal ironworks could be set up to exploit its rich
seams of iron ore and its extensive woods for char-
coal. Similarly, the Crown had extensive claims to
lands in the fens of Lincolnshire and the Isle of
Ely which, if drained, could also be enclosed and
sold or leased for improved agriculture. During
the reigns of James I and Charles I the Crown did
not directly engage in the exploitation of these
resources, but, in return for substantial sums of
money, granted the rights to patentees, courtiers,
noblemen, and associated commercial interests. In
the attempt to recoup their investments through
enclosure and drainage the royal grantees ran into
the riotous opposition from the inhabitants of
unimproved wastes.

By the first quarter of the seventeenth century
undeveloped land in many areas of England was supporting sizeable numbers of cottagers. In some
places such as the forests that ran down the border
of eastern Somerset and western Wiltshire to north
Dorset - Melksham, Pewsham, Selwood and Gillingham -
many of the cottagers were employed in the cloth
industry and supplemented their wages by running
cattle on the waste, poaching game, or helping themselves to wood for building materials or fuel.
Others were employed in woodworking and a variety of
forest crafts. The Forest of Dean had a large population of cottagers who lived off its woods and
wastes as well as a community of free miners who
earned their livelihood digging coal and iron ore.

Many other western and Midland forests - Braydon in
Wiltshire, Feckenham in Worcestershire, Rockingham
in Northamptonshire, Arden in Warwickshire and the
Forest of Leicester - sustained considerable numbers
of poor cottagers who made their livings in crafts,
as day labourers, or from the pastures and
woods.(43) Their existence is often made known to us
from the complaints of their better-off neighbours
who feared rising poor rates. The fens supported a
large population of small holders engaged largely in
pasture farming; access to common was crucial for
their economic wellbeing. There is also evidence
from the fens for the growth of a population of poor
cottagers dependent on wages and on common rights.
Such rights included not only pasturage but fishing,
waterfowling, and access both to turf for fuel and
to materials for basket making.(44)
      Disafforestation or drainage struck hard at the
sources of support for forest and fen communities,
affecting most adversely the livelihoods of marginal
small holders and cottagers who were deprived of
access to unstinted common. In the case of disafforestation, the poor cottagers, who had the big-
gest stake in the continued maintenance of the
unimproved waste, found that the law did not often
recognise their rights to common and to compensation
on its extinction, and on those occasions treated
them as charity cases deserving only a dole out of
the king's grace and bounty. In those instances
where the disafforestation commissioners recognised
the legality of cottagers' claims they were compensated with small plots of one or two acres each. In
comparison, manorial lords, their substantial tenants and freeholders, who could prove rights to
common in forest wastes as appurtenant to their
tenements, were well compensated with land at disafforestation. In addition, landowners probably saw
such advantages for themselves in taking leases of
the newly enclosed grounds that they were, as a
group, largely satisfied with the proceedings.
Opposition to enclosure was left in the hands of the
cottagers. Between 1626 and 1632 there was a
series of riots in Gillingham Forest in Dorset,
Braydon, Melksham and Pewsham Forests in Wiltshire,
Feckenham Forest in Worcestershire, the Forest of
Leicester, and Dean Forest in Gloucestershire,
collectively known as the Western Rising. All these
disturbances, except for those at Dean, were in
opposition to disafforestation. The Dean riots
were aimed at partial enclosures in the forest
which gave control of certain mineral rich areas to

royal grantees and excluded the local miners from
digging iron ore or pasturing their cattle. (45)
In the case of drainage projects, the compensation intended for small husbandmen and cottagers
is not certain, although it could not have been much
and would in no way have compensated them for loss
of access to unstinted commons in the unimproved
fens. The opposition of the poorer commons in the
fens was supported and sustained by discontented
yeomanry and gentry. Landlords actively supported
some drainage projects, and substantial compensation
in the form of a proportion of the drained lands was
assigned to manorial lords and their tenants in all
such schemes. There were, nonetheless, many discontents among vested local interests which sometimes led them to support or encourage rioters.
Discontents included the arbitrary proceedings of
the Crown and some of its leading projectors who
acted with high-handed disregard for established
property rights. At Hatfield Chase and the Isle of
Axholme, where the King was lord of the manor and
conveyed his demesne rights to the projector
Cornelius Vermuyden, the division of the fens was
pushed through the court of Exchequer despite the
tenants' opposition. In some projects, where the
government had to deal with the rights of other
manorial lords, the Crown's legal officers exploited
ambiguities in the law, including a strained interpretation of the Commission of the Sewers that 'was
employed to legitimize drainage operations and to
compel the participation of recalcitrant local landowners'.(46) Prosperous, as well as poor, commoners
had complaints about the practical consequences of
drainage: soil was deprived of the enriching silt
deposits that came with periodic flooding, fisheries
were destroyed, previously dry land was flooded, and
the compensation consisted of poor, infertile land.
At the centre of the protests, uniting many different social levels, was resistance to wholesale
changes in land use that threatened the continued
viability of a thriving pastoral agriculture from
which even the poor could make a living. This was
unlike the situation in forest areas where the
changes caused by enclosure only threatened the marginal poor while the better-off saw advantages for
themselves in taking up and improving forest land
that they could absorb within their existing husbandry practices. Protests over fen drainage began at
Hatfield Chase in 1627 and at the Isle of Axholme in
1628-29, and continued to erupt throughout the
1630s in various locations as other drainage

projects got underway. (47)
Anti-improvement protests shared a number of
common characteristics. The participants had
limited and quite specific aims. Like food rioters,
they directed their anger at abuses which threatened
subsistence rights; they devoted their energies to
the destruction of enclosure or the filling of
drainage works. While the agents or workmen of the
enclosers were occasionally assaulted, the level of
physical violence was low and took the form more of
threats than actual bodily harm. No doubt the most
striking and ritualised riots were those at Dean
Forest in 1631 in which the mining community
expressed its outrage at enclosures in the form of a
skimmington riding. (48) A more typical example is to
be found at Westland Heath, Norfolk, where on 9 July
1630 a crowd of from sixty to eighty people destroyed Sir Augustine Southerton's enclosures.
Southerton had enclosed the heath in order to convert its pastures to corn growing. The rioters,
from nearby Drayton, claimed common of pasture on
the heath; led by two labourers they entered the
property, broke down the fences and pulled up the
hedges. Then the participants set the fence rails
on fire while they shouted and rejoiced accompanied
by the beating of a drum. When the constables
arrived to keep the peace, the rioters threatened to
burn them also. (49)
In response to major disorders such as the
Midland Revolt, the Western Rising and the fen riots,
the government mobilised both its rhetoric and its
machinery of law enforcement. The riots were condemned in general terms as rebellions that ought to
be suppressed with the participants being severely
punished. This response required the mobilising of
the militia or the sheriff's posse to maintain order
and the use of the assizes, special commissions of
oyer and terminer, and Star Chamber to impose punishments. Despite the general similarities of crowd
behaviour in all three situations and the consistent
nature of government response, there are some
interesting differences that are worth elucidating.
In their expressed attitudes and behaviour, the
Midland rebels were much like the participants in
food riots and in the various other protests that we
have seen treated as rebellion. First of all, they
claimed to have official sanction for their actions.
The leader of the rebels in Northamptonshire, John
Reynolds, who took the name Captain Pouch, insisted
that he carried in his pouch authority from the King
to destroy enclosures; in fact when his pouch was

searched after his arrest 'therein was onely a peece of greene cheese'. But more generally, the Midland rebels could point to long-standing governmental opposition to conversion of arable to pasture as sanction for their action; as recently as the dearth of 1597 there had been a new anti-enclosure statute. On one occasion, the rebels told the magistrates of Warwickshire that they would disperse once they heard that the King would remedy their grievances over enclosure. Like the Oxfordshire Rebellion of 1596, the Midland Revolt was a protest occasioned by the scarcity of grain in an area where agricultural improvers were active and where the authorities appeared to be lax in enforcing the tillage statutes.

While local officials tried to persuade the Midland rebels to disperse peacefully, the representatives of the Crown, including the Earl of Shrewsbury, regarded this outbreak as a rebellion that required the use of the trained bands, 'which will run over and cut in peeces a thousand of suche naked roges as thos are'. In the end, although the militia proved (as usual in these situations) reluctant to act, there was a military engagement between the rebels and a number of gentlemen with their servants in which about forty or fifty rebels were killed and a number of prisoners hung and quartered as rebels in arms against the King. The Midland Revolt, like the Oxfordshire Rebellion of 1596, had triggered fears among royal officials of real social turmoil, and no doubt raised apprehensions of a new Kett's Rebellion. (50) Government officials were acutely aware of the potentially dangerous consequences of popular action, even when presented as supportive of the law. In a 1608 Star Chamber ruling on an enclosure riot, the members of the court observed that it was dangerous 'to geve waye to the popular sorte to take the sworde of Justice into there handes, they must not be there owne Judges and especially the offence ys greate to execute busynesses in the nighte, albeit thinges lawful, and theise small beginnings would be nypped in the budde, which yf they were well looked into by the Justices of the peace, in time they woulde be stayed, or else they will growe in little time to the popular rebellyons of Northamptonshire'.(51)

At the same time, the Crown remained officially committed to the enforcement of the statutes in favour of tillage. The Midland Revolt provides another illustration of how a crisis - a depression, a harvest failure, a major riot, a rebellion - could

energise government into enforcing its own policies.
On the heels of the revolt, a commission was established to gather evidence on enclosure in the
Midland counties. This was followed by the prosecution of a number of enclosers in Star Chamber.
But it must be acknowledged that this was the last
major attempt by the Crown, except for a brief
effort in the 1630s, to enforce the laws against
enclosure. (52)

Matters were quite different with regard to the
fen and forest rioters. Although there is some
evidence that rioters in the fens claimed to have
royal sanction for their activities, this was generally a difficult fiction to maintain when drainage
and disafforestation were being carried out in the
King's name and substantially for his benefit. Most
forest and fen protests do not have the attributes
of quasi-official acts designed to enforce royally
sanctioned policies. Rather they appear to be
expressions of community indignation against arbitrary and inequitable treatment at the hands of the
Crown and its projectors, who were often strangers
intruding into the life of the community. Official
opinion on the riots described them as rebellions,
but there was no use of force approaching that
exercised in the Midland Revolt. Prudence, dictated
by the unreliability of the local militia, the hostility of sheltering local communities, and
inhospitable terrain, made local officials reluctant
to use force against forest and fen rioters. There
also might have been a greater awareness of the
limited aims of the protesters. Punishments generally never went beyond the pillory, a stiff fine, and
the occasional period of imprisonment. (53)

Despite the comparatively mild official reaction
to the Western Rising and the fen disturbances,
there could be no positive ameliorative response by
the Crown to the needs of the riotous poor
commoners. Although the Crown remained committed in
its opposition to depopulating conversion of arable
to pasture, the policies that it pursued in forest
and fen were carefully distinguished from depopulating enclosure. Not only the government and its
projectors, but also a number of social commentators, regarded enclosure of waste as a positive
benefit to the commonwealth. Wasteland, such as
forest and fen, was viewed as the nursery of an idle
and disorderly population of poor, who lazed about,
gaining a living from the commons, spending most of
their time in haunting alehouses and in committing
crimes. Enclosure and drainage would turn the land

to improved agriculture and sustain a population of honest and substantial husbandmen. This would bene-fit the commonwealth in numerous ways: eliminate poverty and idleness, increase the number of tax-paying subjects, provide a pool of able-bodied from whom armies could be raised, and increase royal revenues.(54) Thus the good of the commonwealth, the fiscal needs of the king, and the private interests of projectors coincided neatly, and no matter the level of opposition the improvement of waste marched on.

A sullen calm descended over most forests and fens in the late 1630s, but one striking character-istic of the people in both areas was doggedness in pursuit of their aims. As soon as the members of England's elite found themselves preoccupied with the political crisis that led to Civil War, the inhabitants of forests and fens took advantage of the times to riot once again and destroy the works of enclosers and drainers. In the years between 1642 and 1649 riots erupted in all those western forests which had been the scene of the riots in 1626-32; they also occurred in forests like Neroche and Selwood in Somerset that had been disafforested without much violent opposition earlier in the reign of Charles I. At the same time, protests again took place in most of the fen areas that had been the location of rioting in the 1630s.

In their need for revenue, the governments of Commonwealth and Protectorate resorted to an exploi-tation of Crown rights similar to that of the defunct Stuarts. In 1653 and 1654 Acts of Parliament authorised the sale of most remaining royal forests. Although cloaked in parliamentary guise, this was in substance a revival of disaffor-estation. The result was riots by the discontented inhabitants of Needwood Forest in Staffordshire between 1657 and 1659, and of Enfield Chase, Middlesex, in 1659. The standing military forces available to the Protectorate forcibly suppressed the protests. The Protectorate also turned to a Stuart-like policy of exploiting the mineral resources of the Forest of Dean, thereby alienating its inhabitants who rioted in 1659, ostensibly in support of the restoration of the monarchy but actually in favour of the restoration of their com-mon rights. An Act of Parliament in 1649 revived drainage in the Great Level of the fens. Like its predecessors, this project of the early 1650s pro-voked riotous resistance from the local commoners; so too did new attempts in the same period to revive

the draining of other fen areas. As in the case of
contemporary riots against disafforestation, soldiers had to be called upon to maintain order. (55)
     During the period 1640-60 rioters concerned with
subsistence issues do not appear to have had any
clear commitments to either side in the political
conflicts of the day. Popular attitudes were dominated by burning local issues such as enclosure and
drainage and by the desire to return to the unregulated enjoyment of common rights on the undeveloped
waste. The riots in the Stour valley of Essex in
August 1642, which were aimed at the homes and properties of locally prominent individuals, many of
whom were Catholics, had much more to do with the
depressed state of the New Drapery and the chronic
poverty of clothworkers than it did with what one
historian argues was a popular, pro-Parliament
sentiment. As another historian, Clive Holmes,
notes: 'if the opportunity for the riots was provided by the confusion and uncertainty attendant
upon the political crisis, the motive, at least in
the Stour valley, was an economic crisis of serious
dimensions'. (56)
     The interests of poor cottagers who desired
access to unimproved waste attracted little attention from the major supporters of Parliament and of
subsequent republican regimes. As in the reigns of
the first two Stuarts, hard fiscal necessity dictated the enclosure and sale of forests during the
early 1650s. At the same time, there was a considerable pamphlet literature produced by social commentators forcefully advocating the enclosure of
waste ground and its conversion to improved arable
farming. These advocates of improvement, who were
genuinely concerned with the commonweal, argued for
enclosure in terms much like those used to justify
disafforestation and fen drainage under the monarchy. Improvement would result in an increase in
grain supply, a growth in the number of honest,
sober, able-bodied and tax-paying husbandmen, and,
above all, in a solution to the problem of poverty.
The social reformers of the mid-seventeenth century
were convinced that poor commoners were leading
lives of idleness, beggary, thievery and drunkenness. Their manners could only be reformed through
improvement of the waste that one commentator
likened to 'howling wilderness' and 'a deformed
chaos.' Although the proposals differed in detail,
they were broadly similar in outline. Much of the
enclosed land was to be leased or sold to husbandmen and yeomen, but a proportion of it was to be set

aside in small holdings for some of the idle who
would be transformed into industrious husbandmen.
Workhouses, financed from the rents paid for the
improved lands, would employ the rest of the poor.
These proposals were considerably more enlightened
and public spirited than Stuart disafforestation and
drainage schemes in which the Crown and its projectors were the main beneficiaries. Nonetheless, the
authors of improvement schemes in the 1650s saw the
poor as objects to be disciplined and reformed, not
as fellow citizens with viewpoints that needed
examination let alone advocacy.(57)

More radical popular groups like the Levellers
had surprisingly little to say on the question of
enclosure and drainage. Given the large volume of
words poured forth by John Lilburne, Richard
Overton, William Walwyn and others, their statements on fens and enclosure are miniscule indeed.
They consist of brief demands for the laying open of
enclosed commons and fens for the use of the poor,
buried within two pamphlets which are concerned
largely with other matters of genuine interest to
the Levellers: political, religious and constitutional issues.(58) Nowhere do the Levellers offer
any extended discussions of the economic and social
problems that pressed upon the rural poor. In 1650,
John Lilburne did take up the case of the manorial
tenants of Epworth in the Lincolnshire fens. Nonetheless in his pamphlet The Case of the Tenants of
the Manor of Epworth he appears as the shrewd
advocate arguing the case on behalf of the husbandman and yeomen of Epworth, rather than as the social
revolutionary defending the customary rights of the
poor.

It is a measure of the improvement idea's per-
vasiveness that the most extensive proposal on waste
land with any Leveller associations is much like
those emanating from groups like Samuel Hartlib and
his associates. In Several Proposals for Peace and
Freedom John Jubbes advocated the enclosure of
forests and fens, with a quarter of the improved
land to be set aside as small holdings for the poor.
Even the much more radical William Covell, who was
deeply concerned with the poverty of the inhabitants
of Enfield Chase, believed the only solution lay in
the enclosure and tillage of the soil accompanied by
the establishment of manufactories in which the poor
and idle would work.(59) The only apparent supporters in print of the rural labouring poor were the
Diggers. Yet even these advocates of community property in land had little to say in favour of unim-

proved waste. Their interests lay in advancing tillage and in gaining access to commons so that they
could be ploughed and improved by the labouring
poor. In their own words: 'we shall not strive
with sword and speare, but the spade and plow and
such like instruments to make the barren and common Lands fruitful'. The Diggers intended that the
common people 'shall have the freedom to improve the
Comons and waste Lands free to themselves'. It
appears that no one was willing to argue the case on
behalf of the rural cottagers who wished unlimited
access to unimproved waste and to be left to the
uninterrupted enjoyment of their largely autonomous
way of life.(60)

Even after the Restoration some forest and fen
dwellers continued with their stubborn resistance to
enclosure and drainage. A variety of fen disturbances occurred regularly during the late seventeenth century: in 1661-3, 1667, 1669, 1697 and
1699. In 1671 an anti-enclosure riot took place at
Mailescott woods, Dean Forest. This is of particular interest in demonstrating the continuity and
consistency of popular protests. The Crown's grant
of Mailescott woods to Sir Edward Villiers, half-
brother to the Duke of Buckingham, and its subsequent enclosure had provoked the Dean riots of 1631
and a second outbreak in 1632.(61) Although violence
against the enclosure of waste occurred sporadically
in the late seventeenth century and throughout the
eighteenth century, there can be no doubt that the
opposition in later periods was only a pale reflection of the resistance that took place in the years
between 1626 and 1659.(62)

It would be misleading, however, to say that
poor cottagers on the waste had totally lost their
struggle. Instead, beginning with the Restoration,
the conflict between Crown and commoners took a
different form. This can be illustrated in the
example of Kingswood Chase, Gloucestershire, on the
outskirts of Bristol. Here, at least as early as
the beginning of the seventeenth century, local
manorial lords began to exploit the coal measures on
the waste. In the process, they encouraged the
establishment of an ever growing community of miners
living in cottages. By the end of the seventeenth
century the mining community numbered from three
hundred to five hundred households, each with its
small patch of enclosed garden or backside, carved
out of the waste. Title to the waste was a disputed
matter in the early seventeenth century. The ad-
visers of the first two Stuarts regarded the coal-

rich wastes of the Chase as royal demesne, part of
the ancient Forest of Filwood. In their view
Kingswood ought to bring in revenues to the Crown
like the ore-rich lands of Dean Forest just across
the Severn. The local manorial lords, for their
part, claimed that they had title to the waste,
and that, at best, the Crown had only hunting
privileges - the right to the Chase. After about
thirty years of complex and inconclusive legal
wrangling, the Crown by the 1630s appears to have
given up on its attempts to establish title to the
waste of Kingswood. At the Restoration, Charles II
attempted to revive his hunting rights in the Chase
and to apply the forest laws within its
boundaries.(63)

In 1670 Charles II granted his hunting rights in
Kingswood to Sir Baynham Throckmorton who restocked
the Chase with deer. The grantee was also given
responsibility for enforcing the forest laws which
prohibited encroachments that interfered with hunting. Encroachments included the sinking of coal
pits, the felling of trees, and the erection of
cottages with enclosed gardens. Throckmorton and
his assignees attempted to implement this grant, but
they only produced a long conflict with the miners
and their employers. There was one major riot in
1670 when a crowd of four hundred people attacked
the house of a deputy keeper of the Chase and
assaulted the sheriff's men blamed for prosecuting
those who erected cottages on Kingswood's wastes.
By the beginning of the eighteenth century, the deer
in the Chase had either been killed or driven off,
and the holder of the royal hunting rights had
quietly surrendered his claims.(64)

The conflict at Kingswood was one example of the
many struggles that took place within the bounds of
royal forests between those who desired to maintain
a hunting preserve and those who tried to win a subsistence from the waste. On the eve of the Civil
War the people who lived around Windsor and Waltham
Forests engaged in large-scale slaughter of
deer.(65) After the Restoration, except in the case
of a few forests with suitable supplies of ship
timber, the Crown appears to have given up on any
systematic attempt at fiscal or economic exploitation. Instead, the government of Charles II, in its
attempt to revive the forest laws and restock
forests with deer, re-established the idea of forest
as hunting preserve and with it the traditional
notion of the chase as the perquisite of royalty.(66)
At the same time, the Crown reinforced hierarchy and

extended patronage by granting hunting rights and
the privilege of erecting deer parks to members of
the aristocracy. This emphasis of the restored monarchy on hunting as the exclusive preserve of Crown
and aristocracy gave to poaching and the destruction
of park rails a self-conscious edge of social protest that they had never quite possessed before.
Indeed, the conflicts between poachers and forest
and park rangers appear to have become more violent
in the late seventeenth century.(67) The monarchy
under Charles II, in fact, laid the groundwork for
the later Walpolean forest regime that has been the
subject of a memorable work by E. P. Thompson.(68)

IV

This essay has been concerned with certain forms
of popular protest in seventeenth century England,
those that might be called traditionalist in character. But it has certainly not dealt with all forms.
Riots and disturbances occurred with some frequency
in the city of London and its suburbs. Many were
the work of apprentices and often took place in festival times which encouraged the temporary loosening
of order and overturning of hierarchy. In the early
seventeenth century the most frequent were the
Shrove Tuesday riots aimed at brothels and playhouses. There was also a history of metropolitan
riots aimed against foreigners, that started with
the Evil May Day riots of 1517. By the early seventeenth century, the anti-foreign sentiments of the
London populace had become intertwined with anti-
Catholicism so that there were occasional attacks on
the Spanish ambassador and his entourage, the most
visible and hated symbol of a dangerous foreign
Catholicism. During the early 1640s popular anti-
Catholicism in London was focussed increasingly on
the royal court including the Catholic Queen and the
Laudian Church.(69) A process was under way, first
in London and then in certain provincial areas, that
would make anti-Catholicism the means of involving
the people in politics. But the role of the crowd
and anti-Popery in the London demonstrations of
1641-2, and the complex history of popular inter-
ventions in politics from that moment through the
anti-Popery demonstrations·and the Exclusion Crisis
of Charles II until the Duke of Monmouth's Rebellion
and beyond are important topics that demand far
greater elucidation than can be given them here.
In surveying the more typical and traditional
forms of popular protest in the seventeenth century,

certain common themes emerge. Protests were largely
the work of wage earners, especially those in rural
industries, and were concerned with matters of subsistence. The participants had a complex and ambivalent relationship with government and its policies. On the one hand, there was the attempt to
obtain a favourable official response to a variety
of complaints against transportation of grain or
enclosure. Protests often took the form either of
attempts to enforce the law or appeals to the authorities for aid. On the other hand, there were
rebellions which appear to have been extreme versions of the more limited protests. Here the
participants were driven to violent actions by the
failures of officialdom - corruption, laxity, or the
lack of appropriate response to the needs of the
people - that had already been brought to their
attention, either through petition or through riot.

It is worth noting the continuity in themes that
stretches between the disorders of the fourteenth
century and those of the eighteenth. The behaviour,
the social status, the expressed aims and attitudes,
and no doubt the economic vulnerability of rioters
in those four centuries, remained remarkably similar. In this regard, the historian of popular
protest finds ground for agreement with James Sharpe
when in a recent survey of work on the history of
crime he declared, 'If the opinions I have formed of
current writings on the history of crime in the late
Middle Ages and early modern periods are correct, it
would seem that crime, the methods used to suppress
it, and certain characteristics of the system of law
and order likewise showed broad similarities between
the fourteenth and eighteenth centuries'.(70)

1. The foregoing was based upon the examinations and indictments in WRO, QS Great Roll, Trinity 1614, nos. 147, 157,
   160-2, 167-71.
2. APC, 1613-14, pp. 457-8.
3. APC, 1613-14, pp. 652-3.
4. The classic works on the eighteenth-century food riot are
   G. Rudé, The Crowd in History, 1730-1848 (NY, 1964) and
   E. P. Thompson, 'The Moral Economy of the English Crowd
   in the Eighteenth Century', P. and P., 50 (1971). A more
   recent treatment which includes an up-to-date bibliography is in J. Stevenson, Popular Disturbances in England
   1700-1870 (1979). Food riots in earlier periods are
   treated in M. Beloff, Public Order and Popular
   Disturbances 1660-1714 (Oxford, 1938); J. Walter and K.
   Wrightson, 'Dearth and the Social Order in Early Modern
   England', P. and P., 71 (1976); P. Clark, 'Popular
   Protest and Disturbance in Kent, 1558-1640', Economic
   History Review, xxix (1976); Sharp, In Contempt;
   J. Walter, 'Grain riots and popular attitudes to the law:
   Maldon and the crisis of 1629', in J. Brewer and J.
   Styles (eds.), An Ungovernable People (1980); A.
   Charlesworth (ed.), An Atlas of Rural protest in Britain
   1548-1900 (1983).
5. Calendar of the Patent Rolls Edward III, 1345-48, pp.
   376, 381, 388, 392; J. G. Bellamy, The Law of Treason in
   England in the Later Middle Ages (Cambridge, 1970), pp.
   67-8, 218.
6. Guides to harvest quality include W. G. Hoskins, 'Harvest
   Fluctuations and English Economic History 1480-1619',
   Agricultural History Review, xii (1964); idem, 'Harvest
   Fluctuations and English Economic History 1620-1759',
   Agricultural History Review, xvi (1968); P. Bowden,
   'Agricultural Prices, Farm Profits and Rents' and
   'Statistical Appendix', in J. Thirsk (ed.), The Agrarian
   History of England and Wales, 1500-1640 (Cambridge,
   1967); C. J. Harrison, 'Grain Price Analysis and Harvest
   Qualities, 1465-1634', Agricultural History Review, xix
   (1971).
7. A. B. Appleby, 'Disease or Famine? Mortality in
   Cumberland and Westmorland, 1580-1640', Economic History
   Review, xxvi (1973); idem, Famine in Tudor and Stuart
   England (Stanford, 1978). In ch. 9 of the latter work,
   Appleby surveys recent work on the effects of the harvest
   failures of 1597 and 1623 on the populations of a variety
   of English regions and continental countries.
8. The only report from the J.P.s of a north-western county
   for any of the scarcity years between 1586 and 1631 that
   I have been able to find is one from Cumberland dated 22
   March 1587, in BL, Lansdowne MS. 52, no. 45.
9. Sharp, In Contempt, pp. 15-30; Charlesworth (ed.),
   Atlas, pp. 77-9; Records of the County of Wiltshire, ed.

B. H. Cunnington (Devizes, 1932), pp. 182-3, 200-1.

10. Sharp, In Contempt, pp. 15-30; Walter, 'Grain riots', *passim*.

11. For discussions of the Book of Orders, see A. Everitt, 'The Marketing of Agricultural Produce', in Thirsk (ed.), Agrarian History, pp. 581-6; Walter and Wrightson, 'Dearth'; Sharp, In Contempt, pp. 50-3; P. Slack, 'Book of Orders: The Making of English Social Policy, 1577-1631', TRHS, xxx (1980); R. B. Outhwaite, 'Dearth and Government Intervention in English Grain Markets, 1590-1700', Economic History Review, xxxiv (1981).

12. See the discussion of this topic, accompanied by numerous illustrative examples, in Everitt, 'Marketing', pp. 568-73.

13. Examples of proclamations prohibiting export of grain are to be found in Tudor Royal Proclamations, ed. P. Hughes and J. Larkin (New Haven, 1969), ii, pp. 362-3, iii, pp. 61-2, 169-72; Stuart Royal Proclamations, ed. J. Larkin and P. Hughes (Oxford, 1973-83), i, pp. 186-8, 285-6, 521-2, ii, pp. 230-1, 271-2, 312-14.

14. Most of the proclamations listed in note 13 instruct J.P.s to prevent fraudulent export of grain. See also APC, 1586-87, pp. 45-6, 69-70, 110-11, 159; APC, 1587-88, p. 26; APC, 1595-96, p. 133; APC, 1596-97, pp. 226-7, 257-8; APC, 1597-98, pp. 144-5, 230-1; APC, 1598-99, p. 655; APC, 1630-31, pp. 125-6.

15. APC, 1586-87, pp. 259, 264, 338-9, 342, 383-4; APC, 1595-96, pp. 19-20, 221; APC, 1596-97, pp. 516-17, 534-5, 558-9; APC, 1597, pp. 3, 84-5.

16. PRO, SP 12/254/10, 62; SP 12/262/151; APC, 1586-87, pp. 319-20; Clark, 'Popular Protest', pp. 373-5.

17. APC, 1586-87, pp. 359-60, 391-2; APC, 1596-97, pp. 269-70; APC, 1597-98, pp. 42-4, 237; APC, 1599-1600, pp. 347-8; APC, 1630-31, pp. 120-1, 126.

18. T. Wright (ed.), Queen Elizabeth and Her Times (1838), i, p. 478, ii, pp. 462-3; E. P. Cheney, History of England from the Armada to the death of Elizabeth (1926), ii, pp. 33-4; J. Bellamy, The Tudor Law of Treason: An Introduction (1979), pp. 78-81; Clark, 'Popular Protest', p. 379.

19. Calendar of the Patent Rolls Edward III, 1345-48, pp. 376, 381, 388, 392.

20. Clark, 'Popular Protest', pp. 368-9; Walter, 'Grain riots', p. 53; Beloff, Public Order, pp. 58-66; Charlesworth (ed.), Atlas, pp. 80-2.

21. Calendar of the Patent Rolls Edward III, 1345-48, pp. 381, 388, 392.

22. Clark, 'Popular Protest', pp. 374-5; Walter, 'Grain riots', p. 83.

23. Clark, 'Popular Protest', p. 370; Walter and Wrightson,

'Dearth', p. 33.

24. SRO, QSR 61/i/38, 78.
25. The Life and Times of Anthony Wood, ed. A. Clark (1891-1900), iii, pp. 421-2. See also N. Luttrell, A Brief Historical Relation of State Affairs, 1678-1714 (Oxford, 1857), iii, p. 88.
26. Sharp, In Contempt, pp. 30-1.
27. Walter and Wrightson, 'Dearth', pp. 33-4.
28. The foregoing was based upon Walter, 'Grain riots', *passim*; Sharp, In Contempt, ch. 3.
29. The notion of theatre comes from K. Wrightson, English Society 1580-1680 (1982), pp. 174, 182. The following section is much indebted to the stimulus provided by Wrightson's fine survey of 'tumults and mutinies' on pp. 173-82.
30. Sharp, In Contempt, pp. 43-50; Wrightson, English Society, pp. 178-9.
31. APC, 1595-96, pp. 88-9; HMC: Salisbury MSS, xiii, pp. 168-9; Wright (ed.), Queen Elizabeth, ii, pp. 462-3.
32. Cheney, History, ii, pp. 33-4; Bellamy, Tudor Law of Treason, pp. 78-81; Clark, 'Popular Protest', p. 379; Walter, 'Grain riots', pp. 71, 77; Sharp, In Contempt, pp. 20, 27, 44, 48-9.
33. Walter, 'Grain riots', p. 71.
34. Calendar of Patent Rolls Edward III, 1345-48, p. 388.
35. Bellamy, Tudor Law of Treason, pp. 18-21, 78-81.
36. Sharp, In Contempt, pp. 36-42; J. Samaha, 'Gleanings from local criminal court records: Sedition among the "Inarticulate" in Elizabethan Essex', JSH, viii (1975), 72-4.
37. One can hardly do better than to read the Penguin edition of Langland's Piers the Ploughman for a sampling of the medieval moralists' indignation. For example, on p. 47 there is a powerful attack on middlemen and an exhortation to magistrates to regulate the market in the interest of the poor.
38. R. B. Dobson, The Peasants' Revolt of 1381 (1970), pp. 21-6; R. A. Griffiths, The Reign of Henry VI (Berkeley, 1981), pp. 614-15.
39. Western Circuit Assize Orders 1626-1648, ed. J. S. Cockburn (Camden Soc., 1976), pp. 272-3, 288; Latimer, Annals, pp. 221, 230, 285.
40. Wrightson, English Society, p. 174.
41. J. Thirsk, 'Enclosing and Engrossing', in Thirsk (ed.), Agrarian History, pp. 232-5, 247-55; E. F. Gay, 'The Midland Revolt and the Inquisitions of Depopulation of 1607', TRHS, xviii (1904). See also L. A. Parker, 'The Agrarian Revolution at Cotesbach, 1501-1612', in Studies in Leicestershire Agrarian History (Leicester, 1948); HMC: Buccleuch MSS, iii, p. 118.
42. PRO, STAC 8/310/18 (a riot at Winterslowe, Wilts);

PC 2/50, pp. 401, 549, SP 16/403, pp. 81-2 (Hatfield, Essex); PC 2/49, pp. 39, 45, 84-5, 92, 208, 229-30, 236, 307, PC 2/50, pp. 560-2, SP 16/368/80, 81, SP 16/423/103 (Caddington woods, Hertfordshire and Bedfordshire); J. Rushworth, Historical Collections, iii, Appendix, pp. 53-4 (Westland Heath, Norfolk). See also Wrightson, English Society, p. 175 and Clark, 'Popular Protest', p. 369.

43. For evidence on cottagers, see P. A. J. Pettit, Royal Forests of Northampton 1558-1714 (Northants RS, 1968), ch. 8; V. H. T. Skipp, 'Economic and Social Change in the Forest of Arden, 1530-1649', in J. Thirsk (ed.), Land, Church and People, (Reading, 1970); idem, Crisis and Development: An Ecological Case Study of the Forest of Arden 1570-1674 (Cambridge, 1978); Sharp, In Contempt, pp. 156-74, 180-90.

44. J. Thirsk, English Peasant Farming (1957), pp. 114-16; C. Holmes, Seventeenth Century Lincolnshire (Lincoln, 1980), pp. 19-21; Wrightson, English Society, pp. 126-7.

45. Sharp, In Contempt, pp. 126-55, 201-7.

46. Holmes, Lincolnshire, pp. 121-30. (The quotation is from p. 126.) See also K. Lindley, Fenland Riots and the English Revolution (1982), pp. 23-56.

47. Lindley, Fenland Riots, pp. 10-20, 71-107.

48. Sharp, In Contempt, pp. 95-6, 105. See also Martin Ingram's essay on rough music in the present collection.

49. Rushworth, Historical Collections, iii, Appendix, pp. 53-4; PRO, E159/473, Trin. 9 Chas. I, rot. 27.

50. Gay, 'Midland Revolt', pp. 216-17, 240-1; Larkin and Hughes, Stuart Royal Proclamations, i, pp. 152-8, 161-2.

51. J. Hawarde, Les Reportes del cases in Camera Stellata 1593-1609 (1894), pp. 346-7.

52. Thirsk, 'Enclosing and Engrossing', pp. 235-7.

53. Sharp, In Contempt, pp. 96-125; Lindley, Fenland Riots, pp. 57-71.

54. I have surveyed contemporary opinion on waste land in a paper 'Common Rights, Charities and the Disorderly Poor', to be published in G. Eley and W. Hunt (eds.), Reviving the English Revolution (forthcoming). See also Lindley, Fenland Riots, pp. 2-5.

55. D. O. Pam, The Rude Multitude: Enfield and the Civil War (Edmonton Hundred Historical Society, Occasional Paper no. 33, 1977); Sharp, In Contempt, pp. 220-56; Lindley, Fenland Riots, pp. 108-87.

56. C. Holmes, The Eastern Association in the English Civil War (Cambridge, 1974), p. 44; B. Manning, The English People and the English Revolution (1976), pp. 171-83.

57. Examples of the pamphlet literature in favour of enclosure include the following: S. Taylor, Common Good (1652); A. Moore, Bread for the Poor (1653); E. G., Waste Land's Improvement (1653). The last work is reprinted in

J. Thirsk and J. P. Cooper (eds.) <u>Seventeenth Century Economic Documents</u> (Oxford, 1972), pp. 135-40, and is the source of the quotations in the foregoing paragraph. See also C. Webster, <u>The Great Instauration</u> (1975), pp. 465-83.

58. The passages are to be found in <u>Appeale from the Degenerate Representative Body</u> and <u>The Petition to the Commons of England</u>, in D. M. Wolfe (ed.) <u>Leveller Manifestoes of the Puritan Revolution</u> (NY, 1967), pp. 194, 288.

59. Wolfe (ed.), <u>Leveller Manifestoes</u>, p. 319; W. Covell, <u>A Declaration unto the Parliament</u> ... <u>with the Method of a Commonwealth</u> (1659).

60. G. H. Sabine (ed.), <u>The Works of Gerrard Winstanley</u> (NY, 1965), pp. 286, 302.

61. PRO, PC 2/63, fo. 67; KB 9/927/230; Beloff, <u>Public Order</u>, pp. 77-80.

62. Stevenson, <u>Popular Disturbances</u>, pp. 42-3; Charlesworth (ed.), <u>Atlas</u>, pp. 41-4, 48-54.

63. H. T. Ellacombe, <u>The History of the Parish of Bitton</u> (Exeter, 1881), pp. 178-200; R. W. Malcolmson, 'A set of ungovernable people: the Kingswood colliers in the eighteenth century', in Brewer and Styles (ed.), <u>An Ungovernable People</u>, pp. 85-91.

64. Ellacombe, <u>History</u>, pp. 201-8.

65. <u>Journal of the House of Lords</u>, iv, pp. 595, 602, 608, v, pp. 25, 37-8, 61, 612, 625; ERO, QSR 318/33-42; QSR 319/319, 323-40.

66. See, for example, the revival of the forest laws at Waltham Forest and the New Forest, in PRO, SP 29/278/85-8, SP 29/281A/66-7.

67. Examples of riotous destruction of park rails and killing of deer are to be found in PRO, PC 2/68, pp. 127, 139; KB 9/915/94; KB 9/928/318-19; KB 11/3/46; KB 11/4/63; KB 11/7/5; KB 11/9/52; KB 11/10/72.

68. E. P. Thompson, <u>Whigs and Hunters</u> (1977).

69. K. J. Lindley, 'Riot Prevention and Control in Early Stuart London', <u>TRHS</u>, xxxiii (1983); Manning, <u>English People</u>, pp. 1-98.

70. J. A. Sharpe, 'The history of crime in late medieval and early modern England: a review of the field', <u>Social History</u>, vii (1982), p. 203.